# Mapping BRICS Media

*Mapping BRICS Media* is the first comprehensive and comparative study of the emerging media landscape in the world's most dynamic markets. This pioneering collection focuses on one of the key topics in contemporary international relations – the emergence of BRICS (Brazil, Russia, India, China and South Africa) – a grouping that includes some of the world's largest populations and fastest growing economies.

The volume brings together leading scholars, mainly from the BRICS nations, to examine how the emergence of the BRICS media will impact on global media and communication. Contextualizing the rise of the BRICS nations within the broader shifts in global power relations, the chapters investigate the unprecedented growth of the BRICS media within a 'multi-polar' world, evaluating the media landscapes in the individual BRICS countries, their histories and their journalism practices, as well as analyzing emerging inter-BRICS media relationships.

Accessible and comprehensive, the book provides a critical guide to the complex debates about the impact of the 'rise of the rest' on the media globe and how far this poses a challenge to the Western-dominated world order and its media systems.

**Kaarle Nordenstreng** is Professor Emeritus of Journalism and Mass Communication at the University of Tampere, Finland. He is author or editor of over 30 books in English, most recently *Communication Theories in a Multicultural World* (coedited with Clifford Christians, 2014).

**Daya Kishan Thussu** is Professor of International Communication at the University of Westminster in London. Author or editor of 16 books, most recently *Communicating India's Soft Power: Buddha to Bollywood* (2013), he is the Managing Editor of the journal *Global Media and Communication*.

## Internationalizing Media Studies

Series Editor: Daya Kishan Thussu
*University of Westminster*

# Mapping BRICS Media

Edited by
Kaarle Nordenstreng and
Daya Kishan Thussu

Routledge
Taylor & Francis Group

LONDON AND NEW YORK

First published 2015
by Routledge
2 Park Square, Milton Park, Abingdon, Oxon, OX14 4RN

and by Routledge
711 Third Avenue, New York, NY 10017

*Routledge is an imprint of the Taylor & Francis Group, an informa business*

© 2015 Kaarle Nordenstreng and Daya Kishan Thussu for selection and
editorial matter; individual contributions the contributors

*British Library Cataloguing in Publication Data*
A catalogue record for this book is available from the British Library

*Library of Congress Cataloging in Publication Data*
A catalog record for this book has been requested

ISBN: 978-1-138-02624-7 (hbk)
ISBN: 978-1-138-02625-4 (pbk)
ISBN: 978-1-315-72621-2 (ebk)

Typeset in Bembo
by Taylor and Francis Books

# Contents

# Figures and Tables

## Figures

## Tables

# Notes on contributors

**Leonardo Custódio** is a Brazilian doctoral student at the University of Tampere, Finland. His dissertation project analyzes the experiences of young activists from favelas of Rio de Janeiro who have used media technologies for mobilization and social change. Since 2012, his research has been funded by the Academy of Finland through the Finnish Doctoral Programme of Communication Studies. He also works as part-time assistant in the BRICS project.
www.uta.fi/cmt/en/contact/staff/leonardocustodio/index.html

**Pieter J. Fourie** is Professor Emeritus and Research Fellow in Communication Science and the previous head of the Department of Communication Science, University of South Africa, Pretoria. He was awarded a DLitt et Phil degree in Communication Science by the University of South Africa in 1982. He is the editor-in-chief of the oldest South African research journal in Communication Science, namely *Communicatio: South African Journal for Communication Theory and Research* (published by Routledge), the author of a number of South African text books and research articles in media studies and media semiotics, among them a three-volume book series in its 2nd edition *Media Studies* (Juta, 2009).
www.unisa.ac.za/Default.asp?Cmd=ViewContent&ContentID=1247

**Zhengrong Hu** is Professor of Communication at the Communication University of China (CUC), Beijing. He is also Vice President of CUC and Director of the National Center for Radio & TV Studies. His Doctoral Degree is from Renmin University of China. His research areas are media policy and institutional transition, media development strategy and the political economy of communication. He has been a visiting scholar at University of Durham, Britain (2001), Simon Fraser University, Canada (2002–2003), Jonkoping International Business School, Sweden (2005), and a research fellow at Shorenstein Center on the Press, Politics and Public Policy, Kennedy School of Government at Harvard University (2005) as well as Leverhulme Visiting Professor at University of Westminster (2006).
www.huzhengrong.net/about/

**Savyasaachi Jain** teaches at Swansea University in Britain. He has been a journalist, television current affairs producer and documentary filmmaker, whose work has been noticed internationally. As an international trainer he has conducted workshops for journalists from nearly four dozen countries on behalf of various UN and intergovernmental organizations, led international media development projects and supervised more than 50 international co-productions for radio and television. He is completing his PhD at the University of Westminster, researching professional standards and the political economy of the news media in contemporary India.
www.swansea.ac.uk/staff/academic/artshumanities/ltm/savyasaachijain/

**Deqiang Ji** is Assistant Professor at the National Center for Radio & Television Studies at the Communication University of China (CUC), Beijing. He has been a member of several research teams on China's international communication and the political economy of global communication. He is chief editor of a leading academic website for Chinese media and communication studies (www.chinamediaresearch.cn). He has published widely articles on China's international communication, history and structure of global communication, the political economy of social media in transitional China (three co-authored with Zhengrong Hu). He is one of the editors of the first bluebook for China's international communication (2014).
http://rirt.cuc.edu.cn

**Jyrki Käkönen** is Professor in International Relations and European Studies at the Institute of Political Science and Governance in Tallinn University, Estonia, and Jean Monnet Professor, emeritus in the School of Management at the University of Tampere, Finland. He was the director of the Department of Political science and International Relations at the University of Tampere (2002–2007) and the director of Tampere Peace Research Institute (1988–1998). His current research interest is in the changing international order and how the transition challenges Eurocentric IR approaches. Among his recent publications is a 2011 article, 'Interpreting the Transforming World: Perspective from Peace Research', *New Global Studies* 5(3).
www.uta.fi/jkk/pol/yhteystiedot/kakonen.html

**viola candice milton** is an Associate Professor in Media Studies at the University of South Africa's Department of Communication Science. She completed her doctoral studies at Indiana University in 2005, with her dissertation focusing on issues of Public (Service) Broadcasting and HIV/Aids intervention. Her current research focuses on the negotiation of media policy in South Africa as well as issues of media, citizenship and identity. She most recently co-authored *New Voices over the Air: The Transformation of the South African Broadcasting Corporation in a Changing South Africa* with Eric Louw. She is the executive editor for *Communicatio: South African Journal for Communication Theory and Research*.
www.unisa.ac.za/Default.asp?Cmd=ViewContent&ContentID=14215

**Musawenkosi Ndlovu** is Senior Lecturer in Media Studies at the University of Cape Town and a Mandela Mellon Fellow at the W. E. B. Du Bois Institute for African and African American Research, Harvard University. He has taught at the University of South Africa's Department of Communication Science and in the institution that became Tshwane University of Technology's Department of Journalism. Musa holds a PhD in Media and Cultural Studies from the University of KwaZulu-Natal. He publishes in various areas of youth, media and politics, international communication and South African media and culture.
http://cfms.uct.ac.za/staff/dr-musa-ndluvo/

**Kaarle Nordenstreng** is Professor Emeritus of Journalism and Mass Communication at the University of Tampere, Finland, as well as honorary professor at the universities of Moscow and St. Petersburg. He has been a consultant at UNESCO (1969–1981), Vice-President of the International Association for Mass Communication Research (IAMCR) (1972–1988) and President of the International Organization of Journalists (IOJ) (1976–1990). He has written or edited 60 books in Finnish or English, including a classic study on the international flow of TV programmes *Television Traffic: A One-way Street?* (with Tapio Varis, UNESCO, 1974) as well as a contemporary prize-winning *Normative Theories of the Media: Journalism in Democratic Societies* (with Clifford Christians, Theodore Glasser, Denis McQuail and Robert White, University of Illinois Press, 2009).
www.uta.fi/cmt/en/contact/staff/kaarlenordenstreng/index.html

**Raquel Paiva** is Associate Professor of the School of Communication at the Federal University of Rio de Janeiro, where she is coordinator of the Laboratory for the Study of Community Communication. She is a first rank researcher (1-A) in the National Research Council of Brazil and has directed two major research institutions in Brazil – Intercom and Compós. She is also a journalist and has published a dozen books, mainly in the area of community communication and alternative communication. One of her most widely known books is the *Common Mind – Community, Media and Globalism* (1998).
http://buscatextual.cnpq.br/buscatextual/visualizacv.do?metodo=apresentar&id=K4795690A7

**Svetlana Pasti** is a Docent and senior researcher at the Tampere Research Centre for Journalism, Media and Communication at the University of Tampere, Finland, since 2012, a docent in journalism since 2013. Previously, she has been a researcher in various projects of the Academy of Finland, the Finnish Ministry of Education and the European Union, related to media and journalism in Russia and Central Europe. Her research focuses on Russian media, generations in journalism, professional culture of journalists and comparative research in the BRICS countries. She has

authored *A Russian Journalist in Context of Change: Media of St Petersburg* (2004), *The Changing Profession of a Journalist in Russia* (2007), in addition to several book chapters and journal articles. She is on the editorial board of *Central European Journal of Communication*.
www.uta.fi/cmt/en/contact/staff/svetlanapasti/index.html

**Fernando Oliveira Paulino** is Professor at the University of Brasilia. He is part of the Communication Policy Lab (LaPCom-UnB) and member of the Community Media and Citizenship Project of the National Council for Scientific and Technological Development (CNPq). He is also a board member and working group coordinator in the Association of Latin-American Communication Researchers (ALAIC). He has published a number of articles and books on communication and citizenship, ethics and policies of communication. His most recent book *Public Communication in Debate: Ombudsman and Radio* (in Portuguese, 2013) analyzed his experience as former public radio's ombudsman (2008–2012).
http://buscatextual.cnpq.br/buscatextual/visualizacv.do?id=K4768512J6

**Jukka Pietiläinen** is Docent at the University of Tampere, Finland, and a senior researcher at Aleksanteri-Institute (Finnish Centre for Russian and Eastern European Studies) at the University of Helsinki. Earlier, he has been researcher at University of Tampere, where he defended his doctoral dissertation on regional newspapers in post-Soviet Russia. His research is focused on Russian media and society, international news flows and language policy. Current projects include research on Russian magazines, independent regional newspapers in Russia, foreign news in Russia and Russian elections. He is the editor of a forthcoming book: *Creating a New Russia: Magazines and Social Change in Russia*.
https://tuhat.halvi.helsinki.fi/portal/en/persons/jukka pietilainen%2858e61dd8-5589-4a48-9b68-78552f42f964%29.html

**Jyotika Ramaprasad** is Professor and Vice Dean for Graduate Studies and Research in the School of Communication at the University of Miami. Her current research interests are journalist profiles and communication for social change. Her surveys of journalists in Asia and Africa have been published in *Gazette*, *The Harvard International Journal of Press/Politics*, and *Asian Journal of Communication*. Her work in communication for social change has been published in *Social Marketing Quarterly* and *Journal of Health and Mass Communication*. She is on the editorial board of *Journalism and Mass Communication Quarterly* and *Mass Communication and Society*.
http://com.miami.edu/profile/Ramaprasad,Jyotika

**Muniz Sodré** is Professor Emeritus at the Federal University of Rio de Janeiro where he has been teaching since 1970. He is also a first rank researcher (1-A) in the National Research Council of Brazil – CNPq. He lived in France firstly as a student at the *Institut Français des Sciences de l'Information* (Sorbonne-2) and at the *Centre d'Études des Communications de Masse* (CECMAS), where he met Roland Barthes, Georges Friedmann, Edgar Morin and Eliseo Verón. He has made Semiotics and Communication his special study and has published over 36 books on media, culture, education and literature, some of which are benchmarks in Brazilian communication studies. He was President of the Brazilian National Library from 2005 to 2011. http://buscatextual.cnpq.br/buscatextual/visualizacv.do?metodo=apresentar&id=K4783959Y6

**Colin Sparks** has been Professor of Media Studies at Hong Kong Baptist University since 2011. Prior to taking up that post he was Professor of Media Studies and Director of the Communication and Media Research Institute at the University of Westminster. While his doctoral degree is in Cultural Studies, his work is better placed within the tradition of political economy. He has written extensively on different aspects of the media, notably the popular press, the impact of new media, globalization and comparative media. His most recent book is *Globalization, Development and the Media* (Sage, 2007). He is on the editorial board of several scholarly journals, including *Media, Culture and Society*, of which he was one of the founders.
journalism.hkbu.edu.hk/staff/profColinSparks.php

**Joseph Straubhaar** is the Amon G. Carter Sr., Centennial Professor of Communication, Director of Media Studies in the Radio–Television–Film Department, and Director of the Latino and Latin American Media Studies Program at the University of Texas at Austin. His current research concerns the globalization of television and new media, the BRICS, television in Brazil, media and migration, and ICTs and development in Brazil and Texas. He is the author of *World Television: From Global to Local* (Sage, 2007), editor of *Inequity in the Techno-polis: Race, Class, Gender and the Digital Divide in Austin* (University of Texas Press, 2011) and co-author of *Latin American Television Industries* (Palgrave/Macmillan, 2013).
http://rtf.utexas.edu/faculty/joe-straubhaar

**Dmitry Strovsky** has a PhD in Political Science and is Professor at the Journalism Faculty at Ural Federal University in Ekaterinburg, Russia. He has written extensively in Russian and in English on issues concerning the historical and contemporary evolution of the Russian mass media and the relationship between politics and media. Strovsky has received numerous fellowships including the Fulbright Scholarship (2005) and scholarships of the Academy of Finland, and has taught at universities in the United States, Finland, Sweden, the Czech Republic and China. He is also a columnist for the Ural version of *Novaya Gazeta*, one of few liberal outlets in contemporary Russia.
http://usu-ru.academia.edu/DmitriyStrovsky

**Daya Kishan Thussu** is Professor of International Communication and Co-Director of the India Media Centre at the University of Westminster in London. He is the founder and managing editor of the Sage journal *Global Media and Communication*. Among his main publications are: *Electronic Empires* (1998); *International Communication – Continuity and Change*, third edition (2015); *War and the Media: Reporting Conflict 24/7* (2003); *Media on the Move: Global Flow and Contra-flow* (2007); *News as Entertainment* (2007); *Internationalizing Media Studies* (2009); *Media and Terrorism: Global Perspectives* (2012), co-edited with Des Freedman; and *Communicating India's Soft Power: Buddha to Bollywood* (Palgrave, 2013). He is series editor for two Routledge book series: Internationalizing Media Studies and Advances in Internationalizing Media Studies. In 2014, he was honoured with a 'Distinguished Scholar Award' by the International Studies Association.
www.westminster.ac.uk/about-us/our-people/directory/thussu-daya

**Elena Vartanova** is Professor, Dean and Chair in Media Theory and Media Economics at the Faculty of Journalism, Lomonosov Moscow State University. Her research interests include media systems in Finland and other Nordic countries, information society, post-Soviet transformation of Russian media, media economics, journalism and mass communication theories. Vartanova is the author of eight academic monographs and nearly 200 research articles in Russian and international academic journals. She is the Editor-in-Chief of the Faculty research journal Medi@lmanac, online research magazine *Mediascope* and bulletin for experts MediaTrends. She is President of the Russian National Association of Mass Media Researchers.
www.vartanova.ru/

**Herman Wasserman** is Professor of Media Studies at the University of Cape Town, South Africa. He has published widely on media in post-apartheid South Africa, including the monograph *Tabloid Journalism in South Africa: True Story!* (Indiana University Press) and the edited collections *Popular Media, Democracy and Development in Africa* (Routledge); *Press Freedom in Africa: Comparative Perspectives* (Routledge) and *Reporting China in Africa* (forthcoming, Routledge). He edits the journal *Ecquid Novi: African Journalism Studies* and sits on the editorial board of several other international journals.
http://cfms.uct.ac.za/staff/prof-herman-wasserman/

**Peixi Xu** is Associate Professor at the Communication University of China (CUC), Beijing. He has obtained a Doctoral degree from CUC and a Licentiate degree from University of Tampere, Finland. His research interests include international communication, citizen participation and new media.
www.uta.fi/cmt/en/contact/staff/peixixu/index.html

**Yuezhi Zhao** is Professor and Canada Research Chair in Political Economy of Global Communication at the School of Communication, Simon Fraser

University, and a Senior Fellow at the Asia Pacific Foundation of Canada, Vancouver. She is also Changjiang Chair Professor and founding director of the Institute for Political Economy of Communication at the Communication University of China (CUC), Beijing. Her books include *Communication and Society: Political Economic and Cultural Analysis* (in Chinese, 2011), *Communication in China: Political Economy, Power and Conflict* (2008), *Global Communications: Toward a Trans-cultural Political Economy* (co-edited, 2008), *Democratizing Global Media? One World, Many Struggles* (co-edited, 2005), *Media, Market, and Democracy in China* (1998), as well as *Sustaining Democracy?* (co-authored, 1998).

http://pages.cmns.sfu.ca/yuezhi_zhao/

# Introduction

## Contextualizing the BRICS media

*Daya Kishan Thussu and Kaarle Nordenstreng*

More than a decade has passed since the BRIC acronym entered the international lexicon. It was coined in 2001 by Jim O'Neill, a Goldman Sachs executive, to refer to the four fast-growing emerging markets – Brazil, Russia, India and China. South Africa was added, at China's request, in 2011, thus expanding BRIC to BRICS. Although in operation as a formal group since 2006 and holding annual summits since 2009, the BRICS countries have largely escaped academic scrutiny in a comparative and transnational perspective, partly because of the difficulty posed by the range of different political systems and socio-cultural norms, as well as stages of development, within this group of large and diverse nations. In the field of media and communication, virtually no comparative academic work on the BRICS phenomenon has yet been undertaken.

This pioneering study assesses the impact of the exponential growth in media in some of the world's fastest growing major economies on the geo-political environment, and poses questions about the impact this might have on global communication. Have the media in the BRICS countries contributed to enriching the political, cultural and economic discourse globally, providing an antidote to Western-dominated media frames? Can the BRICS media – in all their forms – be deployed to enrich a global dialogue? Will the growing globalization of the BRICS media help to redress the imbalance in global news flow and thus contribute to further internationalization of media and communication studies?

Despite the emergence of the media in the BRICS countries, it is still the case that the US continues to dominate and define the global media scene, being the largest exporter of media content across the increasingly interconnected and digitized globe. The American medias' imprint on the global communication space is profound, by virtue of the ownership of multiple networks and production facilities – from satellites to telecommunication hubs, from cyberspace to real space. Yet other players – including the BRICS nations – have emerged in the last two decades to complement, if not challenge, the US hegemony in this field. In the so-called 'post-American world', the globalization of media from BRICS nations is arguably the most significant development. The emergence of such groupings, coinciding with the relative economic decline of the West, has created the opportunity for emerging powers such as China and India to participate in global governance structures hitherto dominated by the US-led Western alliance (Narlikar, 2010; Brütsch and Papa, 2013; Carmody, 2013). Indeed, it has been argued that the centre of economic gravity could be shifting away from the West, influencing the Obama administration's view that the 'pivot' of US foreign policy is moving to Asia, thus informing its efforts at 'rebalancing' international relations.

## The rise of the BRICS

As a 2013 report from PricewaterhouseCoopers, *World in 2050 – The BRICs and Beyond: Prospects, Challenges and Opportunities,* notes:

> China is projected to overtake the US as the largest economy by 2017 in purchasing power parity (PPP) terms and by 2027 in market exchange rate terms. India should become the third 'global economic giant' by 2050, a long way ahead of Brazil, which we expect to move up to 4th place ahead of Japan. Russia could overtake Germany to become the largest European economy before 2020 in PPP terms and by around 2035 at market exchange rates.
>
> (PwC, 2013)

The United Nations Development Programme's 2013 *Human Development Report* predicts that by 2020 the combined economic output of China, India and Brazil will surpass the aggregated production of the US, Britain, Canada, France, Germany and Italy (UNDP, 2013: 123).

There may be reasonable grounds for such prospects, as BRICS nations have many strengths (Wilson and Purushothaman, 2003; O'Neill, 2011). In demographic terms, the BRICS countries have a great advantage as they account for 43 per cent of the global population: nearly 20 per cent of the world's population resides in China; nearly 18 per cent in India; Brazil accounts for nearly 3 per cent; Russia about 2.2 per cent of the global population; and South Africa 0.7 per cent. The BRICS nations are geographically extensive, covering nearly 30 per cent of the world's land mass: Russia occupies 17 million square kilometres, China 9.3 million, Brazil 8.5 million, India 3.2 million and South Africa 1.2 million square kilometres (BRICS Report, 2012).

Two of the five BRICS nations – Russia and China – are permanent members of the United Nations Security Council, while all its members play a prominent role in Group of Twenty (G20), the Non-Aligned Movement (NAM) and the Group of 77 (G77) (O'Neill, 2011). Within BRICS, members are also part of such groupings as IBSA (India, Brazil and South Africa) and RIC (Russia, India and China). Three BRICS nations – Russia, China and India – possess nuclear weapons, while Brazil and South Africa have deliberately given them up in the post-Cold War world. Politically, the BRICS nations offer a range of political systems: with more than 800 million registered voters, India is the world's largest, most established and institutionalized democracy with a parliamentary system, while Brazil, after two decades of military dictatorship (1964–85), has emerged in the past quarter of a century as a robust democracy, based on a presidential system. South Africa is that continent's most successful democratic experiment, despite the grim legacy of apartheid. After years of socialism, as the system was called when the supreme power was held by the Communist Party, in the past three decades, Russia has moved towards a 'managed' democracy. China remains a one-party state, a system of government that distinguishes it from the other BRICS countries.

Table 0.1 pulls together central indicators of the BRICS countries and their media. Data on media need to be treated with caution, not only because published statistics are often incomplete, but also because the types and characteristics of media differ from country to country, depending on their history and politics. However, the number of newspapers and magazines, as well as Internet penetration rates, are included to demonstrate their scale of magnitude in different BRICS nations. A comprehensive picture of the media landscapes is provided by individual chapters on each member country in part two of this book.

Despite differences in their political systems, all five countries, in their own ways, have embraced economies that are essentially capitalistic and, to various degrees, integrated into the US-dominated global economy, as demonstrated by the fact that the BRICS countries are in possession of 40 per cent of the global foreign exchange reserves – estimated to be $4.4 trillion – and account for 21 per cent of the global GDP, which has increased threefold in the past 15 years. Over the past decade, according to UNCTAD, Foreign Direct Investment (FDI) in-flows to BRICS more than tripled to an estimated $263 billion in 2012. Their share in world FDI flows reached 20 per cent in 2012, up from 6 per cent in 2000. BRICS countries have also become important investors, their outward FDI has risen from $7 billion in 2000 to $126 billion in 2012, or nine per cent of world flows, having steadily grown in the past decade, from merely one per cent (UNCTAD, 2014). Although the impressive figures do not match the powerful Western nations, the trend they represent is significant, as noted by the UNDP Human Development Report titled *The Rise of the South*:

> Economic exchanges are expanding faster 'horizontally' – on a South–South basis – than on the traditional North–South axis. People are sharing ideas and experiences through new communications channels and seeking greater accountability from governments and international institutions alike. The South as a whole is driving global economic growth and societal change for the first time in centuries.
>
> (UNDP, 2013: 123)

Table 0.1 BRICS political-economic and media indicators

| Country | Population (million) | GDP ($ trillion) | Socio-political context | Media system | Number of newspaper and magazine titles | Internet penetration, % of population | Ad-spend ($ billion) | Main global presence |
|---|---|---|---|---|---|---|---|---|
| Brazil | 203 | 2.2 | Presidential democracy, Colonial history, Deep social inequality | Commercial, Limited public service, Abundant community media | 11,000 | 52 | 15.9 | Telenovelas |
| Russia | 148 | 2.1 | Presidential democracy, Imperial history, Socialist legacy, Social inequality | State control, Commercial, Limited public service, Multi-lingual | 59,000 | 61 | 10.3 | RT |
| India | 1,236 | 1.9 | Parliamentary democracy, Colonial history, Deep social inequality | Commercial, Strong public-service, Multi-lingual | 94,000 | 20* | 5.9 | Bollywood |
| China | 1,356 | 9.2 | One-party state, Indirect colonial experience, Socialist legacy, Social inequality | State control, Commercial, Limited public-service | 12,000 | 49* | 40.9 | CCTV News |
| South Africa | 48 | 0.3 | Parliamentary democracy, Colonial history and apartheid, Deep social inequality | Commercial, Strong public-service with community media, Multi-lingual | 1,000 | 49 | 4.4 | Entertainment, mainly in Africa |

*Figures for 2014. All other figures for 2013, compiled from several sources: BRICS governments, World Bank, UN, ITU, UNESCO, ZenithOptimedia.

In the *Fortune 500* ranking, the number of transnational corporations (TNCs) based in the BRIC (Brazil, Russia, India and China) countries has grown from 27 in 2005 to 96 in 2012, indicating a rapid internationalization of BRIC big business (Goldstein, 2013). China's Huawei, a telecommunications equipment firm, is the world's largest holder of international patents, while Brazil's Petrobras is the fourth largest oil company in the world, with an annual turnover of $90 billion. In 2012, the Tata group became the first Indian conglomerate to reach $100 billion in revenues, more than half of it generated overseas – it is one of the largest foreign investors in Britain (Goldstein, 2013). By 2030, according to the World Bank, two-thirds of global savings and investment will be in developing countries, including the BRICS in that category, compared with one-fifth in 2000 (World Bank, 2013).

## The BRIC(S) agenda for a new world order

The first BRIC summit, held in 2009 in Ekaterinburg in Russia amidst the global financial crisis – which was triggered by excessively deregulated capitalism under the conditions of neo-liberalism – was to express demands for reform of the international financial institutions and banking system. By the third summit in China in 2011, the BRIC agenda had become increasingly political, with its leaders demanding constraints from the West in its aggressive policy towards Libya. The Delhi Declaration of the fourth summit in 2012 expressly had a political tone, criticizing the West for its intransigent policies over Libya, Syria and Iran. The declaration issued at the end of fifth BRICS summit held in Durban in 2013 noted that 'the prevailing global governance architecture is regulated by institutions which were conceived in circumstances when the international landscape in all its aspects was characterised by very different challenges and opportunities' and called for the objective of 'progressively developing the BRICS into a full-fledged mechanism of current and long-term coordination on a wide range of key issues of the world economy and politics' (BRICS5, 2013).

One striking manifestation of such a mechanism was the announcement of the establishment of a BRICS Bank to fund developmental projects, potentially to rival the Western-dominated Bretton Woods institutions, such as the World Bank and the International Monetary Fund. In addition, they also announced a new $100 billion fund – the 'Contingent Reserve Arrangement (CRA)' – to withstand currency turmoil and provide potential succour to developing and fragile economies, as well as a BRICS Business Council, to promote business cooperation by exploiting potential synergies and complementarities. At the 2014 summit in Fortaleza in Brazil, the 'New Development Bank', with an initial subscribed capital of $50 billion, and the $100 billion Contingent Reserve Arrangement were formally announced. Given that the bank will be headquartered in Shanghai, and that China has made the largest contribution – $41 billion – to the CRA, with Russia, India and Brazil contributing $18 billion each, and South Africa putting in $5 billion, the bank will further enhance China's domination of the BRICS group.

Although the idea of BRIC was initiated in Russia, it is China that has emerged as the driving force behind this grouping. The peaceful 'rise' of China as the world's fastest growing economy has profound implications for global polity and economy (Wang, 2010; Shambaugh, 2013). Since 2006, China has been the largest holder of foreign-currency reserves, estimated in 2013 to be $3.3 trillion. On the basis of purchasing power parity (PPP), China's Gross Domestic Product (GDP) in 2014 surpassed that of the United States, making it the world's largest economy, according to the IMF. 'No longer is China an emerging great power', observes a commentator, 'it is a "risen" one' (Layne, 2012: 212). When the country opened up to global businesses in the late 1980s, its presence in the international corporate world was negligible, but by 2013 China had 95 companies in the *Fortune Global 500* – for long a preserve of Western companies – just behind the US (128), while three of the top ten global corporations were Chinese (*Fortune*, 2014).

China's economic success story has many admirers, especially in the developing world, prompting the talk of replacing the 'Washington consensus' with the 'Beijing consensus' (Halper, 2010). In Africa, the Chinese presence has notably increased, observed *Der Spiegel*, a leading German magazine, in a three-part series published in November 2013. There were 2,000 Chinese companies operating in the resource-rich continent, it noted, and more than a million Chinese citizens were living in sub-Saharan Africa. Since 2000, trade volumes between China and Africa have grown 20-fold, reaching $200 billion in 2012 (Grill, 2013). China is also one of India's largest trading partners, and aims to achieve a target trade volume of $100 billion by 2015. The 2014 mega deal between Russia and China – a $400 billion pact that will provide 38 billion cubic meters of natural gas per year to the world's most energy-hungry nation for three decades – is the most significant intra-BRICS economic transaction to date, indicating the emerging Moscow–Beijing economic alliance, outside and beyond Western influence. Overall, between 2002 and 2012, intra-BRICS trade flows have grown from $27.3 billion to $282 billion, and are estimated to reach $500 billion by 2015 (UNCTAD, 2013).

It has been suggested that China is working 'within the system' to transform the post-1945 international order set up by the Western powers and wants to use such groupings as BRICS as a global bargaining chip to diminish and eventually displace the Pax-Americana. China is operating, observes a seasoned China-watcher, 'both within and outside the existing international system while at the same time, in effect, sponsoring a new China-centric international system which will exist alongside the present system and probably slowly begin to usurp it' (Jacques, 2009: 362).

It is evident that the BRICS countries are able to exert leverage within the UN system and the World Trade Organization, and are helping to shape the revisions of global governance rules, which were devised, defended and implemented largely by the West (Narlikar, 2010). As large, continental-size powers, BRICS countries are capable of redefining rules in such areas as global trade, intellectual property rights, cyber security and commerce, climate change, health and energy policy, among others (Wu, 2012; Hurrell and Sengupta, 2012; Ebert and Maurer, 2013; Harmer and Buse, 2014). Their aim, it has been suggested, is to 'consolidate a multipolar world' (Carmody, 2013: 133).

As intra-BRICS trade and economic exchange strengthens, their collective bargaining power will increase, as will their capacity to insulate their economies from the US-dominated Western economy. Despite many and clear differences in their foreign policy goals, BRICS nations demonstrate interesting similarities on many transnational issues, for instance the Brazilian notion of 'Responsibility while Protecting' (RWP) to replace the 'Responsibility to Protect' (R2P) doctrine deployed to legitimize Western military intervention in Libya. In the proposal, which received widespread support among UN members, intervening powers could be held accountable for deaths and damage that they might cause while protecting civilians (Burges, 2013). Respecting national sovereignty thus remains a key foreign policy attribute among BRICS nations. Both China and India continue to project themselves as developing countries and champions of the global South. As a founding member of the Non-Aligned Movement, India has traditionally seen itself on the international arena as an articulate voice of the global South, particularly during the 1970s and 1980s in debates about a New World Information and Communication Order (NWICO) (Nordenstreng, 2012). A developmental agenda – both domestically as well as in the context of the global South – has defined Brazilian foreign policy under President Lula (2003–10) and his successor, Dilma Rousseff (Matos, 2012).

It can be argued that the restrictive trade policies of the BRICS nations and their belief in a heightened role of the state have contributed to limiting the liberalizing progress of the multilateral WTO regime, for example during the Doha Round of trade talks (Carmody, 2013). The recent appointment of Brazil's Roberto Azevedo – against Western wishes – as WTO Director General, further highlights their growing influence in the international arena. An analysis based upon BRICS votes in the UN General Assembly for the period 1974–2011, showed 'a high and now growing degree of cohesion' among BRICS and their efforts to be 'seen as leading spokespersons for the developing world' (Ferdinand, 2014: 387). As a Brazilian scholar notes:

> By the mid-2000s, Brazil, Russia and South Africa could all identify with the developmental-multipolar discourse of China and India. The move from a liberal-unilateral to a developmental-multipolar set of social claims was a truly 'discursive alignment' that created the conditions of possibility for the emergence of BRICS. Indeed, development and multi-polarity are the cornerstones of the BRICS initiative.
>
> (Mielniczuk, 2013: 1087)

One outcome of such an alignment is that the BRICS countries have demonstrated policy cohesion, for example, during the 2009 UN Copenhagen conference on climate change, where prominent BRICS nations, such as China and India, insisted that they represented the interests and views of the developing nations, arguing that reducing emissions was the responsibility of the developed countries, who should make deeper, legally binding emissions cuts and help the most vulnerable nations to pay for the expenses of mitigating and adapting to the effects of global warming (Gilboy and Heginbotham, 2012; Hurrell and Sengupta, 2012; Wu, 2012). Similarly, during the 2011 UNESCO decision to grant Palestine full membership, the BRICS countries voted in favour, despite heavy lobbying by US diplomats. During the UN vote on Crimea in 2014, Brazil, India, China and South Africa either voted against or abstained from criticizing their BRICS partner, Russia.

Despite meeting regularly at the highest level since 2009, the BRICS is a relatively new and informal group, without a charter or a fixed secretariat. Its members also have to accommodate intra-group geo-political and economic rivalries. They have so far not succeeded in reforming the Western-dominated international financial institutions – the US dollar continues to be the dominant global currency, while the hegemony of neo-liberal ideology endures. Even though the group was conceived as an alternative to American power, none of the five member nations are eager for confrontation with the US, the country with which they have their most important relationship (Yardley, 2012). Indeed, China is one of the largest investors in the US, while India, Brazil and South Africa demonstrate democratic affinities with the West – as witnessed in their attitude towards issues surrounding Internet governance. India's IT industry is particularly dependent on its close ties with the US and Europe (UNCTAD, 2012). One columnist writing in the *International Herald Tribune* had dismissed BRICS as 'an artificial bloc built on a catchphrase' (Ladwig, 2012) and there remains wide diversity in the BRICS group, both within the large countries, such as Russia and India, and between them, as well as considerable tensions, for example, between China and India. Apart from the contentious border dispute and disagreements on Tibet, both countries vie for resources and the leadership role of the global South (Cheru and Obi, 2010; Mawdsley and McCann, 2011; Pant, 2012).

It has been suggested that, given that all BRICS countries pursue free-market capitalism, they will follow the liberal international system, thus reflecting the 'ultimate ascendance' of the liberal world order (Ikenberry, 2011). According to UNCTAD, 42 per cent of BRICS outward FDI stock is in developed countries, with 34 per cent in the European Union (UNCTAD, 2013). As Zakaria has argued, the US will remain the 'pivotal power' in international politics for a long time because there is 'still a strong market for American power, for both geopolitical and economic reasons. But even more centrally, there remains a strong ideological demand for it' (Zakaria, 2008: 234). Others have cautioned against such formulations, suggesting that the age of Western hegemony is increasingly diminishing: though the US is likely to remain a major anchor in world politics, it will have to share its responsibilities with the emerging powers (Acharya, 2014). Will the ascendance of BRICS lead to greater circulation of its media and thus affect the dominant discourses emanating from the US?

## An Americanized global media?

Despite the unprecedented growth of media and communication industries in the BRICS nations, particularly in such large countries as China, India and Brazil, the global media continues to be dominated by the US. Given its formidable political, economic, technological and military power, American or Americanized media are available across the globe, in English or in dubbed or indigenized versions. The US medias' imprint on the global communication space, by virtue of the ownership of multiple networks and production facilities, gives the US a huge advantage (Castells, 2009). As during most of the twentieth century, the US remains today the largest exporter, both of the world's entertainment and information programmes and of the software and hardware through which these are distributed across the increasingly digitized globe (Thussu, 2015).

According to the 2013 report from the International Intellectual Property Alliance, the core copyright industries – computer software, video games, books, newspapers, periodicals and journals, motion pictures, recorded music and radio and television broadcasting – are worth more than one trillion dollars, demonstrating impressive growth from $884.81 billion in 2009 to $1,015.64 billion in 2012. In the US, these industries employed over five million people in 2012 and accounted for more than 6 per cent of the GDP and overseas sales of $142 billion (Siwek, 2013). In 2012, four out of the five top entertainment corporations in the world were US-based (the remaining one also had strong links with US-based media corporations), evidence of the existence of a Pax-Americana, a trend which has become pronounced in the era of digital and networked entertainment (*Fortune*, 2014).

These corporations have benefited from the growth of markets in large BRICS countries such as Brazil, China and India. In almost all media spheres the US media giants dwarf their global competitors: from entertainment and sport (Hollywood, MTV, Disney, ESPN); to news and current affairs (CNN, Discovery, *Time*), to financial media (Bloomberg, *Fortune*, *Wall Street Journal*) and social media (Google, YouTube, Facebook, Twitter). US entertainment and information networks – sources of its 'soft' power – cannot be separated from American global economic, political and military supremacy, expressed in its more than 1,000 military bases across the globe and its enormous defence budget (more than $600 billion in 2013, according to the London-based International Institute of Strategic Studies), unmatched by any other nation. It is American hard power that impacts on many countries and helps spread the American way of life, supported by its formidable soft power reserves – from Hollywood entertainment giants to the digital empires of the Internet age. As Joseph Nye has remarked, US culture 'from Hollywood to Harvard – has greater global reach than any other' (Nye, 2004: 7).

In the past two decades, the US-inspired commercial media system has been globalized, a phenomenon that Hallin and Mancini have characterized as the 'triumph of the liberal model' (Hallin and Mancini, 2004: 251). While the opening of media and communication markets where there was previously state control has meant more dynamic media, the challenging of state censorship and a widening of the public sphere, it has also contributed to the concentration of media power among private corporations. The exponential growth of multichannel networks has made the global media landscape multicultural, multilingual and multinational. Digital communication technologies in broadcasting and broadband have given viewers in many countries the ability to access simultaneously a vast array of local, national, regional and international media in various genres (Castells, 2009). As UNESCO's *World Culture Report* notes:

> While it is undeniable that globalization has played an integrative role as a 'window on the world', mostly to the profit of a few powerful international conglomerates, recent shifts prompted by technological innovation and new consumption patterns are spurring new forms of 'globalization from below' and creating a two-way flow of communication and cultural products.
>
> (UNESCO, 2009: 131)

## The rise of the BRICS media – contra or complementary?

In parallel with the political and economic rise of BRICS, its media too have grown rapidly in recent years. According to the World Association of Newspapers and News Publishers, the circulation of daily newspapers has continued to demonstrate growth in Asia and Latin America of more than 6 per cent in the period 2009–13, at a time when Europe experienced a decline of 23 per cent and North America witnessed a decline of nearly 20 per cent. In this period, newspaper circulation rose over 7 per cent in Asia, the Middle East and Africa, and more than 6 per cent in Latin America, while it fell by over 10 per cent in North America and 23 per cent in Europe (WAN-IFRA, 2014). The growth in media has also contributed to the rise in advertising revenue among BRICS countries as consumerism escalates, though, in comparison to mature markets, such as the US, Europe and Japan, it still remains small (Ciochetto, 2011). According to a PwC report, in the next three years China will become the world's second-largest book as well as TV market after the US and will overtake Japan to become the third-largest market for filmed entertainment after the US and Britain (PwC, 2014).

Audio-visual media retain an important position as an instrument of global influence and, ever since international broadcasting became a part of the foreign policy agenda during the Cold War, control of the airwaves has been fought over. Until the globalization of television and telecommunication, international broadcasters fulfilled an important information gap, especially in countries where media were under strict state control. With the deregulation and digitization of communication and the entry of powerful private providers, the media landscape has been transformed, offering new challenges and opportunities (Castells, 2009).

There are various types of new media flows, some reinforcing old colonial patterns (notably Britain's BBC World Service and BBC World News, and France's Radio France International, TV5 and France 24), while others are emerging from the BRICS nations. Inspired by the success of Qatar's Al Jazeera, Russia has also raised its international broadcasting profile by entering the English-language news world in 2005 with the launch of the Russia Today (RT) network, which, apart from English, also broadcasts 24/7 in Spanish and Arabic, claiming to have a global reach of more than 550 million people. RT also has a documentary channel as well as a YouTube presence. Its tag line – 'question more' – indicates that the channel questions the dominant Western media discourses and covers international affairs generally from an anti-US perspective, though its coverage of other BRICS nations remains limited and it is widely seen as little more than a voice of the Kremlin, where ultimate editorial control rests. This soft version of propaganda has a long history: during the Soviet era, Moscow managed a massive propaganda machine, supporting anti-colonial movements and progressive causes around what was then called the Third World. Since the disintegration of the Soviet Union, and after recovering from the transition to a capitalist system, Moscow has again expanded its media to reach a global audience (Sherr, 2012).

Though the BRICS nations claim to protect and promote the interests of the developing countries, their media has not yet reached the level of Al Jazeera English, which does privilege the global South in its coverage of international affairs, having emerged since its launch in 2006 as a broadcaster of substance and providing a space for a wider conversation in the global communication arena (Seib, 2012; Figenschou, 2014). With nearly 300 round-the-clock news channels and a strong tradition of English-language journalism, Indian perspectives on global affairs are accessible via such channels as News 18 India, part of the TV-18 group, as well as NDTV 24x7. Both are private networks, while the Indian state broadcaster Doordarshan remains one of the few major state news networks not available in important global markets at a time when global television news in English has expanded to include inputs from countries where English is not widely used, including Japan and Iran (though in August 2014, plans to launch Doordarshan's global channel were announced). Paradoxically, Indian journalism and news media in general is losing interest in the wider world – particularly in other BRICS nations – at a time when Indian industry is increasingly globalizing and international engagement with India is growing across the globe (Thussu, 2013).

Arguably the most significant development in terms of BRICS is the growing presence on the international news scene of Chinese television news in English for a global audience, promoting the Chinese model of development with an extensive and intensive programme of external communication: 'As China has looked outside its borders, it has altered its image across much of the globe, from threat to opportunity, from danger to benefactor' (Kurlantzick, 2007: 5). The image makeover is rooted in an official discourse aimed at projecting the Chinese version of globalization as a peaceful process, and at the same time, to ameliorate the country's image, especially in the West, as a one-party state which suppresses freedom of expression and curtails human rights (Lai and Lu, 2012; Zhu, 2012; Shambaugh, 2013; Stockman, 2013).

Under China's $7 billion external communication programme, including broadcasting and online presence, Chinese media have expanded across the globe: by 2012, CCTV News was claiming 200 million viewers outside China and broadcasting in six languages, including Arabic. Xinhua, among the largest news agencies in the world, with more than 10,000 employees in 107 bureaus, launched the English-language TV channel, CNC World, which plans to expand into 100 countries (Xin, 2012). Xinhua has 28 offices in Africa, more than any international news agency (Grill, 2013). However, as one observer noted: 'CCTV has yet to be the international authority on China, let alone being a credible alternative to the BBC, CNN, or Al Jazeera on world affairs' (Zhu, 2012, 194).

These examples of news from BRICS provide interesting sites for an oppositional discourse on global news: RT's coverage of the Syrian conflict, for example, is strikingly different from the dominant US–UK media discourse (the only military base that the Russians have in the strategically significant Middle East is in Syria). CCTV is gaining viewers as, 'instead of airing the usual disaster reports, the station tends to broadcast "good news" from Africa and portrays China as a "true friend"' (Grill, 2013). And yet, in terms of audience, news networks have a relatively small impact on global media flows, most of which is centred on entertainment, which continues to be dominated by the US, though others players are increasingly visible.

For nearly three decades, Brazil's successful television industry, centred on the *telenovela* format, has spread to most of Latin America, as well as internationally: it is exported to more than 100 countries across the globe – dubbed and adapted and inspiring many television mini-series. Brazilian entertainment is particularly popular within the Lusophone world, where it continues to dominate the media (Sinclair and Straubhaar, 2013). Such Brazilian media conglomerates as the Rio-based Globo group have not only shaped domestic media but also have had a strong political influence within Brazil (Porto, 2012). By hosting the 2014 FIFA World Cup and the 2016 Summer Olympics, Brazil's popular culture is likely to be noticed more than ever before. South

Africa remains the least developed media market among the BRICS nations, though in recent years, apart from the greater visibility of its pan-African network M-Net, the country's film production has grown significantly: from five in 2005 to 60 in 2012, with such films as *Tsotsi*, winning the 2006 Oscar for Best Foreign Language Film (FICCI-KPMG Report, 2014).

If Brazil has a prominent place in television entertainment, India's Bollywood is the most visible BRICS media product globally. According to industry estimates, the Indian entertainment and media industry was worth $29 billion in 2013 (FICCI-KPMG Report, 2014). 'Bollywood', a $3.5 billion industry, is the world's largest film factory in terms of production and viewership, in more than 70 countries (Athique, 2012; Gera Roy, 2012; Schaefer and Karan, 2013; Kohli-Khandekar, 2013; FICCI-KPMG Report, 2014). Indian films have been in circulation around the globe since the 1930s, primarily consumed by the 35-million strong South Asian diaspora, scattered across all continents. During the Cold War years, Indian films were widely circulated in the Soviet Union (Rajagopalan, 2008) and in China, where the escapist musical melodramas were considered by the Communist authorities to be a useful alternative to state propaganda and a cheap substitute for Hollywood. In more recent years, the box office success in China of the 2009 Indian college comedy *Three Idiots* demonstrates the level of interest in Indian cinema; at the same time, Hong Kong-produced Chinese action films have been popular among the Indian audiences (Srinivas, 2003). In 2012, Zee became the first Indian television network to beam its programmes into China. Bollywoodized content has even reached Brazil: one prominent example was the hugely successful India-themed Brazilian soap opera *India – A Love Story*, screened in prime-time in 2009 on TV Globo, which won an International Emmy Award for best telenovela (Thussu, 2013).

While the one-way vertical flow of international television programmes, mainly from the US to other parts of the world as documented by two UNESCO-sponsored studies (Nordenstreng and Varis, 1974; Varis, 1985), has intensified in the era of digitized globalization, it has nevertheless been encountered by multiple and horizontal flows, as 'subaltern' media content providers have emerged to service an ever-growing geo-cultural market (Thussu, 2007). Such contra-flows in international communication raise interesting and important questions about what constitutes the global in global media. Are these new global players necessarily opposed to the US–UK hegemony or are they following the same market-driven, infotainment-oriented model with its roots in the commercial media system of the US? Are these media instruments for soft power? Does the impressive growth of media in the BRICS countries and their greater visibility across the globe indicate the end of globalization as Westernization? There is no doubt that the availability of journalistic material emanating from major non-Western centres of global media production complicates the discourse about international media. What kind of paradigms and theoretical frameworks are required to make sense of this altered reality?

## BRICS and global media research

The academic study of media and communication – relatively new subjects in the BRICS nations – is rapidly growing in these countries. By 2014, more than 800 communication and media programmes were being run in Chinese universities, paralleled by the publication of many Chinese-language journals in the field, as well as China-related material in international journals (see Keane and Sun, 2013). In India too, the growth of media has led to the mushrooming of mostly vocational media research institutes and interesting research is beginning to emerge (Sundaram, 2013). China and India offer potentially lucrative markets for courses in media and communication, as both countries are large suppliers of postgraduate and research students to Western universities. Already many Western universities are developing new courses and collaborative projects with institutions of higher education in China and India, and a few initiatives on intra-BRICS academic exchanges have also begun. At the 2014 Brazil summit, the Indian Prime Minister Narendra Modi suggested setting up a BRICS university.

The increasing mobility of students and faculty and the organization of short courses and exchange programmes have also contributed to this intercultural and international communication. Intellectual curiosity about BRICS nations is often confined to specialists at a time when internationalization should be an integral part of teaching and research in media and communication, given the global nature of the subject and globalization of media and communication industries. Such an altered academic environment demands what Appaduari has called 'deparochialization of the research ethic – the idea of research itself' (Appadurai, 2001: 15).

Can the growth of media and communication studies in BRICS contribute to broadening research concerns and agendas in this relatively new field? Research in the media and communication arena has been traditionally influenced by Eurocentric essentialism. The BRICS communication challenge is difficult to analyse within traditional Western originated and oriented media theory – whether liberal or critical, though both have useful insights to offer (Curran and Park, 2000; Hallin and Mancini, 2012). This calls for original and innovative methodological approaches and theoretical interventions, as well as a radical re-evaluation of pedagogic parameters, taking historical, cultural and socio-psychological factors into consideration.

One research area where a BRICS contribution might be particularly valuable is development communication. Apart from Russia, the other four BRICS nations, despite their robust economic growth – almost double-digit for nearly a decade in the case of China – continue to be home to very large number of poor and disadvantaged people (Zhao, 2008; Kohli, 2012). India was the first country to use television for education through its 1970s SITE (Satellite Instructional Television Experiment) programme. New digital media technologies could be deployed to promote the Gandhian notions of community living and sustainable development. Brazilian experience of community media, South Africa's emphasis on public service broadcasting and China's aid for developing countries in Asia and Africa, especially in such areas as telecommunication, may contribute to promoting a Chinese version of development discourse: the China Great Wall Industry Corporation has been offering expertise and funding to develop satellite and other space programmes. Traditionally, the development discourse has been devised and developed in the West and conforms to a Western sensibility of what constitutes development. Would a BRICS development perspective be less affected by the colonial mindset? Already, in many developing countries in Latin America (Armony and Strauss, 2012) and Africa (Sauvant *et al.*, 2010; Cheru and Obi, 2010; Mawdsley and McCann, 2011; Chan, Lee and Chan, 2011; Lai and Lu, 2012) these debates have occupied policy and media agendas.

The dominant strands of research in global media and communication have traditionally been conducted within a Western, or more accurately, an American, framework. It is pertinent to ask whether such a framework is adequately equipped – both theoretically and empirically – to comprehend the complexity of a new globalization that challenges established ways of thinking about international media and communication (Thussu, 2009; Chen, 2010; Curtin and Shah, 2010; Wang, 2011; Esser and Hanitzsch, 2012; Christians and Nordenstreng, 2014; Iwabuchi, 2014). In an increasingly mobile and globally networked and digitized world, media and communication studies have been transformed, as South–South and, increasingly, South–North cultural flows erode US cultural hegemony. And BRICS, given their size and scale, could be a crucial element in this process.

Industry estimates say that the number of Internet users in India is set to reach 600 million by 2020, making it the biggest 'open' Internet access market in the world. In 2012, with only 12 per cent of its population able to access the Internet, India was already second only to the US in terms of usage of English on the net. According to a PwC report, China and India will account for 47 per cent of net new mobile Internet access subscribers between 2013 and 2018 (PwC, 2014). It is interesting to speculate what kind of content will be circulating on the World Wide Web and in which language when 90 per cent of Chinese and an equally high percentage of Indians get online (in 2014, 45 per cent of China's and nearly 20 per cent of India's billion plus population were using the Internet) (Internet World Stats, 2014). It is particularly striking in the context of India's 'demographic dividend': more than 65 per cent of Indians are below the age of 30. As their prosperity grows, a sizeable segment of young Indians are going online, producing, distributing and consuming digital media, especially using their skills in the English language, the vehicle for global communication and increasingly for global higher education. The combined economic and cultural impact of China and India, aided by their extensive global diasporas, may create a different form of globalization – a 'Chindian' communication space (Sun, 2009; Kapur, 2010; Isar, 2010; Amrith, 2011).

Will the BRICS media emerge as an alternative to the US media or supplement them? It is safe to suggest that, at least in the short-term, the multi-faceted US domination of the world's media is likely to continue. We may agree with Tunstall that *The Media Were American* (Tunstall, 2008) and that the rise and ripening of media from BRICS nations will further internationalize media studies and contribute to de-Americanizing international media. Given the formidable media hard- and software that the United States wields, it is unlikely in the foreseeable future, though the challenges and opportunities that the BRICS media offer would suggest a serious engagement with the emerging communication cultures from major countries, demanding a re-evaluation of the field of global media studies.

## The book in outline

This edited collection brings together leading scholars from the BRICS nations and those with deep interest in and knowledge of these countries, representing a range of academic voices, to examine and discuss how the emergence of the BRICS media will impact on global media and communication. It contextualizes the role of the BRICS media in a 'multi-polar' world, evaluates the media landscape and journalism practices in the BRICS nations, drawing on empirical material. By interrogating the relationship between the inter-BRICS media and media practices and perceptions, this volume aims to be an accessible and comprehensive guide to the complex debates about the impact of the 'rise of the rest' on the media globe. Finally, although it offers a range of perspectives concerning core issues surrounding emerging trends and tendencies in international journalism, it adopts a critical approach in relation to the dominant justifications for and analyses of the BRICS phenomenon.

The book, it is hoped, will make a theoretical and empirical intervention in the ongoing debates about the problems and prospects of comparative communication research and thus contribute further to the internationalization of media and communication, thus conforming to the basic intellectual tenet of this series on Internationalizing Media Studies.

The book is divided into three parts, each having a brief introduction from the editors. The first part – debates and concepts – is aimed to provide an international relations perspective on the rise of the BRICS nations and their impact on global politics and communication. Chapters in this part consider the geo-political and economic contexts of the BRICS nations and the coherence of the concept itself. The second part of the book looks at the media systems and landscapes among the BRICS five. Although the media in the BRICS countries have demonstrated huge growth, their study remains largely neglected in international media scholarship. The chapters provide hitherto unpublished material on some of the most dynamic and differentiated media systems in the world. The final part of the book takes an explicitly comparative framework to explore journalism practices as well as examine intra-BRICS media coverage. Based on interviews with journalists working in the BRICS countries as well as content analysis of media coverage, the chapters in this part provide both a starting point and an argument for further important transnational and comparative media research on the BRICS countries.

The final chapter focuses on digital futures, given the unprecedented growth of online media in some of the larger BRICS nations, notably China and India. The global presence of the BRICS media is likely to expand exponentially with the growing convergence of mobile communications technologies and content via an altered and multi-lingual Internet. What implications will such digital connectivity have for global news flows, information and communication agendas, both in the BRICS countries and beyond?

The book is based on a major four-year project funded by the Academy of Finland entitled 'Media systems in flux: The challenge of the BRICS countries' (http://uta.fi/cmt/tutkimus/BRICS.html). The project starts by mapping BRICS and its media, continuing to examine the media systems with a focus on both traditional mass media and new online media as additional platforms for public sphere. The project examines – by extensive and comparative empirical research – the media systems in the BRICS countries, including journalists as strategic actors and television drama as strategic content. The current book is the first of four volumes foreseen to report results by 2017.

## Acknowledgements

Edited volumes, such as this one, which involves an international group of scholars working in different languages and within distinct intellectual traditions, entail a great deal of coordination. We are very thankful to all our contributors – members of the BRICS project team (http://www.uta.fi/cmt/tutkimus/BRICS/members.html) – for their valuable chapters and to Liz Thussu for her help with editing. We also want to record our profound gratitude to Natalie Foster and her team at Routledge for their professional support.

## Note

There is now a burgeoning literature on the BRICS, their geopolitics and geo-economics and their impact on global governance. In 2012, ministries of finance and central banks in the BRICS nations published *The BRICS Report: A Study of Brazil, Russia, India, China and South Africa with Special Focus on Synergies and Complementarities*. Inter-BRICS dialogue is also growing, for example in India (Observer Research Foundation, 2013) and South Africa (Kornegay and Bohler-Muller, 2013), while the Rio de Janeiro-based BRICS Policy Center produces regular documents about the grouping. For useful data on BRICS countries also see Brazilian Government's Fundação Alexandre de GusmãoBrasília the *Bibliographic Catalogue: Brazil, Russia, India, China and*

South Africa – BRICS, 2nd Edition, revised and expanded in 2011. BRICS is being increasingly noticed outside the five countries, too. See, for example, the 2013 special issue on 'Rise of New Powers' of the journal *International Affairs,* Volume 89, Number 3, as well as 2013 special issue on 'Dreaming with the BRICS? The Washington Consensus and the New Political Economy of Development' in *Review of International Political Economy* Volume 20, Issue 2. Also useful is the special section on 'BRICS and the politics of global health' in the 2014 issue of *Contemporary Politics,* Volume 20, Issue 2. Other recent work includes, the 2013 special issue 'Foreign Policy Strategies of Emerging Powers in a Multipolar World' of *Third World Quarterly,* Volume 34, Number 6, and the 2014 issue of *Oxford Development Studies* on 'Rising Powers' and Labour and Environmental Standards: Challenges to the Global Governance of Consumption, Production and Trade. A BRICS Academic Forum has also been set up to provide policy input. In addition, BRICS resource sites have been set up in universities and other agencies as shown at http://www.uta.fi/cmt/tutkimus/BRICS/materials.html.

## References

Acharya, Amitav (2014) *The End of American World Order.* Cambridge: Polity.

Amrith, Sunil (2011) *Migration and Diaspora in Modern Asia.* Cambridge: Cambridge University Press.

Appadurai, Arjun (2001) Grassroots Globalization and Research Imagination, pp. 1–21, in Arjun Appadurai (ed.) *Globalization.* Durham, NC: Duke University Press.

Armony, Ariel and Strauss, Julia (2012) From Going Out (*zou chuqu*) to Arriving In (*desembarco*): Constructing a New Field of Inquiry in China-Latin America Interactions, *The China Quarterly,* 209: 1–17.

Athique, Adrian (2012) *Indian Media: Global Approaches.* Cambridge: Polity.

The BRICS Report (2012) *The BRICS Report: A Study of Brazil, Russia, India, China and South Africa with Special Focus on Synergies and Complementarities.* New Delhi: Oxford University Press.

BRICS5 (2013) *BRICS Fifth Summit Declaration and Action Plan,* www.brics5.co.za/.

Brütsch, Christian and Papa, Mihaela (2013) Deconstructing the BRICS: Bargaining Coalition, Imagined Community, or Geopolitical Fad?, *Chinese Journal of International Politics* 6(3): 299–327.

Burges, Sean (2013) Brazil as a bridge between old and new powers? *International Affairs,* 89(3): 577–94.

Carmody, Pádraig (2013) *The Rise of the BRICS in Africa: The Geopolitics of South-South Relations,* London: Zed Books.

Castells, Manuel (2009) *Communication Power.* Oxford: Oxford University Press.

Chan, Gerald; Lee, Pak and Chan, Lai-Ha (2011) *China Engages Global Governance: A New World Order in the Making?* London: Routledge.

Chen, Kuan-Hsing (2010) *Asia as Method: Toward Deimperialization.* Durham: Duke University Press.

Cheru, Fantu and Obi, Cyril (eds.) (2010) *The Rise of China and India in Africa: Challenges, Opportunities and Critical Interventions.* London: Zed Books.

Christians, Clifford and Nordenstreng, Kaarle (eds.) (2014) *Communication Theories in a Multicultural World*. New York: Peter Lang.

Ciochetto, Lynne (2011) *Globalisation and Advertising in Emerging Economies: Brazil, Russia, India and China*. London: Routledge.

Curran, James and Park, Myung-Jin (2000) Beyond Globalization Theory, pp. 3–18 in James Curran and Myung-Jin Park (eds.) *De-Westernizing Media Studies*. London: Routledge.

Curtin, Michael and Shah, Hemant (eds.) (2010) *Reorienting Global Communication: Indian and Chinese Media Beyond Borders*. Chicago: University of Illinois Press.

Ebert, Hannes and Maurer, Tim (2013) Contested Cyberspace and Rising Powers, *Third World Quarterly*, 34(6): 1054–74.

Esser, Frank and Hanitzsch, Thomas (eds.) (2012) *Handbook of Comparative Communication Research*. New York: Routledge.

Ferdinand, Peter (2014) Rising Powers at the UN: An Analysis of the Voting Behaviour of BRICS in the General Assembly, *Third World Quarterly*, 35(3): 376–91.

FICCI-KPMG Report (2014) *The Stage is Set: FICCI/KPMG Indian Media and Entertainment Industry Report 2014*. Mumbai: Federation of Indian Chambers of Commerce and Industry.

Figenschou, Tine Ustad (2014) *Al Jazeera and the Global Media Landscape: The South is Talking Back*. New York: Routledge.

*Fortune* (2014) 'Fortune Global 500', *Fortune*, July.

Gera Roy, Anjali (ed.) (2012) *The Magic of Bollywood: At Home and Abroad*. New Delhi: Sage.

Gilboy, George and Heginbotham, Eric (2012) *Chinese and Indian Strategic Behavior: Growing Power and Alarm*. New York: Cambridge University Press.

Goldman Sachs (2007) *BRICs and Beyond*. New York: Goldman Sachs Global Economics Department.

Goldstein, Andrea (2013) The Political Economy of Global Business: The Case of the BRICs. *Global Policy* 4(2):162–72.

Grill, Bartholomäus (2013) Billions from Beijing: Africans Divided over Chinese Presence, *Der Spiegel*, 29 November.

Hallin, Daniel and Mancini, Paolo (2004) *Comparing Media Systems*. Cambridge: Cambridge University Press.

Hallin, Daniel and Mancini, Paolo (eds.) (2012) *Comparing Media Systems Beyond the Western World*. Cambridge: Cambridge University Press.

Halper, Stefan (2010) *The Beijing Consensus: How China's Authoritarian Model Will Dominate the Twenty-first Century*. New York: Basic Books.

Harmer, Andrew and Buse, Kent (2014) The BRICS: A Paradigm Shift in Global Health? *Contemporary Politics*, 20(2): 127–45.

Hurrell, Andrew and Sengupta, Sandeep (2012) Emerging Powers, North–South Relations and Global Climate Politics, *International Affairs* 88(3): 463–84.

Ikenberry, John (2011) *Liberal Leviathan: The Origins, Crisis, and Transformation of the American World Order*. Princeton, NJ: Princeton University Press.

Internet World Stats (2014) 'Asia', www.internetworldstats.com/stats3.htm (accessed 9 June 2014).

Isar, Yudhishthir Raj (2010) 'Chindia': A Cultural Project. *Global Media and Communication* 6(3): 277–84.

Iwabuchi, Koichi (2014) De-westernisation, Inter-Asian Referencing and Beyond, *European Journal of Cultural Studies*, 17(1): 44–57.

Jacques, Martin (2009) *When China Rules the World: The End of the Western World and the Birth of a New Global Order*. London: Allen Lane.

Kapur, Devesh (2010) *Diaspora, Development, and Democracy: The Domestic Impact of International Migration from India*, Princeton: Princeton University Press.

Keane, Michael and Sun, Wanning (eds.) (2013) *Chinese Media*. London: Routledge. Four volume set.

Kohli, Atul (2012) *Poverty amid Plenty in the New India*. Cambridge: Cambridge University Press.

Kohli-Khandekar, Vanita (2013) *The Indian Media Business*. Fourth edition. New Delhi: Sage.

Kornegay, Francis and Bohler-Muller, Narnia (eds.) (2013) *Laying the BRICS of a New Global Order: From Yekterinburg to e'Thekwini*. Pretoria: African Institute of South Africa.

Kurlantzick, Joshua (2007) *Charm Offensive: How China's Soft Power is Transforming the World*. New Haven: Yale University Press.

Ladwig, Walter (2012) An Artificial Bloc Built on a Catchphrase, *The International Herald Tribune*, 27 March.

Lai, Hongyi and Lu, Yiyi (eds.) (2012) *China's Soft Power and International Relations*. London: Routledge.

Layne, Christopher (2012) This Time It's Real: The End of Unipolarity and the Pax Americana. *International Studies Quarterly* 56, 203–13.

Matos, Carolina (2012) *Media and Politics in Latin America: Globalization, Democracy and Identity*. London: I.B. Tauris.

Mawdsley, Emma and McCann, Gerard (eds.) (2011) *India in Africa: Changing Geographies of Power*. Oxford: Fahamu Books.

Mielniczuk, Fabiano (2013) BRICS in the Contemporary World: Changing Identities, Converging Interests, *Third World Quarterly*, 34(6) 1075–90.

Narlikar, Amrita (2010) *New Powers: How to become one and how to manage them*, London: Hurst.

Nordenstreng, Kaarle (2012) The New World Information and Communication Order: An Idea That Refuses to Die, pp. 477–99, in John Nerone (ed.) *Media History and the Foundations of Media Studies, Volume 1, The International Encyclopedia of Media Studies*, Oxford: Wiley-Blackwell.

Nordenstreng, Kaarle and Varis, Tapio (1974) *Television Traffic—A One-Way Street? A Survey and Analysis of the International Flow of Television Programme Material*, Reports and Papers on Mass Communication, no. 70. Paris: UNESCO.

Nye, Joseph (2004) *Power in the Global Information Age: From Realism to Globalization*. London: Routledge.

Observer Research Foundation (2013) *A Long-Term Vision for the BRICS*, www.bricsforum. com/wp-content/uploads/2013/09/long-term-vision-for-BRICS1.pdf (accessed 10 June 2014).

O'Neill, Jim (2011) *The Growth Map: Economic Opportunity in the BRICS and Beyond*. London: Portfolio/Penguin.

Pant, Harsh (ed.) (2012) *The Rise of China: Implications for India*. New Delhi: Cambridge University Press.

Porto, Mauro (2012) *Media Power and Democratization in Brazil: TV Globo and the Dilemmas of Political Accountability*. London: Routledge.

PwC (2013) *World in 2050. The BRICs and Beyond: Prospects, Challenges and Opportunities*. January. London: PricewaterhouseCoopers.

PwC (2014) *PwC Annual Global Entertainment and Media Outlook*. London: Pricewaterhouse-Coopers.

Rajagopalan, Sudha (2008) *Leave Disco Dancer Alone! Indian Cinema and Soviet Movie-going After Stalin.* New Delhi: Yoda Press.

Sauvant, Karl; Pradhan, Jaya Prakash; Chatterjee, Ayesha and Harley, Brian (eds.) (2010) *The Rise of Indian Multinationals: Perspective of Indian Outward Foreign Direct Investment.* New York: Palgrave Macmillan.

Schaefer, David and Karan, Kavita (eds.) (2013) *Bollywood and Globalization: The Global Power of Popular Hindi Cinema.* London: Routledge.

Seib, Philip (ed.) (2012) *Aljazeera English: Global News in a Changing World.* New York: Palgrave Macmillan.

Shambaugh, David (2013) *China Goes Global: The Partial Power.* New York: Oxford University Press.

Sherr, James (2012) *Soft Power? The Means and Ends of Russian Influence Abroad.* Washington: Brookings Institution Press.

Sinclair, John and Straubhaar, Joseph (2013) *Television in Latin America.* London: BFI.

Siwek, Stephen (2013) *Copyright Industries in the U.S. Economy: The 2013 Report*, Incorporated, prepared for the International Intellectual Property Alliance (IIPA), November. Available at www.iipa.com.

Srinivas, S. V. (2003) Hong Kong Action Film in the Indian B Circuit, *Inter-Asia Cultural Studies* 4(1): 40–62.

Stockman, Daniela (2013) *Media Commercialization and Authoritarian Rule in China.* New York: Cambridge University Press.

Sun, Wanning (ed.) (2009) *Media and the Chinese Diaspora: Community, Communications and Commerce.* London: Routledge.

Sundaram, Ravi (ed.) (2013) *No Limits: Media Studies from India.* New Delhi: Oxford University Press.

Thussu, Daya Kishan (2007) Mapping Global Media Flow and Contra-Flow, pp. 11–32, in Thussu, Daya Kishan (ed.) *Media on the Move: Global Flow and Contra-Flow*, London: Routledge.

Thussu, Daya Kishan (2009) Why Internationalize Media Studies and How, pp. 13–31, in Thussu, Daya Kishan (ed.) *Internationalising Media Studies*, London: Routledge.

Thussu, Daya Kishan (2013) *Communicating India's Soft Power: Buddha to Bollywood.* New York: Palgrave Macmillan.

Thussu, Daya Kishan (2015) *International Communication – Continuity and Change*, third edition. London: Bloomsbury Academic.

Tunstall, Jeremy (2008) *The Media Were American.* Oxford: Oxford University Press

UNCTAD (2012) *Information Economy Report 2012: The Software Industry and Developing Countries.* New York: United Nations Conference on Trade and Development.

UNCTAD (2013) The Rise of BRICS FDI and Africa, *Global Investment Trends Monitor*, 25 March, New York: United Nations Conference on Trade and Development.

UNDP (2013) *The Rise of the South: The 2013 Human Development Report.* New York: United Nations Development Programme.

UNESCO (2009) *World Culture Report.* Paris: UNESCO.

Varis, Tapio (1985) *International Flow of Television Programmes*, Reports and Papers on Mass Communication, No. 100. Paris: UNESCO.

WAN-IFRA (2014) *Trends in Newsrooms 2014.* Paris: The World Association of Newspapers and News Publishers.

Wang, Georgette (ed.) (2011) *De-Westernizing Communication Research: Altering Questions and Changing Frameworks.* London: Routledge.

Wang, Jian (ed.) (2010) *Soft Power in China: Public Diplomacy through Communication.* New York: Palgrave Macmillan.

Wilson, Dominic and Purushothaman, Roopa (2003) *Dreaming with BRICs: The Path to 2050.* Goldman Sachs Global Economics Paper, No. 99. New York: Goldman Sachs.

World Bank (2013) *Capital for the Future: Saving and Investment in an Interdependent World.* Washington: The World Bank.

Wu, Fuzuo (2012) Sino-Indian Climate Cooperation: Implications for the International Climate Change Regime, *Journal of Contemporary China*, 21(77): 827–43.

Xin, Xin (2012) *How the Market is Changing China's News: The Case of Xinhua News Agency.* Lanham: Lexington Books.

Yardley, Jim (2012) For Group of 5 Nations, Acronym Is Easy, but Common Ground Is Hard, *The New York Times*, 29 March, page A4.

Zakaria, Fareed (2008) *The Post-American World.* London: Allen Lane.

Zhao, Yuezhi (2008) *Communication in China: Political Economy, Power and Conflict.* Lanham: Rowman & Littlefield.

Zhu, Ying (2012) *Two Billion Eyes: The Story of China Central Television.* New York: The New Press.

# Part I

# Debates and concepts

## Introduction

The rise of the BRICS configuration has evoked much interest among policy makers and the corporate world, as it includes the world's fastest growing economies. How will their ascendance impact on global power relations and international communication and media? Chapters in this part of the book tackle this question from a range of perspectives, encompassing international relations, critical communication studies and cultural studies.

In an overview of the BRICS phenomenon, Jyrki Käkönen, a Finnish international relations expert with expertise on Euro-Asian relations, considers how the BRICS grouping might influence global politics. He reviews the role of the BRICS countries as an organization in international relations, drawing on official documents. The major question he raises pertains to whether their fast economic growth and interest in a multi-polar international system would make BRICS a coherent and effective international actor. It is apparent that all BRICS members have their own national interests and have realized that BRICS is a useful idea for advancing those interests. On the other hand, Käkönen argues, the five BRICS members are a diverse combination of countries with very different civilizational and cultural backgrounds. It is not easy to assume, the chapter suggests, that BRICS would be an organization able to change the international system when its members have varying expectations and ideas about how to reconfigure the world order. For Käkönen, the most important BRICS countries are China and India, given their size and scale for current and future economic growth, coupled with their civilizational attributes. However, both nations have contrasting political systems and competing and even contradictory interests with regard to a new multi-polar international order.

In his chapter, Colin Sparks – a British media scholar currently based in Hong Kong – examines characteristics of the BRICS countries in order to explore whether they constitute a unified group or are simply a convenient label for what he argues is essentially a geo-political category. In terms of scale, there are vast differences between the countries, he notes, with China and India having media systems that are much larger than those of the other BRICS members. The balance within those systems is also uneven, particularly with regard both to the penetration of new media and the role that they play in the different societies. Economically, while all of the BRICS media systems are funded primarily by advertising revenues, the balance between expenditure differs from country to country. The chapter highlights the differences among the BRICS five in terms of freedom of the media, security for journalists and levels of political intervention. Sparks notes that the evidence suggests that many of these characteristics are common across developing countries, and that the BRICS grouping does not display sufficient differentiation to constitute a coherent and distinct category.

The differences within the BRICS configuration are also highlighted in the chapter by Yuezhi Zhao – a Chinese scholar on international communication working in Canada with another base in Beijing. Her chapter considers how the neo-liberalized and reconstituted states of the BRICS formation are shaping a new international communication order in the context of the profound crisis and power shifts in the global economy. Drawing upon both original empirical research and secondary literature, Zhao provides an overview of the roles of the BRICS states – both in their singularity and in their potential collective action – in transforming the existing global communication order. Her analysis focuses on three recent Internet-related cases in an attempt to discern emerging trends and patterns that may be indicative of shifting power relations and/or normative orientations in global communication: the Chinese-initiated Internet Roundtable for Emerging Countries in September 2012 in Beijing, which managed to secure the formal participation of only four of the five BRICS countries (Brazil, Russia, China and South Africa); the respective roles and positions of the BRICS states at the World Conference on International Telecommunications in Dubai in December 2012; and, finally, the Brazilian project to build an undersea cable to link BRICS nations and its hosting of the April 2014 NetMundial conference about Internet governance.

The final chapter in this part, by Joseph Straubhaar – a US media scholar specializing on Brazil – examines the role of the BRICS countries as emerging media powers at the regional, transnational and global levels. Having written extensively on the globalization of media cultures, Straubhaar starts with a theoretical review of the concepts behind the idea of emerging media powers – using BRICS countries as examples – such as critiques of dependency and imperialism, as well as national and global policy debates about measures to change one-way flows. He also examines the move to exporting national content to geo-cultural regions and transnational diasporas, or cultural-linguistic spaces and current perspectives on large emerging nations as part of the global and transnational structures of contemporary media. The chapter then briefly compares and contrasts the BRICS countries in their distinct paths as emerging regional, transnational and global media powers. Together, the four chapters offer a macro-level analysis of some of the key implications of the rise of the BRICS nations on the global scene – from international politics to global media and from Internet governance to global cultural flows.

# Chapter 1

# BRICS as a new constellation in international relations?

*Jyrki Käkönen*

The original designation of Brazil, Russia, India and China as the 'BRIC' countries was the idea of a Goldman Sachs economist in 2001 to promote the four growing economies as promising investment opportunities for global investors. It also made a clever acronym.[1] In 2009 BRIC changed from an abstract concept into an institution in world politics, with the Russian invitation for the heads of these four countries to come together for their first summit in Yekaterinburg. In 2011 South Africa joined the group at the third summit in Sanya, China, and the acronym became BRICS.

BRICS members are all seen as having growing economies in contrast to the traditional centres of the world economy in the West, which, since the 2008 global financial crisis, have all experienced slow or non-existent growth. Therefore the discourse around BRICS has been mainly economic (Sharma, 2012: 9) and BRICS members themselves have contributed to this focus on economic aspects: the first report by BRICS experts was essentially about the global economy and the economies of the member countries (BRICS Report, 2012).

Although there is disagreement on the sustainability of this growth, it seems clear that BRICS countries will occupy a leading, even a dominant, position in the world economy in the coming years (Wansleben, 2013) and it is self-evident that individual BRICS countries, if not BRICS as an institution, are 'part of [the] global geopolitical landscape' (Laidi, 2011: 1). Furthermore, BRICS members understand themselves as actors in a world that is 'undergoing far-reaching, complex and profound changes' (Joint Statement by the 3rd Summit, 2011). It is possible that the concept of BRICS would have little meaning if it were not for the challenge that these so-called rising powers pose to the international order constructed by the West since the Peace of Westphalia in the mid-seventeenth century on the basis of national sovereignty and non-intervention. Therefore, discussing BRICS countries and BRICS as an institution means discussing a change in the international order and the relative decline of the US' dominant position in that order. The issue here is to discuss whether BRICS has a role in changing the international order and, if so, what kind of role it might have.

The idea of changing the international order is supported, for instance, by US National Intelligence Council's global trends reports. The latest report does not predict how the international system will look in the future, but it takes it as given that in 2030 the system will no longer be the same as we know it today (US National Intelligence Council, 2012). Analysts like Jacques (2012), Kupchan (2012) and Tharoor (2012) support this view, although from different perspectives. In any case, BRICS represents major emerging states (with the exception of Russia) and in this sense it could be an agent of change, even for the transition of power from the North to the South. Therefore the question is whether BRICS as an institution is willing to change the rules of the international system.

Theories of international relations, such as world system analysis, power transition theory, the theory of hegemonic war and the long cycle theory, predict that the rising powers will challenge the predominant order (Barma *et al.*, 2009: 257). Changing the international order is closely connected to the issue of peace and war in international politics (Green and Kliman, 2011: 33) and so the issue of the role of BRICS assumes great significance. The rise of China alone has produced many studies evaluating whether it will be peaceful or lead to major conflicts in the international system. In addition, history suggests that new powers, particularly if autocratic, do not rise peacefully (ibid.: 33). However, Green and Kliman (2011: 34) also remind us that there are scholars who suggest that power transitions do not necessarily result in conflict: the probability of conflict depends on the nature of the existing order.

If the existing order is hegemonic, the rising power does not have much of an option other than war to secure its interests. But if the order is rule-based and has well-developed processes – e.g. there are international institutions which can provide the ascendant power with options to increase its voice and influence – then war is not inevitable, although the rising power will have an interest in creating a new order that is more conducive to its preferences (ibid.).

To be an effective organization – either in changing the world order or in increasing its voice in the existing order – BRICS has to fulfil several criteria. As a first criterion, BRICS already represents several emerging states, but whether there is sufficient trust between members for them to be capable of collective action (Brütsch and Papa, 2012: 6), remains to be seen. To survive as an institution, BRICS should also be flexible enough to minimize intra-coalition frictions (ibid.: 5). Furthermore, the aim here is also to try to find out whether BRICS really is an organization for advancing the collective interests of the emerging states or whether it is more an institution used by its members for advancing their individual interests. If the latter, BRICS is hardly a new major player in international relations.

## BRICS as an international organization

According to BRICS' first expert report, BRICS countries accounted for more than 40 per cent of the world's population and around 25 per cent of the world's gross domestic product (GDP) in 2010 (BRICS Report, 2012: ix). In this sense, it is more representative than the G7, which plays a determining role in world politics and the world economy. However, it is worth pointing out that it is often China that accounts for BRICS' statistics. For instance, BRICS' share in global output is 15 per cent, of which China contributes 61 per cent (Cameron, 2011: 2). If current economic trends are sustained, BRICS will represent the majority of the world economy in the future. According to different estimations, BRICS' share of global GDP will already surpass that of the G7 by 2020, or 2032 at the latest (Goldman Sachs, 2007: 157; Brütsch and Papa, 2012: 1; Jacques, 2012, 163). Again, China's economy is the key player: China is already expected to be the largest national economy by 2017 in terms of purchasing power parity (PPP). At the same time, BRICS countries are responsible for about 30 per cent of total global $CO_2$ emissions, thanks to China (Goldman Sachs, 2007: 106).

From the members' perspective, BRICS is currently 'a platform for a dialogue and cooperation amongst the member countries' (Joint Statement by the 4th Summit, 2012). But in order to be something more than this, BRICS needs institutions (BRICS Report, 2012: 177). The idea is that BRICS should be more than an annual meeting for discussion. In the South African Summit a goal was agreed to develop BRICS into a fully-fledged mechanism of current and long-term coordination on a wide range of key issues of the world economy and politics (Joint Statement by the 5th Summit, 2013).

## The objectives of BRICS

The following analysis is derived from the reports of BRICS annual summits and sets out how BRICS members see the purpose of their cooperation, in relation both to their own aims and to the existing international order. The Indian think-tank report *Nonalignment 2.0* (2012) analyses the background to the role of BRICS on the international scene. According to the report, central international institutions, such as the United Nations (UN) and those of Bretton Woods, are creations of the post-Second World War political settlement and are constrained by the circumstances of their origin. In this sense they are the products of an era that was dominated by the West and are now therefore inappropriate in a world that has seen both the end of European empires and the rise of Asia's economic dynamism (Khilnani *et al.*, 2012: 33). Thus, from the perspective of the rising powers, existing international institutions are not necessarily capable of advancing their interests.

Brazil, China, India and Russia are already among the 10 largest shareholders in the International Monetary Fund (IMF) (Jacques, 2012: 483) but BRICS countries control only 14.4 per cent of the votes in the IMF, while the EU and the US control 29.3 per cent and 16.5 per cent respectively (Brütsch and Papa, 2012: 14). China and India are demanding the democratization of international institutions (*A Shared Vision*, 2008). In the 4th BRICS Summit in 2012, member states collectively demanded a comprehensive reform of the UN, including its Security Council, with a view to making 'it more effective, efficient and representative so that it can deal with today's global challenges more successfully' (Joint Statement by the 4th Summit, 2012). As a world body with all countries represented, BRICS sees the UN as the centre of global governance and multilateralism, and therefore making its institutions more representative is very important for BRICS (Joint Statement by the 5th Summit, 2013).

Since the 1st BRIC Summit in 2009, the reform of international financial institutions has also been on the BRICS agenda (Joint Statement by the 1st Summit, 2009). Without this reform, the legitimacy of the IMF and the World Bank is problematic, since they hardly represent the growing weight of BRICS and other developing countries (Joint Statement by the 2nd Summit, 2010, the 4th Summit, 2012, and the 5th Summit, 2013). For the same reason, BRICS wants to give a central role to the G20 rather than the G7 in global economic governance (Joint Statement by the 2nd Summit, 2010, and the 3rd Summit, 2011).

In addition to the reform of these international institutions, other important goals include the condemnation of terrorist acts in all forms and manifestations (Joint Statement by the 1st Summit, 2009, the 2nd Summit, 2010, the 3rd Summit, 2011, the 4th Summit, 2012, and the 5th Summit, 2013) and the recognition of the threat of climate change, which requires a strengthening of global action (Joint Statement by the 2nd Summit, 2010). Thus, BRICS gave their support to the development and use of renewable energy resources (Joint Statement by the 3rd Summit, 2011). Non-renewable energy is a basic source of $CO_2$ emissions, but increased energy will be a vital resource for improving the living standards of people in BRICS countries. Therefore BRICS is committed to expanding the use of clean and renewable energy to meet the increasing demand of its economies and people, and to respond to climate concerns (Joint Statement by the 2nd Summit, 2010, and the 4th Summit, 2012). Reducing the negative impact of climate change is also important for BRICS countries in terms of food security (Joint Statement by the 2nd Summit, 2010), because they have large populations, many of whom are malnourished. They are also key importers and exporters of agricultural commodities (Goldman Sachs, 2007: 265).

BRICS countries are also concerned about ongoing conflicts, but in solving such conflicts the independence, territorial integrity and sovereignty of the countries concerned have to be respected (Joint Statement by the 4th Summit, 2012). According to BRICS members, every country has the right to choose its own path of social, economic and political development (*A Shared Vision*, 2008; Russian Federation, 2008: 6). Furthermore, BRICS members are concerned about the poorest countries, and they present themselves as the voice for all emerging nations (Joint Statement by the 1st Summit, 2009, and the 3rd Summit, 2011).

All in all, BRICS summit reports indicate that BRICS cooperation is closely connected to an understanding that the world is going through fundamental and dynamic changes, as a Russian foreign policy report (2008) indicates. But BRICS does not seem to have any solutions to present for solving global problems. What it wants is the reform of various international institutions in order to provide a rightful place and voice for emerging nations with regard to defining the norms and rules of international interaction. However, it is easy to agree that the reform of international institutions challenges the dominant position of the US and the whole of the West in international relations. At the same time, BRICS has an interest in sticking to traditional Westphalian values, such as respecting first and foremost the sovereignty of every country. This is in the national interest of BRICS countries, but simultaneously supports the stability of the existing international order (see, for instance, Russian Federation, 2008: 5).

To expand and deepen economic, trade and investment cooperation among BRICS members is an essential goal. The idea is that building these synergies could advance each member's industrial development and employment objectives (Joint Statement by the 3rd Summit, 2011, and the 4th Summit, 2012). BRICS' Academic Forum (2012) also emphasized the promotion of cultural cooperation and connectivity between BRICS members.

## Diversity in BRICS

In the introduction it was indicated that one precondition for an organization to be effective is cohesiveness. An organization can also be useful to its members if the members complement each other politically and economically. In this section the extent of diversity within BRICS is briefly discussed, on the basis of some key characteristics of each country taken from the BRICS Report from 2012 and the Goldman Sachs Report from 2007, while additional aspects will be drawn from existing studies.

Brazil is characterized as a country that specializes in agriculture (Cameron, 2011: 3): it has 60 million hectares of arable land and the potential cultivable land is over 400 million hectares (BRICS Report, 2012: 3, 106). Among the BRICS countries, Brazil is an exporter of agricultural products, especially to China (Harris, 2005: 23), among which biofuel is increasingly important. The Brazilian aviation enterprise Embraer is an example of innovation where Brazil is ahead of other BRICS members. On a global scale, Embraer comes in third place after Boeing and Airbus (BRICS Report, 2012: 117).

China is represented as the manufacturing workshop (BRICS Report, 2012: 3; Pieterse, 2008: 708; Cameron, 2011: 3). In terms of industrialization, China is far ahead of the other BRICS countries and China's economy is export-oriented (BRICS Report, 2012: 5). 'China also has about 12 per cent of world's mineral resources' (ibid.: 3), although this is not enough for China's growing economy, which is dependent on imported resources. An interesting aspect in the information on China is the reference to its ageing population: 'China will become an aged society in 2027' (Goldman Sachs, 2007: 47); this is a factor that might limit China's future growth.

In the case of India, its strong service sector is emphasized (BRICS Report, 2012: 3; Cameron, 2011: 3). Among the BRICS members, India is also a software powerhouse (Pieterse, 2008: 708). Furthermore, Goldman Sachs presents India as a country that is industrializing at such a fast pace that by 2020 over 100 million new people will have entered its labour force (Goldman Sachs, 2007: 13–14). Connected to this industrialization will also be fast growth in the urbanization of India. By 2020 it is estimated that 140 million people will have moved to urban areas (ibid.: 19). Still, compared to other BRICS members, India will remain a low-income country for several decades (ibid.: 25).

Among the BRICS members, Russia is represented as an energy resource base as it has about 20 per cent of the world's gas and oil resources (BRICS Report, 2012: 3). In addition, Russia specializes in commodities (Cameron, 2011: 3). However, prospects for Russia are not necessarily as bright as for other BRICS members. Russia is set to face a dramatic population decline from its current 140 million to just 109 million by 2050 (Goldman Sachs, 2007: 37). Due to its energy resources Russia is export-oriented (BRICS Report, 2012: 3). Finally, South Africa has a large mineral base and is one of the leading rare mineral producers (BRICS Report, 2012: 3, 5; Pieterse, 2008: 708).

Even in a political and cultural sense the emerging BRICS countries are diverse. China and Russia are authoritarian states, while Brazil, India and South Africa are democratic states. Already this makes it problematic for BRICS to rally around shared values (Cameron, 2011: 3). China and India are much older civilizational states rather than nation states in the Westphalian sense, which may better describe Brazil and South Africa (Schwengel, 2008: 768). Russia lies somewhere in between the two. The BRICS states are religiously and culturally diverse and it is difficult to find a common set of values for identity-constructing cooperation. Even a colonial past does not connect all the BRICS members. It is therefore hard to find a common denominator that would make BRICS a cohesive international organization.

In an economic sense, however, this diversity makes BRICS economies complementary, and there is great potential for increasing cooperation for the benefit of BRICS members. BRICS could develop into a trading block. Another thing that connects all the BRICS members in spite of their diversity is that they have all chosen their own individual path towards a modern society (Kupchan, 2012: 86–145). Furthermore, BRICS countries, even the democratic ones, diverge from the liberal vision of Western countries (Laidi, 2011: 2).

### What is BRICS for its members?

For Brazil, being in BRICS reflects its interest in increasing South–South trade, especially with developing economies like India and South Africa (Kliman, 2012: 58). From a Brazilian perspective, it is also possible to understand its membership of BRICS as a channel to alternative financing. Even before BRICS formally existed, China and Brazil agreed to an investment of

$4 billion to improve and expand Brazilian railways, roads and ports (Harris, 2005: 24). And, in a wider sense, BRICS is an intermediary political installation between the West – particularly the US – and Latin America (Laidi, 2011: 11).

For China, BRICS allows a chance 'to share its sovereigntist approach' (Laidi, 2011:10). Otherwise China already has the capability to act on its own as a global power, unlike other BRICS members. In the BRICS context, India has joined the block of emerging powers, which is likely to increase India's weight in global negotiations (Kliman, 2012: 59). But India is not committed solely to BRICS. India is simultaneously exploring other avenues of strategic engagement, such as the Indian Ocean region (Khilnani *et al.*, 2012: 35). For India it could also be feasible to establish multiple bilateral free trade areas with all countries that currently contribute the greatest amount to global growth: not only BRICS members, but also Turkey, Indonesia and Nigeria (ibid.: 26).

Although BRICS was established by a Russian initiative, Russia is the least typical BRICS member. It is not an emerging power but a former superpower keen to regain some of the political status it lost with the collapse of the Soviet Union. Russia considers itself to be one of the leading states in the world, as it still has a permanent seat in the UN Security Council (Russian Federation, 2008: 5). For Russia, BRICS is a coalition that allows Russia to associate itself with a wider group 'when interacting with the West' (Laidi, 2011: 7). Russia seems to think that BRICS will become 'one of the key pieces on the global chessboard' (Lavrov, 2012: 1). Therefore Russia supports BRICS as a new model of global relations, overriding the old East–West and North–South divides, and BRICS will be, for Russia, a key foreign policy priority (Lavrov, 2012: 2). Russia also takes it more or less for granted that all BRICS members share a common interest in reforming the international monetary and financial system (ibid.: 2–3). However, for Russia, BRICS is just one means of achieving a strong position in the world community and a channel for flexible participation in international structures (Russian Federation, 2008: 1, 3).

BRICS is not the only means whereby Russia can enhance its role in world politics. The Asia–Pacific region has increasing significance for Russia due to the fact that, geopolitically, it is part of that region (Russian Federation, 2008: 14). Therefore a Russia–India–China troika is also important for Russia (ibid.: 5–6, 14). Furthermore, the Shanghai Cooperation Organization (SCO) has a special place in Russian–Asian policy. It provides an opportunity to develop friendly relations with China and India after India attained observer status in the SCO (ibid.: 14). Russia, as well, intends to build a strategic partnership with China. But it also wants to develop its relations with Turkey, Egypt, Algeria, Iran, Saudi Arabia, Syria, Libya, Pakistan and other leading regional states (ibid.: 14). Although in Latin America Russia seeks to establish a strategic partnership with Brazil, it is also keen to 'broaden its political and economic cooperation with Argentina, Mexico, Cuba and Venezuela' (ibid.: 15). All these interests support the argument that BRICS is more a strategic tool for Russia in maintaining and improving its position in global politics, rather than a means for transforming the whole international order.

For South Africa, BRICS is the continuation of the historic Bandung Conference (South Africa in BRICS, 2013: 3). In this sense, it represents South–South cooperation against the domination of the West. Joining BRICS increases the prestige of South Africa, especially in the African context. In the context of BRICS, South Africa has defined its role to ensure that the rest of the African continent will gain from its BRICS membership (ibid.: 1).

From this brief survey of some of the defining characteristics of BRICS members it is possible to conclude that BRICS as an institution is used to advance the national interests of its members and for 'individual gains than for a more equitable and fair global order' (Brütsch and Papa, 2012: 2). BRICS is not necessarily the main priority in the members' external or global policies. Although BRICS cooperation promotes the relevance of each of its members, according to Cameron 'it is not a cohesive group in major political, security, economic or trade issues' (Cameron, 2011: 2). As Laidi has said, BRICS members form a heterogeneous coalition of often competing powers that share one common interest: 'to erode the Western hegemonic claims' (Laidi, 2011: 1).

## BRICS' role in changing the international order

It is quite evident that the rise of China and India has already changed some aspects of the international system. 'The rise of Brazil, South Africa or South East Asia is not presented as a second generation' of tiger economies 'but as first generation of emerging powers' (Schwengel, 2008: 770). The issue is no longer about small or medium-sized capitalist success stories, but about states that also have the potential for political influence and are not satisfied with their current roles in the international order. For these emerging powers, the existing international order, with its set of rules and common practices, has been imposed by the dominant states of the past (Barma et al., 2009: 527). While BRICS is represented as an organization interested in reforming the existing international order, it is also possible that BRICS has already constructed an alternative international order through its members establishing mutual connections (ibid.: 526). The emergence of an alternative or shadow order will undermine the position of the current dominant powers. This again might affect the way that order and stability will diminish while the existing hegemon declines, at least in a relative sense (ibid.: 540). And, as already mentioned above, both history and theory suggest that the combination of rising powers and a declining hegemony can have a crucial and sometimes even violent effect on international politics (ibid.: 525).

### Does BRICS challenge the existing order?

In an economic sense there is no doubt that the international order is already changing. China, India and Brazil are expected to continue to rise. Middle-range powers like South Korea, Indonesia, Turkey, Egypt, Iran and South Africa are also becoming increasingly important. And in the near future Africa and Latin America might experience rapid growth, while Japan and Europe will decline and the US will have sluggish growth (Khilnani *et al.*, 2012: 31; Kupchan, 2012). In terms of PPP, China is projected to overtake the US as early as 2017, and in terms of market exchange rate by 2027. India still comes behind China, but is expected to become the third 'global economic giant' by 2050 at the latest, and sometime after that Brazil will move to fourth place ahead of Japan. At the same time, Russia could overtake Germany as the largest European economy in terms of PPP by 2020, and in terms of market exchange rate by around 2035.

The changing rank order of national economies challenges the role and influence of the current leading powers but does not necessarily change the system itself. However, there are already signs of increasing South–South trade connections. More than '40 per cent of the South's global trade is accounted for intra-South trade' (Pieterse, 2008: 709). According to Barma *et al.*, rising powers have found each other to be increasingly important as trading partners in the last 25 years and China and India have become important partners for the smaller rising powers (Barma *et al.*, 2009: 532). Brazil has a trade pact with India and South Africa, reducing the influence of traditional industrial nations (Harris, 2005: 22). For South Africa, the trade with other BRICS members has given it a chance to diversify its export structure and reduce the negative trade balance (South Africa in BRICS, 2013: 5).

At the same time, the role of the US dollar as a reserve currency of central banks has been in decline. In 2002, a total of 73 per cent of reserve currencies were still in dollars but in 2006 it was down to 60 per cent (Pieterse, 2008, 709). According to Pieterse, the role of the IMF has also been in decline. In 2003 IMF lending was $70 billion and in 2006 it was only $20 billion (ibid.: 710). The US is no longer self-evidently the dominant power in the world economy, but China is not yet ready to challenge the US and make renminbi into an alternative reserve currency (Brütsch and Papa, 2012: 15–16). However, it is possible that the new global economic regime will be based on BRICS. According to Jacques, this potential regime would be inherently more democratic than the current regime, which is based on the Bretton Woods system (Jacques, 2012: 510-11).

One problem for BRICS is whether potentially antagonistic states are willing or even able to transform 'their combined economic power into a collective geopolitical power' (Brütsch and Papa, 2012: 1). It has been suggested that the BRICS members 'lack the strategic posture and depth for challenging the US leadership or entrench [*sic*] a new world order' (ibid.: 4), and that Brussels does not consider BRICS members to be capable of acting together on any major global issues (Cameron, 2011: 2). However, emerging powers have also been prepared to overlook the sovereignty issue: over the last 20 years, the rising powers have found themselves voting together in the UN (Barma *et al.*, 2009: 533).

On the Libya issue, BRICS took a common stand (Brütsch and Papa, 2012: 1) and stated that NATO had contravened the 1973 UN resolution (Laidi, 2011: 8). Laidi points out that BRICS as a political group has two permanent seats in the UN Security Council and three nuclear powers (Laidi, 2011: 5).

According to Kliman, the emerging powers are challenging the traditional rules-based system. For instance, US maritime hegemony is already under pressure. Beijing's construction of a blue-water navy and its aggressive claims in the South China, East China and Yellow Seas threatens the existing stability. Furthermore, Brazil, India and Turkey have also vitalized their maritime practices (Kliman, 2012: 57).

After the Second World War, the rise of powers such as Germany, Japan and the four tiger economies occurred under US hegemony and did not transform the world order in the way that the rise of China and India might (Schwengel, 2008: 769). The current rising powers 'can route around the existing order' and establish an alternative order coexisting with the still dominant order (Barma et al., 2009: 537). The point here is that the rise of Asia is dependent on neoliberal globalization but 'unfolds outside the neoliberal model' (Pieterse, 2008: 707).

### Does BRICS have a vision of an alternative international order?

It is hard to find any signs of a preferred future international order in the BRICS' Summit Reports. Rather, the values of the Westphalian model are reinforced in their demands to respect the independence, sovereignty, unity and territorial integrity of all nations (Joint Statement by the 3rd Summit, 2011). Therefore it is no wonder that Laidi (2011: 2) has said that BRICS is more a defensive than offensive coalition (Laidi, 2011: 2). BRICS' powers have done little to really challenge the Euro–US domination of the international system. This task has been left to states like Bolivia, Venezuela and Iran (Palat, 2008: 721).

According to Laidi, BRICS members cannot agree on a position in international power games, although they do not have any 'problem collectively contesting the Western dominance' in world politics (Laidi 2011: 7). It seems that the rising powers do not want either conflict or assimilation, although in the rhetoric of BRICS members it is possible to find 'ideas about an order and governance that are not suited to liberal' international order (Barma et al., 2009: 539).

BRICS members, excluding China, have neither 'embraced the existing order, rejected it, nor offered any detailed alternative' (Kliman, 2012: 53–54). They eagerly say no to Western states on different occasions without being able to propose any alternative solutions (Laidi, 2011: 9). For instance, Brazil, China, India and South Africa have been eager to 'challenge the US-led invasions of Afghanistan, and Iraq, or Israel's invasion of Lebanon and continuing occupation of Palestine' (Palat, 2008: 721–22). However, instead of any alternative proposals for solving such crises they appear to wish to uphold the 'principle of inviolable sovereignty, or neo-Westphalianism' (Barma *et al.*, 2009: 538).

Although it seems to be hard to find any clear BRICS vision about an alternative international order, BRICS members express their determination to translate their 'vision into a concrete action' (Joint Statement by the 3rd Summit, 2011). The only concrete action until now has been the decision to establish the New Development Bank in the 5th BRICS Summit in South Africa in 2013, a decision that was formalized at the Brazil Summit in 2014. The main goal of the Bank is to finance infrastructure projects in BRICS countries and in other developing countries (Joint Statement by the 5th Summit, 2013). Chinese banks have already become more important institutions in financing the developing world than the World Bank (Jacques, 2012: 480).

While BRICS may have a limited view of the future world order, China has a clearer vision. In 2005 the Chinese philosopher Tingyang Zhao proposed the traditional Chinese tribute system (the *Tianxia* system) as a model for reorganizing the international order (Zhao, 2006; 2009). Since then the idea has received support as well as criticism, and it has developed into the basis for a Chinese school in International Relations. In the traditional system the Middle Kingdom was the centre of the world, which was hierarchically organized. In India there is also an expectation that when India grows more prominent it will define a 'vision of international norms and rules and decide what norms to throw its weight behind' (Khilnani *et al.*, 2012: 35).

## Reactions to maintaining the hegemony

Although it seems to be evident that the US will remain the most powerful and influential country for around another two decades, the international order is changing (see, for instance, Kupchan, 2012; US National Intelligence Council, 2012). US hegemony is no longer unquestioned and the world is becoming multipolar and more complex, independently of what role BRICS may play in changing or challenging the existing international order. In any case it seems to be clear that the dominance of the West will diminish, although it is less clear how rapid this change will be (Kliman, 2012: 63).

For the US and the whole of the West, the reasons are mainly external, i.e. the rise of the rest of the world. The real problem, according to Kupchan, is not only that the US is internally polarized and incapable of producing a long-term cohesive external policy, at the same time the European Union is incapable of taking on any kind of global role, experiencing serious internal problems and lack of proper leadership (ibid.: 146–81). In order to maintain an influential role in constructing the future international order, the West has to adapt to the realization that the Western modernization model is not necessarily universal, and that the future world will be more pluralist than it can currently envision.

The West also has to accept that the rules-based international order reflects a balance of power that no longer exists. The West is over-represented in international institutions and therefore has to step back and give more space to emerging powers (Kliman, 2012: 62). In order to be a decisive actor in transforming the international order the US needs partners, especially from the group of emerging states (ibid.: 53). This can be seen as a factor threatening the fragile cohesion of BRICS as an international organization. The fact that BRICS do not have much in common and have diverse interests can be used by the US to maintain its position as one of the leading powers.

For Kliman the most promising partners for the US (or the West) are Brazil, India, Indonesia and Turkey, which all are strategically located democratic countries (Kliman, 2012: 57). An alliance with these four states may not be an option, since two of them are BRICS members and two others are more interested in hitching their cart to China (ibid.: 62–63). The problem here is that China currently has much more to offer these four developing states than the US and, furthermore, any such US alliance from a Chinese perspective would be seen as an attempt to block China's rightful rise.

In order to make a partnership with these four states seem attractive, the West has to be prepared to reform the international order. And Kliman's proposal is that if the West is in partnership with at least these four countries it could be possible to produce a global order that would 'safeguard international security and prosperity' (ibid.: 58). In a wider sense, the issue would be to safeguard the interests of the West as well as the Western model of modernization.

In India it is understood that it is natural for the US to have an interest in changing the international landscape by building partnerships with countries like Brazil, India and Indonesia (Khilnani *et al.*, 2012: 31, 32). But from an Indian perspective a partnership with the US is not at all clear, since India does not agree with some of the new international norms like the Responsibility to Protect (ibid.: 37), or with the US policy towards Iran. India is interested in maintaining flexibility in its foreign policy and this might be true even in its membership of BRICS.

From an Indian perspective, China and the US will always be superpowers, but alongside them will be several relevant hubs of power. India has to be in a position where no other state, not even the US, is able to influence it or make it act against its own interests or will (ibid.: 10). Then again, India is engaged in competition with China both in Asia and globally, and does not have any interest in combating the US. Therefore the US is a likely alliance partner for India. But India does not have any interest in becoming a casualty in Sino–American relations.

Finally, it is important to question how integral Russia will be to BRICS. In its foreign policy strategy of 2008, Russia called for the building of a truly unified Europe without any dividing lines. In fact, Russia is looking further west, beyond the Atlantic Ocean, to emphasize the interaction between Russia, the EU and the US. This cooperation could 'strengthen the position of the Euro-Atlantic states in global competition' (Russian Federation, 2008: 12). In this way Russia is associating itself with the West. Cameron has argued that 'Russia's natural place is with the mature Western economies rather than among aggressive and much poorer, emerging economies' (Cameron, 2011: 4).

## Is BRICS just China and India?

It seems evident that the global economic order is first and foremost being challenged by China and India, which are not only nation-states but global regions and ancient civilizations. They are located between the traditional North and South, creating 'semi-central societies'. These two powers have re-entered global history (Schwengel, 2008: 767–68). As Pieterse remarks, after a few hundred years of the historical exception of Western hegemony, China and India are back (Pieterse, 2008: 713). Thus when we talk about global change the issue is essentially about China and India, who are also building relationships with countries beyond BRICS. In addition to BRICS some institutions use the term 'E7' (Emerging 7), which comprises Brazil, China, India, Indonesia, Mexico, Russia and Turkey. It has been estimated that E7 will overtake the G7 countries as early as 2017 in terms of PPP, and by the end of 2050 E7 will be 75 per cent larger than G7 countries. However, much of the growth in E7 will be driven by China and India. By 2050 China, India and the US will be 'the three largest economies in the world' (PwC, 2013: 8).

China is becoming increasingly dominant in BRICS. China is the primary trading partner for Brazil, India and South Africa (Laidi, 2011: 10). In 2010, China was the biggest foreign investor in Brazil (Jacques, 2012: 437). Large international corporations are relocating their research and development facilities to China and India due to the 'massive reservoir of cheap scientific and engineering talent' (Palat, 2008: 725). China and India have also signed many agreements with governments in Africa, Latin America and the Middle East to secure much-needed resources of raw materials and fossil fuels for their growing economies (Palat, 2008: 726).

China has already established itself as the largest exporting nation. It has more than $2.5 trillion surplus in its foreign trade, which has given it the opportunity to invest abroad (Green and Kliman, 2011: 37). One consequence of this is that Chinese exports have displaced local production in some African states, and Chinese companies prefer to 'employ Chinese workers in Africa and provide poor working conditions when they employ African workers' (Palat, 2008: 728). Whether good or bad, discussions about China refer to a Chinese presence in different parts of the world. India is behind China in this respect, while the other BRICS members seem to have only a minor role in global transactions.

Officially China and India are good friends whose relations are based on the so-called Five Principles of Peaceful Co-existence – *Panchsheel* – dating from the 1950s. Both states are committed to realizing peace and the progress of humankind. They also support regional integration in Asia (*A Shared Vision*,

2008). However, an interesting aspect of the China–India Shared Vision is that it mentions India's aspiration for a permanent seat in the UN Security Council, but it does not give China's support for this (*A Shared Vision*, 2008). In general, China opposes any increase in the number of permanent members in the UN Security Council, since the first potential beneficiary would be India (Laidi, 2011: 10).

The US has explicitly supported India in having a permanent seat in the UN Security Council. From the US perspective, India has a potential that other states do not have in counterbalancing the increasing Chinese influence in the changing international order (Laidi, 2011: 12). China's objection and the US support for Indian interests puts India in a difficult position. As already indicated, India is not necessarily keen on a partnership with the US. A friendship would be enough for India, since China is suspicious of India's partnerships, and sees improved Indian ties with the US in zero-sum terms (Khilnani *et al.*, 2012: 32).

According to Cameron, China and India are strategic competitors inasmuch as they are friends and even allies (Cameron, 2011: 3). India is particularly worried about China's military rise and its obvious interest in encircling India with strategic ports in Myanmar, Bangladesh, Sri Lanka and Pakistan (Pant, 2010: 55). China has also been active in India's backyard in Nepal and Mauritius (Jacques, 2012: 440), and China's military presence increased in Tibet in early 2000. China and India also share a disputed Himalayan border. All these factors mean, at least from the Indian perspective, that there is a tension in China–India relations.

There is also the issue of China–India rivalry for Russia's natural resources (Cameron, 2011: 4), and a similar competition for Central Asian influence and resources (Brütsch and Papa, 2012: 2). Both countries are also eager to secure African resources, therefore 'Africa should be a major focus area for India in both economic and political terms' (Khilnani *et al.*, 2012: 35). India's increased dependence on external resources has made the Indian Ocean extremely important for Indian security. By securing the supply of vital resources and trade routes, India 'should be in a position to dominate the Indian Ocean region' (ibid.: 38; 41).

Although China talks about peaceful development, this will remain for the foreseeable future a major foreign policy and security challenge for India. From an Indian perspective, China is the only major power directly in India's geopolitical space (Khilnani *et al.*, 2012: 13). Therefore it might be in Indian interests to preoccupy China with its immediate geopolitical theatre, and also to encourage the US, Japan, Australia, Indonesia and even Vietnam to be more active in the Asia–Pacific theatre, especially in the South China Sea region. This could in turn reduce China's presence in the Indian Ocean and South Asia (ibid.: 13, 16, 32).

India sees itself as a global power in its own right. The scale and success of the Indian economy 'will leave an extraordinary footprint on the whole world and define future possibilities for the entire human kind' (Khilnani *et al.*, 2012: 7) and the whole world is 'increasingly looking to India to shape global norms' (ibid.: 36).

## Conclusion

It is easy to agree with Schwengel that the US is no longer the sole guarantor of the global market or a globally accepted hegemon, 'neither by the elites nor by the common people' (2008: 770). An interesting aspect in the current situation is that the major dividing line is between two different kinds of capitalism, overlapped with a civilizational divide (Pieterse, 2008: 716). But it is far from evident whether BRICS as an organization is capable of challenging US dominance and able to construct a new international order.

Common to all BRICS members is a fast-growing economy, an interest in multi-polarity and antipathy towards the US hegemony, but this is not necessarily enough to make a coherent and influential institution. Then again, Brazil, Russia and South Africa have more in common with the West than China and India. China and India represent different civilizations and can therefore be challengers of the existing Western-dominated international order.

The diversity within BRICS makes it possible for the US or the North Atlantic axis to divide BRICS and continue to rule the world. For Brazil, Russia and South Africa, a reform of the institutions that are vital in the governance of the current international order could be enough. This is one factor that undermines the potential power of BRICS as an international arrangement. The other factor is the Sino–Indian rivalry. This rivalry makes it possible for the US to use India in the emerging Sino–US race for the leading position in the future international order.

It is still difficult to see BRICS as an institution that would seriously challenge the existing international order. It is rather an institution for advancing the diverse individual national interests of the member states. Some of the BRICS countries might be satisfied with increasing their voice and role in global politics and within regional structures. This would democratize international regimes but not necessarily change their order or values, even if the further modernization of the rising powers would be more of an indigenous process and would therefore increase plurality in the global system.

Although BRICS as an institution does not necessarily challenge the existing international order, there are elements in BRICS that can provide the basis for an alternative world order. It is even more likely that, on a China and India axis, it will be possible to intensify South–South cooperation and to replace the existing order with one that would better reflect international realities. China and India are the two BRICS members for whom the reform of the international regime would not be enough. They both talk about changing the rules of the game, although both lean on the growth-oriented market economy.

Finally, how peaceful or violent the transition process will be depends first on how possible reforms will be accepted by rising and declining powers. First of all, are the declining powers ready to adapt to the new realities, when the existing order has been understood as normal for some two hundred years? Second, does the reform accommodate the rising powers enough for them to be satisfied? Reforms might be enough for the US, Brazil, Russia and South Africa but not necessarily for China and India.

Further complicating the issue will be discussion about the hegemony changing simultaneously with the change of the whole global order. In this case it is not BRICS but China that is the potential hegemon under discussion. There are currently many states in the global South that are ready to jump on the bandwagon with China, but at the same time are less interested in Chinese hegemony within the global system.

The Ukrainian crisis in the summer of 2014 demonstrates a stronger cohesion of BRICS members than indicated in the analysis above. None of the BRICS countries has joined in the sanctions on Russia imposed because of its role in the crisis. It is also hard to find any critical comments on Russia's role in this by any other BRICS member. One could argue that due to Western sanctions on Russia, inter-BRICS relations have in fact deepened.

## Note

1   The acronym refers to the construction of something new – a new international order (see O'Neill, 2013: 22–3).

## References

A Shared Vision (2008) *A Shared Vision for the 21st Century of the People's Republic of China and the Republic of India*, Statement issued after meeting between Indian and Chinese Prime Ministers. Beijing: January 14.

Barma, Naazneen; Chiozza, Giacomo; Ratner, Ely and Weber, Steven (2009) A World without the West? Empirical Patterns and Theoretical Implications. *Chinese Journal of International Politics* 2(4): 525–44.

BRICS Report (2012) *The BRICS Report: A Study of Brazil, Russia, India, China, and South Africa with Special Focus on Synergies*. New Delhi: Oxford University Press.

Brütsch, Christian and Papa, Mihaela (2012) Deconstructing the BRICs: Bargaining Coalition, Imagined Community or Geopolitical Fad? *CRP Working Paper* No. 5 October. Cambridge: Centre for Rising Powers, Department of Politics and International Studies, University of Cambridge.

Cameron, Fraser (2011) The EU and the BRICs. *Policy Paper 3*: February. Brussels: EU-Russia Centre.

Goldman Sachs (2007) *BRICS and Beyond*. New York: Goldman Sachs Global Economics Group.

Green, Michael and Kliman, Daniel (2011) China's Hard Power and the Potential for Conflict in Asia. *SERI Quarterly*, April.

Harris, Jerry (2005) Emerging Third World Powers: China, India and Brazil. *Race & Class* 46(3): 7–27.

Jacques, Martin (2012) *When China Rules the World: The End of the Western World and the Birth of a New Global Order.* London: Penguin.

'Joint Statements of the BRIC/S Countries Leaders':
1st Summit, 16 June 2009, Yekaterinburg, Russia
2nd Summit, 16 April 2010, Brasilia, Brazil
3rd Summit, 14 April 2011, Sanya, China
4th Summit, 29 March 2012, New Delhi, India
5th Summit, 27 March 2013, Durban, South Africa

Khilnani, Sunil; Kumar, Rajiv; Mehta, Pratap Bhanu; Menon, Prakash; Nilekani, Nandan; Raghavan, Srinath; Saran, Shyam and Varadarajan, Siddharth (2012) *Nonalignment 2.0: A Foreign and Strategic Policy for India in the Twenty-First Century.* New Delhi: National Defense College and Centre for Policy Research.

Kliman, Daniel (2012) The West and Global Swing States. *The International Spectator: Italian Journal of International Affairs* 47(3): 53–64.

Kupchan, Charles (2012) *No One's World: The West, the Rising Rest, and the Coming Global Turn.* New York: Oxford University Press.

Laidi, Zaki (2011) The BRICS Against the West? *CERI Strategy Papers* N° 11 – Hors Série, November.

Lavrov, Sergei (2012) *BRICS: A New Generation Forum with a Global Reach.* Moscow: Ministry of Foreign Affairs.

O'Neill, Jim (2013) *The Growth Map: Economic Opportunity in the BRICs and Beyond.* London: Penguin.

Palat, Ravi (2008) A New Bandung? Economic Growth vs. Distributive Justice Among Emerging Powers. *Futures* 40(8): 721–34.

Pant, Harsh (2010) *The China Syndrome: Grappling with an Uneasy Relationship.* New Delhi: Harper Collins.

Pieterse, Jan Nederveen (2008) Globalization the Next Round: Sociological Perspectives. *Futures* 40(8): 707–20.

PwC (2013) *World in 2050: The BRICs and Beyond: Prospects, Challenges and Opportunities.* London: PriceWaterhouseCooper, January.

Russian Federation (2008) *The Foreign Policy Concept of Russian Federation.* Approved on 12 July 2008. Moscow: Ministry of Foreign Affairs.

Schwengel, Herman (2008) Emerging Powers as Fact and Metaphor: Some European Ideas. *Futures* 40(8): 767–76.

Sharma, Ruchir (2012) Broken BRICs. *Foreign Affairs*, 91(6): 2–7.

South Africa in BRICS (2013) BRICS (Brazil, Russia, India, China, South Africa). Pretoria.

Tharoor, Shashi (2012) *Pax Indica: India and the World of the 21st Century.* New Delhi: Allen Lane.

US National Intelligence Council (2012) *Global Trends 2030: Alternative Worlds.* Washington: US National Intelligence Council. Available at www.dni.gov/nic/globaltrends.

Wansleben, Leon (2013) Dreaming with BRICs: Innovating the Classificatory Regimes of International Finance. *Journal of Cultural Economy* 6(4): 453–71.

Zhao, Tingyang (2006) Rethinking Empire from a Chinese Concept 'All-under-Heaven' (Tian-xia). *Social Identities* 12(1): 29–41.

Zhao, Tingyang (2009) A Political World Philosophy in Terms of All-under-Heaven (Tian-xia). *Diogenes* 56(1): 5–18.

# Chapter 2

# How coherent is the BRICS grouping?[1]

*Colin Sparks*

## Introduction

The concept of BRICS is very widely used today, both inside and outside the world of scholarly discussion, and it needs to be understood in the context of current changes in international relations. The shape of the world economy is unquestionably shifting, as is the global political and military balance. The centuries-old domination of the West is passing, and with it the more or less politely disguised looting and coercion that have been its unlovely foundations. However, it is another, very large, step from recognizing that this epochal shift is under way to arguing that it can best be understood as the emergence of a particular group of countries that can, in any useful sense, be considered as a single type of economy, still less a single type of society with a single type of media.

The BRICS grouping is certainly a political and diplomatic reality, united by some common aspirations and substantial trade flows. Closer examination, however, reveals not only well-known tensions between some of its leading members, but also quite substantial differences in the scale and dynamics of the economies in question. An even closer look at their main social and political structures, and particularly at the nature of the media and of their relationships to social and economic power, reveals differences so large as to call into question the utility of trying to see them as anything other than a somewhat ad hoc grouping of governments that are at least as different as they are similar. Moreover, the factors they do have in common are seldom exclusive to the group itself, but are rather more general features of a broad range of societies that are undergoing similar social and economic changes.

This chapter therefore begins with a brief rehearsal of some of the economic realities that have forced BRICS to the attention of the Western world before moving on to consider the relationships between their media and other centers of economic and political power. Throughout, the discussion draws comparisons with both other developing countries and those of the developed world, notably the United States (US). The latter is the largest economy and possesses by far the richest media system in the world today. As the incumbent "global hegemon," it is inevitably the measure against which other societies are judged and judge themselves. If the balance in the world is indeed shifting, then that shift must inevitably involve re-adjustments on the part of the currently dominant society. The chapter concludes that there is little basis for considering BRICS either a unique or a coherent grouping in the developing world, and that there are other, more illuminating, ways to analyze the shift in the balance of world power.

## Economic scale and rates of growth

The most obvious fact concerning the economic scale of the BRICS countries is that they vary greatly in size. As Figure 2.1 demonstrates, according to the International Monetary Fund (IMF), the Chinese economy is, at purchasing power parity (PPP), more than 2.5 times larger than India's, more than 5 times larger than Brazil's or Russia's, and more than 20 times the size of South Africa's. In fact, in 2013, the size of China's economy, at nearly 80 percent of that of the US, was closer to the world leader than to any of its fellow BRICS. A similar picture of China far outstripping the other countries emerges for its share of global GDP at PPP. Of the five, only China and Russia are net exporters, and while in China's case the surplus is largely generated through manufactured goods, Russia's exports are predominantly hydrocarbons (IMF, 2014).

Such a static picture might be seen as misleading: after all, the expansion and contraction of economies is a constant reality in the contemporary world. Figure 2.2 presents the IMF's projections for the future size of the BRICS and US economies at PPP. Note that, from 2014 onward, these figures are *projections*, and that there are strong historical reasons to expect major revisions to the figures in the future. All these figures are subject to the unpredictable

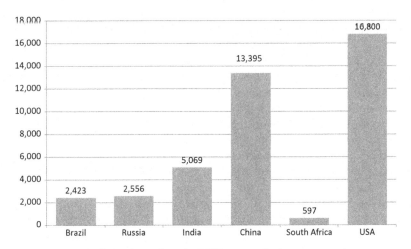

*Figure 2.1* 2013 gross domestic products in US$bn at purchasing power parity
Source: IMF World Economic Outlook Database (Note: figures for China and South Africa are IMF estimates)

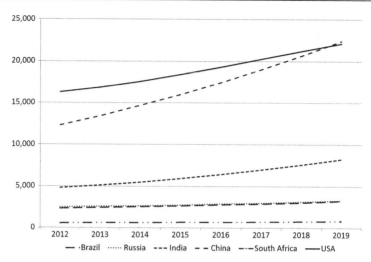

*Figure 2.2* Projected growth of GDPs in US$bn at purchasing power parity
Source: IMF World Economic Outlook Database

rhythms of the world trade cycle, which are highly unlikely to have a uniform effect across all six countries under review. For example, recent movements in the price of natural gas might significantly change estimates of growth rates for Russia. Similarly, powerful arguments concerning the ability of the Communist Party to retain its exclusive control of the country, at least in its current form, contend that internal factors may negatively impact Chinese growth. Nevertheless, these figures are the closest we have to "official" estimates of future growth.

Perhaps the most striking feature of Figure 2.2 is the prediction that, in purchasing power parity terms, the Chinese economy will be larger than the US's by 2019, but the concern here is with the projected rates of growth rather than absolute figures.[2] While all of the economies will grow significantly, China will grow more rapidly than any of the other countries, with its economy 83 percent larger in 2017 than in 2010. The growth rates projected for the other four countries are not as high: Brazil will grow by 38 percent; Russia by 32 percent; India by 72 percent; South Africa by 37 percent. The US is projected to grow by 36 percent. Even though most are projected to grow faster than the US, the latter is starting from a very much higher level and as a consequence the absolute gap between the size of the US economy and the size of these four countries is in fact projected to grow during this period. Setting these figures in context, during the same period Indonesia is projected to grow by 69 percent, Vietnam by 68 percent, Malaysia by 59 percent, and Thailand by 49 percent (IMF, 2014). All these developing economies are already larger than that of South Africa, so it is difficult to see any rational basis, at least in terms of economic scale or pace of growth, for including the latter in the BRICS grouping rather than any of the others.[3]

From the point of view of scale and growth, then, the concept of BRICS is of little utility. Wide divergence within this group is identifiable with regard to the balance between extractive and manufacturing industries, to current size, and to past and projected growth rates. One could easily construct other groups, perhaps with less catchy acronyms, to better capture the economic dynamic of the "rise of the rest."

## Wealth and poverty

Upon consideration of how these economic fruits are distributed amongst the populations of the respective countries, one finds much greater similarities, albeit similarities that are hardly unique to BRICS. As Figure 2.3 demonstrates, these are all relatively poor countries compared to the US. In fact, the distribution of per capita income per country differs greatly from that of the actual scale of the economies. The two giant developing economies are poorer per head than are the three much smaller BRICS; their relatively large absolute GDPs are a function of them being considerably more populous than the others. According to the United Nations Development Programme (UNDP), Russia (more correctly, the Russian Federation) and Brazil are classified as having a "high" level of human development, while South Africa, India, and China fall into the category of "medium" human development (UNDP, 2013: 143–146).

One area where the BRICS do display a higher degree of convergence is the way in which the limited available per capita income is distributed: they all tend to be unequal societies. Using the "Gini income coefficient," a simple but very widely used measure of economic inequality in a society, Table 2.1 demonstrates

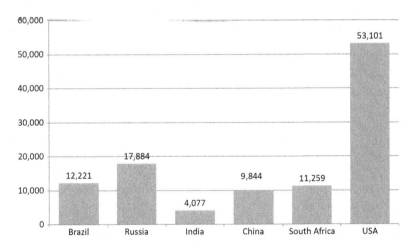

*Figure 2.3* 2013 gross domestic products per capita in US$bn at purchasing power parity
Source: IMF World Economic Outlook Database (Note: figures for China, South Africa, and the USA are IMF estimates)

*Table 2.1* Estimated Gini income coefficients

| Country | UNDP 2000–2010 |
| --- | --- |
| Brazil | 54.7 |
| Russia | 42.3 |
| India | 33.4 |
| China | 42.5 |
| South Africa | 63.1 |
| USA | 40.8 |
| Hong Kong | 43.4 |
| Sweden | 25.0 |
| Japan | 24.9 (1993) |

Source: Apart from Japan, *United Nations Development Programme Human Development Report 2013.* 152–154. The Japanese figure is the most recent available in the World Bank *Poverty and Inequality Database* 2014.

the relative degrees of inequality. To give some perspective on this measure, two other countries are included for comparison. Conventional wisdom has it that a Gini income coefficient of more than 40 (sometimes written as 0.4) signifies a society where economic inequality has reached levels that may be expected to provoke social unrest and, by this measure, of the BRICS only India has an income distribution below the threshold. These figures place South Africa and Brazil among the most unequal societies in the world, while China and Russia fall into the same category of high inequality as the US and Hong Kong. None compare to the North European social democracies, which are, like Sweden, marked by much lower levels of inequality.

In fact, there is evidence that these figures paint too rosy a picture of the level of inequality, at least in the case of China. Official figures have the Gini coefficient peaking at 0.491 in 2008 and falling to 0.474 in 2011, but credible unofficial estimates put it as high as 0.61 in 2012, in a grouping with Brazil and South Africa (Agence France Presse, 2013; Holland, 2012). Again, however, these groupings are not exclusive to the BRICS, as numerous other societies in the world also face rampant inequality. Basing groupings on a combination of geographical and cultural proximity, for example, Brazil would be alongside, although rather more unequal than, Argentina (44.5), Uruguay (45.3), Chile (52.1), and Mexico (48.3) as well as several other Latin American countries. Alternatively, Thailand (40.0) could be placed alongside China, while Indonesia and Vietnam have distributions quite similar to India's (UNDP, 2013: 152–154). The BRICS are unequal societies, and some are extraordinarily unequal, but this factor does not single them out as a unique, coherent group.

Many of the commonplace explanations given for these figures, notably in the case of China, do not stand up to even cursory scrutiny, as the additional figures in the table help to demonstrate. The very high degree of inequality in China cannot be attributed to some supposed "East Asian" social model. Japan, whose last reported Gini coefficient was 24.9, is unquestionably both an East

Asian society and significantly more equal than China (World Bank, 2013). Neither is it ascribable to the very real imperfections of the Chinese version of capitalism (rampant corruption, persistent state intervention, extreme exploitation of workers and peasants, etc.), since it is in the same category as the US and Hong Kong, the latter of which is regularly praised by none other than the Heritage Foundation as "the freest economy in the world" (Lau, 2013).[4] Political perspectives do not seem a satisfactory explanation either: China and the US have rather different political systems but similar levels of inequality, and Sweden, the social democratic paradise incarnate, has a low level of inequality similar to that of Japan, which has been ruled by a rightist party for most of the last 60 years.

Severe income inequality is one aspect of a more general feature of the BRICS nations (and many other developing economies). A relatively small proportion of the population enjoys approximately the same standard of living, and opportunities to purchase luxury goods, as do denizens of the advanced world, while a large proportion of the population lives in very serious poverty. These disparities—which are sometimes not obvious to the visitor who is met at the airport by charming, fluent, English speakers, often respectful former students, and whisked in a smart car from a modern airport to a well-equipped university campus to a delicious dinner to a luxury hotel and next day back to the airport—are one aspect of what is often called the "combined and uneven development" of such economies. Alongside modern production and consumption, and essential to its functioning, older forms of production and consumption continue to thrive.

In sum, then, the evidence from measures of income and inequality suggests that, whereas all of the BRICS are relatively poor (they are, after all, developing countries) and very unequal countries, these elements are neither unique nor sufficiently proximate to form the basis for a grouping clearly distinguished from other poor and developing countries marked by economic inequality.

## Poverty, inequality, and the media

A major factor influencing the shape of the media in any given country is the source and scale of available revenues, which relate directly to the economic factors considered above. The primary forms of commercial revenue available to the media are advertising and subscription.[5] The former was historically the major source of support in market economies, but various forms of subscription are of increasing importance in the developed world, at least for television. For both sources, the scale of the economy as a whole, the level of per capita income, and the distribution of that income are significant factors.

In the case of the BRICS countries, all the major media depend primarily on commercial revenues, particularly advertising income, which invariably relates, albeit indirectly, to the scale and structure of an economy. Figure 2.4 displays figures for advertising spending (adspend) across BRICS and the US at

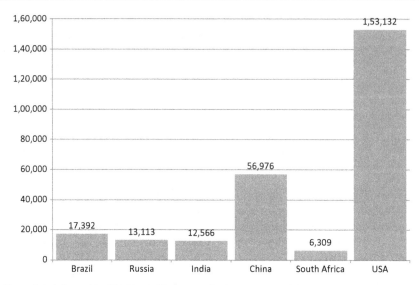

*Figure 2.4* Adspend in 2012 in US$m at purchasing power parities
Source: World Advertising Research Centre

purchasing power parities for 2012, the most recent year available. China has overtaken Brazil with the largest adspend of any of the BRICS countries, but its total is still only 37 percent of that of the US, even though China's economy as a whole is 80 percent of the size of the US's. In current dollar terms, the disparity is even greater: calculated thus, China's adspend is only 25 percent of that of the US. In fact, all the BRICS countries' advertising industries are proportionately smaller, compared to the US, than are their economies. This is evidence of immature advertising industries, which in all the BRICS nations nonetheless experienced relatively rapid expansion during the decade 2001–2011, in contrast with the US, whose industry contracted 15 percent in constant dollar terms over the period. Of course, the choice of dates means that the US figures reflect sharp cyclical movements in the economy that had a major impact on advertising revenues, but were not present in the Chinese case. However, even according to these figures, which tend to overstate the rate of convergence, only by about 2030 will advertising expenditure in China surpass that in the US in dollar terms (World Advertising Research Centre, 2014).

The second important way the overall economic structure of the BRICS countries affects advertising revenues is through the distribution of disposable income. As we saw above, the BRICS are all relatively poor countries, so the figures given in Figure 2.5 are hardly surprising: per capita adspend is a function both of total wealth and of population size. Consequently, countries with a high total adspend and a huge population, like China, have a very low per capita adspend. A country with a high adspend and a relatively small population, like the US, has a very high per capita adspend. The US's per capita adspend is

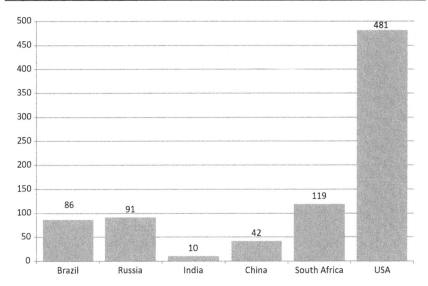

*Figure 2.5* Per capita adspend at US$ purchasing power parities
Source: derived from World Advertising Research Centre

thus more than 10 times larger than that of China and nearly 50 times greater than India's. Once again, in dollar terms the gap is very much greater.

These characteristics are neither distinctive of BRICS nor supportive of the claim that they are a unique grouping, as the same features appear in many other developing countries. They do, however, have important consequences for the media. The enormous absolute scale of US advertising expenditure means, of course, that it can support a wide range of high-cost media directed at its home population. At the same time, the high per capita adspend means that even media that target relatively small sections of the audience can command high advertising income. The high individual income of Americans also means that the subscription base of different media can display similar characteristics: the US media consumer is rich enough to pay both for media that command a very large audience and for media that have much smaller audiences. Taken together, these two factors mean that in the US there is enough available revenue to support both high cost mass media and high cost niche media. As we shall discuss below, recent developments have introduced some important modifications to this picture but it still remains the case that the US audience is large enough and rich enough to support an astonishing range of expensive media.

Across all the BRICS countries, the relatively low per capita adspend, combined with very high levels of income inequality, means that what advertising expenditure there is will likely be highly concentrated amongst the relatively small number of people who enjoy higher incomes. The mass of the population is only attractive to advertisers to the extent that it can be delivered in very large numbers, since individually none of them have more than limited purchasing power. The absolute size of the mass audience, however, also affects the absolute revenue that advertising can generate: a vast number of very poor people can still generate a large income even if the amount per head is tiny. China and India do possess these vast audiences and thus media directed at a mass of the population can generate substantial advertising revenue.

It follows that, although the media in some of these countries do command relatively large audiences, they are not on average very rich, and consequently the producers do not enjoy access to the very substantial financial resources that underlie the success of the US cultural industries. The economies of scale enjoyed by the latter are not due solely to the relatively large size of their domestic market, but to its being both large and rich: high production values can be discounted across an audience that is, in absolute terms, very much smaller than that available to, for example, Indian or Chinese media. In the latter cases, it is only media directed at very large audiences that can expect to generate the kinds of revenues that can sustain high production values. Even so, there is still a considerable disparity in the revenues that can be generated. In 2013, the top-grossing Hollywood movie, *Frozen*, earned a world-wide revenue of $1,232.6 million of which $400 million was from domestic audiences. The top-grossing Chinese movie on the same list, *Lost in Thailand*, earned $197 million worldwide (at number 41 in the global list of revenues).[6] The most successful Bollywood movie, *Dhoom 3*, earned $88 million worldwide (Box Office Mojo, 2014).

Second, the size of the population and the distribution of incomes, and thus of likely adspend, mean that even though media in these countries that address a mass audience must operate with financial resources that are scant compared to those available in the US, those that address an elite audience are in a much more equal position. Wealthy consumers in China or India form a small proportion of the total population of those countries, but they nevertheless are large in absolute size: even after the Xi regime's crackdown on corruption, China in 2013 accounted for 47 percent of the world's luxury spending and forms by far the largest single market (Chang, 2014). Magazines and other niche media directed at these groups can thus potentially command total revenues that approach those of their US counterparts.

Third, because of the low income of the mass of the population, the shift from advertising support to subscription as a major source of revenue is likely to be restricted to those media addressing the same elite audiences. The evidence from the developed world is that, in broadcasting, subscription is a much more efficient mechanism of revenue generation than is advertising: globally, revenues from subscription exceeded those from advertising in the five years to 2012 (Ofcom, 2013a). In the UK, advertising accounted for 29 percent of television revenues while subscriptions accounted for 43 percent, although free-to-view channels commanded around 75 percent of the audience (Ofcom, 2013b: 127, 188, 193).[7] The increasing domination of the broadcasting market by subscription services, either through encoded channels or through online pay services, means that unique content (notably premium sports events) and high-cost programming (movies, original dramas) will more and more be available only through this means. In the developed world, disposable income is such that these forms of subscription are widely, if not universally, available (take-up of subscription TV is more than 50 percent in the UK, for example). In the BRICS countries, income distribution is such that subscription-based services will either be relatively very expensive and restricted to an elite audience or fees will be set so low that they will be unable to produce original high-cost programming.

Even more than is the case in the advanced world, the overall media market is likely to be polarized between generic material that reaches a relatively poor mass audience and a more diversified media serving niches within the wealthy elite. Combined and uneven development is part of the pattern of the media as much as of the broader economy.

## Political power and the media

If it is difficult to find compelling reasons for singling out the five members of BRICS as having unique characteristics, either in their economies generally or in basic media economics, it is even more difficult to find distinctive features of the relationship between the media and political power, broadly conceived. Forms of government differ widely. Despite its obvious limitations, India is a long-established political democracy that, since 1947, has only been interrupted for 21 months (June 1975–March 1977). China, on the other hand, remains a state where power has been exclusively and uninterruptedly in the hands of the Communist Party since 1949. Although different factions of the party have sometimes engaged in bitter struggles – notably the Cultural Revolution and, on a much smaller scale, the Bo Xilai debacle in 2012 – the struggles have always been within the party and have never resulted in a substantial shift in the group monopolizing political power. Even the great challenge of 1989, which certainly had the potential to transform the political system, resulted in the victory of the party's conservative wing over both its inner-party opponents and the popular movement. Brazil is today a democracy that emerged from its most recent period of military rule in a long, contested process beginning in the 1980s and only ending, it is sometimes claimed, with the victory of Lula in 2000. South Africa emerged from apartheid and became a democracy in 1994, although it remains a democracy in which one party, the ANC, continues to command overwhelming electoral support. Russia was unquestionably ruled by the Communist Party until 1991, and how democratic the subsequent chaotic years actually were remains questionable. Certainly, since the mid-1990s, the state has been increasingly authoritarian. Thus there is no apparent common political pattern among the BRICS countries, at least at the level of the formal arrangements of power.

Despite these substantial differences, in all cases there is strong evidence of interchange between political, economic, and media power at other levels.

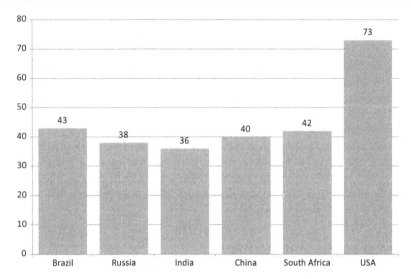

*Figure 2.6* A rough measure of corruption
Source: Transparency International Public Sector Corruption Index 2013
Note: A higher score means less corruption

This finds its most obvious expression in the high levels of corruption present in all of the countries, although once again this is hardly unique to BRICS. Figure 2.6 presents data from a well-respected but unofficial source in which a high score represents a low level of perceived corruption. These indices refer only to perceived corruption in the public sector, but they illustrate the degree to which it pervades these societies. As is clear, the BRICS nations are generally in the middle of the corruption index, between the highest rated countries (the Nordic countries plus New Zealand, all scoring above 85) and the lowest rated (North Korea, Afghanistan, and Somalia, who tie at the bottom with a score of 8). This generalized corruption finds a reflection in the media: common terms for journalists receiving what are in effect bribes include "red envelope journalism" (China), "brown envelope journalism" (South Africa) and "paid journalism" (India).[8]

Rather more nebulous, but equally important, is the relationship between political power and media ownership. In the Chinese case, there is little question that the party-state owns all the legal media and controls them very closely. Furthermore, the people who run the media are appointed and removed at the whim of the party. In Brazil, the direct benefits of close ties between the media and the ruling groups have long been evident, and the restructuring of media ownership in South Africa and Russia has, in different ways, depended upon political interventions. Overall, on the spectrum of the links between political, economic, and media power—which ranges from societies like the US, in which they are relatively indirect and informal, to China or North

Korea, where they are direct and formal—India lies closer to the US while South Africa, Brazil, and Russia are, in different degrees, closer to China, a positioning they share with large numbers of other developing countries.

One of the crudest and least contentious measures of media freedom is the degree to which journalists can conduct their jobs safe from death or imprisonment. Imprisoning journalists is one of the ways that states faced with internal dissent try to control the symbolic landscape, while the murder of journalists is usually, but not always, the work of some non-state body. Nevertheless, the two can be considered in parallel as indicators of societies in which reporting and commenting on public issues is under pressure from social conflict. All of the BRICS nations are societies marked by relatively high levels of violent social conflict, perpetrated by both individual citizens and the state apparatuses. Even democratic India is engaged in a range of internal armed conflicts with disaffected peasants and minority religious groups. In all the other countries, clashes, sometimes armed and often fatal, between sections of the citizenry and the police and army are unfortunately quite common. Predictably, the situation of journalists working in societies with these kinds of economic and political conflicts differs in important respects from that of their counterparts in most of the developed world. Table 2.2 quantifies some of the harm personally suffered by journalists in a range of countries.

Among the BRICS countries, China stands out as the one where the imprisonment of journalists is by far the most common. Worldwide in 2013, in absolute terms, only Turkey, with 40 in jail, had more imprisoned journalists than China. Controlled for size of population, countries like Eritrea (22 in jail) have worse records, but on this measure journalists are far more likely to end up in prison in China than in the other BRICS nations. In this group of societies, the threat to media freedom comes primarily from the state in the form of action that operates within an existing legal system in order to punish some journalists and intimidate others. On the other hand, regarding what the Committee to Protect Journalists (CPJ) considers directly work-related deaths of journalists, Brazil, Russia and India stand out as particularly dangerous societies.[9] China and South Africa, on this measure, are closer to the US,

Table 2.2 Journalists killed and jailed by country

| Country | Imprisoned journalists 2013 | Confirmed murders of journalists 1992–2014 |
| --- | --- | --- |
| Brazil | 0 | 29 |
| Russia | 2 | 56 |
| India | 1 | 32 |
| China | 32 | 2 |
| South Africa | 0 | 3 |
| USA | 1 | 5 |

Source: Committee to Protect Journalists
Figures for murder are from 1992 to June 2014

although it should be noted that the three killings in South Africa all date from 1992–1994. No journalists have been killed since the end of the apartheid regime, and none are in jail today, placing that country in the same very safe category as the Nordic countries. These forms of terror are extra-legal, whether perpetrated by agents of the state or its enemies, but they have a similar function in punishing some journalists and intimidating others. Once again, the BRICS countries neither fall into a single group nor distinguish themselves from many other countries. Four of the countries can be placed in the large group of states where journalists are likely to suffer persecution, but the mechanisms of persecution fall into two different categories. In China it is the state that directly intervenes through its legal system to silence journalists it regards as troublesome. Russia, India, and Brazil, on the other hand, are societies in which the extra-legal murder of journalists is shockingly common. Of the BRICS countries, only in South Africa, despite some ominous rumblings, can journalists still today operate without these particular threats.

"Press freedom," a much more nebulous concept, is clearly open to ideological manipulation. Several well-known attempts are underway internationally to measure the degree of press freedom around the world, but none are readily acceptable as reliable and impartial. Figure 2.7, in which a higher score equates with less media freedom, compares the estimates of the two best known: those by Reporters Sans Frontières (RSF) and Freedom House (FH). The scales and absolute measures differ to an extent that demonstrates how relatively unreliable they are as precise indicators.[10] Notwithstanding their different methodologies, both organizations rate four of the BRICS countries rather poorly. FH rates

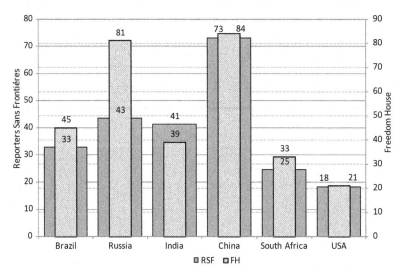

*Figure 2.7* Two rough measures of press freedom
Sources: Reporters Sans Frontières; Freedom House

Russia and China as "not free" and Brazil, India, and South Africa as "partly free." RSF does not have the same classificatory systems. On their scoring, South Africa is reckoned to have a press whose freedom is close to that of the US and Brazil, Russia and India fall into a grouping in the middle range, while China is regarded as significantly less free. The overall picture is one of a wide range in the degree of press freedom in BRICS. Again, this tendency toward less freedom is hardly a unique characteristic of BRICS: in RSF judgment, 41 countries have freer media than South Africa, which both analyses agree has the freest media of the BRICS countries, but another 132, including Italy, have less media freedom. In the judgement of FH, there are 68 countires with freer media than South Africa, but 129 with less media freedom.[11]

Overall, the BRICS countries exhibit some similarities in terms of the media's economic situation, although while all confront a population that is overall relatively poor, the differences in scale between India and China on the one hand and the other three countries mean that media that address a mass audience are able to command significant revenues, even if they are very much smaller than those available to their US competitors. In terms of their relationship to other centers of power, and their relative degree of freedom, conditions in the various BRICS countries are neither particularly close nor distinctive. In none of these latter categories, except perhaps the prevalence of corruption, do BRICS form a coherent grouping, and in this they are regrettably not unique.

## From legacy media to new media

The structure of the media systems in BRICS has, in the past, been similar to that in other developing countries. In all of these countries, television is very widely available, while newspapers remain a minority pursuit. The pattern for advertising revenues follows this quite closely, as Figure 2.8 demonstrates. Just as in the US, and indeed most other countries, in four of the cases, television is the major beneficiary of advertising expenditure; the exception is India, where newspapers have marginally the greater share. However, in BRICS there was until recently no evidence of the rapid decline in newspaper circulation that has been so marked in the developed world. While the average paid circulation of daily newspapers in the OECD countries declined by 2.7 percent between 2000 and 2008, with much greater losses in some major countries like the US, in India it grew by 45 percent, in South Africa by 34 percent, and in China by around 30 percent (OECD, 2010: 24). Circulation in Brazil has also been growing, at a steady but much less spectacular rate (Barbosa, 2012; Folha de Sao Paulo, 2013; World Association of Newspapers, 2009: 265). Figures for newspaper circulation in Russia are unavailable, but the number of daily titles has clearly been growing (World Association of Newspapers, 2009: 772). Much of this overall growth is attributable to changing social structures: Brazil, India, and China are experiencing urbanization, rising living standards, and

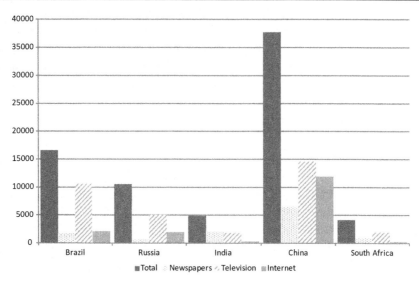

*Figure 2.8* Adspend in 2012 on selected media
Source: World Advertising Research Centre

improved education, all of which are factors which, other things being equal, drive increased newspaper readership.

This pattern is now showing evidence, at least in some of the BRICS countries, of experiencing the same disruptions as have marked the developed world, due to increasing Internet penetration and usage. Recently, there has been some evidence that the tale of constant growth in newspaper readership has come to an end. In China, at least, the rise in newspaper circulation peaked in 2008 and began to fall quite sharply in 2012. One factor in this turn-around is probably the increasing use of the Internet for news and other information. This channel is growing in all of the BRICS countries. Figure 2.9 presents the most recent International Telecommunications Union figures for the percentage of individuals in each country using the Internet in 2012.[12] As before, no single clear, discernible pattern unites the BRICS nations or distinguishes them from many other countries. Brazil and Russia have rather more than half their populations with Internet access; China and South Africa are approaching this level; India records a substantially lower proportion. In percentage terms, none of them approaches the US. In absolute terms, however, China has the world's largest population of Internet users and India, even with its low penetration rate, is close to the US with the third largest online population. The physical basis certainly exists for new media to have a major impact upon patterns of media behavior and on the business models of legacy media.

Comparisons of usage are much more difficult, in part because of the problematic status of the available statistics, which tend not to provide equivalent figures for equivalent time periods. Comparison is particularly complicated by

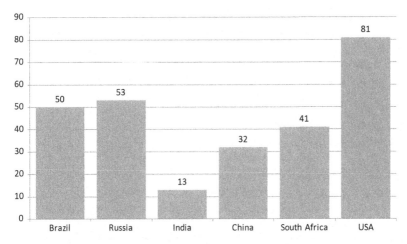

*Figure 2.9* Percentage of individuals using the Internet as of 2012
Source: International Telecommunications Union

the fact that in China, many well-known international online brands like
Facebook, Google, and Twitter are either refused legal entry or eclipsed by
their national competitors. A similar situation with local competition prevails
in certain other segments in other countries, notably Russia. One comparison
that can be drawn, at least in general terms, is between usage of Twitter and that
of its Chinese equivalent, generically known as Weibo. While the US is home
to by far the largest number of Twitter users in a recent measure, India has the
third highest number, followed by Brazil in fifth and Russia in sixth place.
South Africa, with by far the smallest population of the BRICS countries,
ranks 26th (Alexa: The Web Information Company, 2013). As for China, it had
around 300 million individuals, 55 percent of total Chinese Internet users, with
registered accounts across the range of equivalent services at the end of 2012
(Xinhua, 2013).[13] These figures, cautiously interpreted, suggest that microblogging is particularly important within BRICS, although again this is not a
defining feature, since Mexico, Indonesia, and Turkey are also amongst the 10
countries with the most current users.

Microblogging, of course, can mean different things in different contexts.
Although everywhere it is used by political activists as a mechanism for self-
organization, and by states as a mechanism for surveillance, the impact of
Weibo in China requires some additional comment. In terms of the extent of
its penetration of daily life in China, Weibo does not appear to differ qualitatively
from the different usages of Twitter around the world. Just as elsewhere, Chinese
Internet usage, including Weibo usage, spans a very wide range of activities,
including commerce, leisure, travel, search, gossip, gaming, and so on (Lai and
To, 2012; Sullivan, 2012). On the other hand, Weibo is also the site of genuine
popular discussion, sometimes highly politicized, about breaking news of

public interest. Unlike in the press and on television, which are censored in advance, stories expressing critical views and reporting sensitive incidents can appear on Weibo, although they are likely to be removed as soon as the censors realize their import (Li, 2013). So, for example, a struggle over censorship at the famous magazine *Southern Weekend* found a public airing on Weibo (Hille and Hook, 2013; Kennedy, 2013). In a society where frequent outbursts express popular discontent ("mass incidents"), and incompetence and corruption are ingrained patterns of behavior for officials and businesses, such crises occur regularly, impacting social media in ways that are extremely rare in traditional media.[14]

The extent to which this represents a transformative potential can certainly be exaggerated: some senior party officials, like Executive Vice-President of the Central Party School Li Jingtian, have told Western reporters that Weibo has a role to play in curbing official corruption (Orlick and Baker, 2013). Admittedly, a certain amount of publicity, whether in the traditional media or online, can help the leading party bodies identify, and exercise better control over, their corrupt, incompetent, and unruly subordinates, but it certainly has disruptive effects as well. The clearest example of this dynamic was the high-speed rail disaster in Wenzhou in July 2011. Despite many casualties, official media were very reluctant to cover the event; meanwhile it was vigorously reported and debated on Weibo. Eventually, this pressure resulted in much more extensive and thorough coverage in the official media (Branigan, 2011).[15] More recently, the new leadership has taken a more proactive attitude towards the potential of the Internet, exerting pressure on popular Weibo posters to adopt a more conciliatory tone and attempting to use the Internet as a propagnda instrument putting forward a positive view of the country and the party's role in leading it towards the realization of the "Chinese Dream" (Yang, 2014).

In the developed world, the Internet's most marked economic impact on traditional media has been the flight of advertising revenues from printed newspapers to online locations, mostly search sites. As we saw above, the proportion of advertising going to the Internet was, in four of the five countries involved, relatively small; the exception being China. The trend, however, tells a different story. As Figure 2.10 demonstrates, there is something of a crisis in both China and Russia, although it displays a rather different profile in each case. For China (2012) and Russia (2010), Internet advertising exceeded that in newspapers. Up until very recently, however, this shift did not pose the same sort of problem that it has done elsewhere in the developed world, notably in the US. This was largely because overall advertising revenues were still rising in both of these countries. Total advertising revenues, including both that in the print editions and online, for newspapers in the US fell by 45 percent between its peak in 2005 and 2012. The fall in China (2012) did not begin until rather later, in 2012, when the overall fall was 7 percent. In the Russian case, after a sharp fall in 2008, related more to general economic

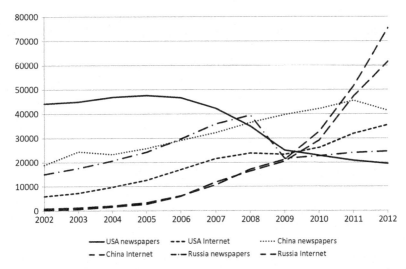

*Figure 2.10* Advertising expenditure on newspapers and Internet in local currency for the
USA, Russia and China, 2002–2012
Source: World Advertising Research Centre

conditions than to Internet penetration, newspaper advertising in Russia continued to rise year on year, albeit slowly. Anecdotal evidence suggests that the
fall in both circulation and advertising revenue in China in 2013 has been
much more severe than what went before, and newspapers are facing very
serious economic situations.

Overall, the evidence from a study of the new media demonstrates no clear
and distinctive patterns that can be attributed to common features unique to
BRICS. Internet penetration is growing everywhere, but this is not unique in
the developing world. The level varies greatly from country to country, and it
correlates quite well with per capita income. Levels of microblogging usage
seem very high in all the BRICS countries, but in no other respect do they
form a clearly defined bloc. The economic impact of new media compared to
the old is also highly varied. Outside of China, where advertising expenditure
on new media has reached a proportion comparable to that in the US, it is still
substantially below that of television, although it has also surpassed that of the
press in Russia. Only in China, so far, do we have any evidence that these
changes have had an impact on the audiences for, or income of, the legacy media.

## Conclusions: positive and negative features of the category "BRICS"

Whatever its popular appeal to bankers, journalists, politicians, or the general
public, the BRICS concept has severe weaknesses from the viewpoint of scholarly
enquiry. It is hard to find a single major dimension, in economics, politics, or

media, in which these five countries are (a) uniform and (b) collectively distinct from other developing countries. As this chapter has shown, the BRICS countries display common characteristics in very few factors of their general political and economic structures, or in their media. Moreover, many of the features they do display in common, for example pervasive corruption or the popularity of microblogging, are scarcely unique to this grouping alone, but rather are usually shared with many other developing countries. Even where a common category appears to single them out, as with the density of microblogging, closer examination might reveal that different social dynamics are at work in each case.

It is therefore very tempting simply to say that the concept of BRICS is empty and should be discarded as useless for analytic purposes. Yet that entirely justified response still fails to explain why so many people with so many different occupations, social researchers among them, have found the concept useful. Part of the answer lies in the fact that the concept is a geopolitical reality, albeit a new and relatively powerless as a body compared with established blocs like NATO or the EU. More important, however, is its powerful rhetorical significance, owing to the clear label it puts upon a process that is long-term and diffuse but undoubtedly real. Whatever reservations people might have, and however dubious certain predictions about the future may be, the economic geography of the world has changed fundamentally in the last quarter-century. The international political structure is already changing, and it is reasonable to assume that culture will also eventually begin to reflect these growing forces. This multidimensional "rise of the rest" is what the use of "BRICS" as a slogan captures: these countries, taken as the vanguard of this changing order, have helped force its reality on many people, some of whom are most reluctant to accept the extent of the changes.

On the other hand, use of this category can obscure more than it reveals. The above analysis demonstrates the deep differences between the constituent countries of the BRICS bloc. Most strikingly, in terms of the scale and pace of growth of its economy and the nature of its political and media systems, China stands out as different in degree from all of the others, a reality that corresponds to the birth of BRICS as an international grouping. China was and is the moving force and the dominant player in this initiative. Chinese pre-eminence is partly a matter of scale and partly a matter of growth rates. The Chinese economy is vastly bigger than the economies of the other BRICS countries, and China is also growing much faster; indeed, the gap grows larger every day. In some important respects, the US is a more obvious comparator for China than are the other BRICS nations. In most respects, this disparity of scale between China and the rest will continue indefinitely, primarily because of the sheer size of the Chinese population. In the longer term, the only other society that can expect to reach the same absolute size is India, which has an almost equally large, and faster growing, population.

Whether it is BRICS, all developing countries, or just the potential giants of China and India together that are under consideration, or whether a more immediate view restricts the field to China, clearly the processes of social and economic change in question will be neither smooth nor painless. They will have huge ramifications both for the countries in question and for the shape of the world order. Previous shifts in global economic power have resulted in sharp international conflicts with a huge human and material cost. In the near term, it is unlikely that the conflicts that are all too evident over barren rocks in the East and South China Seas will result in the same global cataclysm as occurred twice in the last century. For one thing, the military balance is today so overwhelmingly in favor of the incumbent power that even the most blinkered militarist can see that there could only be one outcome to any major armed conflict: according to the Stockholm International Peace Research Institute (SIPRI), US military expenditure in 2013 was more than three times higher than that of China (SIPRI, 2014).

Less intense conflicts, however, are already underway and are likely to increase. For our purposes, cultural conflict is the most relevant dimension to explore. Conflict and potential conflict in the cultural area spans both China and the US, on a spectrum ranging from higher education to popular culture. Potential for cultural conflict has risen sharply since the Chinese government launched its "going out" strategy in an attempt to gain what it considers to be 'soft power'. For example, one part of this strategy, the highly successful initiative to establish Confucius Institutes in universities around the world, has been the subject of attack and controversy in the US (Redden, 2012). On a more popular level, in November 2012 Hollywood released a remake of *Red Dawn*. The original, released in 1984, hinged on a Soviet invasion of the US, but the remake has North Koreans in the aggressor's role. Given that North Korea's estimated population is about 24.5 million, as compared with around 314 million for the US, it may be wrong to consider this film as a realist text. In earlier versions of the remake, the invaders were Chinese; apparently the nationality was changed for commercial reasons (*Global Times*, 2011). The substitution of China for the former USSR as a potential occupying power clearly has some appeal in the US. On the Chinese side, such reversions to the simpler narratives of the high Cold War tend to be less institutional, finding expression in apparently spontaneous popular protests against Western misreporting on China and other perceived slights. The official line, even when articulated in the rather threatening terms of *Global Times*, is that "China is sincere in pursuing peaceful development," although "the possibility that in the future China will become tougher cannot be excluded" (*Global Times*, 2013).

In this chapter the stress has been on the differences between the constituents of the BRICS bloc, but there is one dimension that they share with each other and with a much broader group of countries: they all rest upon systems that, at their foundation, ruthlessly suppress the majority of their populations. All these countries face serious internal opposition, and all have notoriously corrupt governmental systems. The same problems—minorities facing discrimination, persistent oppression of women, peasants robbed of their land, workers subject to exploitative regimes and sometimes cheated of their wages—are found in all these countries. So, too, is the same brutal repression of organized dissent, often effected through armed force; and so, too, is brave and determined resistance.

That the economic center of the world will shift is largely certain, although it remains unknown whether the BRICS will be the sole beneficiaries of this change. We can hope for two things: first, that geopolitical shifts do not have the same disastrous consequences for the world that they did in previous episodes; and second, that the workers and peasants of the emerging economies succeed in winning for themselves at least the same limited control over their lives that those in the declining West still enjoy. Indeed, one can even hope they will show people everywhere how to win a great deal more freedom and autonomy.

## Notes

1 The current chapter is a substantially revised and re-worked version of the article "Deconstructing the BRICS" that appeared in the *International Journal of Communication* 8 (2014), 392–418. The pdf of the original article is available at http://ijoc.org/index.php/ijoc/article/view/2049/1074.

2 To underline the fact that these are projections and are subject to sometimes quite drastic revisions, in the first version of this article (published in the *International Journal of Communication* in January 2014) and using figures available in 2012, the IMF projections were for China's GDP measured in purchasing power parities to surpass that of the US in 2017. It is more than possible that future revisions will further postpone the crossover point, but the evidence of the last thirty years suggests quite strongly that it will be reached at some time in the not-too-distant future.

3 Some international organizations have also queried whether the economic differences between BRICS mean that the term is misleading and have proposed alternatives. For example, the OECD uses the term "BIICS", deleting Russia and inserting Indonesia (OECD, 2010).

4 Like China (and the US), Hong Kong's Gini coefficient has been increasing. According to the city's Census and Statistics Department, it reached 0.537 in 2011 (Chong and Lee, 2012).

5 State subsidy, of course, is another source of income for some media in some countries—for example the BBC in the UK—and private subsidy is important in others—for example, in the US, *The Washington Post*. In none of the cases under consideration, even China, is this form of financing central to the media systems.

6 According to an alternative source, the most successful Chinese movie of the year was *Journey to the West: Conquering the Demons*, which "amassed 1.25 billion yuan ($205 million) at the domestic box office during the 2013 Spring Festival" (Shi, 2014).

7 The remaining 22 percent was a state subsidy, in the form of a licence fee, granted to the BBC. The latter accounts for roughly 33 percent of the total audience. In fact, the share of audience gained by the free-to-view advertising supported channels was around 40 percent. To be complete, some 25 percent of the advertising revenue went to subscription channels.

8 The official term in China, Professor Zhao informs me, is *youchang xinwen*, which is best translated as "paid journalism." "Red-envelope journalism" is the more popular term. If a phenomenon has both an official and unofficial terminology, it is probably rather pervasive.

9 The formal definition reads:

> We consider a case "confirmed" only if we are reasonably certain that a journalist was murdered in direct reprisal for his or her work; was killed in crossfire during combat situations; or was killed while carrying out a dangerous assignment such as coverage of a street protest. Our database does not include journalists killed in accidents such as car or plane crashes.
>
> (CPJ, 2014)

Other cases still under investigation that the CPJ considers possibly linked to professional issues number nine in Brazil, 24 in Russia, 22 in India, and three in China. In South Africa there are none; in the US, one. Other news workers, including "translators, drivers, guards, fixers, and administrative workers" have been killed in similar circumstances, but the CPJ has collected these figures only since 2003 (CPJ, 2014). In the countries reported here, only India has cases (three) in the "confirmed" category.

10 The scales and rankings may differ but both are agreed, unsurprisingly, that the Nordic countries dominate the ranks of the freest press environments. The objectivity and independence of FH's judgments have sometimes been called into question, e.g., by Herman and Chomsky (2008: 26).

11 Italy, with 31 points and also "partly free" comes in at 64, a sliver above South Africa.

12 There are more recent estimates available, for example from Internet World Stats (www.internetworldstats.com/) but I have decided to use the figures from the ITU on the grounds that, so far as possible, this paper has employed "official" figures rather than commercial estimates. In fact, although estimates for 2014 are generally higher, they follow more or less the same pattern. For example, Internet Live Stats, basing themselves on ITU data, estimate the populations at 1 July 2014 will be: Brazil, 54 percent; Russia, 59 percent; India, 19 percent; China, 46 percent; South Africa, 47 percent; US, 87 percent (www.internetlivestats.com/internet-users-by-country/).

13 "Registered accounts" does not mean active users.

14 The number of mass incidents in China is a matter of debate. Estimates rise year by year; one high estimate is around 200,000 for 2012. According to *Legal Daily*, as excerpted by *Danwei*:

> It's worth noting that in 13.3 per cent of mass incidents new media Weibo was used as an organizational tool. One can see that the nature of mass incidents is changing with the development of the internet, and there are more and more methods of organizing people who have never met before into an interest group that encourages a mass incident to break out.
>
> (Goldkorn, 2013)

15 The China Media Project has collected images of the disaster posted on social media (Bandurski, 2011).

## References

Agence France Presse (2013) *Beijing to Release Own Gini Inequality Index*, January 20. Retrieved from www.scmp.com/news/asia/article/1132424/beijing-release-own-gini-inequality-index.

Alexa: The Web Information Company (2013) *Twitter.com*. Retrieved from www.alexa.com/siteinfo/twitter.com.

Bandurski, D. (2011) *Images on Social Media Chronicle Days of Disaster*. Retrieved from http://cmp.hku.hk/2011/07/26/14149.

Barbosa, M. (2012) *Newsaper Circulation in Brazil Grows 3.5 per cent in 2011*. Retrieved from www1.folha.uol.com.br/internacional/en/finance/1039340-newspaper-circulation-in-brazil-grows-35-in-2011.shtml.

Box Office Mojo (2014) *2013 Box Office Grosses*. Retrieved from www.boxofficemojo.com/yearly/chart/?view2=worldwide&yr=2013&p=.htm.

Branigan, T. (2011) *Chinese Anger Over Alleged Cover-up of High-speed Rail Crash*. Retrieved from www.guardian.co.uk/world/2011/jul/25/chinese-rail-crash-cover-up-claims.

Chang, L. (2014) *China World's Biggest Luxury Consumer*. Retrieved from www.chinadaily.com.cn/bizchina/2014-02/21/content_17298225.htm.

Chong, D. and Lee, A. C. (2012) *Haves and Have-Nots*, June 20. Retrieved from www.scmp.com/article/1004440/haves-and-have-nots.

Committee to Protect Journalists (CPJ) (2014) *Terminology*. Retrieved from http://cpj.org/killed/terminology.php.

Folha de Sao Paulo (2013) *Newspaper Circulation in Brazil Grows: Folha Takes the Lead*. Retrieved from www1.folha.uol.com.br/internacional/en/finance/1220366-newspaper-circulation-in-the-country-grows-folha-takes-the-lead.shtml.

Freedom House (2012) *Global Press Freedom Rankings*. Retrieved from http://freedomhouse.org/report/freedom-press/freedom-press-2012#.VFdrLmcVE6J. Accessed October 28, 2014.

*Global Times* (2011) *US Vision of Villains v. Heroes not Just on Screen*. Retrieved from www.globaltimes.cn/content/634541.shtml.

——(2013) *Xi's Message Shows Consistent Diplomacy*. Retrieved from www.globaltimes.cn/content/759261.shtml.

Goldkorn, J. (2013) *Legal Daily Report on Mass Incidents in China in 2012*. Retrieved from www.danwei.com/a-report-on-mass-incidents-in-china-in-2012.

Herman, E. and Chomsky, N. (2008) *Manufacturing Consent: The Political Economy of the Mass Media*, second edition. London: The Bodley Head.

Hille, K. and Hook, L. (2013) Battle over Censorship Spreads, *Financial Times*, January 9.

Holland, T. C. (2012) *China Now Reaching the Same Levels of Inequality as Johannesberg*, December 11. Retrieved from www.scmp.com/business/article/1102451/china-now-reaching-same-levels-inequality-johannesburg.

IMF (2014) *World Economic Outlook Database, April 2014*. Washington: International Monetary Fund, Retrieved from www.imf.org.

Kennedy, J. (2013) *Guangdong Censor's Clumsy Hatchet Job Sparks Fierce Backlash*, January 3. Retrieved from www.scmp.com/comment/blogs/article/1118939/guangdong-censors-clumsy-hatchet-job-sparks-fierce-backlash.

Lai, L. and To, W. M. (2012) The Emergence of China in the Internet Market. *IT Professional*, 14(1): 6–9.

Lau, S. C. (2013) *Hong Kong Again Named World's Freest Economy*, January 10. Retrieved from www.scmp.com/news/hong-kong/article/1124621/hk-again-named-worlds-freest-economy.

Li, J. (2013) *Censor-row Paper Honours Stories That Were Banned Blog Post Showing Summaries of Unpublished Southern Weekly Articles Honoured Soon Deleted*. Retrieved from http://0-search.proquest.com.hkbulib.hkbu.edu.hk/docview/1270842136.

OECD (2010) *Economic Policy Reforms: Going for Growth 2010*. Paris: Organisation for Economic Co-operation and Development.

Ofcom (2013a) *Global TV Industry: Revenue by Source*. London: Office of Communication.
——(2013b) *The Communications Market 2013*. London: Office of Communication.
Orlick, T. and Baker, G. (2013) *Chinese Official Alludes to Severe Penalty for Bo*, January 23. Retrieved from http://0-search.proquest.com.hkbulib.hkbu.edu.hk/docview/1272368160.
Pew Center's Project for Excellence in Journalism (2012) *Digital: News Gains Audience but Loses Ground in Chase for Revenue*. Retrieved from http://stateofthemedia.org/2012/digital-news-gains-audience-but-loses-more-ground-in-chase-for-revenue.
Redden, E. (2012) *Confucius Says …* Retrieved from www.insidehighered.com/news/2012/01/04/debate-over-chinese-funded-institutes-american-universities.
Reporters Sans Frontières/Reporters Without Borders (2012) *Press Freedom Index 2011–2012*. Paris: Reporters Sans Frontières.
Shi, B. (2014) *Hollywood Takes a Hit*. Retrieved from http://english.entgroup.cn/news_detail.aspx?id=2194.
SIPRI (2014) *SIPRI Military Expenditure Data Base*. Stockholm: Stockholm International Peace Research Institute.
Sullivan, J. (2012) A Tale of Two Microblogs in China. *Media, Culture and Society*, 34(6): 773–783.
UNDP (2013) *Human Development Report 2013*. New York: United Nations Development Programme.
World Advertising Research Centre (2014) *Adspend Database: Table Builder*. Retrieved from www.warc.com.
World Association of Newspapers (2009) *World Press Trends 2009*. Paris: World Association of Newspapers.
World Bank (2013) *Poverty and Inequality Database*. Retrieved from http://databank.worldbank.org/data/views/variableSelection/selectvariables.aspx?source=poverty-and-inequality-database.
Xinhua (2013) *China's Internet Users Reach 564 Million*. Retrieved from http://news.xinhuanet.com/english/sci/2013-01/15/c_132104473.htm.
Yang, G. (2014) The Return of Ideology and the Future of Chinese Internet Policy. *Critical Studies in Media and Communication*, 31(2): 109–13.

# Chapter 3

# The BRICS formation in reshaping global communication: possibilities and challenges[1]

*Yuezhi Zhao*

This chapter examines the possibilities of the BRICS countries in reshaping the current global communication order as an emerging power bloc. Beginning by making a case for taking the BRICS formation seriously, the chapter then offers preliminary case studies that may serve as signposts from which to observe whether the BRICS countries are emerging as a potential power bloc in reshaping global communication in the realms of infrastructure building and global Internet governance.

## Clearing the ground: why take the BRICS concept seriously?

It is easy to take a cynical view of the attempt to engage the BRICS concept seriously in studying contemporary global communication. In his article, 'Deconstructing the BRICS', Colin Sparks has made the observation that the BRICS are not a homogenous group of countries and that they do not pose a serious challenge to US hegemony or Western domination. In this view, the differences between the BRICS countries are so 'large as to call into question the utility of trying to see them as anything other than a somewhat ad hoc grouping of governments that are at least as different as they are similar' (Sparks, 2014: 393). Consequently, rather than being a 'unique or coherent group' that will shift the balance of world power, 'the primary value of the term [BRICS] is to draw attention to the fact that the world is shifting' (ibid.: 414). Outside the communication field, international studies scholar Vijay Prashad, in an earlier and more sympathetic assessment in the book the *Poorer Nations*, recognized the counter-hegemonic potential of the BRICS by characterizing it as 'the first formation in thirty years to challenge the settled orthodoxy of the Global North' (Prashad, 2012: 12). However, as noted elsewhere (Zhao, 2014), Prashad, whose book appeared in 2012, was also quick to underscore the major limitations of the BRICS platform. Apart from the lack of a 'new *institutional* foundation for its emerging authority', an '*ideological* alternative to neoliberalism', as well as an 'ability to sequester the military dominance of the United States and NATO', he noted in particular how a continuing neoliberal orientation in the domestic policies of these countries had meant the 'obscene' situation of the supposed 'locomotives of the South' pulling the 'wagons of the North' with 'sales of commodities and low wages to workers accompanying a recycled surplus turned over as credit to the North' (Prashad, 2012: 10–11).

There is certainly more than a grain of truth in these assessments. After all, unlike the twentieth-century Non-Aligned Movement (NAM), which constituted itself as a conscious Third World counter-hegemonic bloc demanding a New International Economic Order (NIEO) and a concomitant New World Information and Communication Order (NWICO), it was Jim O'Neill (2001) of Goldman Sachs who first coined the term 'BRIC' in 2001. Considering both the timing and authorship of the concept, there is no question that the initial 'BRIC' term carried with it the birthmark of an expansionary, even triumphant, global capitalist logic in a post-Cold War global order. Among other things, this logic truncates history and reduces the four vast and historically complex countries of Brazil, Russia, India and China to the status of 'emerging markets' or new growth zones for neoliberal capitalist expansion and investment. Indeed, the very characterization of the BRIC countries as 'emerging markets' in a unipolar post-Cold War US-dominated global capitalist order registered the devastating defeats of the two major anti-systematic movements in the twentieth century: the international communist movement of universal human emancipation that counted the USSR and China as its main protagonists, and the 'Third World' as a 'utopian project' of what Prashad (2012) called the 'Darker Nations' of Africa, Asia and Latin America in a struggle for national independence and autonomous development, in which India played a leading role.

In fact, contrary to Prashad's expectation, the BRIC countries, in O'Neill's original formulation, were not imagined to be the 'locomotives of the South' to begin with. Rather, they were imagined and shaped by the post-Cold War capitalist global political economy to be the locomotives of neoliberal global capitalism. Moreover, even though the era of neoliberal capitalism has been widely characterized as 'digital capitalism' or 'informationalized capitalism' (Schiller, 1999 and 2007) and 'communicative capitalism' (Dean, 2009) in which information and communication play a pivotal role as both a site of capital accumulation and a site of social struggle, there was nothing in the initial BRIC concept that foregrounded media and communication specifically as either a site of geopolitical struggle or as a platform of accumulation for global capitalism. In fact, although China and India have both featured ICT-driven neoliberal growth since the 1980s, information and communication have not figured prominently in the more resource-oriented Russian and Brazilian economies.

However, the above discussion does not mean that we need to carry the metaphorical nature of the initial BRIC concept to its logical end by concluding that, since we cannot see through a 'BRIC' for a crystal clear vision of the world and its future direction, and since there has not been any clearly articulated BRIC agenda in the area of media and communication, it is futile or perhaps even foolish to try to gain a perspective on the evolving structure of global communication through the BRICS nations.

To begin with, while the metaphor of a BRIC conveys a pre-configured and solidified structure, this is certainly not the case here. Despite all the differences and limitations, as noted respectively by Sparks and Prashad in the above cited publications, that the leaderships of the initial BRIC countries of Brazil, Russia, India and China would first assume a BRIC identity and then start a process of pro-actively constituting itself as a potential geopolitical bloc is certainly noteworthy. That these countries would, by 2010, have invited South Africa to join them and thus transform the singular BRIC to the plural BRICS is also not insignificant. Notwithstanding Prashad's 2012 critique of these countries' economic integration with the Global North, that the 2013 BRICS summit hosted by South Africa would foreground a continental development agenda for Africa under the theme of 'BRICS and Africa – Partnerships for Integration and Industrialization' seems to indicate that these countries are serious about a developmental reorientation toward the Global South, especially Africa. Moreover, by the July 2014 summit in Brazil, these countries had announced the establishment of a $100 billion New Development Bank as an alternative to the World Bank for financing infrastructure projects and the BRICS Contingent Reserve Arrangement as an alternative to the IMF to provide relief for short-term liquidity pressures of group countries. With these two 'signature initiatives', observations have been made that 'the BRICS club of emerging powers' are 'walking the talk', proving themselves 'beyond a shade of doubt that the BRICS is not a glorified talk shop, but a powerful instrument for recasting the world order' (Chand, 2014). In other words, there is already enough evidence to demonstrate that this formation is building institutional alternatives to a US dominated global financial capitalist order. Finally, just as the 2013 Summit featured a strong African regional developmental agenda, the 2014 Brazil Summit not only featured Argentine President Cristina Kirchner as a special guest (*Buenos Aires Herald*, 2014), but also included a BRICS–UNASUR (Union of South American Nations) Summit, whereby leaders of BRICS countries discussed issues of common concern with leaders of the South American regional bloc.

This is further illustrative of the possibility that BRICS may turn out to be more fluid and stretchable than the metaphor allows, and may indeed gradually turn itself into an engine of growth for the Global South. Of course, it is also possible that it may even outgrow its initial cast as a stepping stone to something else. That the much-anticipated 'BRICS Bank' would be officially called the 'New Development Bank' is certainly indicative of the inclusive intention of the BRICS countries. Moreover, as Prashad observed in a 21 July 2014 interview with *Russia Today* in response to news about the creation of the BRICS Bank, not only was it a 'frontal challenge to the IMF and the World Bank', but also its commitment to the principle of equal voting power by each of the BRICS countries against the drawback of China's disproportionate economic power underscored an advancement in terms of global democracy (Prashad, 2014).

Second, Prashad is certainly correct in pointing out that BRICS does not offer an ideological alternative to neoliberalism. Moreover, this seems to remain true in the post-2008 era, when neoliberalism suffered from a devastating blow. For example, while the current Chinese leadership seems to continue to pursue a 'signaling left and turning right' approach by proclaiming its commitment to socialism on the one hand and pushing for deepening market reforms on the other, the April 2014 election of the pro-business Hindu nationalist party Bharatiya Janata Party leader Narendra Modi as the Indian Prime Minister seems to signal a decisive ascendance of a more extreme version of what Prashad (2012) had characterized as 'neoliberalism with Southern characteristics' in India.

However, just as it is important to recognize how the 'BRIC' group has evolved in the past decade, it is also important to look further back to appreciate the historical relics or the mud, so to speak, that has contributed to the making of today's BRICS states, and to appreciate how these historical legacies continue to cast a long shadow in these countries' future transformations. To recast a point about the early history of these countries from a bottom-up perspective, it is perhaps worthwhile to note that these are five countries that carry with them the rich and powerful historical memories of the epic struggles against colonialism, slavery, apartheid, fascism and even capitalism.

From a normative perspective, that these countries today all practice some version of neoliberalism and share all the sins that Sparks (2014) has identified – staggering inequalities, corrupt governmental systems, the ruthless oppression of dissent, the exploitation of workers and the discrimination of minorities – has only made the collective memories of these past struggles, including the historical solidarities and animosities that these countries forged in these struggles, all the more poignant and relevant. For example, China and Russia have recently announced that they would jointly launch activities in celebration of the 70th anniversary of the end of the Second World War and the victory over fascism in 2015 (Liu and Lu, 2014).

This is illustrative of the fact that these two countries are re-forging some kind of ideological solidarity out of their shared historical struggles within the international communist and anti-fascist movements in the twentieth century. Similarly, China has tried to court India to reestablish the long historical connections between the two peoples through the 'rebuilding of the maritime silk road' rhetoric. This rhetoric, articulated against the drawback of the post-2008 American state's 'pivot to Asia' geopolitical move and the new manifestations of the Western 'divide and conquer' strategy in Asia, is also noteworthy. To be sure, geopolitical or geo-culturally inspired 'soft power' initiatives such as these do not constitute an effective articulation of the kind of anti-neoliberal counter-hegemonic ideological alternative that Prashad criticized the BRICS for lacking. However, just as anti-neoliberal and perhaps even anti-capitalist social forces within each of these countries have to rebuild radical anti-system movements and reshape their respective states to serve popular needs one brick at a time, solidarities and alliances between and among these BRICS countries have to be forged one brick at a time, out of the complex interplay of elite divisions and popular struggles as well as the particular articulations of domestic and transnational politics at specific historical conjunctures.

In addition, it is true that the BRICS formation has not foregrounded information and communication as a distinct arena for alternative development and policy formation. There is also no ready-made NWICO type of movement for international communication scholars to reference. However, there is no question that the realm of information and communication has figured prominently in the ongoing contestations over the evolving global order, and the BRICS countries, in their singularity or in collectivity, have been on the forefront of these struggles. For example, as I will describe in more detail in the next section, there have been initial reports about a BRICS communication infrastructure in the form of a BRICS under sea fiber-optic cable.

Post-2008 changes within the US-led global capitalist order have provided favorable conditions for the BRICS countries to challenge US unipolar domination. On the one hand, the 2008 Wall Street-originated, global financial crisis has accentuated the role of the BRICS as important nodes of global political economic power. This, among other factors in a rapidly transforming global political economy, including Russia's willingness to reassert its geopolitical power, first in Syria and then in Ukraine, and the Chinese Communist Party's ability to regroup and reassert itself both nationally and internationally under the leadership of Xi Jinping after a paralyzing transition struggle in 2012, have made it increasingly difficult to simply think of the BRICS countries as 'emerging markets' for a Western-centric capitalist global order.

Not surprisingly, in the aftermath of the Syria crisis in 2013, it has been suggested that there is a distinct possibility that the group may move from an economic agenda to a political agenda. On the other hand, former US intelligence contractor Edward Snowden's revelations of the US National Security Agency's (NSA) pervasive surveillance of electronic communication since June 2013 have provided an unprecedented opportunity for the BRICS countries to pursue a long-standing agenda of decentering the ideological and institutional supremacy of the US in global communication, particularly in the Internet. Indeed, it is perhaps not an exaggeration to say that the Snowden-triggered implosion of the US imperial information surveillance state has created a hegemonic crisis in a US-dominated global Internet governance model. Consequently, we have an opportunity to study how and why the BRICS countries have or have not seized this opportunity to organize a counter-hegemonic offensive.

This last point also underscores an important qualification regarding academic politics and intellectual positioning that we need to make clear at the onset: whether to 'construct' or 'deconstruct' BRICS is inevitably not a value-free or geopolitically neutral scholarly exercise – even though, as academics, we are fully aware of the limited 'real world' impact of such an undertaking. By writing this chapter and contributing to an emerging BRICS media and communication studies literature, we have taken the BRICS idea seriously and contributed to its circulation in the academic realm. This is not because we have simply bought into an original Goldman Sachs idea, but because the term has long gone beyond its initial meaning in the past decade.

The questions I would like to pose in this chapter, then, are the following: what can we expect from the newly neo-liberalized and reconstituted states in the BRICS formation, in terms of a new global communication order in the context of a profound global economic crisis and a radical realignment in the global political economy in the post-2008 era? What are the struggles that have been waged over the future shape of global communication between the US on the one hand and the BRICS countries on the other – or, perhaps equally important, what have prevented the BRICS from forming themselves as a collective entity in global communication vis-à-vis the US? To put it in another way, if the forging of the BRICS group as a potential counter-hegemonic bloc in global communication is itself part and parcel of an ongoing geopolitical struggle, then, how are such struggles being played out around and through the BRICS states? The remaining part of this chapter explores these questions by examining the words and deeds of the BRICS countries – mostly in their potential collective/coordinated action – in the realm of global communication. Specifically, the next two sections look at collective BRICS attempts at infrastructure development in the form of a BRICS cable and their attempts at alternative policy formation in global Internet governance.

Before going further, however, a few methodological qualifications are due. First, while the Snowden revelations serve as a pivotal point in this analysis, the discussion is not strictly limited to the post-Snowden period. Second, the distinctions concerning the infrastructural and policy realms are more analytical than empirical. Clearly, these areas are not mutually exclusive. Moreover, at this stage, it is inevitable that there is more talk than anything else. Third, the sources for this study are primarily the world's news media. In a way, this chapter can be seen as both a preliminary attempt to view a changing global communication landscape through the words and deeds of the BRICS countries and as an analysis of global news discourses about the BRICS nations in communication-related matters. As it is the case with this book, it is important to underscore the research-in-progress nature of this chapter; its view of the possibilities and limits of the BRICS in reshaping the global communication order is ultimately shaped by its sources. The limits of this study will be seen immediately in the next section, with regard to the BRICS cable.

## Tracing the BRICS cable: how far will it go?

What one learns and does not learn about the BRICS cable is perhaps illustrative of the hope and follies, or possibilities and limits, of BRICS. This is also a dimension of BRICS that seems to come closest to Jim O'Neill's original BRIC vision – as emerging markets and as sites of investment and speculation. And what better way to realize the speculative potential of BRICS than a BRICS cable that links these countries in different continents to facilitate direct communication and business in this era of digital or communicative capitalism. According to a *Bloomberg Business Wire* story (2012), the BRICS cable is a 34,000 km, 2 fibre pair, 12.8 Terabit per-second capacity, state-of-the-art, submarine, fibre-optic cable system that will link the five BRICS countries and the United States. Stretching from Vladivostok in Russia to Miami in the US, via Cape Town in South Africa, Chennai in India, Shantou in China and Fortaleza in Brazil, it will also interconnect with the WACS cable on the West coast of Africa and the EASSY and SEACOM cables on the East coast of Africa, and thus 'give the BRICS countries immediate access to the 21 African countries and give those African countries access to the BRICS economies' (*Bloomberg Business Wire*, 2012).

Though not from one of the four countries of the initial BRIC formation, South African businessman Andrew Mthembu was 'the man driving the new submarine telecommunications cable to connect the BRICS countries' (McLeod, 2012). As both former deputy group CEO at Vodacom and former chairman of Broadband Infraco, Mthembu is the current chairman of the technology group i3 Africa and Imphandze Investments, the two entities involved in promoting the BRICS cable. News reports identified Mthembu as having been involved in another submarine cable, the West African Cable System (WACS) before embarking on the BRICS cable project.

According to one report, the BRICS cable project 'came about following suggestions at the March 2011 BRICS summit in China that SA [South Africa] was punching above its weight as the smallest of the economies in the grouping.' When 'questions were being asked about what value SA brought to the table … Mthembu put forward the idea of the cable system as a way of reducing reliance on links across Europe and [the] North Atlantic.' That is, it would 'provide a shorter, cheaper and potentially more secure route for traffic flowing between the BRICS nations and the US' (McLeod, 2012).

This report went on to describe the project's development, including how France's Axiom and America's Terabit Consulting were contracted to do feasibility studies and how the consultants concluded an internal rate of return (IRR) of 24 per cent without debt and an IRR of 38 per cent with a 60–40 debt-to-equity split. The report further cited Mthembu as saying that this is 'phenomenal' and that the demand 'will be driven to a large extent by China', as it expands to 'become the leading destination for internet traffic by about 2030' (ibid.). A Reuter's story that was widely circulated online dated the project's initial conception slightly later in May 2011 (*Independent Online*, 2012). Nevertheless, subsequent press reports in English and Chinese all confirmed that the project received high-level support at the 2012 and 2013 BRICS summits in New Delhi and Durban respectively.

In the Chinese language press, a 4 May 2012 article on the *China Electronic Journal* (*Zhongguo dianzi bao*) reported how the cable received support of the BRICS countries and how the project would not only save nearly 40 per cent of costs for these countries to communicate with each other, but would also increase the security of intra-BRICS communications by bypassing other countries. The report further noted four additional infrastructure projects aiming at establishing South Atlantic linkages between Africa and South America (Bai, 2012). Nearly a year later, on 29 March 2013, the *China Information Industry Net* (*CNII*) posted a story saying that the project will be the 'largest strategic investment of the BRICS countries' and that South African media regarded this project, along with the proposed establishment of the BRICS Development Bank and the BRICS Contingent Reserve Arrangement, as the three major achievements of the Durban BRICS summit (*CNII*, 2013). As well, a 3 April 2013 *Shantou Daily* report confirmed this development from a local angle by underscoring the fact that the southern Chinese city of Shantou will be the only landing point of the BRICS cable.

Within the English language media, in addition to various news reports, a slick promotional video for the project, the BRICS Cable Video (Imphandze Subtel Services, 2013), is available on YouTube. Featuring a pair of highly professional-looking black male and brown female narrators, the video provokes excitement for anybody who is familiar with the colonial and imperial legacies of the international communication infrastructure, a system in which telephone calls and Internet traffic between Southern countries in the same continent has to pass through European and North Atlantic nodes. A 1 March 2013 article by Rajeev Sharma on the *Russia Beyond the Headlines* website heralds the project in the following enthusiastic language:

> The quotient of success or failure of an international grouping is determined by the level of connectivity among members of the grouping and what steps the body has taken to bridge the gaps. On that count, BRICS has already cemented its place in the comity of nations. A super ambitious BRICS project, already on, is a testimony to the grouping's high success quotient. The project is called BRICS cable. The project, scheduled to be completed by next year, is going to cost $1.5 billion, to be shared by the five member countries depending upon the work involved in each country. The grandiose nature of the project can be ascertained from the fact that once completed the 34,000-km-long BRICS cable, stretching from Vladivostok in Russia to Miami in the US, will be the third longest undersea telecommunications cable in the world.
>
> (Sharma, 2013)

Similar to other reports, Sharma goes on to outline the two main points that the BRICS cable addresses: at present, BRICS countries have to use hubs in the US or Europe to connect and communicate digitally. Besides adding to costs, this opens them up to having data monitored or stolen. Sharma writes in the following hyperbolic language:

> [t]hese problems will become a thing of the past once the project becomes operational. It adds high strategic value to the entire BRICS grouping and sends a strong signal to the world that this grouping means business and has the technology, the resources, and more importantly the political will, to reduce dependence on the developed world.
>
> (*Sharma*, 2013)

In the aftermath of the Snowden revelations in June 2013, the security dimension of the BRICS cable received further attention. For example, a 28 October 2013 *Voice of Russia* news story carried the sensationalist headline of 'BRICS Countries are Building a "new internet" hidden from NSA.' Underneath a picture of five BRICS country leaders holding hands together at the Fourth New Delhi BRICS Summit in 2012, the opening paragraph of the story read:

> The NSA spying scandal created a need for a cyberspace hidden from the prying eyes of American spooks. While countries like Germany are trying to create a secure cyberspace built on current infrastructure, a consortium of BRICS companies is working to create a 'new Internet'. *The Hindu*, reports that Brazil is building a 'BRICS cable' that will create an independent link between Brazil, South Africa, India, China and Russia.
>
> (*Voice of Russia*, 2013)

That a *Voice of Russia* report would use *The Hindu* as a source to report how 'Brazil is building a BRICS cable' certainly underscores an interesting degree of mediated intra-BRICS connection and information flow. Two days later, a South Africa originated story on the *Mybroadband* website similarly heralds 'an "independent internet" which will not be susceptible to spying by the United States' (*Mybroadband*, 2013). The story not only reported that the South Africa government's Department of Communication 'said that it supports the BRICS cable system because it gives meaning to the political agreement between these emerging countries by providing infrastructure that can be used to conduct transactions amongst these nations', but also how the project's profile 'was lifted when the President of Brazil, Dilma Rousseff publicly announced the creation of an internet which is independent of the US and Britain' (ibid.). For its part, the Chinese language Internet also registered various local newspaper reports about the BRICS cable as a means to evade US surveillance in late October 2013. These stories repeated previous reports about the project, confirming projections about the early 2014 construction of the cable and the mid-2015 completion of the project, as well as the hope of the Brazilian President that this cable would allow the people of the BRICS countries to evade US surveillance. Like the above cited *Voice of Russia* story, these stories also cited a 24 October 2013 *The Hindu* story as their source (*Jinzhuanwuguo*, 2013).

However, perhaps symptomatic of a potential flop, while the *Mybroadband* story reported government support of the BRICS cable, it included a line saying that '[t]he BRICS cable's Andrew Mthembu did not respond to questions about the development of an "independent internet system"' (*Mybroadband*, 2013). Indeed, even though the construction of the BRICS cable was supposed to start by early 2014, there has been a conspicuous lack of updates in the global news circuits about any progress of the project since October 2013. The latest reference one can find about this project is in a 13 February 2014 *BRICS Post* news story. Describing itself as a UK registered not-for-profit company and 'an international news and views website' with a mission to 'deliver reliable, insightful news, opinion, and expert analysis from the five BRICS countries' and a commitment to 'build a platform to unravel the intricacies and complexities of information flow from these countries' (*BRICS Post*, 2014), this web paper had reported on the BRICS cable in the same way that it had been reported by other sources (*BRICS Post*, 2013). Rather than featuring any progress of the BRICS cable, however, the *BRICS Post*'s 13 February 2014 story focused on the Brazil–Europe Internet Cable project instead. According to this report, Brazil's state-owned telecom provider, Telebras, had announced a joint venture with Spain's IslaLink Submarine Cables to construct a cable between the northeastern Brazilian city of Fortaleza and the Iberian Peninsula. The project is budgeted at $185 million and construction was scheduled to begin in July 2014. That is, rather than connecting with fellow BRICS countries, this cable is about how Brazil would bypass the US by rerouting its online traffic directly to Europe (*BRICS Post*, 2014). Although this report did mention in passing that 'Brazil and its fellow BRICS partners are also moving ahead with building a massive undersea cable that would connect all members', there has not been any further news reporting on the progress of the BRICS cable. Most notably, the BRICS cable website www.bricscable.com, which was up and running with several pages of information about the project as late as March 2014 (last accessed on 7 March 2014), had disappeared by early April 2014, with a message saying that '[t]his domain has expired. If you owned this domain, contact your domain registration service provider for further assistance'. Attempts to reach i3 Africa through email to find out more about the current status of the BRICS cable project have not yielded any responses as of this writing.

Can it be the case that the BRICS cable project has run into a major obstacle and is not going anywhere? If so, what might be the reasons? Is it possible that China has dropped out of the project? In light of the recent report about the Brazil–Europe cable, can it be the case that rather than building both the Brazil–Europe Internet Cable and the BRICS cable, as the *BRICS Post* had us to believe, Brazil has found it more compelling to connect itself with Europe at this point? Or perhaps the whole thing is no more than a promotional gimmick in the global financial news circuits?

## From Beijing to San Paulo: BRICS and the challenges of challenging US 'cyber-hegemony'

Compared with the effort to build a BRICS cable to circumvent US domination of the Internet infrastructure, reshaping Internet governance has been a far more central and herculean challenge in contemporary global communication. As Dan Schiller has effectively argued, borrowing a term by Milton Mueller, US state and capital have worked together to sustain the status quo of American 'unilateral globalism' over the management and system development of the Internet (Schiller, 2014: 356). This has been maintained in a two-pronged strategy. On the one hand, the US champions the ideology of human rights and the doctrine of 'Internet freedom,' an Internet age re-articulation of the 'free flow' doctrine that the US had effectively deployed during the Cold War era to defeat the NWICO movement, and posits itself as being the country 'best suited to manage the global Internet because of its unique historical commitment to free speech rights' (ibid.: 357). Even though such a claim 'ignores incontrovertible historical and contemporary realities' (ibid.: 357), it remains a powerful American ideological weapon. On the other hand, the American state continues to assume governmental power in the formal and informal management of the Internet through entities such as IANA (Internet Assigned Numbers Association), VeriSign, and ICANN (Internet Corporation for Assigned Names and Numbers).

For their part, many nations, such as Kenya, Egypt, India, Mexico and China, have voiced their dissatisfaction at the status quo of global Internet governance and have demanded changes (ibid.: 358–359). As Bhuiyan (2014), among others, has argued, the two-phase World Summit on the Information Society (WSIS) in 2003 and 2005 served as the occasion and platform for a first concerted effort by states in the Global South to challenge US domination in Internet governance. By the time of the World Conference on International Telecommunications (WCIT-12) in Dubai in December 2012, the global struggle over Internet governance had reached a new stage, when 89 attending countries 'openly challenged the US domination over the Internet by calling to place this critical international communication infrastructure under the jurisdiction of the International Telecommunications Union (ITU), a UN agency' (Shen, 2014). Indeed, as Hong Shen has noted, the geopolitical–economic struggles over Internet control had intensified to such an extent that Gordon Crovitz (2012) of the *Wall Street Journal* framed 'an opposition between the countries in favor of the existing governance structure and the countries supporting more governmental control as "digital cold war"' (Shen, 2014: 1).

BRICS countries, most notably China and Russia, have been on the forefront of such challenges. However, it is also clear that given the sustained US deployment of a 'divide and conquer' strategy, real political economic divisions within and among the BRICS countries, as well as the hegemony of the US championed human rights and 'Internet freedom' discourse, it is highly unlikely that we will see the formation of a unified BRICS challenge against the US in Internet governance at this point. Indeed, China, which now hosts the world's largest Internet population, has gained such a notoriety in the global media arena for its curtailment of human rights and Internet freedom that the mere mention of the terms of 'China' and 'the Internet' immediately connotes control and repression in the Western imagination, and any attempt to articulate an alternative or non-neoliberal ideology as the guiding principle of global communication seems to be doomed. On the one hand, because 'US backing for speech rights itself has been incomplete and contingent' (Schiller 2014: 357) the US position is morally bankrupt. On the other hand, because the Chinese state's domestic Internet censorship regime has served to suppress the struggles of China's lower social classes against the Chinese state's subordination to neoliberal policies, that have disproportionately benefited domestic and transnational capitalistic and bureaucratic interests, the Chinese model does not serve as a viable ideological model to move forward with either. Looking beyond China, it is also clear that no other BRICS countries offer any persuasive ideological alternative for global communication govern- ance. 'Freedom' versus 'control', 'US/Google v. China' remains the dominant ideological framework in global communication.

For its part, China, which, in Sparks' view, not only 'stands out as different in degree from all of the others' in the BRICS formation and 'was and is the moving force and the dominant player' in the BRICS initiative (Sparks, 2014: 410), has pursued a complex and pragmatic strategy in global Internet governance. As Hong Shen (2014) has persuasively demonstrated, the popular label of an authoritarian 'cyber-sovereignty' doctrine does not fully explain China's actual approach of both building upon and revising the existing extraterritorial global Internet governance structure. Moreover, the Chinese position on global Internet governance has evolved over time, as the Internet becomes increasingly vital to China's political economic development and as the Chinese state continues to transform itself by trying to fashion the appropriate domestic and global institutional frameworks for the Internet in the context of changing domestic and international political economic environments. Specifi- cally, Shen noted an evolving trajectory of both frictions and adjustment, or a 'mixture of resistance and compliance' (Shen, 2014: 9) between China and the US-dominated global Internet governance regime between 1987 and 2012. In 2012, in the aftermath of the high-profile 'Google v. China' conflict that pitted Hilary Clinton's 'Internet freedom' crusade against the Chinese state's demand for the US to stop exercise its 'information imperialism' or 'network hegemony' over China, and in the months leading to the WCIT-12 in Dubai in December 2012, China's State Internet Information Office (SIIO) hosted a series of bilateral and multilateral roundtables on Internet governance with various countries.

The ostensible absence of BRICS as a unified bloc on these roundtables is revealing. Some of the roundtables, such as the one with Britain, had been launched as early as 2008, so the year of 2012 saw the fourth roundtable between these two countries. Others, notably one called 'Internet Roundtable for Emerging Countries' and one with South Korea, were launched in 2012. In the news reports, both were billed as annual events. However, whereas the December 2012 China–South Korea first Internet roundtable in Beijing was followed by a second one in December 2013 in Seoul, the 2012 'Internet Roundtable for Emerging Countries' has not been followed with any new event at the time of writing.

More intriguing, however, is the actual naming and making of this particular 2012 Internet roundtable. Why 'emerging countries', not 'BRICS'? Apparently, the 'I' in the BRICS, i.e., India, was missing at the 18 September 2012 roundtable in Beijing. According to a China Radio International report, it was China which 'proposed that roundtable discussions for Internet development should be launched in newly emerging economies' (China Radio International, 2012). The report went on to say that the call attracted Russia, Brazil and South Africa, while India 'dispatched an official from its embassy in China to the event as an observer' (ibid.). This was clearly intended to be a high-profile bloc building meeting. Deputy ministerial level officials from Russia, Brazil and South Africa participated. Wang Chen, Director of SIIO, made a keynote speech, arguing that 'developed nations should help rather than practice "hegemony of the cyber-world" on the advantage of their advanced technology' (ibid.). Furthermore, Liu Yunshan, the CCP's Political Bureau Standing Committee member in charge of ideology, met the foreign guests. Nevertheless, the fact that India was not a participant of the meeting was a clear indication that BRICS would not be a relevant unit in the geopolitically highly sensitive area of global Internet governance even though, interestingly, two months later, on 28 November 2012, the BRICS nations did seem to come together as a bloc in the Chinese city of Fuzhou, at the less politically-oriented and more broadly based 8th World Multimedia and Internet Summit, where they signed the 'BRICS Countries Fuzhou Proclamation for Collaboration in Digital and Creative Industries' (Wu, 2012).

In a way, India's absence at the September 2012 higher profile Beijing roundtable was not surprising. As others have observed, the Indian government has been highly ambivalent and inconsistent in its articulation of a clear position on Internet governance in the crucial period leading to the December 2012 WCIT-12. So much so that it even backtracked from 'its support for a UN Committee on Internet Related Policies supported by Russia and China as an alternative to the ICANN' (Thomas, 2014: 467; see also Schiller, 2014: 359). As Thomas went on to explain, the Indian government's ambivalence to some extent 'has been shaped by the disquiet expressed in the domestic IT sector and by civil society' (Thomas, 2014: 467). Citing this as an example and the fact that close to 80 per cent of India's software experts are tied to the US market, Thomas concluded, '[t]here is little evidence of BRICS being more than an ideological gathering of nations, given that the economies of the BRICS nations are integrated with the global economy and in some ways are tied to US interests' (ibid.: 467).

While it takes interview data, if possible at all, to identify the exact reason for India's non-participation at the September 2012 Beijing roundtable, it is reasonable to speculate that, beyond the positions of the Indian domestic IT Industry and civil society, and the alignment of their economic and ideological interests with the US, there were important geopolitical and ideological obstacles for China and India to work together on global Internet governance. Geopolitically, the US counts on India as a key player in its 'pivot to Asia' strategy, which aims predominantly at containing China. Ideologically, the identity of India as the world's largest democracy and the image of China as the world's largest authoritarian state may also play a role in preventing India from even wanting to be seen as being in collaboration with China on global Internet governance.

The Snowden revelations have significantly undermined the credibility of the American state's championship of human rights and 'Internet freedom'. All the BRICS countries were the targets of the NSA's far-reaching surveillance operations, and they all voiced criticisms against the US in response to the Snowden revelations. However, given that Brazilian President Dilma Rousseff was herself a target of the NSA's surveillance operations, it was not surprising that her government's response to NSA's far-reaching espionage has been the most vocal and condemning from the BRICS countries. In her well-known critique at the opening of the general debate of the 68th Session of the UN General Assembly in New York in September 2013, she referred to the US's 'global network of espionage' as 'a situation of grave violation of human rights and of civil liberties; of invasion and capture of confidential information concerning corporate activities, and especially of disrespect to national sovereignty.' She asserted that she could not 'but defend, in an uncompromising fashion, the right to privacy of individuals and the sovereignty of my country. In the absence of the right to privacy, there can be no true freedom of expression and opinion, and therefore no effective democracy. In the absence of the respect for sovereignty, there is no basis for the relationship among Nations' (Rousseff, 2013). Furthermore, Rousseff argued that it was time to ensure that cyberspace was not 'used as a weapon of war, through espionage, sabotage, and attacks against systems and infrastructure of other countries' (quoted in *The Mercury*, 2013).

But to what extent have the Snowden revelations served as a catalyst for the possible constitution of BRICS as a unified bloc on global Internet governance, which has increasingly become a focal point of geo-political economic conflict (Schiller, 2011)? The evidence is not promising. To be sure, there is some early indication of an emerging consensus among the BRICS countries on the single issue of cyber-security. For example, on 7 July 2013, a month after

Snowden's appearance in Hong Kong in June 2013, the *South China Morning Post*, in reporting the gathering of the BRICS security officials in Vladivostok, Russia, suggested that Snowden's revelations 'appear to be pushing its rivals closer together', and that Meng Jianzhu, secretary of the Chinese State Council's political and legislative affairs committee, had spoken of an emergent 'cybersecurity consensus' among the BRICS countries (Wang, 2013). The news story not only made a mention of the group's collaboration on the BRICS cable within this context, but also went further to cite Jin Canrong, a well-known Chinese academic spokesperson on global affairs, as saying how 'the consensus on cybersecurity at the BRICS forum shows its desire to become a "power-wielding" group' (ibid.).

However, as the eventual shaping of Brazilian President Rousseff's NETmundial – the Global Multistakeholder Meeting on the Future of Internet Governance – has revealed, the BRICS countries were definitely not a 'power-wielding' group as far as coming up with a comprehensive alternative Internet governance model is concerned. While India was missing at China's much more modest 2012 'Internet Roundtable for Emerging Countries' in Beijing, NETmundial did not count Chinese and Russian representatives as members of its High-Level Multistakeholder Committee. Compared with China's low-key bilateral or multi-lateral Internet roundtables, NETmundial represented an ambitious effort by the outraged Rousseff to spearhead the search for an alternative global Internet governance model in protest against the US in the aftermath of Snowden's revelations, and took place in São Paulo between 23 and 24 April 2014. The NETmundial committee, which oversaw the overall strategy of the event and promoted 'the involvement of the international community around the themes that will be discussed at the meeting' (http://netmundial.br/about/), drew ministerial level representatives from the following 12 countries: Argentina, Brazil, France, Ghana, Germany, India, Indonesia, South Africa, South Korea, Tunisia, Turkey and the US. Furthermore, according to Nothias (2014), almost half of the participants were from the corporate sector, making its claim to be truly dedicated to 'multistakeholderism' 'really about launching the next stage of US global multistakeholder domination over the Internet'.

In terms of NETmundial's outcomes, critical observers covering the event for media outlets, ranging from *Wired* to the *Huffington Post*, have telling titles, such as *NETmundial: Disappointed Expectations and Delayed Decisions* (Marques, 2014); *For More Internet, and More Democracy, Forget NetMundial and ICANN* (Nothias, 2014); *Big business was the winner at NETmundial* (Powles, 2014) to name a few. Brühwiller (2014) writes in the Swiss newspaper *Neue Zürcher Zeitung*, 'The final document of the international Internet governance conference NETmundial in Sao Paulo is not revolutionary.' The Western-civil-society-based Internet governance activist community, in particular, characterized the final document as much too weak and 'more like a set of corporate standards', in which the voices of the US government, along with that of lobbyists from the corporate sector, sound strong on issues ranging from intellectual property to net neutrality (Marques, 2014). Regarding mass surveillance, NETmundial's *raison d'etre*, O'Brian (2014) writes:

> For all its commitment to transparency and openness, governments, including the United States government, had the last say in a closed meeting at the very end of NETmundial. Even before then, the targets of Rousseff's and the Internet technical community's ire set about weakening an initial strong draft document, as obtained by WikiLeaks before the public consultation.

Again, it would take interviews and more corroborated research to find out exactly why and how China and Russia did not send ministerial level representatives to the meeting, and what role the US government and corporate entities, as well as ICANN, played in shaping the final results of the event. Nevertheless, the following observation, made by Nothias (2014) in a *Huffington Post* article, offers both a powerful critique of 'multi-stakeholderism' in its latest manifestation at NETmundial and a glimpse of the neutralization of a potential Brazilian-led counter-hegemonic challenge against the status quo:

> [R]ather than asking 'What can we expect from it?', perhaps we might ask instead whether this future might be more promisingly reformed by political, technical and architectural innovations than by a preach to a so-called multistakeholder choir convened in Sao Paulo. Since Fadi Chehadé, Chair and CEO of ICANN, flew to Brazil in October 2013 to soften President Dilma Rousseff's outrage after her famous anti-digital-US-surveillance speech, Netmundial has been part of the visible US effort to embrace Brazil into its political multistakeholder (MS) digital discourse. [ ... ] So, thanks to Chehadé's smooth assistance, Rousseff accepted to organize a conference jointly with ICANN. It provided a victory for Rousseff's external politics, by embedding Brazil in a so-called MS conference, while also giving ICANN another victory, because as co-organizer of such a conference it has been able to influence any kind of decision related to choice of content, committee, secretariat, panelists, speakers and ultimately any critical outcome.

It is also noteworthy that NETmundial did not receive much coverage in the Anglo-American mainstream media. Searching for 'NETmundial' on their online archives as well as the commercial news archive at LexisNexis, for example, resulted in zero hits for articles on news outlets ranging from *The Guardian*, *The Times*, to *The Los Angeles Times*. *The New York Times* only mentioned it in a two liner in its 'Your Wednesday Briefing' (Hassan and Shannon, 2014). *The Washington Post* did publish four articles on its website. However, the title of one of these articles, *How China and Russia Are Trying to Undermine the Internet, Again* (Fung, 2014), is telling of the prevailing framework and illustrative of the 'digital cold war' discourse: the demonization of China and Russia on an event that did not even count these two countries as high-level participants.

Underscoring a profound ideological gap between the Western and Chinese media on this 'emergent geopolitical flash point' (Schiller quoted in Shen, 2014: 2), a widely circulated Chinese story on NETmundial, authored by Xin Lian for the *China Daily* network, runs the following headline: 'Foreign Media: At NETmundial in Brazil, China Treated as Guest of Honor.' The report, self-described as just summarizing international media coverage but clearly betraying the Chinese official view of the event, made the following observations. First, contrary to the official report of having arrived at a wide range of principles, it only reached some partial non-compulsory guidelines after much quarrelling and the intensive contestation of different views. In particular, and significant for this analysis, it mentioned how Russia, Cuba and India opposed the passage of the final document, which Brazil as the co-host was keen to push through. In this way, the Chinese report registered a clear intra-conflict within the BRICS countries on this occasion. Second, while the US – the current 'network hegemon' – kept a low profile and was the target of protests despite its success in keeping cyber-surveillance off the official agenda, China, which only sent a bureau-level official (one level lower than a ministerial level official) to attend the meeting, was popular and much sought after by other delegates. This, according to the report, was because China's position was considered 'very important' by both sides of the controversy. Indeed, it noted how China's top official at the meeting was the second speaker on the opening day. Third, according to the report, many countries, including the ones that had repeatedly criticized Chinese Internet management in the past, had begun to show a keen interest in the 'Chinese experience'. Moreover, 'the Chinese model of Internet management is influencing some countries, especially some emerging countries' (Xin, 2014).

An Australian official suggested that perhaps China should host the next meeting. A Russian official spoke publicly on how the Snowden event had marked the beginning of the 'dissolution' of US-dominated Internet governance as part of the overall major realignment of global power relations, as the American claim to Internet freedom and security had been totally discredited. The report concluded by noting how foreign countries have shown 'curiosity' at China's establishment of the Xi Jinping-led CCP Leadership Group on Internet Security and Informatization in February 2014 and how the success and failure of China's reform in this area would be relevant to others (Xin, 2014).

## Concluding remarks

This excursion into the potentialities of the BRICS countries in shaping the current global communication order leaves much to be desired, both in terms of the chapter's research methodology, but also, more importantly, in terms of the hopes and follies of BRICS in reshaping global communication as a potential power bloc. The BRICS cable understandably generated media hype, but there is no concrete progress report on its actual construction as of the time of writing. Although the 14–16 July 2014 6th BRICS Summit was held in Fortaleza, the Northeastern Brazilian city that also happens to be the Brazilian landing point of the BRICS cable, English and Chinese language news reports of the summit hardly included any updates on the current state of the BRICS cable project. The Snowden revelations – and one should not forget the respective roles of Hong Kong as China's special administrative region, and more importantly, Russia, in the entire event – galvanized long-standing opposition by non-Western countries, especially China and Russia, to a US-dominated global Internet governance order, and created a counter-hegemonic opening in this area. However, from Beijing in September 2012 to San Paolo in April 2014, there is enough ground to believe that profound geopolitical differences, entrenched economic interests, US pressures, as well as the enduring power of the US-state-led and Western-media-supported, 'democracy v. authoritarian', 'freedom v. control' ideological framework, have prevented the BRICS countries from even appearing together or co-hosting a potentially counter-hegemonic meeting on global Internet governance.

Not only was India's visible absence at the September 2012 Beijing 'Internet Roundtable for Emerging Countries' indicative of the profound division between China and India, but also the 12-country, top-sponsor list of the Brazilian initiated NETmundial did not include China and Russia. If India had been the target of intensive US lobbying against its potential alliance with other BRICS countries on this issue, from reports of the Brazil–Europe Internet cable to the eventual co-sponsorship of Brazil and ICCAN of NET-mundial, is it too far-fetched to say that Brazil is the other key target of the US and the West's divide and conquer strategy as far as BRICS is concerned?

Furthermore, that the Chinese media would report a division between Brazil and India and Russia over NETmundial's final document is also a matter of concern as far as any potential BRICS 'united front' in global Internet governance is concerned. Given that Brazil, India and South Africa have been known to have worked more comfortably together as democracies in the area of media and ICTs, can it be the case that, rather than truly committing to any kind of internationalism or even multilateralism, all the BRICS countries, or, for that matter, many other similar groupings, have likewise been used as a mechanism for stressing bilateral bargaining between these countries – and the US in particular – and the US-dominant Western capitalist order in general?

The US-dominated old order is no doubt unravelling, and the 2008 US financial meltdown and Snowden revelations have accelerated such unravelling economically, politically and ideologically. In the aftermath of the defeat of the world communist movement, the death of the 'Third World' project and more than thirty years of neoliberal global capitalist integration, the desires of the BRICS countries – as with that of many other countries outside the

West – for a new global information and communication order in the way that led to the formation of the NWICO movement in the last century, however, cannot be taken for granted. Meanwhile, as can be seen from the limited Western news reports about the shaping of NETmundial, the US, as the current hegemon, is no doubt working tirelessly to prevent any potential emergence of a broad-based counter-hegemonic alliance. The BRICS countries, even without their potential formation as a unified bloc, each have a pivotal role to play in this unfolding struggle.

While there is still a lot to watch at the level of elite politics, including the annual summitry of the BRICS states, in the end, the political will and political orientation of each state will matter significantly. As Prashad (2014) has observed, whether it is in the 'odd' use of the US dollar as the holding currency for the BRICS Bank, or in the failure of BRICS leaders to take a more aggressive position against the US for its backing of Israel in the Middle East in the aftermath of the new round of Israeli bombing of Gaza in July 2014, there is a lack of 'courage' and 'confidence' among the BRICS leaders in challenging US domination of the global order and in articulating an alternative vision of the world. He may be right in saying that it will take time for these countries to no longer 'look over their shoulders' but to 'look ahead'. However, what counts most will be ongoing bottom-up struggles by progressive social forces inside these countries that are capable of challenging the domestic dominant power blocs within each country against their complicity with, and vested interest in, the US-led transnational capitalist global order.

## Note

1 I would like to acknowledge Birgit Schroeder for her research assistance in the preparation of this article. Her research provided invaluable initial material on the BRICS cable and parts of the analysis on NETmundial. She has also been a trusted interlocutor for me to bounce off some of my initial ideas in this chapter.

## References

Bai, X. (2012) Jinzhuanwuguo zhici 3qianwanmei haidi guanlan xiangmu [BRICS countries support 30,000 km undersea cable project]. *Zhongguo dianzibao* [China Electronics Journal], 4 May. Retrieved from: www.cableabc.com/news/201205041000234.html.

Bhuiyan, A. (2014) *Internet Governance and the Global South: Demand a New Framework.* London: Palgrave Macmillan.

*Bloomberg Business Wire* (2012) 'BRICS cable unveiled for direct and cohesive communications services between Brazil, Russia, India, China and South Africa', 16 April. Retrieved from: www.bloomberg.com/apps/news?pid=newsarchive&sid=aDLKQqIM.ZZ0.

*BRICS Post* (n.d) *About US*. Retrieved from: http://thebricspost.com/about-us/#.U5MzxyhZ98E.

——(2013) 'Fact file: South Africa says BRICS cable will boost trade', *The BRICS Post*, 26 February. Retrieved from: http://thebricspost.com/fact-file-south-africa-says-brics-cable-will-boost-trade/#.U5I_vldZ98G.

——(2014) 'Brazil-Europe Internet cable to cost $185 million', *The BRICS Post*, 13 February, Retrieved from: http://thebricspost.com/brazil-europe-Internet-cable-to-cost-185-million/#.U5I8B1dZ98E.

Brühwiller, T. (2014) 'Ein roter Faden für das Netz', *Neue Zürcher Zeitung*, 25 April. Retrieved from: www.nzz.ch/aktuell/international/auslandnachrichten/ein-roter-faden-fuer-das-netz-1.18290215.

*Buenos Aires Herald* (2014) 'Russia invites Argentina to BRICS summit, ratifies support in Malvinas case', *Buenos Aires Herald*, 28 May.

Chand, M. (2014) 'Walking the talk: India to be first CEO of BRICS Bank, Shanghai will host NDB', *India Writes*, Retrieved from: www.indiawrites.org/diplomacy/walking-the-talk-indian-to-be-first-ceo-of-brics-bank-shanghai-will-host-ndb/.

China Radio International (2012) 'Meeting aims at better Internet development', *China Radio International*, 18 September. Retrieved from: http://english.cri.cn/6909/2012/09/18/3241s722902.htm.

CNII (2013) 'Jinzhuan guojia tuijin guanglan jihu, jiangjian 3.4wan qianmi haidiguanlan' [BRICS Countries Push Ahead Optical Cable Plan, will build 34,000 meter undersea optical cable], *China Information Industry Net (CNII)*, 29 March. Retrieved from: www.cnii.com.cn/broadband.2013-03/29/content_1119349.htm.

Crovitz, G. (2012) 'America's first big digital defeat', *The Wall Street Journal*, 16 December.

Dean, J. (2009) *Democracy and other Neoliberal Fantasies: Communicative Capitalism and Left Politics*. Durham: Duke University Press.

Fung, B. (2014) 'How China and Russia are trying to undermine the Internet, again', *The Washington Post*, 23 April.

Hassan, A. and Shannon, V. (2014) 'Your Wednesday briefing', *The New York Times*, 23 April.

Imphandze Subtel Services (2013) 'BRICS cable video', 21 March. Retrieved from www.youtube.com/watch?v=OkQI4bJcDGw.

*Independent Online* (2012) 'Investors mull $1.5bn BRICS cable', *Independent Online*, 4 June. Retrieved from: www.iol.co.za/business/international/investors-mull-1-5bn-brics-cable-1.1311484?source–safindit#.U5D-M1dZ98E.

Jinzhuanwuguo ni lingbi guanglan(2013) 'xiwan duoguo meiguo jianting', *Hangzhou Daily Press Group*, 27 October. Retrieved from: www.shm.com.cn/ytwb/html/2013-10/28/content_2954226.htm.

Liu, Y. and Lu, J. (2014) 'Putin: China and Russia will jointly commemorate the 70th anniversary of anti-fascism victory', *Xinhua Net*, 25 May. Retrieved from: http://news.ifeng.com/a/20140525/40445014_0.shtml.

Marques, S. (2014) 'NETmundial: Disappointed expectations and delayed decisions', *Index on Censorship*, 30 April.

McLeod, D. (2012) 'The inside story of the $1.5bn BRICS cable', *TechCentral*, 3 May. Retrieved from: www.techcentral.co.za/the-inside-sotry-of-the-15bn-brics-cable/31530/.

*Mercury* (2013) 'The West has been bypassed. or has it? Talk has been rife of an undersea cable linking Brazil, Russia, India, China and South Africa. But is it true?' *The Mercury*, 27 September, p.11. Retrieved (from LexisNexis): www.iol.co.za/mercury.

*Mybroadband* (2013) 'South Africa's "independent Internet" plans with BRICS', *Mybroadband*, 30 October. Retrieved from: http://mybroadband.co.za/news/internet/90617-south-africas-independent-Internet-plans-with-brics.html.

Nothias, J. C. (2014) 'For more Internet, and more democracy, forget NetMundial and ICANN', *Huffington Post*, 23 April.

O'Brian, D. (2014) 'Human rights are not negotiable: Looking back at Brazil's NET-Mundial', 25 April. Retrieved from Electronic Frontier Foundation website: www.eff.org/deeplinks/2014/04/netmundial.

O'Neill, J. (2001) 'Building better global economic BRICs', Global Economics Paper No. 66. Retrieved from Goldman Sachs website: www.goldmansachs.com/our-thinking/archive/archive-pdfs/build-better-brics.pdf.

Powles, J. (2014) 'Big business was the winner at NETmundial', *Wired*, 28 April.

Prashad, V. (2012) *The Poorer Nations: A Possible History of the Global South*. London: Verso.

——(2014) 'BRICS bank to rival western bank monopoly', interview with Vijay Prashad. Russia Today, 21 July. Retrieved from: www.youtube.com/watch?v=ZoNUsaC1G4M.

Rousseff, D. (2013) 'Speech at the plenary of the sixty-eighth General Assembly of the United Nations', 24 September. Retrieved from: www.un.org/press/en/2013/ga11423.doc.htm. Accessed 5 March 2014.

Schiller, D. (1999) *Digital Capitalism: Networking the Global Market System*. Cambridge, Mass: MIT Press.

——(2007) *How to Think about Information*. Urbana: University of Illinois Press.

——(2011) 'Geo-political economic conflicts and network infrastructures', *Chinese Journal of Communication* 4(1): 90–107.

——(2014) 'Rosa Luxemburg's Internet? For a political economy of state mobilization and the movement of accumulation in cyberspace', *International Journal of Communication* (8): 355–375.

Sharma, R. (2013) 'BRICS cable: Connecting continents, brick by brick', *Russia Beyond the Headlines*, 1 March. Retrieved from: http://in.rbth.com/economics/2013/03/01/brics_cable_connecting_continents_brick_by_brick_22617.html

Shen, H. (2014) 'Beyond cyber-sovereignty? China and global Internet governance, 1987–2012'. Paper presented at the 2014 International Communication Association Annual Convention, Seattle, USA, 22–26 May.

Sparks, C. (2014) 'Deconstructing the BRICS', *International Journal of Communication* (8): 392–418.

Thomas, P. (2014) 'The ambivalent state and media in India: Between elite domination and public interest', *International Journal of Communication* (8): 466–482.

*Voice of Russia* (2013) 'BRICS countries are building a "new Internet" hidden from NSA', *Voice of Russia*, 28 October. Retrieved from: http://voiceofrussia.com/2013_10_28/BRICS-countries-are-building-a-new-internet-hidden-from-NSA-7157/. Accessed 5 March 2014.

Wang, A. (2013) 'BRICS emerging economies to expand co-operation on Internet security', *South China Morning Post*, 7 July.

Wu, H. (2012) 'Closure of world multi-media and Internet summit', BRICS signed proclamation. Retrieved from *NetEase*, 29 November: http://news.163.com/12/1129/07/8HFA3T7T00014JB6.html.

Xin, L. (2014) 'At the Brazilian Internet conference, China treated as a guest of honor', *China Daily*, 5 May.

Zhao, Y. (2014) 'Communication, crisis, and global power shifts: An introduction', *International Journal of Communication* (8): 275–300.

# Chapter 4

# BRICS as emerging cultural and media powers[1]

*Joseph Straubhaar*

## Defining BRICS

When Goldman Sachs economist Jim (James) O'Neill coined the term 'BRIC' (Brazil, Russia, India, China) in a 2001 paper, it was partly in response to the September 11 attack. He wrote that 9/11 had highlighted 'on a truly global basis' the 'need for general international economic and political co-operation' (O'Neill, 2001) and he wanted to emphasize the need to draw these key nations more closely into global governance.

O'Neill suggested that these four countries had grown so much in power and importance in the global economy that membership of the G7 club of industrialized nations 'might need to be significantly changed' – that these new emerging countries were now part of the core of the world economy, and need to be consulted and represented in all central deliberations. That certainly represents a change in thinking from world systems or dependency theories, which saw Brazil as part of a partially developed semi-periphery, and China and India as a part of the impoverished periphery. O'Neill concluded that, regardless of which measure was used, the relative strengths of economies were changing and that 'China especially' should be in the 'G7 Club' (O'Neill, 2001). He also suggested that if Canada were in, then Brazil, Russia and India should be too, since in terms of GDP PPP (purchasing power parity), the BRICs and G7 in 2000 made up the world's top eleven economies with Canada ranked eleventh (O'Neill, 2001). In 2010, South Africa was added to the 'BRIC' group, which became BRICS.

In 1999, the Finance Ministers and Central Bank Governors of the world's 20 leading economies began meeting as the G20. So the emphasis in this text on the BRICs nations to the exclusion, for example, of countries like Mexico, Spain, South Korea, Indonesia, Australia, Taiwan, Turkey, Thailand and the Netherlands, which, in order, rounded out O'Neill's (2001) top 20 economies by GDP PPP is, as already noted, somewhat arbitrary. However, it does permit a focused study of four countries' media in a political–economic context that throws light on the more general dynamics of global media developments in recent years, a trend away from US-media-centric production and English-language dominance towards dispersed, multi-centric and regionalized media systems that are shaped as much by culture as they are by political economy.

## From dependent nations to emerging powers

The BRICS nations are emerging in a somewhat, but far from completely, transformed world or global system. As recently as 30 to 40 years ago, all of the BRICS countries, except Russia (then the dominant part of the Soviet Union), were seen as part of the periphery of a world system dominated by the core industrialized capitalist economies (Wallerstein, 1979). Some of the BRICS countries – Brazil and perhaps South Africa – were seen as part of what Wallerstein called the semi-periphery; large developing countries which showed some growth and limited autonomy in some areas, but were still essentially dependent on the core countries, especially in economic matters. However, Wallerstein then saw both China and India as part of the periphery, countries without much overall development on the edge of the world capitalist economy. As part of the Soviet Union, Russia was then seen as one of the two superpowers in the duality of the Cold War, the centre of its own system of allies and countries economically and militarily dependent on it. In some ways, China was off the global economic map, seen as a still largely socialist country deliberately disengaged from the world economic system, seeking a more autonomous form of development.

In a related assessment, Cardoso (1973) called the condition of countries like Brazil, or India, 'associated dependent development', i.e., associated with and dependent on the core countries, such as the US and Western Europe. They might grow and develop, but their development would be fundamentally dependent on, and conditioned by, the core economies. Some dependency theorists of the era were even more pessimistic about the prospects for much economic growth or other forms of development for what were then seen as 'Third World' or peripheral, dependent countries (Cockroft et al., 1972; Dagnino, 1973).

However, by 2001, not quite 30 years later, a Goldman Sachs economist called attention to the fact that large emerging markets were growing faster than the G7 'core' countries: the US, the UK, France, Germany, Italy, Canada and Japan (O'Neill, 2001). O'Neill called particular attention to what he called the BRIC countries – Brazil, Russia, India and China. Depending on the measurement, those countries had about 8 per cent of global GDP in 2001, which, depending on the measure, has risen since then, particularly as the BRIC and other emerging economies suffered less and recovered faster in the current recession than did the G7, at least up until a couple of years ago (Dorgan, 2013). O'Neill called for incorporating the BRIC formation into global economic governance, which has happened as they became a central part of what is now the G20 expanded group of 'core' countries (2001).

One strength of the BRIC concept is its focus on the state. In the giddy formulations of second-wave globalization theory, post-1991, the state was all but ignored (Ohmae,1995; Strange 2001). More current analysis has rethought this assumption, since even weak states have managed to survive, in part because they and global systems, such as the UN, major multinational corporations and global NGOs, have become interdependent, with global actors often propping up weak states in Africa, for example, because they need them to deliver services or help to extract resources (Bayart, 1993). In this sense, Bayart notes that globalization and state systems have become mutually constitutive (Bayart, 2007). Waisbord and Morris and others have also noted that the state is a key part of the global system, particularly important for media, creating crucial conditions, such as national markets, educated consumers, etc., that transnational and global advertisers and global media rely on (Waisbord, 1998; Morris and Waisbord, 2001).

The issue of the transformed nature of the global system, between BRICS and the former core, raises an interesting question of what it means to be a core country in the global system now. While useful in that it recognized the existence of regional subsystems and strong national dynamics outside the capitalist core, Wallerstein's world systems theory came to be seen by many as too economistic, or estimating economic determinacy too highly, not taking sufficient account of cultural and other dimensions of globalization (Boyne, 1990). At about that time, Straubhaar raised the question of whether countries could have different degrees of power and (inter)dependence, an asymmetrical interdependence, based on his analysis of how Brazil, for example, could be dependent on core powers in finance and technology, but increasingly autonomous, or even emerging as a regional and global export power, in areas like media production (Straubhaar, 1991).

In a related analytical approach that has shown enduring theoretical appeal, Appadurai (1990) created a highly influential argument that globalization could be seen as consisting of five crucial landscapes, or 'scapes', which, while related, were also to a substantial degree disjunct, which is to say that they had their own separate dynamics and trajectories, not necessarily primarily determined or driven by economic forces (1990). Those (land)scapes of financial, technological, ethno/migration, media and ideological globalization, provide an interesting starting point for analyzing China, India, the rest of the BRIC nations and other emerging powers like Mexico and South Korea, which subsequent Goldman Sachs reports have tentatively added to BRIC, for analytical purposes (Goldman Sachs, 2007). Coupled with the theory of asymmetrical interdependence, in which countries may gain power in one global (land) scape more than another, this gives us several useful analytical or theoretical tools for understanding BRICS, as an interaction of several powerful emerging cultural and media producers (Brazil, Russia, India, China and South Africa), as well as their interaction with other emerging powers, such as Mexico or South Korea.

## Theoretically unpacking global, transnational, regional, national, local

Another key theoretical idea for understanding the BRICS countries as global and regional actors, as well as powerful nation states, is to nuance the differences between these spheres and landscapes. Appadurai (1990) put all of his scapes at a global level, but what if many of the more important developments and interactions are not fully global in scale, but are more regional or transnational. Acknowledging this opens up a new terrain of multiple media spaces of production, flow, identification and identity that are emerging in what might be seen as a multi-layered system of global or world television. For example, a partial mapping of some prominent current levels of global film, television and Internet flow can be seen in recent work (Straubhaar, 2008).

One of the reasons for this analysis by levels is to disaggregate the word 'global', which is often used in so many ways as to begin to lose meaning. Perhaps the most important parts of a global system, the ones that most definitions of globalization tend to focus on, are: the increasing interconnection of the global financial system, in which a crisis in Argentina can end up causing a crisis in South Korea; the increasing interconnection of the world though technologies of transportation and communication, such as air travel, global shipping, communications satellites and the Internet; and that most people across the world tend to be aware of world events and are aware of, perhaps even impacted by, other cultures. Not quite as consensual but widely held is the larger sense that the whole world is now one unit, for purposes of analysis and understanding, and needs to be thought of in unitary, holistic terms; and the increasing prevalence of commercial, capitalist models for all kinds of institutional and individual activity, including media, which reflects one of the key points anticipated in the cultural imperialism paradigm, too.

A practical way of thinking of the word 'global' is to think about what things literally have global reach. An increasing number of entities have a truly global reach. Still at the top of global system in terms of length of relative dominance, volume of flow, money actually made and presumed cultural impact are the cultural and informational industries of the US, whose continuing production and export is based in Hollywood's structural and cultural power. That is particularly true in film, where US films or others co-produced by or distributed by Hollywood dominate film screens in most countries, as Miller et al. show (Miller et al., 2005). As Straubhaar (2007) and others have demonstrated, US television shows are still quite prominent in the television schedules of many countries, although much less prominent, especially in prime viewing hours, than the equivalents in film. While US dominance of the Internet and the World Wide Web was notable in its early years, the growth of web pages, social media postings, etc. in languages other than English and from producers outside the US has been considerable.

Another powerful group of truly global actors includes the BRIC countries, plus a number of others. These are national television, film, news and Internet producers who have become globally important exporters, particularly in certain key genres and in reaching specific global audiences, such as telenovelas (from Latin America), anime (from Japan), Bollywood (from India), martial arts (from China and Hong Kong), etc., which have fewer programmes placed in overall global television schedules than does the US, but are very significant, often beating the US in some regions or genre specialties (B](tereyst and Meers, 2000; Iwabuchi, 2002).

Global format producers are another distinct category that provides a significant fraction of imported television formats on which national production is often actually based (Moran, 2004; 2009). In television, these work with national or regional partners to locally produce versions of global formats like *Big Brother*, *Pop Idol*, *Who Wants to Be a Millionaire*, etc., which appear as national production in most studies and policy analyses, but are in fact really a new category of their own. In fact this kind of production, which is neither fully global or fully local, but a complex blend of forces from both, is a good example of another major cultural and theoretical trend, that of the hybridization of elements from global forms and institutions, transnational or regional ones, and national or local ones (Kraidy, 2005). The BRICs countries are not strongly represented in this category yet, but Brazil and India at least have produced some formats for license, and some other emerging media powers, like Argentina and South Korea, have done more.

Another emerging global force is transnational or global genre producers and audiences in global film and television genres like travel, documentaries, nature and historical issues. These producers tend to be centred in the UK and the US, but there are strong equivalents in Japan and elsewhere. They are also among the most avid global co producers, often incorporating several national and transnational producers in joint original productions. They are also open to minor co-production, adapting an existing documentary to a national market by including local footage or localized narration. These kinds of productions are very visible in an also rapidly increasing array of global and regional cable channels, including co-productions with most of the BRICS (Mjøs, 2010).

Geo-cultural regional film, television and Internet producers and spaces are based on shared languages, histories and geographic proximity. These kinds of producers are particularly prominent in the television schedules of some countries, which belong to large geo-cultural groups, like Spanish-speaking Latin America (Sinclair *et al.*, 1996; Straubhaar, 2007). In these regions that link geographic proximity and cultural commonalities, several of the BRICS countries are emerging strongly. India is the dominant producer for South Asia (Pendakur and Subramanyam, 1996), and one of the dominant producers for Central Asia, along with Russia. Brazil is one of the dominant producers, along with Mexico, for Latin America, showing also that historical and cultural ties can overcome linguistic differences, since Brazilian programmes have to be dubbed into Spanish for Latin America (Sinclair and Straubhaar, 2013). The Hong Kong region of China has been a major exporter to much of Asia for decades, and China also exports to neighbouring countries. Russia is a less prominent global exporter, post 1991, but focuses on its neighbours (Dolinskiy, 2013). South Africa has become a major exporter of TV programmes and satellite TV channels to Africa, particularly southern Africa (Wasserman, 2011).

Transnational cultural-linguistic television producers and spaces, consisting of former colonial powers and colonies, and their migrants elsewhere, like the Anglophone or Spanish-speaking spaces (Sinclair, 1999), have also become increasingly important cultural spaces where BRICS countries have emerged as powerful exporters and actors. Brazil is the dominant cultural exporter to the Portuguese-speaking or Lusophone world – Angola, Mozambique, Portugal and several smaller countries – where its television programmes, movies and music are more popular than those of the US (Sinclair and Straubhaar, 2013). India and China both have significant diasporic populations spread worldwide, who take much of their media intake from exports, channels and websites from the home countries. Geographically based regional cultural trade blocs, like the European Union or NAFTA, can also encourage transnational TV trade and flow within the bloc (Galperin, 1999). Finally, national television is still dominant in many countries, particularly where national markets are well developed and where national regulatory requirements and government incentives also support it (Straubhaar, 2007).

## Disjunctures between cultural and economic landscapes

In the past, some current emerging powers were seen as perhaps important culturally, but not really economically. Brazil and India have long been major producers and minor exporters in television and film, respectively. China and India have both had enormous long-term cultural influence throughout Asia and, more recently, notable cultural presence globally (Thussu, 2013). Economically, however, Brazilians used to joke about themselves that they were a country of the future and always would be. While these three and other large developing countries, including South Africa, had long been seen as potentially interesting markets for core powers, as well as sources of raw materials and cheap labour, their potential for any sort of major economic growth, let alone the accumulation of any real economic power, had always been seen as quite limited.

China, however, began to emerge as an increasingly important economic partner for core countries and their major corporations. An economic analysis by the government of New Zealand notes, '[i]n a period of less than 30 years, China has evolved into one of the world's fastest-growing economies, increasingly outwardly-oriented and market-driven' (Government of New Zealand, 2010). India is seen as an emerging power in a more limited set of areas, notably high-technology outsourcing and services, and its education system at the top is seen as a major economic asset, producing many of the world's best regarded engineers. Brazil continues to be seen primarily as a major agricultural exporter, with recognition that its agriculture is increasingly industrialized and efficient, with some high-tech exports in aircraft and metals.

In sum, perhaps the most striking aspect of the recognition since 2000 of China, India, Brazil and other emerging powers is now precisely in the global economic landscape, where their importance had earlier been doubted. However, their importance and growth has now come within a global system that all of the BRIC countries had in various ways resisted prior to the 1980s and 1990s. As the USSR, Russia had, along with the People's Republic of China, been the primary alternative to the world capitalist system until the late 1980s, but Wallerstein had presciently anticipated that neither would likely be able to resist the draw of an otherwise completely dominant global capitalist system (Wallerstein, 1979). Although not trying to challenge the world capitalist system, Brazil tried for semi-autonomy through import substitution industrialization. India did, too, coupled with a more socialized, government-driven overall economic structure. South Africa, under apartheid, struggled against sanctions placed on it by many of the core countries, also focusing on import substitution. All five of the BRICS countries came to accept far more of the rules of an emerging global capitalist economy, but all five have continued to employ state capitalist enterprises, elements of state economic control and intervention and, in the case of Brazil, increasing welfare transfer payments to the poor, more than the standard advice of the World Bank might prefer.

So, let us look systematically at the financial and economic landscape of the BRICS countries as a base for then considering the other landscapes. This includes the disjuncture, which we will argue separates the increasingly powerful mediascapes of these five countries – and other emerging powers – from the more asymmetrically interdependent, or indeed even dependent natures of some of their economies and technoscapes.

## Financial/economic landscape

In a push for economic development after the 1940s, Brazil, India and South Africa all tried import substitution, with large state sectors and growing private sectors, with more of a mix of capitalism and socialism in India (Watkins, 2013; Evans, 1979; Drèze and Sen, 1996). Most of Latin America, including Brazil, stagnated throughout the 1970s, due to the oil price shocks and increases in the dollar value of their debt (Solimano and Soto, 2005). China went through a series of economic ups and downs, including several severe crises, through the mid-1970s (Brandt and Rawski, 2008). Russia, as part of the USSR, began to fall back in its economic competition with the US and Western Europe. South Africa and India also went through some economic stagnation in the 1970s–1980s.

Brazil, Russia, India, China and South Africa all moved towards greater liberalization of economic competition, privatizing some state firms and deregulating some sectors of the economy in the 1980s and 1990s. After the late 1970s, a distinctly different economic strategy was introduced in China, moving it towards a modified capitalism, with the de-collectivization of agriculture, opening up to foreign investment and the allowance of more entrepreneurship. By the 1980s and 1990s, there was increasing privatization, decentralization of economic policies to local levels and growth of special economic zones, with increasingly fast economic growth but also rapidly increasing geographic and economic inequalities (Brandt and Rawski, 2008). In Russia, a rapid shift towards open capitalism in the 1990s created a chaotic social and economic situation, in which many entrepreneurs became rich, but the wealth did not spread to workers or the middle class (Riasanovsky and Steinberg, 2010) as it did in China. In fact, many in Russia became impoverished, which led to retrenchment under President Vladimir Putin (ibid.).

Brazil started fairly rapid change in 1990 with the neo-liberal policies of President Collor, which were stabilized and moderated somewhat in various sectors – like film production – under the Cardozo and Lula governments. The latter governments also created education incentives, like the *Bolsa Escola* (paying parents to keep children in school) and other stabilization programmes, which, coupled with increasing economic growth from the mid-1990s, created many new consumers (Baer, 2001; Amann and Baer, 2006). India also began to liberalize in a somewhat more gradual manner after 1991, opening some sectors to foreign investment and global integration, especially those linked to new technologies (OECD, 2007).

South Africa was pushed towards change by the economic unsustainability of its internal racist apartheid system, in part due to international economic sanctions against the regime. A transition in 1990–1991 led to an initial internal focus on improving housing, jobs, education and health for black citizens, along with a programme of affirmative action known as Black Empowerment. The end of apartheid improved relations with African neighbours and potential foreign investors. South Africa began opening its economy to global invest-ment and increased South African investment in neighbouring countries (Feinstein, 2005).

In all these BRICS countries, except possibly Russia, a major outcome of economic change in the 1990s and 2000s was substantial growth in the lower middle class and middle class. This middle-class growth created a basis for an expanding consumer economy, along with growth in advertising and in media (Court and Narasimhan, 2010). In Brazil, some 40 million people rose from working class or working poor, although the World Bank, in a comparative analysis of the new lower middle class in Latin America, noted that many of this new group were in danger of falling back out of the middle class, depending on circumstances and events (2010). Much larger numbers of people have risen in social mobility to the lower middle class in China and India.

Another factor to consider are the increasingly complex economic relationships between the BRICS countries themselves. China and India are much larger in population and in their economic roles in the global system than the other three. China overshadows the others not only in size and economic development, but also in multidimensionality of roles as it emerges as a new sort of great power. For example, China has overtaken the US as the number one trading partner of Brazil. While the relationship has contributed to Brazilian economic growth, its nature – exporting raw materials to China and importing manufactured goods – looks uncomfortably to many Brazilians like the asymmetric or even dependent relationships it has long had with the US and the core countries of Europe. A Brookings report observes that, 'even with advantageous trade relations, there is a pattern of growing imbalances and asymmetries in trade flows that are more favourable to China than Brazil. Therefore, China and Brazil are bound to be competitors … ' (Pereira and Neves, 2011: iii).

## Technological landscape

All of the BRICS countries have worked on improving their technological infrastructure rapidly. In 2013, according to figures from International Telecommunications Union, Russia led with Internet penetration of 61 per cent, followed by Brazil 52 per cent, China 46 per cent and India 13 per cent (ITU, 2014). Mobile phone penetration is increasing even more rapidly in all four (ibid.). While all are working hard on technology infrastructure, compared to many other developing economies, the BRICS countries are beginning to specialize individually in different aspects of the global technoscape in ways that differentiate them. India has developed a very sophisticated telecom, industrial and personnel infrastructure for outsourcing of technology related services, such as telemarketing, telephone inquiries and tech support for users in other countries. This builds on unique strengths, such as a large population educated and relatively fluent in English, unavailable to other BRICS countries.

China and, to a slightly lesser degree, India have emerged alongside some other smaller nations, like South Korea and Taiwan, as major producers of technological goods. All those have also now tried to move up the technological value chain from being efficient, low-cost centres for high-tech manufacture, to being centres for research and development, design and other high-value technological processes. Brazil tried early, in the 1970s and 1980s, under the earlier economic model of autonomous import substitution, to become self-sufficient in computers (Evans, 1992), but failed to anticipate that conditions in this area were shifting from autonomous national champion industries to a highly integrated globalized network of producers. In a way, their failed effort was decisive evidence that emerging markets in technology were having to cope with a global technoscape in manufacture that was far more integrated at a global level than could have been imagined in the 1970s.

Furthermore, companies and their ownership are only part of the technology landscape. Global interactions using technology owned by a variety of institutions are getting very complex. For much of the 2000s, Brazilian and Indian users had essentially hijacked Google's Orkut social network, so that most of its users communicated in Portuguese or Hindi. Google eventually gave up trying to rebrand Orkut to do better in the US market and moved its headquarters to São Paulo to take advantage of the global market they had. Using several generations of technology, foreign corporations like Murdoch's Star TV satellite service in the 1990s, or Google's search programmes in the 2000s, have tried to break into the Chinese market and open up more direct access to Chinese audiences and users. But the Chinese government has largely foiled all such attempts (although many users figure out ways around the so-called 'great Firewall of China') and has kept some companies like Facebook out of its market altogether. To get into India with any success, Murdoch's Star TV had to partner with an Indian production company, Zee TV, which knew what Indian audiences actually liked, i.e. locally produced series, soaps and news. In the long run, global Star TV may have served more to launch Zee TV as a major player in India than anything else. So did a much earlier partnership by Time Life, Inc. in Brazil. In the 1960s, it helped launch TV Globo, now a rising regional and global powerhouse, but gained very little from the partnership itself. A Time Life executive years later confessed to this author in a personal interview that the local partner, backed up by its government, had essentially taken advantage of them, making good initial use of Time Life's technology and money, then kicking them out just when the Globo network really became profitable.

## Migration and diaspora

While perhaps less visible than the emerging manufacturing might of China and the dominant services outsourcing role of India, both these countries exercise another strong role in another global landscape that differentiates them from other emerging powers. That is the visibility, economic and cultural power of their diasporas across many parts of the globe, especially to other core countries. The Indian diaspora reaches many countries with a variety of types of emigrants, some highly-skilled and educated professionals, others working as labourers in a variety of nearby countries (Parekh et al., 2003). The same is true of the Chinese diaspora, which is represented in the US, for example, by a variety of people ranging from high-tech inventors and businessmen to small shopkeepers and working-class tradespeople. There are Russian, Brazilian and South African diasporas of some importance, but much smaller and less significant in the global landscape than those of China and India.

Much of the literature on diaspora has to do with migrants' own ongoing formation of identity (Braziel and Mannur, 2003), which is clearly of central importance. However, it might be interesting to begin to think of the diasporas as a source of not only economic but cultural power, both on behalf of the migrants themselves, and the home countries they come from. In interviewing with and about migrants in Austin, Texas, for example, we are beginning to find that the Indian, Chinese and Korean diasporas are coming to be highly regarded not just as useful members of high-tech, higher education and other important industries, but as cultural assets to their communities and as useful cultural links to their home countries.

Diasporas also represent a solid foothold in many other countries for the cultural and industries of their home countries. This seems to increase first with satellite TV and now broadband Internet. Taplin notes that, with increased broadband access, 'the cultural Diasporas of the major competitive filmmaking powers (China, India, Russia and Latin America) would be able to access their country's movies regardless of location' (Taplin, 2007:176).

## Cultural and media exports and reach

Brazil, India, China and other emerging powers are also becoming important in the global mediascape as exporters of cultural products with a broad global reach, beyond their diasporas, to more general audiences in multiple continents. Bollywood and regional film industries in India actually make more movies than the US, and increasingly distribute many of them globally, too. The same is true of the *telenovelas* (prime-time soap operas) of Brazil, the martial arts series of Hong Kong and China, and the Bollywoodish prime-time TV soap operas of India. Brazil and India are also significant global exporters of music, too. China and India export games and other software. While perhaps not significant global exporters on the same scale, Russia and South Africa are very significant as regional media exporters and powers in their regions, central Europe and central Asia, and southern Africa.

At first, the BRICS countries and others were notable for being among the first to produce many of their own media and cultural products, effectively doing import substitution for the television, music and/or films of Hollywood. The 1970s produced major research, such as the Nordenstreng and Varis report for UNESCO (1974), which concluded that most countries were importing most of their television, mostly entertainment and largely from the US. Other studies also showed an unbalanced news flow (Boyd-Barrett, 1977; 1980).

However, even then, China, India and Russia did not fit that pattern. China and Russia resisted almost all imports, including most news, especially from the dominant centres in the Western core countries. India imported news but much less film and music. Brazil moved during the 1970s to substitute its own music and television for most of what had been imported, but continued to be more dependent on outside news and film. Furthermore, the size and affluence of the home markets of these rapidly emerging media producers is increasing faster than most of the existing core countries, which will add to the solidity of their home base for media production (Taplin, 2007).

Several of these countries not only protected and grew their own markets and cultural industries, but also moved towards exporting. Brazil has been a relatively major television programme exporter, especially in *telenovelas*, since the 1980s (Straubhaar, 1991), particularly in Latin America, where it has long been a dominant exporter (along with Mexico) (Marques de Melo, 1992) but reaching over 100 markets globally as well (Rêgo and La Pastina, 2007). However, compared to the continuing television exports of the US, the Brazilian and Mexican roles in what have been called global media contra-flows (Thussu, 2007), are perhaps more limited than initially expected (Biltereyst and Meers, 2000).

India had always produced and exported film and television in its near region (Pendakur and Subramanyam, 1996; Ray and Jacka, 1996). It began to go well beyond that in the 1990s, exporting film and television throughout many developing countries in Asia and Africa (Pendakur and Subramanyam, 1996). In the 1990s and 2000s, Indian film in particular began to reach more global markets (Lorenzena and Täube, 2008), following its diaspora, but also going well beyond it, to draw in viewers from the larger audiences of many countries, including the US (Taplin, 2007). China is going through a similar process, building on a strong and growing home market, on a widespread and affluent diasporic audience, and on a cadre of stars and directors, including both those from Hong Kong and China, who are increasingly well-known in Western markets, well beyond the Chinese diaspora itself (ibid.).

Regions can be complex for the BRICS nations, however. National systems see regional media emerging within their borders and transnationally across them, their neighbours, their linguistic communities, etc. For example, Chinese national media seem very strong, but television attention is being drawn away from national television channels to regional channels, run by regional governments, that offer increased diversity in entertainment and news. At the same time, Chinese audiences are also drawn to television programmes from culturally similar, or culturally proximate (Straubhaar, 1991) neighbouring nations, particularly South Korea, which is rising now as a regional and global exporter of television drama (Huang, 2011).

One important theoretical and analytical point is to disentangle what is national, what is global and what is obviously transnational. It seems clear that emerging global media powers are usually even more powerful in a specific regional or cultural linguistic market that is culturally proximate (Straubhaar, 1991), geographically proximate or both. Several of the emerging media and cultural exporters discussed here are even stronger in markets or cultural spaces that are regional (geographically contiguous spaces or markets like South or East Asia) or cultural-linguistic, i.e. geographically dispersed but culturally and linguistically linked markets or spaces, such as the widely dispersed Anglophone or Lusophone cultural markets (Straubhaar, 2007).

While India is a rising film export power globally, it has long been dominant in South Asia (Ray and Jacka, 1996). The same is true with Brazil and Mexico in Latin American television (Sinclair, 1999). While Japan previously grew into a dominant regional exporter of cartoons, comics, games, pop music, etc. (Iwabuchi, 2002), South Korea is now making strong inroads across East Asia as part of what has been called the 'Korean Wave' (Dator and Seo, 2004; Taplin, 2007).

## Conclusion

It might be theoretically interesting, therefore, to think of emerging media and cultural powers as, first and foremost, those who work from a strong home base, either large or affluent or both. Part of that is the size of their economies. Another is the strength of their states, who are increasingly important in the UN, in the G20, and in their own series of BRICS summits. Second, it seems that emerging powers build next on an important regional or cultural-linguistic market base in which they are to some degree also dominant. Then, thirdly, we may see them emerging as truly global media or cultural export powers, reaching first to diasporas, then to more truly global audiences in the case of China and India, or moving directly to export as in the case of Brazilian television.

It is also worth considering that while the idea of Chindia – as a pairing of two of the most important markets that are both regional and global rivals and trading partners – is definitely interesting, it is also worth considering them both within BRICS. They have several key interests in common, including their relationship to core industrial countries, essentially those of the OECD. China has perhaps changed its relationship to the older core most clearly, in some ways emerging as the world's second most important economy, after the US, and pushing to re-establish different bases for that relationship, in everything from trade to culture and media. China is one of the few countries that can directly challenge and limit the power of global media conglomerates like Murdoch's News Corporation (Curtin, 2005; Shi, 2005). It will be interesting to see if other emerging powers gain a measure of this position or if China is uniquely powerful given its size, market, regulatory power, industrial base, etc.

The BRICS countries and other newly emerging economic, cultural and media powers also have to work out how they relate to each other and to less developing countries (LDCs). Within BRICS, Goldman Sachs speculate that China and India might emerge as relatively stronger in industry and manufacturing, while Brazil and Russia might end up as fairly powerful resource exporters to the other BRICS members, as well as other core countries. In fact, recent evidence shows that Brazil is moving to reduce its growing dependence on China, diversifying exports and rebuilding key industries required to be competitive with China in economic terms (Pomfret, 2010), similar in a way to the complex ways in which India confronts its need to both compete and cooperate with China.

Much like Brazil's complex reaction to both supplying China with raw materials while competing with it in other areas, including media and culture, other developing countries are also trying to sort out their relations with BRICS, Mexico, South Korea, etc. All the BRICS countries had put out political and economic overtures to other developing countries for a long time; India through the Non-Aligned Movement; Brazil, China and Russia by supporting independence and autonomy movements in Africa and Latin America. Brazil, India and South Africa have met to discuss their common interests as large emerging democracies. Lastly, to many smaller countries, all these emerging countries, BRICS plus South Korea, Mexico and a few others may well look like regional or cultural-linguistic hegemons in terms of cultural and media exports and presence. India has a dominant position in South Asia and parts of the Arab Gulf and Africa. Brazil has a large, almost hegemonic presence in both Latin America and diverse parts of the Lusophone world, including Portugal itself. China has been a cultural hegemon in East Asia for millennia. So while the position of these countries may look emerging to the core nations, they may seem very well established, even dominant to others.

## Note

1 The author acknowledges the contribution of John Jirik to an early draft of this chapter.

## References

Amann, E. and Baer, W. (2006) 'Economic Orthodoxy Versus Social Development? The Dilemmas Facing Brazil's Labor Government'. *Oxford Development Studies* 34(2): 219–241.

Appadurai, A. (1990) 'Disjuncture and Difference in the Global Cultural Economy'. *Public Culture* 2(2): 1–24.

Baer, W. (2001) *The Brazilian Economy: Growth and Development*. Westport, CT: Praeger.

Bayart, J. F. (1993) *The State in Africa: The Politics of the Belly*. London, Longman.

——(2007) *Global Subjects: A Political Critique of Globalization*. Cambridge, Polity.

Biltereyst, D. and Meers, P. (2000) 'The International Telenovela Debate and the Contra-flow Argument'. *Media, Culture and Society* 22: 393–413.

Boyd-Barrett, O. (1977) 'Media Imperialism: Towards an International Framework for the Analysis of Media Systems', in James Curran *et al.* (eds.) *Mass Communication and Society*. London: Arnold.

——(1980) *The International News Agencies*. London: Sage.

Boyne, R. (1990) 'Culture and the World System'. *Theory, Culture and Society* 7: 57–62.

Brandt, L. and Rawski, T. (eds.) (2008) *China's Great Transformation*. Cambridge: Cambridge University Press.

Braziel, J. E. and Mannur, A. (eds.) (2003) *Theorizing Diaspora: A Reader*. London: Routledge.

Cardoso, F. H. (1973) 'Associated Dependent-Development: Theoretical and Practical Implications.' in A. Stephan (ed.) *Authoritarian Brazil*. New Haven: Yale University Press.

Cockroft, J. *et al.* (1972) *Dependence and Underdevelopment: Latin America's Political Economy*. New York: Anchor Books.

Court, D. and Narasimhan, L. (2010) 'Capturing the World's Emerging Middle Class'. *McKinsey Quarterly*. Available at: http://www.mckinsey.com/insights/consumer_and_retail/capturing_the_worlds_emerging_ middle_class. Accessed 28 October 2014.

Curtin, M. (2005) 'Murdoch's Dilemma, or "What's the Price of TV in China?"' *Media Culture and Society* 27(2): 155–175.

Dagnino, E. (1973) 'Cultural and Ideological Dependence: Building a Theoretical Framework.' in F. Bonilla and R. Girling (eds.) *Structures of Dependency*. Stanford: Stanford University Press.

Dator, J. and Seo, Y. (2004) 'Korea as the Wave of a Future: The Emerging Dream Society of Icons and Aesthetic Experience'. *Journal of Futures Studies* 9(1): 31–44.

Dolinskiy, A. (2013) 'How Moscow Understands the Role of Media to Achieve Soft Power'. *Promoting Alternative Views in a Multipolar World: BRICS and their Evolving Role in Developing Media Markets*. Berlin: Robert Bosch Stiftung.

Dorgan, G. (2013) Jim O'Neills Bullish BRICS Outlook until 2020 and our Critics. Retrieved from Swiss National Bank's blog: http://snbchf.com/global-macro/jim-oneills-bullish-brics-outlook-until-2020-and-our-critics/.

Drèze, J. and Sen, A. (1996) *India: Economic Development and Social Opportunity*. Oxford: Oxford University Press.

Evans, P. (1979) *Dependent Development: The Alliance of Multinational, State and Local Capital in Brazil*. Princeton: Princeton University Press.

——(1992) *High Technology and Third World Industrialization: Brazilian Computer Policy in Comparative Perspective*. Berkeley: International and Area Studies, University of California at Berkeley.

Feinstein, C. H. (2005) *An Economic History of South Africa: Conquest, Discrimination, and Development*. Cambridge: Cambridge University Press.

Galperin, H. (1999) 'Cultural Industries Policy in Regional Trade Agreements: the Cases of NAFTA, the European Union, and MERCOSUR'. *Media, Culture, and Society* 21(5): 627–648.

Goldman Sachs (2007) *BRICS and Beyond*. Goldman Sachs Global Economics Group.

Government of New Zealand (2010) 'Trade, N. Z. M. o. F. China' Country Information Paper. Retrieved from www.mfat.govt.nz/Countries/Asia-North/China.php.

Huang, S. (2011) 'Nation-branding and Transnational Consumption: Japan-mania and the Korean Wave in Taiwan'. *Media Culture and Society* 33(1): 3–18.

ITU (2014) 'ICT Statistics Database.' Geneva: International Telecommunications Union. Retrieved on 15 August 2014 from www.itu.int/en/ITU-D/Statistics/Pages/stat/default.aspx?.

Iwabuchi, K. (2002) *Recentering Globalization: Popular Culture and Japanese Transnationalism*. Durham: Duke University Press.

Kraidy, M. (2005) *Hybridity, or the Cultural Logic of Globalization*. Philadelphia: Temple University Press.

Lorenzena, M. and Täube, F. A. (2008) 'Breakout from Bollywood? The Roles of Social Networks and Regulation in the Evolution of Indian Film Industry'. *Journal of International Management* 14(3): 286–299.

Marques de Melo, J. (1992) 'Brazil's Role as a Television Exporter within the Latin American Regional Market'. 42nd Annual Conference of the International Communication Association, Miami, FL.

Miller, T. *et al.* (2005) *Global Hollywood 2*. New York: Pearson Longman.

Mjøs, O. J. (2010) *Media Globalization and the Discovery Channel Networks*. New York: Routledge.

Moran, A. (2004) 'Television Formats in the World/the World of Television Formats', pp.1–8 in Moran, A. and Keene, M. (eds.) *Television across Asia: Television Industries, Programme Formats and Globalization*. London: RoutledgeCurzon.

——(2009) *New Flows in Global TV*. Bristol: Intellect.

Morris, N. and Waisbord, S. (eds.) (2001) *Media and Globalization: Why the State Matters*. Lanham, MD: Rowman & Littlefield.

Nordenstreng, K. and Varis, T. (1974) *Television Traffic: A One-Way Street*. Paris: UNESCO.

O'Neill, J. (2001) *Building Better Global Economic BRICs*, New York: Goldman Sachs.

OECD (2007) *Economic Survey of India 2007: Policy Brief*. Public Affairs Division and Directorate. Paris: OECD.

Ohmae, K. (1995) *The End of the Nation State: The Rise of Regional Economies* London: HarperCollins.

Parekh, B. C. *et al.* (eds.) (2003) *Culture and Economy in the Indian Diaspora*. London: Routledge.

Pendakur, M. and Subramanyam, R. (1996) 'Indian Cinema beyond National Borders', in Sinclair, J., Jacka, E. and Cunningham, S. (eds.) *Peripheral Vision: New Patterns in Global Television*. New York: Oxford University Press.

Pereira, C. and Neves, J. A. d. C. (2011) 'Brazil and China: South-South Partnership or North-South Competition?' *Foreign Policy at BROOKINGS*. Washington: Brookings Institution.

Pomfret, J. (2010) 'China Invests Heavily in Brazil, Elsewhere in Pursuit of Political Heft'. *Washington Post*, 26 July.

Ray, M. and Jacka, E. (1996) 'Indian Television: An Emerging Regional Force' in Sinclair, J., Jacka, E. and Cunningham, S. (eds.) *Peripheral Vision: New Patterns in Global Television*. New York: Oxford University Press.

Rêgo, C. and La Pastina, A. C. (2007) 'Brazil and the Globalization of Telenovela' in Thussu , D. K. (ed.) *Media on the Move: Global Flow and Contra-flow*. London: Routledge.

Riasanovsky, N. and Steinberg, M. (2010) *A History of Russia since 1855*. Oxford: Oxford University Press.

Shi, A. (2005) 'The Taming of the Shrew: Global Media in a Chinese Perspective'. *Global Media and Communication* 1(1): 33–36.

Sinclair, J. (1999) *Latin American Television: A Global View*. New York: Oxford University Press.

Sinclair, J. and Straubhaar, J. (2013) *Television in Latin America*. London: BFI.

Sinclair, J.; Jacka, E. and Cunningham, S. (eds.) (1996) *Peripheral Vision: New Patterns in Global Television*, pp.1–15. New York: Oxford University Press.

Solimano, A. and R. Soto (2005) *Economic Growth in Latin America in the late 20th Century: Evidence and Interpretation*. Santiago: Economic Commission for Latin America and the Caribbean (ECLAC).

Strange, S. (2001) 'The Declining Authority of the Nation State', in Held, D. and McGrew, A. (eds.) *The Global Transformations Reader*. Malden: Polity.

Straubhaar, J. (1991) 'Beyond Media Imperialism: Asymmetrical Interdependence and Cultural Proximity'. *Critical Studies in Mass Communication* (8): 39–59.

——(2007) *World Television: From Global to Local*, London: Sage.

——(2008) 'Global Television Flows', *Flow TV*. Austin, TX.

Taplin, J. (2007) 'Crouching Tigers: Emerging Challenges to US Entertainment Supremacy' in *The Movie Business* 1: 167–190.

Thussu, D. K. (ed.) (2007) *Media on the Move: Global Flow and Contra-Flow*. New York: Routledge.

Thussu, D. K. (2013) *Communicating India's Soft Power: Buddha to Bollywood*. New York, Palgrave/Macmillan.

Waisbord, S. (1998) 'The Ties that Still Bind: Media and National Cultures in Latin America'. *Canadian Journal of Communication* 23: 381–401.

Wallerstein, I. (1979) *The Capitalist World Economy*. Cambridge: Cambridge University Press.

Wasserman, H. (ed.) (2011) *Popular Media, Democracy and Development in Africa*. London: Routledge.

Watkins, T. (2013) 'Privatization in South Africa'. Retrieved from www.sjsu.edu/faculty/watkins/southafrica.htm.

# Part II

# Media systems and landscapes

## Introduction

Although the BRICS countries account for 40 per cent of the global population and a quarter of the global GDP, the study of media in these nations remains largely neglected in international media studies. To reflect the global nature of this media, the five chapters in Part II of the book include detailed analyses of media systems and landscapes in each BRICS country, which have some of the world's most dynamic and differentiated media systems. Written by authors from the respective countries, each chapter provides a much-neglected historical context to the rise of media in BRICS nations. From the European colonial legacy – in the case of India and South Africa – to imperial and socialist heritage in Russia and China, to Brazil's case of 'reverse colonialism', the chapters anchor the contemporary media scene within the diverse and rich history that has left a lasting impact on the media scene among BRICS members. The deregulation, digitization and democratization of mass media in recent decades is discussed in detail by each contributor.

In their chapter, Raquel Paiva, Muniz Sodré and Leonardo Custodio look at the Brazilian media system in the context of the particular historical tradition of media patrimonialism and the current debates on media democratization. After providing a brief history of the Brazilian press, they give an overview of the current media structure with efforts for media democratization and explore patterns of media ownership in the country that reflect the highly patrimonial nature of Brazilian society. Patrimonialism is defined as a complex set of relationships among close-knit families or groups to control and consolidate power among a small elite. The chapter underlines the importance of the dominating family-controlled private conglomerates, which define the mainstream media landscape in Brazil, through their control of traditional media (print, radio and television). The authors – who have extensive experience of the Brazilian alternative media space – stress the need for democratization of the media and discuss how community radio stations and the Internet are becoming instruments for the civil society actors for the construction of a more plural and accessible media system.

Elena Vartanova's chapter provides a background to the post-Soviet media system in Russia. Drawing on the latest empirical data, she gives an overview of the history and current state and structure of the Russian media system. The chapter considers emerging trends in media content and the rise of the digital media/social networks in the context of globalization and the growing fragmentation of the Russian society and its rising consumerism. Vartanova explores the effects of the unique nature of Russia, being simultaneously a centre of empire and geopolitical periphery, part of a global culture and evolving market economy, a multi-cultural and multi-linguistic society with a strong Russian orthodox identity. The roles played by press, radio, television and more recently Internet in post-Soviet nation-building is considered in the context of centripetal and centrifugal pressures emanating from different media at national, regional and local levels.

In his chapter on the media system in India, Savyasaachi Jain provides a conceptual map of its features, developments and influences, beginning with a short history of Indian media, tracing its roots in colonial India and in the Indian freedom struggle, and going on to evaluate the impact of the rapid expansion of media since the economic liberalization of the 1990s. The chapter examines the newspaper market, which has grown to overtake China as the largest in the world, as well as the proliferation of hundreds of television channels – more than 800 – and radio stations in the last two decades. A democratic polity, a growing economy and expanding literacy are some key factors for this. However, the advertising revenue for the Indian media industry is smaller than some of its BRICS partners. The chapter highlights the reasons for the high rate of growth of mobile telephony, with more than 850 million subscribers in 2013, and the relatively slow uptake of online media. Jain analyses aspects and issues ranging from ownership, competition and the effect of market forces on the evolving culture of media. The chapter challenges the practicality of characterizing India's multilingual, multi-layered and continent-sized media as one 'national media system'.

Though the media industry in China has demonstrated very impressive growth in recent decades, the media continue to be defined by a system still dominated by the Party-State structure. In their chapter, Zhengrong Hu, Peixi Xu and Deqiang Ji explore the logic inherent in a state-controlled system operating within one of the world's largest media markets. Like the rest of the four BRICS countries, they argue, the Chinese media landscape is undergoing rapid changes. Analysing this in terms of four key historical phases, the authors argue that newspapers, radio, television, the Internet and mobile phones were born in divergent social contexts and bear the birth marks of different eras in terms of ideological orientations, technological imperatives and management styles. After outlining the broad aspects of Chinese media landscape, the chapter illustrates how the rise of grassroots media is giving voice to social forces that are shaking and stirring and thus reconfiguring the media landscape. The chapter juxtaposes the emergence of these grassroots voices with the rise of market forces since the 1978 reform, which broke the monopoly of the state media system. In the most recent phase, the chapter proposes that there is evidence that the state media system is attempting a form of redemption by disassociating itself from national and transnational capital in order to re-establish credibility with the people.

The final chapter in this part by viola milton and Pieter Fourie, focuses on the media system in South Africa, which has evolved from apartheid to a complex and more inclusive system. After providing a brief history of the South African media and an overview of contemporary media regulatory framework, the chapter focuses on the size of the print, broadcasting, online, film and advertising industries in Africa's biggest media market, though smallest among BRICS nations. In a comprehensive analysis, milton and Fourie explore such issues as media ownership and concentration, competition and black empowerment, as well as matters relating to the freedom of the media and threats to freedom of expression. The chapter argues that the governance and independence of public service broadcasting requires a new model replacing the Reithian one (misused under colonialism, apartheid and the present political dispensation). The development of online media, exemplified by the expansion and inter-nationalization of a South African print media group, indicates potential for South African media of not only being pan-African but going beyond the continent. Finally, the chapter highlights the historic and increased role of civil society and non-government media organizations in safeguarding a dynamic, independent and growth-oriented media system.

All five contributions demonstrate the complexity and the dynamic nature of media in BRICS nations. They highlight the trend towards commercialization and internationalization as well as the domestic socio-political tensions that media face, and their impressive current and projected growth trajectories.

# Chapter 5

# Brazil: patrimonialism and media democratization

*Raquel Paiva, Muniz Sodré and Leonardo Custódio*

This chapter analyzes the tradition of media patrimonialism and civil society struggles for media democratization in Brazil, providing a historical overview of the media industry and media conglomerates. At the same time, it shows how different civil society actors have organized and articulated networks to challenge the domination of family-owned media companies. Brazilian media patrimonialism survived and prospered through distinct political periods: the Old Republic (1889–1930), the Vargas Era (1930–1945) and the Military Dictatorship (1964–1984), which are set out below. The chapter then goes on to examine the struggle for media democratization in Brazil from the 1960s to the present.

The term 'patrimonialism' refers to a complex set of relationships between families, clans or groups which aimed to preserve unity through the internal distribution of assets. Raimundo Faoro's classic *Owners of Power* (Faoro, 1973) shows how the Brazilian patrimonial social order has its roots in Portugal. During the colonization process, the circulation of wealth within families was governed by principles established by the Portuguese monarchy at the end of the medieval era. Colonization enabled the monarch to offer wealth and power to the estates of the realm, and this process shaped the constitution of the state and power relations in Brazil. Since the time of colonization, family ties and economic interests have continued to allow certain groups to dominate the political and economic spheres. This patrimonial order is important in understanding the nature of the media in Brazil.

The inauguration of the press was one of the immediate changes made by the Portuguese Crown on the arrival of the royal family in Brazil in 1808 after escaping Napoleon, creating its own official periodical – *Gazeta do Rio de Janeiro*. Simultaneously, the Crown also censored all independent newspapers that did not support the Empire. Nevertheless, in 1821, the Emperor Dom Pedro I abolished censorship, believing that the campaign for independence needed the press to promote its cause. One year later, Brazil became an independent country. By the end of the nineteenth century, the alliance between independent press representatives and the political sphere suited the purpose of different political movements struggling for the Abolition of Slavery (1888) and the Proclamation of the Republic (1889) (Barbosa, 2010).

In the twentieth century, the patrimonial relationship between the press and the political sphere became even more evident. After 1889, the proximity between political elites and media owners created an environment that led to the continual switching between political support and animosity through the news medium. Interestingly, these troubled relationships were a backdrop for the construction of powerful private media conglomerates that have dominated the Brazilian media system for almost a century. The best-known and most widely discussed case of media monopoly is that of the Globo Network (Porto, 2012). Founded in 1925 when the patriarch of the Marinho family purchased the newspaper of that name, Globo has become one of the world's biggest media conglomerates. However, Globo is not the only family-owned media conglomerate in Brazil. The Mesquita family (1902, *Grupo Estado*), the Frias family (1921, *Grupo Folha*), the Civita family (1950, *Grupo Abril*) and the Saad family (1937, *Grupo Bandeirantes*) are also important groups that dominate and control the Brazilian media system. A more particular example of a private media conglomerate in Brazil is Grupo Record, which belongs to the Pentecostal religious group called *Igreja Universal do Reino de Deus* (Universal Church of the Kingdom of God). These companies followed the footsteps of Brazil's first media conglomerate: *Diários Associados*. Its owner, the media mogul Assis Chateaubriand, was considered the Brazilian Citizen Kane in the first half of the twentieth century. Thus, the role of patrimonialism is clearly reflected in how these family-owned or private groups have not only managed to protect themselves from a very unstable political system, but also to become media empires and economic powerhouses during both authoritarian and democratic regimes.

Patrimonialism is certainly not exclusive to Brazil. Waisbord identifies contemporary patrimonialism as one of the characteristics of media systems in democratic countries with a recent history of dictatorships and authoritarian rule. For him, patrimonialism is 'the discretionary use of public resources by political officials to strengthen personal and partisan power and favour allied news organizations' (Waisbord, 2013: 154). The persistence of patrimonialism in Latin America, Waisbord argues, is also due to the constant courting between the private media and the state for economic advantage (ibid.: 159–161). In this sense, Hallin and Papathanassopoulos also give a similar description of the patrimonial characteristic of the Latin American media system. Building from the concept of clientelism, Hallin and Papathanassopoulos argue that, similarly to Southern Europe, Latin American economic elites 'are often deeply enmeshed in party politics' (Hallin and Papathanassopoulos, 2002: 186).

However, media patrimonialism has been challenged. Struggles for media democratization in Brazil have fought against ownership concentration and patrimonial relations. In practice, media democratization takes two forms. On the one hand, democratization relates to the role of the press in pushing for the transition from authoritarian rule towards more democratic forms of governance. In this case, patrimonialism is not automatically in opposition to democratization. For example, the most traditional family-owned media conglomerates in Brazil have adopted progressive attitudes against authoritarian regimes even while constantly shaking hands with those in power. On the other hand, media democratization refers to civil society struggles against the power of dominant media organizations and their patrimonial ties with the political sphere. Sometimes they are the efforts of social organizations like workers' unions, ethnic organizations and residents' associations to protest and make demands. In other cases, organizations make efforts to challenge media ownership concentration and create a plural and diverse media system.

## Media patrimonialism in three political periods

In the twentieth century, we can identify three historical periods in which patrimonial relationships between the press and the political elites are evident. These political periods were witness to (a) the rise of the industrial press; (b) the popularization of radio as a mass medium; and (c) the establishment of television. We refer to these periods respectively as the First Republic (1889–1930), the first era of Getúlio Vargas (1930–1945) and the military dictatorship (1964–1984).

### The First Republic (1889–1930)

The First Republic was the political period that lasted from the demise of the monarchy in 1889 until the military revolution of 1930. The First Republic had two phases: military rule (1889–1894) and civilian rule by the landowners (1894–1930). Perhaps the best description of the patrimonial relationship between the press and the political elite during the First Republic is Nélson Werneck Sodré's account in *The History of the Press in Brazil* (Sodré, 1999). According to Sodré, in the First Republic the press was transformed from artisanal printing into an industrial business. The small-scale newspapers set up by individual publishers to challenge or support the monarchy and the aristocrats, known as *pasquins*, gradually disappeared in the second half of the nineteenth century, as journalistic enterprises rose. After Brazil's independence in 1882, private newspapers proliferated and heated up the political debates of the time. In the period of the abolitionist and republican movements, newspapers did not aim to be impartial: each of the publications indicated their political alliances and ideologies and reflected the growth of popularity of the abolitionist and republican movements, culminating with the Abolition of Slavery (1888) and the Proclamation of the Republic (1889) (Barbosa, 2010).

The political instrumentalization of the press was an important characteristic of both phases of the First Republic. At that time, the press acted according to their political ideologies as well as their business strategies, by supporting politicians in return for privileges (Sodré, 1999; Melo, 2006). In the military rule of the First Republic, the supportive press was free to act while opposing voices were pressurized and censored. In the civilian-oligarchic phase of the

First Republic (1894–1930), the news-making enterprise was also consolidated in the capital – Rio de Janeiro – and the economic metropolis – São Paulo. In the countryside, the press remained artisanal and closely tied to local economic and political elites. The business orientation both of the government and the press led to an awkward combination of capitalist ideology – which prevailed among newsmakers – with the traditional, feudal power of the political elites. This situation meant that some newspapers were in harsh opposition to the regime whilst others published government-friendly information in exchange for financial benefits.

In the 1920s, the dissatisfaction of the urban bourgeois elite (including journalists and media owners) with the backwardness of oligarchic rule generated an oppositional alliance that led to a military coup d'état in 1930, by which Getúlio Vargas came to power. As a first act in office, the military forces under Vargas shut down all opposition newspapers. These early censorship measures were an indication of how the new government would deal with the press – including those journalists and newspapers that supported the coup d'état – in the following decades (Sodré, 1999).

### The Vargas Era (1930–1945)

The relationship between the press and the state during the first 15 years of Vargas' rule was highly paradoxical. Most newspaper owners supported the 1930 military campaign led by Vargas. However, in 1932 most newspapers turned against him in support for a constitutionalist movement. Despite the failure of the constitutionalist movement, a new constitution was created and Vargas was voted in as President in 1934. During the following three years, Brazil enjoyed an apparently liberal democratic environment, in which newspaper owners were able to consolidate and expand their businesses – for example investing in magazines and radio stations – especially with the support of foreign capital. However, in 1937 Vargas and the military employed inflammatory anti-communist propaganda to motivate another coup d'état. The resulting dictatorial regime of the *Estado Novo* (New State) lasted until 1945, during which the censorship of the press was particularly harsh. The regime also used radio for propaganda, combining politics with samba and football broadcasts to disseminate the populist ideology among the urban poor (Martin-Barbero, 1993).

Despite the harsh dictatorial regime, the press expanded into multimedia companies and media conglomerates. Three aspects of patrimonialism facilitated this: market development, radio development and regulation, and censorship. Firstly, the media market developed because of deals between media owners and the government. In order to become and remain profitable and influential, media owners had to be on good or at least tolerable terms with the military ruling elite (Waisbord, 2000). One example in Brazil was the case of Assis Chateaubriand. Two years after having used his publications to support Getúlio Vargas, Chateaubriand's *Diários Associados* supported the oppositional movement. After its defeat, Chateaubriand's main newspaper was seized in the capital and soon the threat was extended to his publications in other states. In order to protect his publishing empire, Chateaubriand allowed his publications to support politicians that were part of Vargas' regime (Sodré, 1999).

Secondly, the development of the Brazilian radio broadcast system was part of the Vargas regime's political strategy. Brazil's first radio broadcast was aired in 1922. One year later, the anthropologist Roquette Pinto – a pioneer and icon in the history of radio broadcasting in Brazil – launched *Radio Sociedade do Rio de Janeiro*, aimed at diffusing social and scientific information for educational purposes. According to the regulations of the period (based on telephony and telegraphy), radio broadcasters could not run advertisements. Consequently, all radio stations in the 1920s were either educational or experimental. However, the perception of radio as a powerful political instrument motivated Vargas to move radio from an amateur practice into a highly profitable, politically influential and thus carefully regulated mass instrument for media owners and the state.

The most important boost for the growth of radio in Brazil was the change in the regulatory regime during the first four years of the Vargas era (1930–1934). In 1931, the government decreed that radio broadcasting services were to be exclusively controlled by the federal government. The regime considered radio to be a powerful propaganda machine in an illiterate country. Thus, radio broadcasting regulation in Brazil aimed at building a unified infra-structure to reach three main goals: to guarantee the supply for the demand for radio sets, to build mass audiences, and to create a means for mobilizing the working class and the poor (Jambeiro, Santos, Ribeiro and Ferreira, 2000).

Despite the clear centralized and protective nature of the regulations, the regime knew that they could not build a nationwide broadcasting infra-structure without private investment. For this reason, the concession of licenses for private broadcasting, advertising and foreign (mostly US-based) investment were also included in the new set of regulatory norms. Some of the 1930s regulations remained in force for the following 30 years, such as 10-year renewable concessions and the obligation to have a national board of directors. In relation to advertising, the regulations allowed a maximum 10 per cent of each programme to be sold as sponsoring ads (Calebre, 2003; Jambeiro *et al.*, 2000). These measures created conditions for foreign (again, mostly US-based) investment in broadcasting infrastructure. In the 1930s, 43 stations were founded, but despite this private expansion of the broadcast industry, the control of the regime was evident. 'The state coordinates, distributes, rationalizes and promotes the radio broadcasting system all over the country while preparing itself, on the other hand, to use it for its own benefit by creating a national programme of official character' (Calebre, 2003).

Media control was guaranteed through censorship mechanisms. During the dictatorial regime of *Estado Novo* (1937–1945), the state's interventions in the media were most evident and had the Second World War as the context, US market expansion as a financing system and a strong anti-communist discourse as a fuel. Thus, inspired by Nazi Germany, Vargas and the military engaged against oppositional voices (politicians and journalists) while simultaneously increasing the governmental use of the broadcasting system for the propagandist construction of a national identity. As soon as the 1937 coup d'état was announced, the parliament was closed and the press suffered a number of oppressive measures. The creation of new newspapers was forbidden, many existing newspapers and magazines were either seized or shut down, and a number of journalists were arrested (Sodré, 1999). In 1939, the military rulers created the Department of Press and Propaganda (DIP). The department's tasks included the creation of state-controlled radio stations or the seizing of existing ones. The best-known example of a private radio station turned into a state-controlled instrument was Radio Nacional (Calebre, 2003).

Radio was the instrument Vargas used both to construct a national identity and to build his populist image as the 'father of the poor'. The President used radio to communicate his political actions, while harnessing elements of popular culture. For instance, it was during Vargas' regime that samba changed from a criminalized activity of the capital's poor into the musical symbol of Brazil. It was also during *Estado Novo* that live football broadcasts helped to build the country's national passion for the sport. Because of the governmental emphasis on and control of radio, the medium enjoyed great popularity during the 1940s and 1950s. The decades became known as the Golden Age of Radio. Radio artists were worshipped as idols and thus were also incorporated in different forms of propaganda for the regime. Among the owners of the press, the strategy was either to support, or at least to avoid conflicts with, the agents of DIP for the sake of their businesses. Censoring agents kept a 24-hour surveillance on private radio stations and newsrooms. In addition, the department also financed newspapers and radio stations that were supportive or not oppositional to the regime (Sodré, 1999).

As a result, censorship was mitigated, because, despite political persecution, the media companies profited and expanded their patrimony. By the end of the Vargas Era in 1945, Chateaubriand's *Diários Associados* was already a media conglomerate. The Marinho Family had expanded their newspaper business into broadcasting with *Rádio Globo* (1943). The Saad Family had also entered the broadcasting business with *Rádio Bandeirantes* (1937). This small group of families managed to resist political interference to become the powerful media corporations of today. Their success indicates a certain level of complicity with the dictatorship to enable their survival and growth commercially and in terms of their patrimony (Barbosa, 2006).

### The 1964–1984 dictatorship

Studies of the relationship between the authoritarian regimes and the media rarely compare the Vargas Era and the 1964–1984 dictatorship (for an exception, see Martin-Barbero, 1993). This is a strange fact considering that the pattern of media patrimonialism in both regimes was very similar, such as the movement that led to the 1964 coup d'état. In 1961, Jânio Quadros was elected President, but renounced his post in less than a year. Vice President João Goulart took his place. Goulart's left-oriented policies and close ties with the organized working class raised suspicions of communism. In response, the military, with the blessing of the United States and local support from the conservative and economically liberal urban elites, seized the power once again. The media – owned by members of the urban elites – also supported what was called 'The 1964 Revolution'. As with the 'Revolution of 1930', another era of censorship and strategic deals between the media and the military regime began.

Another resemblance between media patrimonialism in the two military regimes is in the development of electronic media: instead of radio, the military regime of 1964–1984 focused on television. During the previous 30 years, radio had grown to be the most popular medium in largely illiterate Brazil. It had also allowed newspaper owners and media entrepreneurs to build successful and profitable businesses. Thus, the introduction of television was a natural step forward for the growth of the mass media market when, in 1950, Chateaubriand launched TV Tupi. Throughout the decade, new channels were created in Rio de Janeiro and São Paulo. For example, TV Record (1953), TV Rio (1955) and TV Continental (1959) were followed by a number of others in the early 1960s, like TV Excelsior (1960). In 1965, the Marinho Family inaugurated TV Globo. Within about 15 years, television had already gained great importance in the biggest urban centres. One reason for the success of television was the transplantation of successful radio formats: telenovelas, musical contests, comedy and variety shows and football broadcasts increased the TV audience. The potential of the new medium attracted the attention of the military forces. In comparison to radio in the 1930s, private media companies had already developed television significantly by the time of the coup d'état. However, the infrastructure for nationwide coverage was still precarious in the 1960s. Therefore, both the government and the private media owners were keen that the regime invest in broadcasting.

Under the dictatorships, media infrastructure and media productions reflected the combination of the military strategy for national integration with the profit orientation of media owners. All this was closely observed by the US government (concerned with the spread of communism) and US corporations (interested in increasing market penetration in Brazil). Some of the dictatorships' strategies related to broadcasting regulation. To some extent, the government acted like managers of a system, which was disputed by the influential private companies. After the coup d'état, the military made changes to the Code of Telecommunications in order to increase government control of the tele-communication sector (Mattos, 1982). The military government created the Brazilian Telecommunication Enterprise (EMBRATEL) and later Brazilian

Telecommunications (Telebrás) in order to build a nationwide telecommunication infrastructure. Satellite transmission, for example, was also a product of the military regime. These and other governmental actions (e.g. facilitated bank loans and importation of equipment) benefited the supportive or non-oppositional media companies that received the concession to explore the system (Mattos, 1982).

Like *Diários Associados* in the Vargas Era, Globo was the private company that most benefited from the close ties between the Marinho family and military officials in the 1960s. In the years preceding the coup d'état, Globo had used its newspapers and radio stations in propaganda against the civilian government by portraying it as communist rule in disguise. This expression of loyalty to the military paid off when they came to power. The first reward from the military regime to Globo was permission to launch its own TV station. In 1962, Globo's owner Roberto Marinho had signed a secret agreement with the US company Time Life to build TV Globo as a joint venture. When the deal was announced, it became a scandal, as the Brazilian Constitution did not allow foreign ownership in the country's mass media sector. Nonetheless, one year after the coup d'état, the military government passed a temporary decree to allow foreign ownership. This allowed Globo to establish its television station with the market advantage of having a huge budget due to foreign investment.

In addition to favouring Globo with the concession of stations all over the country, the military regime also made sure that competing stations would not get in their way. For example, the two most powerful stations of the 1960s – TV Excelsior and TV Tupi – were driven out of the market in the 1970s, the former by having its concession renewal denied and the latter being squeezed financially until it became bankrupt (Straubhaar, 1991; Wilkin, 2008; Porto, 2012). Other television networks were set up during the dictatorship period, but concessions were distributed in a way to prevent any of them becoming a significant competitor to Globo. Even after the military regime was over, Globo maintained the position of favoured media conglomerate among those in power. For instance, the first two civilian presidents of the country after the dictatorship were owners of local television stations affiliated to TV Globo: José Sarney in the state of Maranhão and the impeached Fernando Collor de Melo in the state of Alagoas (see Amaral and Guimarães, 1994).

The patrimonial relationship between Globo and the military regime demonstrates another parallel between the 1964–1984 dictatorship and the Vargas Era: censorship benefited the media that played along with the regime. In both cases, the military had a strategy for national development and security. The choice of the press was either to be supportive or to avoid reporting whatever could be considered as oppositional to the regime (Barbosa, 2007). Those who decided to challenge the regime were censored, coerced, exiled, tortured and even killed.

## Struggles for media democratization in Brazil

Although media patrimonialism has existed since the founding of the press in Brazil, the struggle for media democratization in the country can be considered a recent phenomenon. There have certainly been occasions throughout the 200-year history of the press in Brazil when newsmakers and civic actors aligned themselves against hegemonic political forces. The press and media conglomerates have played a crucial role for the democratic transition in Brazilian politics (Sodré, 1999). Nonetheless, the media have aimed at the democratization of politics, not of the media system itself. Paradoxically, the unchallenged and concentrated private media industry was a very important actor in the establishment of Brazil as a democratic country (Matos, 2008). Thus, our understanding of media democratization refers both to the demands for better quality information and plurality in media (Matos, 2012) as well as to a movement that aims at protecting and creating mechanisms within the media system for social groups to exert their right to communicate (Peruzzo, 2011).

Other scholars have attempted to systematize the history of the struggle for media democratization in Brazil. For instance, José Milton Santos (1995) analyzed how the discourses of media democratization were articulated between 1974 and 1994. Santos identified and categorized three periods of media democratization struggle: resistance, conquest and 'indefiniteness'. The period of resistance refers to the creation of ephemeral and alternative newspapers during the military dictatorship. The period of conquest refers to the creation of organized movements to challenge media conglomerates in the field of policymaking throughout the democratic period. Finally, the period of 'indefiniteness' refers to the early 1990s when the political and economic instabilities obscured the demands of civil society (ibid.). In this section, we take advantage of the benefit of hindsight to do a similar exercise of briefly historicizing the struggles for media democratization in Brazil. For this purpose, we look at four different periods: the 1960s–1970s, the 1980s, the 1990s and the 2000s. This chronological framework allows us to analyze how grassroots activists and policy-oriented intellectuals have built parallel but articulated movements for media democratization.

### 1960s–1970s

Important movements for media democratization in Brazil were formed during the military dictatorship after the coup d'état in 1964. The Basic Ecclesial Communities (CEB) formed by progressive sectors of the Catholic Church are one example. For Santos (1995), the CEBs were examples of micro-spaces that developed their own mechanisms for communication and political articulation. Created in the 1960s, the CEBs consisted of small groups of poor people organized in local parishes of urban peripheries and rural areas all over Brazil. During the dictatorship, the CEBs also became spaces of political mobilization, also including non-Christian and non-religious groups (Frei, 1985).

Communication was a very important element for the organizational and political strategies of the CEBs. The use of communication techniques for the education and politicization of the poor had already been used by the Catholic Church in Latin America (Gumucio-Dagron, 2001). Influenced by radical pedagogic methods, the CEBs understood communication as a dialogic and participatory practice rather than a process of transmission of knowledge. The CEBs implemented this philosophy in their production of flyers, posters, films and radio programmes to promote critical awareness among low-income workers and poor populations (see Fávero, 2006; Reimberg, 2012).

Community radio stations formed another grassroots movement during the dictatorship that has been of great importance for the struggles for media democratization in Brazil. The first Brazilian small-scale, local free radio stations were created in the early 1970s, mostly in smaller cities a long way from the large urban centres (Peruzzo, 1998). The pioneers were often young people who were more interested in broadcasting as a free-time hobby than as deliberate political action. Still, some of the young radio broadcasters were arrested for subversion. By the end of the dictatorship, small-scale radio stations had become instruments for local political struggle and for community mobilization. Some stations focused on information of local interest and valued local voices. These radio stations survived the military regime, proliferated all over the country and became an important movement in Brazil.

Finally, another movement of the 1960s–1970s that influenced the Brazilian movement for policy change and media democratization in Brazil were the international debates against media imperialism and ownership concentration (Santos, 1995; Reimberg, 2012). Latin American scholars were among the earliest and most critical contributors to UNESCO debates on a New World Information and Communication Order in the 1970s. At the time, research centres in different countries around Latin America hosted scholars who challenged the expansion especially of the US-based cultural industries. They called for communication policies to increase the balance between foreign and national productions. The Latin American twist in the UNESCO debates was inspired by grassroots communication in the region. The scholars participating in the debates called for more horizontal and inclusive rather than top-down vertical forms of communication (Beltrán, 1979; Cañizales, 2011).

One evidence of the importance of Latin America for the UNESCO debates was the organization of the First Intergovernmental Conference on National Policies on Communication in Latin America and the Caribbean in Costa Rica (1976) (Schiller, 1978; Cañizales, 2011). It was the first time civil society actors and media conglomerates debated communication policies in the region. The conference called for public participation in media and for the recognition of the right to communicate. In response, a number of media companies tried to delegitimize and criminalize the meeting (Quirós and Segovia, 1996). The campaign of the media conglomerates frustrated the outcomes of the conference (Beltrán, 2006). At the same time, these debates inspired civil society actors to challenge the media systems and patrimonial alliances in their own countries. In Brazil, the movement for policy change gained shape in the 1980s.

## 1980s

The democratic transition of the 1980s saw the proliferation of community radio stations and the articulation of policy-oriented movements in Brazil. The end of the authoritarian regime in 1984 led to the creation of thousands of small-scale, community-oriented radio stations all over the country. These stations were established with inexpensive equipment and soon became channels of information, self-representation and articulation of local political actors. The exact number of radio stations in the 1980s is difficult to estimate, but throughout the decade and the following years, private media efforts to criminalize, delegitimize and close what they referred to as 'pirate', 'illegal' and 'clandestine' stations were signals of how fast and extensively community-oriented radio stations were spreading around the country (Peruzzo, 1998).[1]

The end of the dictatorship also coincided with the creation of civil society groups pushing for policy changes in the Brazilian communication sector. In the mid-1980s, scholars and journalists in university departments and professional associations formed the National Front of Struggles for Democratic Communication Policies (FNLPDC). The Front was considered the first movement for media democratization in Brazil. Its early years were important for participants to gain experience to challenge the powerful mainstream media lobbyists and the close ties between media owners and politicians (FNDC, 2011). Some authors suggest that the more intellectualized profile of the policy-oriented movement prevented the more grassroots movements from supporting their cause (cf. Gohn, 2010; Peruzzo, 1998).

Nevertheless, this rather informal movement soon managed to cause significant discomfort among private media owners. They also managed to initiate public discussion of communication policies in Brazil. One example of the outcome of this work was the participation of the movement in the drafting of the Constitution of 1988. The activists proposed policies to reduce the influence of private media organizations in the media system. They also called for policies to increase plurality and citizen participation. However, the lobbying power of the companies prevailed and influenced the final text of the constitutional chapter about communication (Cassol, 2003). But as had happened during the UNESCO debates, the defeat of the movement did not prevent it from growing, articulating with other organized groups and becoming very influential in media democratization debates in the following decades.

## 1990s

In the 1990s, civil society actors for media democratization were able to consolidate the informal movement into nationwide networks. These networks involved community media associations as well as policy-oriented groups. The parallel movements joined forces to increase their participation in and impact on the development of the mass communication sector in Brazil. The community radio sector already consisted of thousands of stations all over the country. Different associations attempted to articulate the sector as an organized movement. For example, the Brazilian Association of Community Broadcasting (ABRAÇO) was created in 1996 and since then has been working to unify 'the struggle of community radio stations for the regulation of the service by the National Congress, for the democratization of communication and for the freedom of expression' (Sóter, 2009). The Brazilian branch of the World Association of Community Radio Broadcasters (AMARC) was created in 1995 with similar democratizing objectives (AMARC, 2004). Policy-oriented movements also changed in the early 1990s. In 1991, the National Forum for the Democratization of Communication (FNDC) emerged as a more institutionalized version of the National Front of Struggles for Democratic Communication Policies (FNLPDC). The FNDC aims at working 'for the planning, mobilization, relationship, formulation of projects, engagement in legal actions and policy for the promotion of democracy in communication' (FNDC, 2011).

The articulation of these associations and networks led to stronger civil society participation in policy debates in the 1990s. The movement for media democratization affected two laws: the Cable Law (1995) and the Community Radio Law (1998). In the case of the Cable Law, even though it was promulgated in 1995, discussions had started in 1991. The process was the first in Brazilian history in which civil society actors were invited to join private media representatives and the government in the discussions to design new communication policies, including the FNDC. Their participation led to a series of developments in media regulation in Brazil. For instance, cable broadcasting was considered a private service with a public character. Therefore, private cable TV operators were obliged to provide free channels for transmission of senate, parliament and other deliberative chambers, as well as free channels for higher-education and community-based institutions (Ramos, 1998).

Three years later, the Community Radio Law also resulted from both the pressure of the increasingly organized sector of small-scale free broadcasters and from the lobbying power of the private media conglomerates. Similarly to the Cable Law, the patrimonial power of the private media companies prevailed. Today, the Community Radio Law constrains more than facilitates the operation of the community radio stations. Nevertheless, the promulgation of the law legitimized and created the official basis for regulating practices that were considered illegal before (Paiva, Malerba and Custódio, 2013). Thus, while the participation of the movement for media democratization in Brazil in the 1990s did not represent a threat to the power of the media conglomerates, the decade was important for the consolidation of civil society actors as subjects in national communication policy-making processes.

## 2000s

The movement for media democratization in Brazil remained active, articulate and influential in the first decade of the twenty-first century. In fact, the President of the Workers' Party, Luiz Inácio Lula da Silva, gave the movement the hope that a federal government would be more receptive and open to the cause of media democratization. In his two terms as President (2002–2010), Lula da Silva included a number of FNDC proposals in his governmental programme. However, the lobbying of private media conglomerates remained highly influential in the spheres of regulation and policy-making. One example of this power was the choice of the model for Brazil's digital television system. Even though the country had invested millions in research and development of a home-made model, the government opted for a Japanese model in the interests of the media conglomerates (Carvalho, 2013). Despite such evidence of the persistent power of the private media conglomerates, the first decade of the 2000s also saw an increase in room for debates about communication policies between representatives of the media conglomerates, the government and civil society actors. One example was the First National Conference on Communication (CONFECOM) in 2009. This meeting was the largest conference ever to see joint discussions by government, civil society and private media to determine the future of communication policies in the country.

The 1st CONFECOM can be considered the most important outcome so far of the struggle for media democratization in Brazil. The Brazilian National Conference on Communications is the most recent in the history of international efforts to democratize national communication policies since the UNESCO debates of the 1970s. The gradual emergence over decades of civil society forces pushing for change, culminating in a federal government with sectors favourable to the cause, has created a context for debates to challenge the private media monopolies. Before and during the 1st CONFECOM, the expectations about the meeting were a combination of excitement and uncertainty among activists. But realistically the meeting was just one more step in the long road towards more democratic and inclusive forms of policymaking and opportunities in the communication sector (Brittos, Rocha and Nazário, 2010).

Nevertheless, despite being an important event in the history of media democratization in Brazil, the 1st CONFECOM was met with old-fashioned reactions from the private media owners. Similar to the UNESCO meeting in Costa Rica in 1976, the privately owned media companies showed concern and disapproval of the conference. The 1st CONFECOM ended with 672 propositions that were considered important by FNDC, but for the private media sector the process seemed like an attempt to threaten the freedom of the press and even to censor their actions. Consequently, various media companies and their supporters tried different measures to undermine and delegitimize the conference. Participating civil society organizations had their funding threatened, the news in mainstream media emphasized the danger of censorship that the meeting implied and during the process representatives of private media companies decided to abandon the meeting (Matos, 2012).

The period after the conference has been marked by the continuation of the disputes between the movement for media democratization in Brazil and the lobbyists of the private media companies. The remainder of the first decade of the 2000s saw the struggle for media democratization in Brazil continue. Civil society has managed to consolidate networks that have proven to be powerful representatives in the policy-making debates in the communication sector. However, the century-old patrimonial relationship between private media conglomerates and the political sphere remains powerful, and continues to dictate the present and the future of the Brazilian media system.

## Note

1 See the diagnostic report by the World Association of Community Radio (AMARC) and the National Movement of Community Radio (MNRC). The report was presented at the Inter-American Commission on Human Rights (IACHR) in Washington (March 2013). The document (in Portuguese) is available at http://artigo19.org/?p=4184.

## References

Amaral, R. and Guimarães, C. (1994) 'Media monopoly in Brazil'. *Journal of Communication*, 44(4): 26–38.

AMARC (2004) 'Quem somos'. Retrieved 19 February 2014, from http://brasil.amarc.org/quemsomos.php.

Barbosa, M. (2006) 'Imprensa e poder no Brasil pós-1930'. [Press and Power in Brazil post-1930] *Em Questão*, 12(2): 215–234.

——(2007) *História cultural da imprensa – Brasil 1900–2000* [Cultural History of the Press – Brazil 1900–2000] Rio de Janeiro: Mauad.

——(2010) *História cultural da imprensa – Brasil 1800–1900* [Cultural History of the Press – Brazil 1800–1900] Rio de Janeiro: Mauad.

Beltrán, L. R. (1979) 'A farewell to Aristotle: "Horizontal" communication'. *Cuaderno no. 48* (UNESCO).

——(2006) 'A humanizadora utopia da democratização da comunicação'. *Revista Brasileira de Ciências da Comunicação*, 29(2): 177–183.

Brittos, V. C.; Rocha, B. L. and Nazário, P. M. (2010) 'Tomando posição: Uma análise política da I conferência nacional da comunicação'. *RECIIS*, 4(4): 45–54.

Calebre, L. (2003) 'Políticas públicas culturais de 1924 a 1945: O rádio em destaque'. *Estudos Históricos*, 31: 161–181.

Cañizales, A. (2011) 'Milestones of communication and democracy in Latin American thought'. *Journal of Latin American Communication Research*, 1(1): 15–32.

Carvalho, J. M. d. (2013) 'La implantación de la televisión digital en Brasil y Chile: Tendencias y asimetrías'. *Cuadernos De Información*, 32(101): 110.

Cassol, D. B. (2003) 'A democratização da comunicação no Brasil: Anotações teóricas e história do movimento'. (Bachelor Degree, Universidade Federal do Rio Grande do Sul).

Faoro, R. (1973) *Os donos do poder*, second edition. Rio de Janeiro: Editora Globo.

Fávero, O. (2006) *Uma pedagogia da participação popular: Análise da prática educativa do MEB – movimento de educação de base (1961–1966)*. Campinas (SP): Autores Associados.

FNDC. (2011) 'Duas décadas de luta pela democracia'. *MídiaCom Democracia: Revista do Fórum Nacional Pela Democratização Da Comunicação*, 12: 12–14.

Frei, Betto. (1985) *O que é comunidade eclesial de base?*, Fifth edition. São Paulo: Editora Brasiliense.

Gohn, M. d. G. (2010) *Movimentos sociais e redes de mobilizações civis no Brasil contemporáneo*. Petrópolis (RJ): Editora Vozes.

Gumucio-Dagron, A. (2001) *Making Waves: Participatory Communication for Social Change*. New York: The Rockefeller Foundation.

Hallin, D. C. and Papathanassopoulos, S. (2002) 'Political clientelism and the media: Southern European and Latin America in comparative perspective'. *Media, Culture & Society*, 24(2): 175–195.

Jambeiro, O.; Santos, S. d.; Ribeiro, A. and Ferreira, S. A. (2000) 'Regulação da radiodifusão: A concessão de frequências no governo provisório de Vargas (1930–1934)'. *EPTIC (Revista De Economia Política Das Tecnologias Da Informação E Comunicação)*, (3): 97–113.

Martin-Barbero, J. (1993) *Communication, Culture and Hegemony: From Media to Mediations*. London: Sage.

Matos, C. (2008) *Journalism and Political Democracy in Brazil*. Plymouth (UK): Lexington Books.

——(2012) 'Media Democratization in Brazil: Achievements and future challenges'. *Critical Sociology*, 38(6): 863–876.

Mattos, S. (1982) *The Impact of the 1964 Revolution on Brazilian Television*. San Antonio (Texas): V. Klingensmith Independent Publisher.

Melo, J. M. d. (2006) *Teoria do jornalismo: Identidades brasileiras*. São Paulo: Paulus.

Paiva, R.; Malerba, J. P. and Custódio, L. (2013) 'Comunidade gerativa e "Comunidade de afeto": Propostas conceituais para estudos comparativos de comunicação comunitária'. *Animus: Revista Interamericana De Comunicação Midiática*, 12(24): 244–262.

Peruzzo, C. M. K. (1998) *Comunicação nos movimentos populares: A participação na construção da cidadania*. Petrópolis (RJ): Editora Vozes.

——(2011) *El lugar de la comunicación comunitaria en las políticas públicas de comunicación en Brasil*, pp. 123–141 in Peruzzo, C. M. K.;Tufte, T. and Casanova, J. V. (eds.) *Trazos de una otra comunicación en América Latina: Prácticas comunitarias, teorías y demandas sociales*. Barranquilla (Colombia): Editorial Universidad del Norte.

Porto, M. (2012) *Media Power and Democratization in Brazil: TV Globo and the Dilemmas of Political Accountability*. New York: Routledge.

Quirós, F. and Segovia, A. (1996) 'La conferencia de San José de Costa Rica (1976)'. *CIC: Cuadernos De Información Y Comunicación*, 2: 63–80.

Ramos, M. C. (1998) 'Televisão a cabo no Brasil: Desestatização, reprivatização e controle público'. *Intexto*, 2(4): 1–20.

Reimberg, C. O. (2012) 'Exercendo o direito de comunicar'. *Extraprensa (USP)*, 10: 88–96.

Santos, J. M. (1995) 'A democratização da comunicação no Brasil nos discursos da sociedade civil brasileira – 1974/1994'. *Ordem/Desordem*, 12: 9–16.

Schiller, H. I. (1978) 'Decolonization of information: Efforts toward a new international order'. *Latin American Perspectives*, 5(1): 35–48.

Sodré, N. W. (1999) *História da imprensa no Brasil* [History of the Press in Brazil], Fourth edition. Rio de Janeiro: Mauad.

Sóter, J. (2009) 'Apresentação'. Retrieved 19 February 2014, from www.abraconacional. org/diretoria/diretoria-2001/.

Straubhaar, J. D. (1991) 'Beyond media imperialism: Assymetrical interdependence and cultural proximity'. *Critical Studies in Mass Communication*, 8: 39–59.

Waisbord, S. (2000) 'Media in South America: Between the rock of the state and the hard place of the market', pp. 50–62, in Curran, J. and Park, M. (eds.) *De-Westernizing Media Studies*. London: Routledge.

——(2013) *Reinventing Professionalism: Journalism and News in Global Perspective*. Cambridge: Polity Press.

Wilkin, P. (2008) 'Global communication and political culture in the semi-periphery: The rise of the Globo corporation', pp. 93–114, in Constantinou, C. M.; Richmond, O. P. and Watson, A. (eds.) *Cultures and Politics of Global Communication*. Cambridge: Cambridge University Press.

# Chapter 6

# Russia: post-Soviet, post-modern and post-empire media

*Elena Vartanova*

Since the eighteenth century, Russia has always played a significant though varying role in European and global politics. As a Eurasian Empire, it has had a strong economic and cultural influence over a vast territory, stretching from the Baltic Sea in the north to the Far East, which was responsible for the rise of Russia as a key actor in regional and global politics, especially in the twentieth century. As the largest territory in the world, connecting different continents, Russia's geopolitical position is strategically important and this, combined with its great wealth of natural resources, explains its role in global industrial development. Population growth in the nineteenth and twentieth centuries and the creation of the Soviet educational system enabled the country to become a global intellectual leader that substantially strengthened the USSR's position among the most powerful economic nations.

In the two last centuries Russia and then the USSR has lived through several waves of radical social transformations from an agrarian society and imperial monarchy (the first part of the nineteenth century) through rapid, though regionally uneven, urban capitalist industrialization to the emergence of a political party system with a strong presence of left-wing Social Democrats under the rule of a monarch (in the second half of the nineteenth century), which, though delayed by World War I, led to a short-lived multi-party democracy (February–October, 1917). After the Bolshevik revolution in October 1917, an entirely new Socialist system based on the Communist Party's ideological monopoly and a state-controlled planned economy was established for almost 80 years. This ended with a period of 'mature socialist' democracy, an economic recession and with President Gorbachev's new policies of (economic) acceleration, (political) 'perestroika' and (media) 'glasnost'.

Introduced in 1985, as top-down Communist party reforms, these resulted in the collapse of the USSR (with a population of 250 million) and the establishment of Russia (with about 143 million inhabitants in 2012) as an independent state. This process was characterized by liberalization in various areas of societal life, the introduction of a market economy and political systems inspired by 'Western' models of liberal democracies (Vartanova, 2012: 119). The bipolar world of the Cold War was shaped by an opposition of the Soviet

Union and the US. However, as Straubhaar pointed out, 'the USSR, along with the People's Republic of China, had been the primary alternative to the world capitalist system only until the late-1980s, but Wallerstein (1979) had ... anticipated that neither would likely be able to resist the draw of an otherwise completely dominant global capitalist system' (Straubhaar, 2010: 253).

After the dissolution of the USSR, and the end of the Cold War, the geo-political situation dramatically changed, making Russia's global position rather different to that of the USSR in the twentieth century. Today, Russia is a federal, semi-presidential republic, comprising 85 federal states, and in terms of land it is still the largest country in the world, with extremely rich natural resources, such as oil, gas, mines, etc., though not all of it is good for agriculture.

After the collapse of the USSR at the end of 1991, a liberal policy was adopted in its most radical form – 'shock therapy' – with simultaneous liberalization of prices for the vast majority of goods and services, rapid privatization of state property (including media and telecommunications companies) and the final abolition of the state monopoly of foreign trade and other economic activities. In the 2000s big business strengthened its position in the economy but in terms of production the fuel, energy and natural resource companies still remain the leaders. The role of the state in the economy has gradually declined, but is still influential. With the 2008 global crisis, the Russian state increased its support to the banking sector and its presence in the real sector of the economy. The level of direct and indirect state involvement in the Russian economy is currently estimated at 50 per cent (*Encyclopedia Myrovoji Industrii SMI*, 2013: 259).

Although Russia lost almost one third of the territory of the Soviet period, it retained a leading role at the regional level, being politically and economically the driver of the Commonwealth of Independent States (11 countries of the former USSR – Azerbaijan, Armenia, Belarus, Kazakhstan, Kyrgyzstan, Moldova, Russia, Tajikistan, Turkmenistan, Uzbekistan and the Ukraine)[1]. Moreover, it is the backbone of the Customs Union and the Collective Security Treaty Organization (CSTO). Russia also plays a significant role in other regional organizations such as the Eurasian Economic Community (EAEC or EurAsEC), the Organization of Central Asian Cooperation (OCAC), the Organization of the Black Sea Economic Cooperation (BSEC), the Shanghai Cooperation Organization (SCO) and many others.

In addition, Russia has risen as a trans-regional religious power due to its growing role in the worldwide unification of the Orthodox Churches and diasporas. Recent attempts to improve the distribution of media products to Russian diasporas and worldwide audiences using the Russia Today TV channel, and the re-positioning of the multimedia news agency RIA Novosty as the internationally oriented media company, demonstrate the goal of influencing the global news agenda 'from the Russian' point of view. Russia has been exploring different ways of positioning itself as one of 'the global powers', from membership of global power alliances such as G8 and G20 to being the leader of the Eurasia and Russian/Orthodox civilization (Huntington, 1996; Gumilev, 2001).

Russian media had a rather late start. Although the first Russian newspaper *Vedomosti* was established in 1703, print media as an industry started to develop only in the 1820s and 1830s with a predominance of magazines. Russian postal distribution was rather underdeveloped until the late-nineteenth century, and so newspapers were limited to the 'capitals' – Moscow and St. Petersburg – and large industrial centres. However, after the social reforms of the 1860s, the peasantry gained its political and economic freedom, which resulted in a rapid development of capitalism, supported by the growth of daily newspapers in major urban centres.

Literary journals were the main form of print journalism and literary criticism was the leading genre until nearly the end of the nineteenth century. The first Russian journalists came from the field of literature, creating a foundation for public debates, particularly on general cultural questions (Mirsky, 1999: 124). The Russian view of literature assumed a much broader social and cultural role for it than in other countries, thus often merging it with journalistic activity (Vartanova, 2012: 136). The history of Russian journalism contains many examples of the journalistic activities of famous writers – Alexander Pushkin, Nikolay Nekrasov, Fyodor Dostoyevsky, Leo Tolstoy and Anton Chekhov (Martinsen, 1998).

The core feature of journalism in the Russian Empire for centuries was the practice of censorship. Pre-publication censorship was introduced in 1804, and from that time Russian journalism never experienced freedom of speech. The liberally minded Tsar Alexander II (1855–1881) did change the basis of this legislation from pre-publication censorship to a more punitive post-publication system based on legal responsibility. Although censorship was abolished by the 1905 Revolution, freedom of speech was only accepted in April 1917 by the Temporary Government with the first Law on Freedom of Information, but this decree was only in force until October 1917. In Soviet Russia and later the USSR (from 1918 until 1991), the censorship system operated under the central censorship office, Glavlit, subordinate to Communist Party media regulation. From 1922 on, it subjected the mass media to preventive censorship, suppressing political resistance by shutting down dissident voices. These long-lived censorship practices contributed significantly to the establishment of the self-censorship mechanisms that still play a role in journalists' newsroom practices.

The development of the Russian Imperial press reflects trends in political, economic and cultural life. Before the reforms of the 1860s, the number of dailies remained rather low: their circulations did not exceed 2,000 copies and they were located mostly in St. Petersburg, Moscow and a few regional centres. But the progress of capitalism stimulated the evolution of the press market. In 1889 there existed 667 publications in the Russian language, in 1901, 1,074 in all languages (900 in Russian), and in 1905, before the First Russian Revolution, 1,795 in total (1,400 in Russian). At its peak, in 1912, more than 2,500 publications were published in Russia, although the statistics from different sources vary. However, until the Socialist Revolution, access to newspapers remained rather low with one newspaper printed per 128,000 Russians.

During the 80 years of its existence, the Soviet Union created a multi-layer media system serving the aims of political propaganda as well as creating unified public opinion, supporting new 'Soviet' identity and promoting Soviet/Russian culture. The Soviet media system was quantitatively well-developed. By 1985, the start of Perestroika, about 8.5 thousand print media outlets were published, with an annual circulation of 180 million copies. The largest newspapers were *Komsomolskaya Pravda* (17 million), *Trud* (18 million), and *Pravda* (10 million). About 13,500 magazines were published in 55 languages of the Soviet nations and ethnic groups, with the circulation of 3.5 billion copies annually. Before the dissolution of the Soviet Union, broadcasting included 180 radio houses, more than 5,000 radio stations and 130 TV programming centres. Availability of the first national TV was almost universal, besides, there were numerous regional stations with local programming and the national educational channel (Channel 4).

While the initial political and economic aims of 'Perestroika' may have failed, its cultural goals are still valued highly by many Russians, and this provokes much nostalgia among older audiences. The Soviet media system was characterized by a high degree of centralization and the absence of the profit motive, which resulted from the ideological role given to media in Soviet society. The structure of the Soviet media remained artificial because it responded to the needs of the integrated and heavily centralized political and financial elite, the 'nomenclatura', which financed the media operation to a great extent. The Soviet media system was characterized by the following:

- top-down control of media outlets, with an emphasis on high-circulation, universally distributed and cheap print media;
- surveillance of content production and control of content flows, particularly of the creative industries – cinema, popular music, fashion;
- planned financing from central state-Communist party resources;
- heavy investment in infrastructure (postal delivery, TV terrestrial network, satellite communication) leading to a high penetration of television and radio;
- no attention to audience needs and very immature advertising.

Journalism in the Soviet Union was described as 'a social activity of collection, transmission and periodical dissemination of information through mass communication channels aimed at propaganda and agitation' (Ovsepyan, 1979: 7). It had a clear normative character: professional norms included the priority of accuracy over topicality and timeliness; the supremacy of feature and polemic genres involving personal judgments and options; and the role of 'publicistics' (political or moral essays with moral reasoning) linking journalism to ideology.

## The contemporary Russian media landscape:
## print v. broadcasting, analogue v. digital, old v. new

Rapid changes in the behaviour, structure and performance of the Russian media have shown that the transition from an old (ideologically driven and print-based) media system to a new (commercialized and digital) one was turbulent. It happened within a historically short period of two decades. Moreover, it occurred in the context of the political and economic decentralization of the country, and this led to the rise of new leaders in media markets at federal and regional levels. This decentralization resulted in dissimilar regional media systems, uneven distribution of media economic wealth, various regional forms of media–state authorities relations, diverse types of mono- and multiculturalism in journalism and different significance of federal media in particular regional markets (Resnyanskaya and Fomicheva, 1999; Pietilainen, 2002; Yershov, 2012).

The general picture of the Russian media, at least in quantitative terms, is highly diverse. In print media, the total number of registered newspaper and magazine titles is 59,000, of which around a third are published. There are about 2,700 radio stations, of which 85.5 per cent are private, 12.6 per cent state and only 1.9 per cent are non-state, non-profit stations. Russian television consists of mainly private, regional or local stations: there are seven state channels and 20 nationwide broadcasters; there are 50 regional channels with their own content but 900 regional stations which broadcast the network programmes of national channels.

Russians are very fond of mobile telephones, with 225.1 million mobile phones in use (SIM cards represent 157 per cent of the population); 70 million people (49 per cent of the population) use the Internet via computers; 25.7 million (18 per cent of the population) use the Internet via mobile phone (including tablets). Russian Internet space contains 4.6 million registered domains/websites (31.9 websites per thousand people). 65.8 million Russians have accounts in social media, and this represents 46 per cent of the population.

As a result of the post-Soviet changes, Russian media now represents a unique combination of heterogeneous processes:

- rapid growth in the number of private media companies operating in all segments of a liberalized media industry, including traditionally popular print and broadcasting media and new areas such as cable and satellite TV, television production, telecommunications, online media, search engines, etc.;
- uneasy coexistence of state interests (state-owned and operated media companies) and overtly commercial interests (private media) with the growing civil sector (significant components in social networks on the Internet);
- clashes of innovative breakthrough technologies (RuNet and mobile telephony) along with the survival of print media outlets using outdated technical facilities (those in the Russian province);
- consequences of political pluralism, which sometimes result in confrontation (governmental, political and oppositional sites);

- a lack of political diversity (media markets in Tatarstan, Kalmykia, Bashkiria, or Kuban), paralleled by state media policies to guarantee cultural diversity in multicultural Russian regions;
- complementary coexistence of elite editions and channels with the media that cater for undemanding mass preferences, of private and state-owned media, of state-loyal federal TV channels and openly opposition newspapers, magazines and Internet media.

Current developments in the Russian media system need to be understood in the context of several key trends of the last two decades. These trends include the rise of television as the core medium of the Russian media system, paralleled by the decline of print media, especially daily newspapers, the growing role of the new media as a reflection of the information society's evolution, and the widening divergence of regional media systems as a reflection of Russia's regional diversity.

### The centrality of television

Television today is the most important source of international, national and even regional information for the majority of Russians. More than 90 per cent of Russians obtain their news from TV, more than 80 per cent watch it every day and about 80 per cent trust television. Terrestrial television in Russia is generally available: 99 per cent of the population receive at least one TV channel, by 2010 the average number of available channels per urban household amounted to two dozen and more than 70 per cent of the population had access to at least seven terrestrial channels.

In the first decade of the twenty-first century, rapid development and increased penetration of non-terrestrial television, already available to 40 per cent of Russians living in large industrial centres, became a crucial tendency in the TV sector. In the contemporary Russian media system, the centripetal function has moved over to the federal (nationally distributed) television, and it has taken upon itself several roles: that of a major instrument of maintaining national identity and supporting national elections; of a universally accessible channel to inform Russians about the events in the world; and of a tool to organize leisure time.

National – federal – television channels cover national politics and mass entertainment and can be divided into three major groups. The first group of 'federal public TV channels' – so decribed by Presidential decree (24 June 2009) – are nationally available, but do not have the programming responsibilities of public-service broadcasters. The group includes:

- state-private owned channel Pervyi kanal (The First Channel), operated by the 'Pervyi kanal' broadcaster;
- state channels Rossija 1, Rossija 2, Rossija K (Culture) and Rossija 24, owned and operated by the VGTRK state broadcaster;

- children's channel Karousel operated by the '*Pervyi kanal*' and *VGTRK*;
- Pyatyi kanal (Channel 5) – the only regional channel from St. Petersburg with national distribution;
- commercial broadcaster NTV, owned by state operated Gazprommedia, an affiliate of the national monopoly GazProm company;
- the state channel TV-Tsentr (TV Centre) owned by the Moscow government.

With the Russian digital switch over planned for 2015, these channels are planned to become free and universally available as part of the first digital multiplex. The state maintains a firm position in the television industry by supporting the technical infrastructure, controlling the financial operations of the state channels and formally and informally influencing news flows.

The second group comprises the entertainment networks (REN TV, CTC, TNT), which have a strong presence in the regional markets. And the third group consists of smaller broadcasters with entertainment and niche focus such as 2x2, TV 3, Peretz, MTV, Yu, Disney, etc. The number of regional TV companies has been increasing and there are about 700 local stations, both public and private.

Major national TV channels are transmitted from Moscow via both terrestrial networks and satellites. Satellite earth stations provide access to Intelsat, Intersputnik, Eutelsat, Inmarsat and Orbita systems. In 2012, about 18 per cent of Russian viewers subscribe to cable platforms, while 12 per cent rely on satellite platforms. The regions most highly developed in this respect are Moscow, St. Petersburg and the 11 largest industrial centres (with populations greater than a million). At the same time, only 10 per cent of the country's population has access to up-to-date, integrated broadband services provided by cable operators (telephone, cable television and the Internet). In 2010, the leading cable platform providers at the national level were the Moscow-based NKS (with 4.7 million subscribers), Comstar (2.4 million), Acado (1.3 million) and the regional providers ER Telecom (880,000) and Moline (870,000).

Direct satellite broadcasting (DBS) is dominated by NTV+, established in 1998 and with a subscriber base of 550,000 in 2010, and Trikolor TV. NTV+ was the first company to try experimental high-definition television broadcasting (HDTV) in Russia. Trikolor TV, formerly Natsional'naya Sputnikovaya Kompaniya, entered the market in 2005 and offered a package of channels distributed in the European part of Russia (west of the Ural Mountains). In 2011, Trikolor TV had 3.1 million subscribers and became the largest satellite TV platform provider in Russia (and all of Eastern Europe, for that matter). Both cable and satellite TV platforms also provide limited IPTV services. In total, the Russian market of pay TV in 2010 was valued at $1.2 billion (RUB 34.9 billion).

As for other media in Russia, television can be analyzed at different levels:

- federal (national, publicly available) television channels tend to cover key issues of national politics and provide mass entertainment, to a general audience, regardless of demand or socio-demographic characteristics, which partly accounts for the presence of global and national advertisers on these channels;

- regional broadcasters have focused on catering for the needs of regional/ local audiences, elites and advertisers, though because of the economic crisis they have had to reduce local programming and news coverage;
- pay TV operators (cable, satellite) tailor their programming and advertising to their target, though fragmented, audience – urban, well-paid, highly educated and internationally concerned (Vartanova and Smirnov, 2010: 80; Televideniye v. Rossii, 2013).

Thus the contemporary Russian media landscape is characterized by the dominance of a few federal broadcasters operating 10 free on-air TV channels transmitted from Moscow. Regional TV stations are relatively insignificant, being in many cases regional affiliates of Moscow entertainment networks. But the competition from 'other' media is growing, although in different regions the challenges are also different:

- in the 'capital' cities (Moscow and St. Petersburg) challenges are coming from (mobile) digital new media;
- in large industrial centres the most visible contenders are online broadband media and cable and satellite;
- in small cities there are almost no alternatives to free on-air federal channels.

### The print media's struggle for survival

Media changes in the 2000s have resulted in the decentralization of the national economy and political life. Being heavily dependent on the centralized production processes and distribution systems of the Soviet era, post-Soviet Russian print media were not able to maintain both cheap and efficient home delivery and timely retail sales systems. As a result, the press in small towns with limited advertising markets had dramatic reductions in circulation and became very dependent on subsidies from local authorities, while newspapers in urban industrial centres began to serve the everyday cultural demands and consumption of the inhabitants, able to link distribution to the transport and trade infrastructure of these cities. The arrival of the global phenomenon of free newspapers, together with the establishment of new lifestyle and consumer habits made this development even stronger.

The pyramid structure of the press market that was at the heart of the ideologically determined and vertically hierarchical Soviet media system has been replaced by a complex of horizontally linked regional local media markets, marked by declining local print media. As the State Agency of Press and Mass Communication reported, 'two thirds of the circulation of socio-political newspapers are created by regional and local editions' (2007: 30). The number of newspaper titles increased significantly from nearly 5,000 (in 1991), to nearly 6,000 (in 2000) and to over 28,000 (in 2012), but the newspaper circulation as a whole first dropped dramatically from 160 million to 109 million (a decrease of 68 per cent) and then increased again to 232 million at time of writing (an increase of 112 per cent), though with the share of nationally distributed newspapers falling to 35 per cent. In many places, newspapers reduced publication from daily to weekly, reflecting the trend in print media from news to entertainment (SMI Rossiji, 2011). The print media also continued to decline under pressure from increasing competition from the Internet and with the impact of the global financial crisis of 2008–2010.

The lack of significant investment in printing and distribution, as well as the uneven development of regional advertising markets, clearly affected the business operations of the newspaper companies. On the one hand, the non-national press became strongly dependent on regional and local authorities, which began to provide large amounts of both formal and informal financial support. On the other hand, the privatized national dailies with established Soviet brands – *Komsomolskaya Pravda, Sovetsky Sport, Moskovsky Komsomolets, Trud, Izvestia* – retained the largest market shares, thus gaining some segments of the advertising market.

The most active private-media holding companies have built themselves up around the well-established titles: Moscow's daily newspapers – *Moskovsky Komsomolets* (Average Issue Readership (AIR): 1.4 million), *Komsomolskaya Pravda* (2.2 million) and *Izvestia* (334,900) – safeguarded their popularity outside the capital by producing inserts in cooperation with regional dailies. These dailies adopted particular content strategies similar to sensational journalism. Other leading publications are state-owned: *Rossijskaya Gazeta* (1 million), *Sport-Express* (523,900), *Sovetsky Sport* (418,900) and *Trud* (196,900). The position of quality newspapers is more problematic. *Kommersant* (219,900) or *Vedomosti* (134,600) cannot compete with local tabloids or nationally distributed mass-circulation dailies.

In contrast, the magazine segment of the print media is a more positive case, being the most globalized and successful medium, though with more limited range than newspapers. Magazine publishing, particularly Russian franchises of global brands, is still more attractive to investors than newspapers and other media because of higher advertising revenues and less expensive distribution. The exposure of Russia to Western consumerism has increased the popularity of publications carrying lifestyle content, which also explains the prevalence of foreign owners in this sector, compared with any other media platform. It is interesting to note that about one third of magazines' circulation is printed abroad – in Finland, Croatia, Poland and Italy.

The bulk of the magazine sector's revenue (60 per cent) comes from the Moscow metropolitan area. In terms of popularity, the publications most in demand are illustrated TV guides: *Antenna/Telesem* (AIR: 10 million), *Telenedelya* (4.3 million), and *7 dnei* (3.7 million). Among women's magazines, *Liza*, a cheap weekly with a mixture of practical advice for working females, recipes and fashion patterns, is the most popular (3.1 million). Glossy magazines represent a comparatively small but vigorous sector of the magazine industry. The German company Burda, American–Russian Hearst-Shkulev Media Group/InterMediaGroup and Finnish-owned company Sanoma Independent Media have adapted international periodicals like *Men's Health, Burda, Harper's Bazaar, Cosmopolitan, Maxim, Esquire, Elle*, etc. for the Russian market.

### The Internet and mobile phone as media innovation

The Russian Internet began to develop between 1993 and 1997, in which period the number of users doubled each year. In 2012, the maximum number of Russian Internet users stood close to 60.41 million (about 55 per cent of the population). The progress of the Internet initially took place in big cities, especially in Moscow, but in recent years the inequality of geographical regions has been steadily decreasing. Now residents of Moscow and St. Petersburg represent less than one third of Russian users.

In the Russian media system, the Internet has become the most open medium, thus closely corresponding to the concept of the public sphere, regardless of attempts by the Russian legislative authorities to introduce special regulation into the field. With its increasing penetration, the Internet, together with its related services, is becoming the most serious challenger to the traditional media: television, radio and the press. According to FOM surveys, in autumn 2012, the Russian Internet monthly audience was about 52 per cent of the adult population, about two thirds (47 million) being daily users. Another study found that an overwhelming majority of urban residents (94 per cent) have access to the Internet, with most connected to broadband networks.

Internet users today are active, generally well-educated and also form the wealthiest market segments. These are professionals, high-school and university students and graduates, people who look to the future, members of the modern audience, that very creative class which sets the tone in the context of the globalizing economy. The most active group of Russian Internet users is young residents of industrialized urban areas. In Russian cities with a population over one million, about 70 per cent of young people under 22 are active Internet users. The digital divide, as defined by various indicators from access to technologies and communication networks to lifestyle and digital literacy, remains a problem in Russia.

However, the main focus of Internet news search and communication in Russia is the social media, which include the blogosphere, social networks, microblogs (Twitter) and the like. As of spring 2010, RuNet comprised 12 million blogs, 10 per cent of which were regularly updated. As the data for 2013 indicates, social networks in Russia became the most popular Internet resource for Russian users (34 per cent of all audiences), followed by search engines and email services. However, the users of social networks are characterized by generational differences. For instance, younger users access fewer networks through mobile devices while older users access more networks from personal computers.

Traditional media companies have also been active on the Internet. There are more than 5 million sites in the Russian-language sector of the Internet, RuNet. Several popular newspapers, like *Nezavisimaya Gazeta*, were already exploring the Internet in 1994. The first online media projects were started by literary postmodernist writers, who launched the *Russky Zhurnal*. Currently the most popular online news media are *Lenta.ru*, *KP.ru*, *Gazeta.ru*, *RG.ru*, *NEWSru.com* and *LifeNews.ru*.

In fact, the Internet as a communication platform has replaced traditional mass media in terms of rapidly delivering information and shaping the political agenda. The Russian Internet today is a unique communication and information channel, which provides the user with maximum freedom of choice and content. Political and intellectual preferences are presented on the Internet in the form of polarized viewpoints. The Internet allows for great freedom of choice of diverse content, ranging from information to education, and serves as an information menu where people can choose any information they want. Major political parties and official state agencies also operate numerous sites, but a diversity of political and cultural views is created by the Internet presence of many oppositional parties. This was demonstrated during the 2010s during several election campaigns, when the provision of news from oppositional parties or protest groups by traditional broadcast media was limited. It is also indicative that online media, especially social networks, have shown their potential for mobilization, becoming an instrument for organizing and coordinating protest activities in Moscow and other large industrial centres (The Russian Awakening, 2012: 11).

## Media for different Russias

In terms of media consumption, access to new digital technologies and the use of digital media, Russia has several media cultures, which correlate with territorial differences in income, demographic features, lifestyles and values. As Zoubarevich argues, today's Russia might be characterized by the coexistence of three layers, representing different levels of economic and social development:

Russia One, as the country of large industrial centres and the middle class;
Russia Two, as the semi-urbanized space;
Russia Three, as 'sleeping' agricultural areas (Zoubarevich, 2013).

Consequently, there is a significant difference in the penetration of new technologies, media demand and use in these three layers. The uneven media realities of the 'three Russias' demonstrates the need to approach the Russian media system differently, bearing in mind the complexity of the country as a federal state, with strong and, at the same time, unequal regional administrative areas, uneven wealth distribution among regions and population, and diversity of cultures and lifestyles.

With programming strategies based on the growing popularity of Russian drama and soap operas, features, cultural and non-political programmes and reliance on imported entertainment formats, television is reflecting the global trend towards infotainment (Rantanen, 2002). Evening news and current-affairs programmes that were popular among intellectuals and civic activists during the 'glasnost' years have clearly lost out to online media. Although politically they are much more free and open than the federal TV channels, this has contributed significantly to the fragmentation and division of the Russian public sphere. However, it should be stressed that over such a vast territory and given the obvious unevenness of the technological infrastructure, television remains the only national mass medium in terms of penetration and access that is available to construct a modern Russian information space and support a common public sphere. Thus television, being an important centrifugal force in Russian politics, plays a key role in the federal/national media system. However, this has resulted in a form of 'division of labour': the central (federal) channels cover national politics and mass entertainment – given their co-operation with global and national advertisers – while the regional media (both audiovisual and print ones) focus on regional/local audiences and advertisers (Rantanen and Vartanova, 2003).

Another particular feature of Russian television, linked to its unique character as a unifying medium, is its crucial mobilizing role during election campaigns. Already in the mid-1990s it became clear that it was not possible to construct a new Russian political system based on a stable multi-party system overnight. Some scholars argued that television had taken over the traditional role that political parties played in the election process in post-Soviet Russia. In a series of elections, the electorate was mobilized by the main national television channels rather than by traditional political organizations. According to media critic Rykovtseva, television constituted an 'airwave (or broadcast) party', while Russian political parties were a much less real phenomenon (Vartanova, 2012: 130).

Print media have lost their leading role in the media system not only because of an economic crisis but mostly by their loss of ability to shape the national 'agenda', a role which has been played, over recent years, by federal television broadcasting. Apart from reductions in distribution, the deterioration of the print media has had negative effects on journalism. Serious political and intellectual public discussions have suffered the most. The national agenda has 'lost' a number of issues important for national identity. Today, only the weekly business magazines are trying to continue the traditions of the quality press, though the discussion of non-economic issues is minimal. Attempts to establish a universal (in terms of the audience) national (in terms of distribution and agenda) news magazine have not progressed far. Although the success of 'Russky Reportyor' in the regions (a project by the 'Ekspert' publishing house) is some sign for optimism, its sales in Moscow and other large cities are far from being satisfactory.

It is clear that neither federal television nor the quality press has fulfilled its potential to formulate the national news agenda. In an attempt to satisfy advertisers' needs, Russian TV has shifted the emphasis to entertainment, with elements of infotainment, a tabloid style and journalism 'on demand'. The print media, in turn, focusing on the needs of regional and local audiences, are trying to outperform the national media in their informational closeness to the audience.

New media in Russia are challenging the traditional media in terms of content, offering not only additional, but also alternative news agendas, broadening the diversity of ideological views, as well as contributing to political and cultural pluralism. Even bearing in mind the continuing 'digital divide' in Internet use in Russia, it is clear that the impact of new media on political and cultural communication in Russia is increasing. Moreover, the political split in the Russian society is more and more being reflected in patterns of media use: young city residents get their news agendas from new media, while middle-aged, politically concerned Russians rely upon TV or print media, especially quality weeklies. This has inspired some scholars to take further the idea of the 'TV party', with the potential for an 'Internet party' as a form of political engagement.

Thus, the structure and roles of different media in the evolving media environment in Russia are far from those described in traditional academic approaches. The mass circulation, print-based press considered by Hallin and Mancini (2012) as the main feature of a modern media system no longer plays an influential role in involving the Russian public in the process of democracy. On the contrary, the powerful role of federal/national television in public communication, together with that of distributing mass entertainment, was vital in the post-Soviet transitional period, in political mobilization and identity building, as well as popular leisure, though this may also be true of other 'transitional societies'. However, this period is now coming to an end with the growing penetration of new media, the diversification of online content, new chances for interactivity of users and the increasing influence of social networks in a hybrid communication and information-gathering system.

## Media and state in Russia: a complex relationship

Media–state relations in Russia have traditionally been at the core of the media system and defined the nature, functions and roles of the media. Moreover, as Trakhtenberg argues:

> [R]elations with the state ... and a broad cultural context within which the Russian media have been developing had nothing in common with the 1st Amendment to the USA Constitution. Moreover, these relations have nothing in common with the whole Anglo-American tradition that

sees proper functioning of the mass media as a fundamental element of the civil society and of the system of representative democracy.

(Trakhtenberg, 2007: 122)

It is certainly symbolic that the first Russian newspaper *Vedomosty* (1703) was initiated and even operated for some time by the reformist tsar Peter the Great. In his attempts to modernize Russia along western European lines, he set up a quality newspaper addressed to the Russian aristocracy. The aim was to harness the press as a means of social and political management, as an indispensable element of the European societal model. Since then, the media in Russia have often been used as tools of social and ideological management, making the tradition of 'press/mass media serving the nation' (in many cases the state) durable and stable in all historical periods from Imperial Russia, through Bolshevik Russia to the USSR, including that of Glasnost (Vartanova, 2012: 131–135).

In the 1990s, academic literature on the evolution of post-Soviet/post-socialist societies and developing countries often suggests there is a model of the so-called transitional period, which integrates the market economy and democratic political system – two interrelated elements of the new society. This 'double teleology', according to Sparks (2013), presupposes similar vectors of socio-economic development in these countries, which are stimulated by regulated processes and which expect a transition towards universal and similar market systems and political structures. It is worthwhile exploring this approach in analyzing the economic developments of the Russian media.

The actual transformation of the Russian media business has called into doubt the correctness of this 'double teleology' approach. For example, a study of regional press and TV markets in Russia after twenty years of transition to the market economy has shown that the formation and vectors of development of independent daily newspapers and broadcast TV channels cannot be explained solely by market forces. The surveys did not reveal any clear correlation with the development of advertising markets, funding availability or local business activities (Vyrkovsky and Makeenko, 2014). This is one of the rare research projects in which Russian media has been analyzed as an industry (especially the industries based on small and medium-sized businesses), which demonstrated that it was not possible to interpret its functioning merely through the prism of the concept of transitional media. It was clear that there was a need for a new angle, and the approach based on institutional economics has become valuable in this analysis.

Supporting the theory of institutionalism, Russian economists doubt that the transitional period should be understood as a simple and linear process of the formation of conceptually new economic and social conditions in the country. The modern Russian economy is the product of historically formed institutions, norms, rules and enforcement mechanisms that have been part of Russia's national socio-economic system regardless of its name or appearance. These institutions contribute a lot to the modern economic mentality of Russian governments (powers), businesses and consumers. The same situation can be observed in the media industry and its key players – entrepreneurs, investors, managers, advertisers, audiences and regulators. One can hardly understand the level of the state involvement in the media industry without taking into account the specifics of national institutions and traditions.

The institutional approach makes evident the substantial role of the state in media economics. It will certainly differ from the role of the state, for example, in Western Europe, where mass media are perceived as part of a specific industry with a high level of social responsibility, which makes it impossible to leave it controlled by the market forces only. That is why in Western Europe a specific media policy is being formed, which is understood as a framework to stimulate particular political and cultural roles of commercial media enterprises and to guarantee public service obligations of media.

The level of involvement of the state in Russia's media industry reflects the historically important role of the state in all spheres of life, including the economy. That is the reason why the media industry in Russia, like a number of other industries, depends greatly on the state, and depends on it not only as a regulator, but also as an owner, investor, distributor of goods, services and finances. Two cases are particularly illustrative, those of the print media and television. In 2012, the Federal Agency on Press and Mass Communications provided about 65 billion RR in financial support to the electronic media and more than 5 billion RR for the print media.

As for television, formally or informally, the state remains the major actor in the sector. Regardless of ownership structures, Russian television is financed primarily by advertising and sponsorship, however, but in ownership and programming it is a mixture of two models: the state-owned and commercial. In 2013, after two decades of debate and anticipation, a public-service channel OTR *(Obshestvennoe televidenie Rossii)* was established, but its programmes and poor economic perfomance caused some concern. By operating the VGTRK broadcaster, the state gained complete control over the nationally distributed TV channels (Rossija 1, Rossija 2, Rossija 24 and Rossija K), radio channels Radio Rossija and Mayak. VGTRK also includes a network of 80 regional television stations and 100 centres for broadcast transmission. Another important player, Gazprom Media, the owner of NTV and TNT, is an affiliate of the state-owned Gazprom company, which also increases the presence of the state in the Russian TV industry.

With regard to theoretical or methodological approaches to studying inter-cultural differences or similarities between the BRICS countries, the institutional approach enables us to say there cannot be any universal model of economic or social development based on Western models. Since the BRICS countries possess historically formed systems of social and economic institutions, and informal collective agreements based on the traditional and cultural differences of these countries, national identity is going to dominate there. Such identity can adjust to various conditions, for instance, the demands of a modern global market economy, but cannot be transformed fundamentally. Thorough analysis of the specifics of the media industries in each country will provide empirical confirmation of this.

## Conclusions

Today's Russian media are far from conforming to a theoretical set of features associated with a 'Western' or 'Global North' media model, even if we recognize that this kind of model never existed in media reality (Sparks, 2013: 123–126). In the last two decades, after the fall of the USSR and the social transformation that followed, Russian media have lived through dramatic changes, which many foreign media scholars have described as 'dual transition' or even 'revolution' (Nordenstreng et al., 2001; McNair, 1994; 2000; Rantanen, 2002; Mickiewicz, 1997; 2008; De Smaele, 1999; Oates, 2006). However, it became clear that although normative ideals are based on a set of prescriptive roles and expected functions, there are not many similar media systems outside the Western world (Hallin and Mancini, 2012) and each of them is 'adapting' to the Western model in a different scope and with different success (Toepfl, 2013: 251). Thus, the only trend that might be identified for the majority of the states is hybridization (Voltmer, 2008).

Simultaneously, Russian media scholars have found evidence of tremendous changes in media structures and practices, although many of them have elements of continuity and long-term development rooted both in the Soviet approaches to the media and journalism, and also in Russian cultural traditions and social norms and informal collective agreements that have influenced public communication and media practices (Zassoursky, 2001; Ivanitsky, 2010; SMI v. Menjajusheisja Rossiji, 2009). Nevertheless, the introduction of market relations and advertising into the media system, together with the liberalization of telecommunications in Russia in the 1990s–2000s, have resulted in the emergence of new business models and new ownership/financing structures, the diversification of media companies, multiplication of channels, convergence of media business and the rise of the new media (Vartanova, Nieminen and Salminen, 2009). All of this has changed the old media–power relations' paradigm and called for a broad discussion of the 'post-communism' media changes and media model in a post-modern context (Ekecrantz, 2007: 75). By describing a post-modernist media–society model, he underlined the interactive relationship between media and audiences, the importance of culture and the downplay of technology, politics and economy (ibid.: 77). Further, he put forward an integrated institutional model in which media are mixing (or linking closely) culture, politics, economy and technology, contributing 'to the restructuring of the whole institutional setup, the social order' (ibid.: 78).

The new model of 'media–culture–political–technological–industrial complex' embraces also national characteristics, and therefore developments in 'post-communism' reflect much more global clash of media civilization and the state. The case of the Russian media obviously demonstrates a merger of 'the old and stale political structures on the one hand, and the modern capitalistic consumer culture of the other' (ibid. 83) and is moving towards further diversification between 'authoritainment' and new media activism. And this, concludes Ekekrantz, has much in common with other regions in the East and West.

It is definitely a challenge to analyze BRICS media within the global context and at the national level. In fact, there should be a comparative and detailed research of media models/systems/ecology beyond the traditional Western world. In certain ways this comparison should be aimed to decrease the normativity of Western media theories and to introduce new approaches to shaping and 'modelling' media systems. Such variables as countries' territories, legacy of the history, nature of a nation state, traditions of culture and levels of multiculturalism, as well as informal agreements between various social actors and forms of civil activism, definitely affect media structures, conduct and performance. Particular attention needs to be given to the media–state relationships in a more positive sense, assessing the state as the 'third force' to support the media system economically (in the context of economic hardships) and in terms of media policies (in conditions of an undeveloped civil society). In addition, since BRICS today remains more an economic than a cultural entity, analysis of BRICS media definitely needs a clear political economy approach, including the analysis of media and power relations in the countries and at the geopolitical level.

With regard to theoretical or methodological approaches to studying intercultural differences or similarities between the BRICS countries, we would argue that there cannot be any universal model of economic or social development on the basis of 'Western' models. As North points out:

> It is the admixture of formal rules, informal norms, and enforcement characteristics that shapes economic performance. While the rules may be changed overnight, the informal norms usually change only gradually. Since it is the norms that provide 'legitimacy' to a set of rules, revolutionary change is never as revolutionary as its supporters' desire ... The implication is that transferring the formal political and economic rules of successful Western market economies to Third World and Eastern European economies is not a sufficient condition for good economic performance. Privatization is not a panacea for solving poor economic performance.
>
> (North, 1990: 366)

Since the BRICS countries possess a historically formed system of social and economic institutions, and informal collective agreements based on the traditional and cultural differences of these countries, national identity is going to dominate there. Such identities can adjust to various conditions – for instance, the demands of the modern global market economy – but cannot be transformed fundamentally.

## Note

1 In 2014 Ukranian parliament started debates on the country's full withdrawal from this organization.

## References

Amsden, A. H. (2001) *The Rise of 'The Rest'. Challenges to the West from Late-Industrializing Economies*. Oxford: Oxford University Press.

Becker, J. (2004) Lessons from Russia: A Neo-Authoritarian Media System. *European Journal of Communication*, 19(2): 139–163.

De Smaele, H. (1999) The Applicability of Western Media Models on the Russian Media System. *European Journal of Communication*, 14(2): 173–189.

Ekecrantz, J. (2007) Post-post-communist Media? A Challenge for Comparative Media Studies, in Vartanova, E. (ed.) *Media and Change*. Moscow: MediaMir; Faculty of Journalism, Lomonosov Moscow State University.

*Encyclopedia Myrovoji Industrii SMI* (2013) (*Encyclopedia of World Media Industries*). Edited by E. Vartanova. Moscow: Aspekt Press.

Grinberg, T. (2005) *Politicheskie Trchnologii: PR I Reklama* (Political Technologies: PR and Advertisement). Moscow: Aspekt Press.

Growth Environment Score (GES) The Global Sherpa. Available at: http://www.global-sherpa.org/bric-countries-brics.

Gumilev, L. (2001) *Etnogenez I Biosfera Zemli* (Ethnogenesis and the Earth's Biosphere). Moscow: Izdatel'stvo ACT.

Hallin, D. and Mancini, P. (eds.) (2012) *Comparing Media Systems Beyond the Western World*. Cambridge: Cambridge University Press.

Huntington, S. P. (1996) *The Clash of Civilizations and the Remaking of the World Order*. New York: Simon and Shuster.

Ivanitsky, V. (2010) *Modernizaciya Zhurnalistiki: Metodologichesky Etjud* (Modernization of Journalism: A Methodological Study). Moscow: Moscow University Press; Faculty of Journalism, Lomonosov Moscow State University.

Jakubowicz, K. (2007) *Rude Awakening: Social and Media Change in Central and Eastern Europe*. New York: Hampton Press.

Martinsen, D. (1998) *Literary Journals in Imperial Russia*. Cambridge: Cambridge University Press.

McNair, B. (1994) Media in Post-Soviet Russia: An Overview. *European Journal of Communication*, 9(2): 115–135.

——(2000) 'Power, Profit, Corruption, and Lies: The Russian Media in the 1990s', in Curran, J. and Park, M. J. (eds.) *De-Westernizing Media Studies*. London: Routledge.

MQuail, J. (2013) *Journalism and Society*. London: Sage.

Mickiewicz, E. (1997) *Changing Channels: Television and the Struggle for Power in Russia*. Oxford: Oxford University Press.

——(2008) *Television, Power and the Public in Russia*. Cambridge: Cambridge University Press.

Mirsky, P. (1999) *The History of Russian Literature from Its Beginnings to 1900.* Evanston: Northwestern University Press.

Nelson, G.; Maniam, B. and Leavell, H. (2013) *BRIC: Overview and Future Outlook.* Available at: http://ehis.ebscohost.com/ehost/pdfviewer/pdfviewer?sid=ac4998da-114b-4205-beb7-32fbf7c6d3a3percent40sessionmgr113&vid=2&hid=107.

Nordenstreng, K.; Vartanova, E. and Zassoursky, Y. (eds.) (2001) *Russian Media Challenge.* Helsinki: Aleksanteri Institute.

North, D. (1990) *Institutions, Institutional Change and Economic Performance,* Cambridge: Cambridge University Press.

Oates, S. (2006) *Television, Democracy and Elections in Russia.* London: Routledge.

O'Neill, J. (2011) *The Growth Map: Economic Opportunity in the BRICs and Beyond.* London: Portfolio/Penguin.

'Our 2013 GES: Surprising the Markets'. Global Economic Paper: 223. Goldman Sachs Global Economics Group. Available at: www.abnamromarkets.nl/fileadmin/user_upload/TA/2013/2013_Growth_Environment_Scores.pdf.

Ovsepyan, R. (1979) *Sovetskaya zhurnalistika I kommunisticheskoye vospitanije trudyashikhsya* (Soviet Journalism and Communist Upbringing of Workers). Moscow: Izd-vo Mosk. Un-ta.

Papatheodorou, F. and Machin, D. (2003) The Umbilical Cord That Was Never Cut: The Post-dictatorial Intimacy between the Political Elite and the Mass Media in Greece and Spain. *European Journal of Communication,* 18(1): 31–54.

Pasti, S. (2007) *The Changing Profession of a Journalist in Russia.* Tampere: Tampere University Press.

Pietilainen, J. (2002) *The Regional Newspaper in Post-Soviet Russia. Society, Press and Journalism in the Republic of Karelia 1985–2001.* Tampere: Tampere University Press.

Rantanen, T. (2002) *The Global and the National. Media and Communications in Post Communist Russia.* Lanham: Rowman & Littlefield.

Rantanen, T. (2013) A Critique of the System Approach in Comparative Media Research: A Central and Eastern Europe Perspective. *Global Media and Communication,* 9(3): 257–277.

Rantanen, T. and Vartanova, E. (2003) Empire and Communications: Centrifugal and Centripetal Media in Contemporary Russia, pp. 147–162 in Couldry, N. and Curran, J. (eds.) *Contesting Media Power: Alternative Media in a Networked World.* Lanham: Rowman & Littlefield.

Resnyanskaya, L. and Fomicheva, I. (1999) Gazeta dlya vsei Rossii (Newspaper for the Whole Russia). Moscow: Fakul'tet zhurnalistiki/IKAR.

Rosenholm, A., Nordenstreng, K. and Trubina, E. (eds.) (2010) *Russian Mass Media and Changing Values.* New York: Routledge.

*The Russian Awakening.* A Joint Paper by the Carnegie Moscow Center. November 2012. Available at http://carnegieendowment.org/files/russian_awakening.pdf. Accessed 5 February 2014.

Sharma, R. (2012) *Breakout Nations: In Pursuit of the Next Economic Miracles.* New York: W. W. Norton.

*SMI Rossiji* (2011) Mass Media in Russia. Edited by Y. Zassoursky. Moscow: Aspekt Press.

*SMI v. menjajusheisja Rossiji* (2009) (Mass Media and Changing Russia). Edited by E. Vartanova. Moscow: Aspekt Press.

Sparks, C. (2013) Global Media Studies: Its Development and Dilemmas. *Media, Culture and Society,* 35(1): 121–131.

Sparks, C. and Reading, A. (1998) *Communism, Capitalism and the Mass Media.* London: Sage.

Splihal, S. (1994) *Media beyond Socialism. Theory and Practice in East-Central Europe.* Boulder: Westview Press.

State Agency of Press and Mass Communication (2007) *Russian Periodical Press Market: Situation, Trends and Prospects.* Annual Report. Moscow: FAPMK.

Straubhaar, J. (2010) Chindia in the Context of Emerging Cultural and Media Powers. *Global Media and Communication,* 6(3): 253–262.

Televideniye v Rossii. Sostojanie, tendencii I perspektivy razvitija (2013) Television in Russia. Condition, Trends and Perspectives. Moscow: FAPMK.

Thussu, D. (2013) India in the International Media Sphere. *Media, Culture and Society,* 35(1): 156–162.

Toepfl, F. (2013) Why Do Pluralistic Media Systems Emerge & Comparing Media Change in the Czech Republic and in Russia after the Collapse of Communism. *Global Media and Communication,* 9(3): 239–256.

Trakhtenberg, A. (2007) Transformation without Change: Russian Media as a Political Institution and Cultural Phenomenon pp. 122–130 in Vartanova, E. (ed.) (2007) *Media and Change.* Moscow: MediaMir.

Vartanova, E. (ed.) (2007) Media and Change. Moscow: MediaMir; Faculty of Journalism, Lomonosov Moscow State University.

Vartanova, E. (2012) The Russian Media Model in the Context of Post-Soviet Dymnamics, in Hallin, D. and Mancini, P. (eds.) *Comparing Media Systems Beyond the Western World.* Cambridge: Cambridge University Press.

Vartanova, E. and Makeenko, M. (2013) *Applicability of the Institutional Approach to State–Media Markets Relations in BRICS Countries: The Case of Russia.* Paper presented at the ICA conference. June 17, London.

Vartanova, E.; Nieminen, H. and Salminen, M. M. (eds.) (2009) *Perspectives on the Media in Russia: 'Western' Interests and Russian Developments.* Helsinki: Aleksanteri Institute.

Vartanova, E. and Smirnov, S. (2010) *Mapping Contemporary Trends in Russian Media Industry,* in Rosenholm, A.; Nordenstreng, K. and Trubina, E. (eds.) *Russian Mass Media and Changing Values.* New York: Routledge.

Voltmer, K. (2008) Comparing Media Systems in New Democracies: East Meets South Meets West. *Central European Journal of Communication,* 1(1): 23–40.

Vyrkovsky, A. and Makeenko, M. (2014) *Regionalnoe televidenie Rossii na poroge cifrovoy epohi.* (Regional television on the threshold of the digital age). Moscow: MediaMir; Faculty of Journalism, Lomonosov Moscow State University.

Wasserman, H. (2013) South Africa and China as BRICS Partners: Media Perspectives on Geopolitical Shifts. *Journal of Asian and African Studies.* 20(10): 1–15. doi:10.1177/0021909613514191.

Wilson, D., Kelston, A. and Ahmed, S. (2010) Is This the 'BRICs Decade'? *BRICs Monthly,* 10(3), 20 May.

Yandex, downloaded 15 January 2013 http://company.yandex.ru/researches/reports/2013/ya_internet_regions_2013.xml

Yershov, J. M. (2012) *Televidenie regionov v poiskach modeley razvitija* (Television in Regions: Finding a Model for Development). Moscow: Izd-vo Mosk. Un-ta.

Zassoursky, I. (2001) *Rekonstruktsiya Rossii. Mass-media i politika v 90-e* (Reconstruction of Russia. Mass Media and Politics in the 1990s). Moscow: Moscow University Press.

Zoubarevich, N. (2013) *Chego zhdat chetyrem Rossiyam?* (Four Russias: What to Expect?) Available at: www.vedomosti.ru/opinion/opinions/2013/09/24/16681621.

# Chapter 7

# India: multiple media explosions

*Savyasaachi Jain*

India is one of the fastest growing countries in the world and the second fastest in the BRICS grouping. India's GDP grew at an average of more than 7.8 per cent per annum in real terms between 2003 and 2012 (World Bank, 2014). The relatively low growth rate of 4.4 per cent in 2013 is projected to again take an upward trend, reaching 6.8 per cent by 2016 (IMF, 2014: 184). Given the context of India's rapidly growing economy, it is to be expected that its media would have also expanded rapidly in recent years; however, the growth of the media sector has been even faster than the economy as a whole. Media growth has consistently outstripped GDP growth by several percentage points in the last decade, achieving growth rates in the double digits (Thussu, 2012; FICCI, 2006; 2008; FICCI-KPMG, 2010; 2011; 2012). This growth is expected to continue at rates of up to 16 per cent per annum (FICCI-KPMG, 2013; 2014). The result is one of the largest – and probably the most energetic and vibrant – media landscapes in the world, which notably deviates from the trend of shrinking news markets in many of the developed economies.

There is no doubt that Indian media are significant – they serve one of every six humans, the largest democratically governed population on the planet. Even with low penetration rates, Indian newspapers reach more people than in any other country. Many of the statistics for Indian media are an order of magnitude larger than other BRICS countries. For instance, there were more than 94,000 publications registered with the Registrar of Newspapers for India at the end of March 2013 (RNI, 2014). The numbers rise every year: 7,337 new publications were registered during 2012–2013 (ibid.). Other media show similar or higher growth figures in terms of numbers of outlets and audiences as well as revenues.

However, the story of the growth of Indian media is one of the great untold – or less told – stories. It has not received as much international scholarly attention as the national media systems of many other countries. India's relatively sheltered economy and, in particular, barriers against international investment in India's news media, undoubtedly have a role to play in this seeming lack of interest. Language differences and the Indian media's limited international reach and impact in the West outside the relatively narrow sphere of diasporic audiences are also important factors. In addition, Indian media are hard to understand or even describe. Data is often unavailable but, more than that, the rapidly multiplying and expanding newspapers, television channels, radio stations and mobile networks reflect a continental scale and diversity. No compartments become readily apparent into which various segments of the Indian media can be neatly boxed and categorized. Bollywood may be the most prolific film factory in the world, but it is just one of more than a dozen regional and language-specific film industries in India.

Across media, multiple languages and layers weave a web of intertwining divergences that defy patterns as soon as they are established. Media operations vary widely on every parameter, including size, financing, patterns of ownership, relationship to power, methods of production, genre and approach. On the one hand there are one-man operations in remote areas producing content on obsolete equipment in a language spoken by a few hundred thousand people and, on the other hand, there are large diversified corporate entities that, among other businesses, own large newspapers, radio stations, web operations and television channels reaching tens of millions and making profits in the billions of rupees. Unlike many other countries, neither corporatization nor political constraints are dominant, homogenizing factors.

This diversity of media and the dozens of languages in which they operate makes it difficult to classify Indian media as one media system. Neither do Indian media behave as one system. The dissimilarities are often more pronounced than resemblances, despite several common overarching frameworks, such as a common national boundary and political system, legal structure and regulatory mechanisms. The diversity is pronounced to the extent that, across India, the media do not exhibit homogeneity with respect to any given sets of parameters, including the four 'dimensions' of Hallin and Mancini (2004) – the development of media markets, political parallelism, journalistic professionalism and state intervention. This chapter examines not only the growth trajectory of Indian media but also some of the diversity they encompass in an attempt to describe this multi-faceted and multi-layered media landscape.

## Historical roots

Building upon long-established communication traditions, news media in modern forms have a history of nearly two and a half centuries in India. The first printing press arrived with the Portuguese in 1556 and was largely used for the printing of religious literature by Jesuit missionaries based in Goa on the western coast of peninsular India (Vilanilam, 2005: 51). The first printed newspaper dates back to 1780, during the colonial period, when an Englishman, James Augustus Hicky, launched the weekly *Bengal Gazette*, also known as the *Calcutta General Advertiser*, in Calcutta (now Kolkata). Hicky's *Gazette*, described as a 'witty and scurrilous newspaper' that carried items of scandal and gossip (Parthasarathy, 1997: 19) had a short life span. Hicky was sued for defamation by the Governor-General of Bengal, Warren Hastings, fined, imprisoned and subsequently deported, and the newspaper ceased publication less than two years after its launch. However, even in this period, other newspapers had already made an appearance, the first of them being the *Indian Gazette*, which was launched a mere few months after Hicky's newspaper. Within a few years, Calcutta had four weeklies and a monthly. The other two Presidencies (settlements) of British India, Madras (now Chennai) and Bombay (now Mumbai) were slightly slower off the mark; but the weekly *Madras Courier* began publication in 1785 and the *Bombay Herald* in 1789. Within half a century, there were nearly 50 publications being published in different parts of the country. A majority of them were in English, and catered to the needs of an expatriate population. Newspapers in Indian languages began to be published several decades after the early beginnings. The first such newspaper, *Digdarshan* (World Vision), first published in 1818, was started by missionaries and it mainly concerned itself with religious matters, but it was soon followed by many others in a number of languages.

Newspapers in colonial, pre-1947, India displayed three strong, persistent trends: resistance to the oppressive legal and governmental regimes; furtherance of social reform campaigns; and a strong tradition of political activism.

The first of these, an antagonistic relationship with the government, began with Hicky's *Gazette* in 1780. Parathasarathy (1997) chronicles the long history of active resistance by both British and Indian editors in the face of repressive licensing and legislative regimes, and the prosecution and deportation of British editors (the tactics of resistance often included appointing editors of mixed Anglo-Indian descent who could not be deported). From the very earliest days, newspapers exhibited a strong streak of watchdog journalism, exposing financial and administrative scandals of the East India Company. They commented strongly on governance and policy issues, even as they took prurient delight in exposing personal scandal. It is noteworthy that many of the issues of authoritarianism and governmental control faced by newspapers in the early decades persisted through the colonial experience and into Independent India. The post-colonial elite preserved the colonial legacy of media laws, regulations and systems of control, either by default or design (Thomas, 2010: 36–37).

The most prominent early exponent of the second persistent trend – that of social reform – was Raja Ram Mohun Roy, under whose influence the first Indian-owned newspaper in English, the *Bengal Gazette*, began publication in 1816. Roy went on to launch and inspire several other newspapers in Bengali and Persian languages. One of the major social reform campaigns he inspired is the one against *sati*, the practice of the immolation of a widow on the pyre of her dead husband. Ironically, many of the progressive and reformist newspapers suffered a decline in readership after the abolition of *sati* in 1829 (Parthasarathy, 1997: 36). Roy also championed other causes, including freedom of expression and of the press. Several other newspapers in different parts of the country followed Roy's inclinations, making social reform a noticeable trend. Attempts to modernize India and Hinduism through appeals to logic and rationalism persisted well into the twentieth century.

It is also recognized that the intellectual base of Roy's social and religious activism laid the base for the more emotionally charged trend that later became manifest as the third prominent movement in pre-Independence media – that of political activism. Indian newspapers played a major role in promoting a spirit of nationalism and directly supported the independence movement, especially after the failed First War of Independence (also called the Sepoy Mutiny) in 1857. Ram (1997, xiii–xiv) characterizes the press's support to the anti-imperialist cause as Stage II of the history of Indian journalism, stretching from 1868–1919. It includes the founding of several long-lasting newspapers that achieved a reach beyond their regions, including *Amrita Bazar Patrika* (1868–1986), *The Statesman* (1875 to the present day) and *The Hindu* (1878 to the present day). Ram defines Stage III as the period between 1919 and 1937 that sees the differentiation of the press into moderate and radical, a reference to their positions with regard to the strategy and tactics of the freedom movement. This phase encompassed the launch of *Hindustan Times* and *The Indian Express*, both of which continue to be published today. Stage IV, from 1937 to the achievement of independence in 1947, sees the maturing of assertive tendencies in the press, according to Ram (ibid.). Many leaders of India's independence movement, including the Father of the Indian Nation, Mahatma Gandhi, and India's first Prime Minister, Jawaharlal Nehru, wrote and published extensively, and newspapers were a critical element of mobilization and activism in the first half of the twentieth century. When India gained independence in 1947, there were several mass circulation newspapers both in English and Indian languages, even though less than one-fifth of Indians were literate.

Independent for India represented a discontinuity in political and governance terms, but not with regard to the media, which continued to exhibit many of the tendencies from the colonial period. The tradition of watchdog reporting, support for social reform and nationalistic zeal continued, albeit in modified forms and to differing extents across the vast and diverse media sector. In the immediate post-Independence era, that is, in the 1950s and 1960s, many newspapers consciously adopted a watchdog role, especially in view of the parliamentary majority enjoyed by the ruling Congress Party (Parthasarathy, 1997). The freedom of the press is not expressly enshrined in the Indian Constitution, but the Supreme Court of India has interpreted it as being implicit within the freedom of speech and expression, which are guaranteed by the Constitution.

In the early decades of independent India, even as they espoused a watchdog role, the media remained an integral part of the nation-building project. This is perhaps also a reflection of the influence of Mahatma Gandhi and the values of 'Gandhian journalism' that he inspired. Newspapers understood their role to be one that incorporated development journalism. Public radio and television – All India Radio and Doordarshan – were expressly mandated to perform a positive social role. All India Radio had emerged in the 1930s from an amalgamation of radio clubs and experimental services (Page and Crawley, 2001) and television broadcasting began in New Delhi in 1959, with a second station being opened in Mumbai only after a gap of 13 years. The initiation of colour broadcasting for the 1982 Asian Games was an important step in television transitioning to its status as a mass medium. A missionary zeal that included residual nationalism and multiple elements of social reform is evident in the media output of this period, equally in journalism, broadcasting and the emerging film industries in different languages.

Despite the committed nature of media during these years, newspaper journalism maintained a largely independent and probing character even as it maintained a close relationship with political institutions. Newspapers were headed by eminent editors who robustly and loudly guarded their freedom – when they were able to. A notable exception occurred during the state of emergency imposed by the then prime minister, Indira Gandhi, from 1975 to 1977. Stringent censorship was imposed and journalists were among those arrested along with activists of opposition parties. Lal Krishna Advani, a political leader who became Information and Broadcasting minister after the Emergency, famously said to editors: 'You were merely asked to bend, but you chose to crawl' (quoted in Ninan, 2007: 273). However, once the Emergency was over, the media reasserted its independence with a vengeance and entered an era of aggressive journalism, fuelled by newspapers such as *The Indian Express* and the newsmagazines *India Today* and *Sunday*.

Doordarshan and All India Radio, though ostensibly granted autonomy as independent public service broadcasters under the Prasar Bharati (Broadcasting Corporation of India) Act, 1990, have found it more difficult to emerge from under the yoke of governmental control over content. Not only are they treated as tools for development, they also serve as instruments to weld the nation together (Mehta, 2008: 25). The government substantially funds the public broadcasting corporation and also plays a role in the appointment of officers in key executive roles. It thus continues to exercise financial, administrative and editorial control.

The early 1990s were an inflection point for Indian media. Several events and circumstances combined to create the conditions for major changes. Chronologically, the first of these was the tentative advent of independent factual television in 1990. The independent current affairs newsmagazines *Eyewitness* and *Newstrack*, which were initially circulated on VHS videocassettes marketed through direct subscription and neighbourhood video libraries, first began to break the monopoly of Doordarshan on visuals of news events. With high journalistic standards and production values, they introduced audiences to the immediacy of television visuals and whetted their appetite. The second event was the first Gulf War, during which, in early 1991, India was first introduced to satellite television through CNN's broadcasts. The third, and most important, of the events was the economic reforms of 1991–1992 that followed on from the near bankruptcy of the Government of India in 1991. The liberalization not only marked a break with the command economy of previous decades but also created fertile ground that subsequently facilitated the emergence of privately-owned broadcasting and market-led media. Thereafter, the changes were rapid. In 1992, the first private television station, Zee Television, ushered in the era of satellite television. The independent journalism introduced by *Eyewitness* and *Newstrack* found an echo in news bulletins that began to appear on the entertainment-focused private channels by the mid-1990s. In 1998, the first 24-hour news channel was launched, marking the breaking point with the past and leading to developments that irrevocably altered the size, reach and character of the media landscape.

This is the age in which Indian media currently exists – an era of sharp growth in media outlets and revenues, energetic but chaotic individualism and market-led journalism.

## Rapid expansion

As the world's largest democracy and second most populous country, it is perhaps no surprise that India also has one of the most vibrant media environments. With more newspapers and 24-hour television news channels than any other country, India combines a larger economic base for its media industries with rapidly increasing audience numbers. The 'argumentative Indian' (Sen, 2005) evidently continues to display a hunger for news.

Double digit growth rates for the media industries have become normal over the past several years. The projections of industry analysts are that between 2013 and 2018, the television industry will grow at a cumulative annual growth rate (CAGR) of 16.2 per cent, print at 9 per cent, films at 11.9 per cent, radio at 18.1 per cent and digital advertising at 27.7 per cent (FICCI-KPMG, 2014: 2). Figure 7.1 shows the growth of the television and print industries as a whole.

## Newspapers

About two decades ago, Robin Jeffrey wrote:

> No other country – indeed no other continent – in the world has a newspaper industry as complex and highly developed as India's. ... In most of the industrialized world, the past decade has seen a reduction in the number and circulation of daily newspapers. But not so in India, where the overall circulation appears to have increased by roughly 140 per cent in the same period.
>
> (Jeffrey, 1993: 2004)

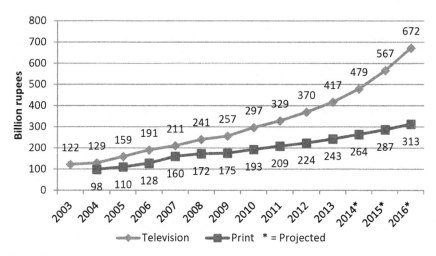

*Figure 7.1* Growth of television and print industries
Source: KPMG analysis (KPMG, 2012: 4); PwC industry analysis (PwC, 2011: 7, 2008: 9)

In terms of the scale of the newspaper industry, the situation today qualitatively remains broadly the same, but in quantitative terms, growth has far outpaced what Jeffrey saw in the early 1990s (WAN-IFRA, 2008; 2010). Since then, the Indian newspaper market has overtaken China's to emerge as the largest (WAN-IFRA, 2011), and *The Times of India* has become the largest circulated English quality newspaper in the world. According to the Indian Readership Survey, conducted in the second quarter of 2012, each day's paper is read by an average of 7.64 million people. However, there are many Indian newspapers in other languages that have far greater reach (Table 7.1).

*Table 7.1* Top 10 dailies in India

| Publication | Language | IRS 2012 Q2 |
|---|---|---|
| | *Average issue readership (AIR) figures in millions* | |
| Dainik Jagran | Hindi | 16.43 |
| Daink Bhaskar | Hindi | 14.45 |
| Hindustan | Hindi | 12.20 |
| Malayala Manorama | Malayalam | 9.71 |
| Amar Ujala | Hindi | 8.61 |
| The Times of India | English | 7.64 |
| Lokmat | Marathi | 7.51 |
| Daily Thanthi | Tamil | 7.43 |
| Rajasthan Patrika | Hindi | 6.76 |
| Mathrubhumi | Malayalam | 6.49 |

Source: Indian Readership Survey 2012, Q2
(IRS measures readership, not circulation)

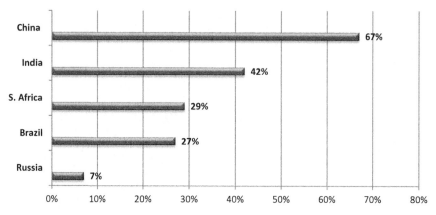

*Figure 7.2* Comparative newspaper reach in the BRICS countries – 2010
Source: World Press Trends, 2011

At the same time, there is a sustained growth in the numbers of newspapers and periodicals. At the end of March 2010, 77,384 newspapers and periodicals were registered with the Registrar of Newspapers for India. This rose to 82,222 by 31 March 2011, to 86,754 a year later, and further to 94,067 in 2013. Unlike in more developed economies, newspapers are a rapidly growing sector in India.

Newspapers reach approximately 42 per cent of Indians (WAN-IFRA, 2011). It ranks second among the BRICS countries in newspaper reach (see Figure 7.2). At a global level, India's figures are close to those of the US (40 per cent), but far lower than those of Germany (70 per cent), Sweden (81 per cent), Venezuela (85 per cent) and Japan (91 per cent). With rising literacy, there is ample scope for expansion of the newspaper market in India.

## Television

Television is one of India's fastest growing sectors, not just among media but among all industries, with double-digit growth both attained and forecast. Television follows the commercial model rather than the public-service broadcasting model seen in Western or Northern Europe. There is a vibrant television news environment dominated by private broadcasters, many of whom are parts of larger media empires.

More than 61 per cent of India's households (143 million households out of a total of 233 million households) have television sets. Though in percentage terms the figure has not grown substantially in the recent past, in reality millions of additional households tune into television every year (see Figure 7.3). More than 64 per cent of these – 92 million households – have access to hundreds of channels via cable and satellite services (see Figure 7.4); the rest can receive only terrestrial signals from the state broadcaster, Doordarshan, which is the

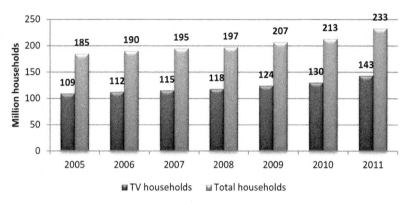

*Figure 7.3* Growth in the reach of television in India
Source: Ministry of Information and Broadcasting

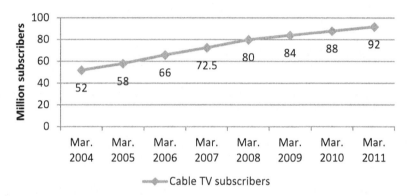

*Figure 7.4* Cable TV subscribers
Source: Ministry of Information and Broadcasting

sole terrestrial broadcaster. Doordarshan broadcasts 35 channels in different languages (Ministry of Information and Broadcasting, 2012: 126).

The average Indian household is of five people, so television reaches more than 700 million people, of whom more than 450 million can watch cable and satellite channels. They are served by about 6,000 multi-system operators who download and supply signals from satellites and 60,000 cable operators (Ministry of Information and Broadcasting, 2012) who provide the last-mile connectivity through physical cables strung from trees and telephone poles. This is a fast-growing sector of the television industry, though one that will witness large-scale business model reconfigurations with the digitization programme currently underway.

Another fast-growing area is that of direct-to-home (DTH) satellite television services. There are six major DTH providers who enable subscribers to

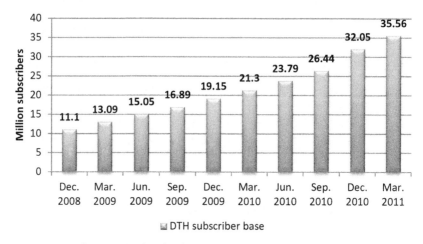

*Figure 7.5* Growth in DTH subscriber base
Source: Ministry of Information and Broadcasting

access satellite signals through Ku-band satellite dishes similar to those of Sky in the UK. As Figure 7.5 shows, the number of DTH subscribers has nearly trebled in the two years between 2009 and 2011.

It is clear that there is substantial scope for further expansion of audiences. Figure 7.6 shows TV penetration in India in comparison with other countries. It is interesting to note that a fellow BRICS country, Brazil, has a much lower newspaper reach than India (see Figure 7.2), but a substantially higher TV penetration rate. Of course, Brazil is a mid-income country, while India is a low-income country. India has a nominal per capita GDP of about $1,570 and a GDP per capita PPP of about $5,350 (World Bank, 2014).

Though private television channels did not begin to proliferate until the late 1990s, more than 600 channels were launched in the first decade of the twenty-first century. The figure continues to rise every year and, in 2014, stands at more than 800.

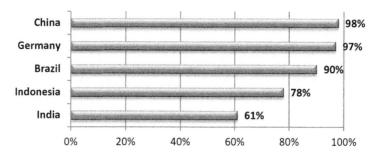

*Figure 7.6* Comparative TV penetration
Source: KPMG Analyses; KPMG, 2012: 10

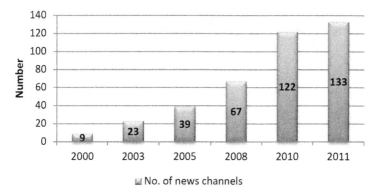

*Figure 7.7* Proliferation of news channels
Source: TAM Peoplemeter Systems

The Ministry of Information and Broadcasting classifies all channels that have news and current affairs content as 'news channels'. By this definition, the list includes 405 news channels and 426 non-news channels. The audience measurement company, TAM Peoplemeter Systems, on the other hand, counts only those that have 24-hour news or a majority of news content, and their figures show that India had 133 news channels – and growing – in 2011 (see Figure 7.7).

## Radio, mobile and the Internet

An overwhelming majority of advertising revenue flows to newspapers and television, now being called legacy media in many media systems, but still ruling the public sphere in India. This is because of structural and historical as well as economic factors. As things stand, print and television continue to get the lion's share of advertising revenue, with radio and the Internet commanding a miniscule share. As a result, newspapers and television in India have not yet begun to experience crippling declines in advertising revenue.

State-owned All India Radio has a geographical coverage of about 92 per cent and it reaches more than 99 per cent of the population with its 432 medium wave, short wave and FM transmitters (Telecom Regulatory Authority of India, 2013). In addition, 148 community radio stations and 242 private FM stations in 86 cities cover about 37 per cent of the geographical area of India. The number of private FM stations is set to grow to 839 licences across 294 cities, with the third phase of licensing to be concluded in 2014. In terms of revenue, private radio grew at 15 per cent in 2012–2013 and is expected to keep growing at an average of 18 per cent per annum over the next six years (FICCI-KPMG, 2014). Private FM stations are music stations for the most part; they are not, as yet, allowed to broadcast any news other than the feed of All India Radio. However, they have been undertaking a number of social initiatives in their attempts to connect with audiences and build community. These campaigns and public-service announcements on health, education, the environment, safety and gender issues, are a staple programming element for private stations.

The big growth story in India in recent years has been the mobile – from an interpersonal communication point of view, but not yet from a media perspective. As Figure 7.8 shows, by March 2013, there were 867 million mobile phone subscribers in India.

There is – as yet – very little commercial or media activity on mobile phones. 3G connections are still relatively expensive compared to calling rates, which have dropped drastically from 32 rupees per minute in the mid-1990s to less than one rupee per minute over the last few years (the latter figure comes to about £0.01 at mid-2014 exchange rates). Because of the high rates for 3G connections, few Indians access the Internet over their mobile phones.

Compared to voice segment's 39 per cent spurt in numbers, the Telecom Regulatory Authority of India (TRAI) describes growth in the Internet as slow. The number of Internet subscribers grew from a little over 16 million to 19.67 million in 2010–2011 (TRAI, 2011), which represents a growth rate of 21.6 per cent. Most of this growth was in broadband connections, and if one considers broadband alone, the growth rate was about 35.6 per cent in 2010–2011 (see Figure 7.9). Thus, the growth rates are not small in themselves, but the size of the sector and the comparison with other countries do make it seem insignificant in relation to other media sectors. The low penetration of the Internet is attributable to infrastructural issues (TRAI, 2011). While the total number of fixed line Internet connections in India is only about

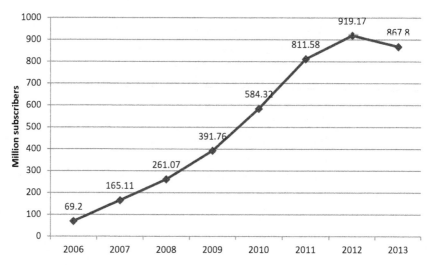

*Figure 7.8* Mobile phone subscribers in India
Source: Compiled from reports of the Telecom Regulatory Authority of India

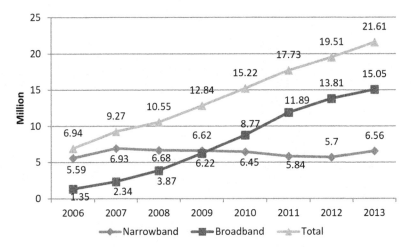

*Figure 7.9* Fixed line Internet connections
Source: TRAI

21 million, the number of users who access the Internet through mobile phones is estimated to be about 143 million (TRAI, 2014).

Though the Internet has not yet begun to have a reach sizeable enough to impact the fortunes of the newspaper and television industries, advertisers have begun to notice it. This segment of the media has begun to attract advertising revenue faster than its growth, partly because it represents a desirable demographic for advertisers. As Figure 7.10 shows, the value of advertising on the Internet is growing rapidly, at rates of up to 50 per cent per annum, but it remains a fraction of that in the television or print industries. There is

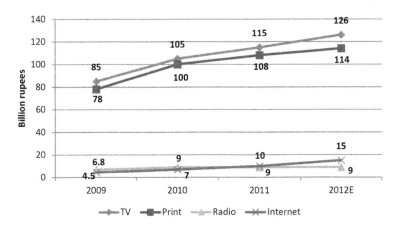

*Figure 7.10* Advertising revenue by media
Source: Pitch Madison Media Ad Outlook, 2012, Edelweiss Research

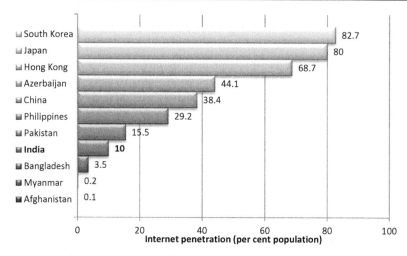

*Figure 7.11* Internet penetration in Asian countries
Source: Boston Consulting Group

substantial scope for growth, and the position of India vis-à-vis chosen Asian countries is represented in Figure 7.11.

So, while print and television revenues are growing, the Internet is beginning to make some inroads into advertising revenues. As Internet penetration increases, this trend will be more pronounced and will be reflected in the business models of the print and television industries. At the same time, it must be stated that because of factors such as the size and stratification of the Indian market, it will be a long time before the bottom lines of the legacy media is seriously hit.

## Engines of growth: population, literacy, urbanization and the economy

India is the seventh largest country in the world, 13 times as large as the UK, with a population of 1.21 billion (Census of India). The sheer size of the population is a major driver of media growth. Along with the growth in number of people, literacy rates are rising. At the beginning of the twentieth century, literacy rates as recorded by the Census of India were very low (5.35 per cent in 1901 and 5.92 per cent in 1911). Substantial progress in literacy in the last 60 years (see Figure 7.12) has been instrumental in increasing the audience for news media. There are marked differences in literacy between different states in India and also between men and women. For instance, in 2011, though 82.14 per cent of men were literate, less than two-thirds of women were able to read and write, leading to a male–female literacy gap of nearly 17 per cent, but as these differentials reduce, larger media audiences will be available.

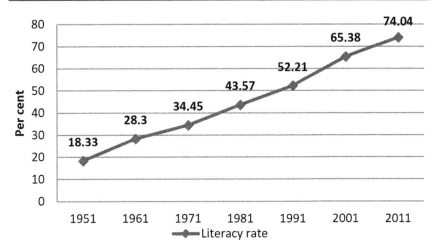

*Figure 7.12* Literacy rates
Source: Census of India

In the last decade alone, India has added more than 217 million people to its literate population (see Figure 7.13). With the audience for news growing at such a rapid pace, Indian media have several years of growth ahead of them before they reach saturation levels. Large numbers of Indians remain in a 'media-dark' zone – for economic reasons, among others. Thus, opportunities for growth of the news media will continue to exist for decades.

At the same time, it must be pointed out that 'literate' does not necessarily mean being educated well enough to read a newspaper. The detailed tabulation from the 2011 census is not yet available, but in 2001, out of the 562 million Indians aged 20 and above, less than one-third had finished middle school and/ or gone on to secondary school and higher education. The other two-thirds were classified as educated to primary level, literate below primary level, literate without any educational level or illiterate (Census of India) – categories where

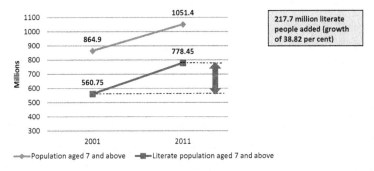

*Figure 7.13* Addition to literate population aged more than seven years
Source: Analysis based on data from the Census of India

consumption of the news media can reasonably be expected to be low. This low level of education among those classified as literate is a limiting factor for the reach of the media – and of course it also has a bearing on the media's approach and treatment of news. However, with a greater thrust on education including the 'Education for All' initiative in recent years, it is expected that the educational levels of literate Indians will rise to a level that brings larger numbers into the catchment area of the news media.

The growth in audiences of news media is also related to migration from rural to urban areas. The trend of urbanization is shown in Figure 7.14. In 1901, only 10.8 per cent of Indians lived in urban areas; this increased to 17.3 per cent in 1951 and 31.2 per cent in 2011 (Census of India). While India has 640,867 villages, which can be remote and hard to access for news media, it now has nearly 8,000 'urban units', which is what the Census calls towns and cities. Between 2001 and 2011, the number of urban units increased from 5,161 to 7,935, a jump of about 54 per cent in a span of merely 10 years. The Census defines urban areas as all residential agglomerations that have a population of at least 5,000, a population density of at least 400 persons per square km. and where at least 75 per cent of male 'main workers' are engaged in non-agricultural pursuits. This clustering of people and the movement from agricultural to non-agricultural livelihoods has obvious implications for the penetration and delivery of news media, whether newspapers or television. There are now 53 cities in India with populations of more than one million. The largest of these – called the four 'metros' in India – are Greater Mumbai (earlier Bombay) (18.4 million), the National Capital Territory of Delhi at 16.3 million, Kolkata (earlier Calcutta) with 14.1 million residents and Chennai (earlier Madras), which comes in at 8.7 million. Several other cities, including Bangalore (8.5 million), Hyderabad (7.7 million), Ahmedabad (6.4 million) and Pune (5 million), are not far behind.

Media consumption has also risen along with income and an upward swing in standards of living. Poverty in India continues to remain at abysmal levels.

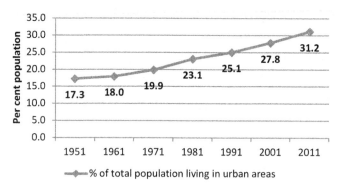

*Figure 7.14* Urbanization in India
Source: Census of India

About one-third of all Indians – that makes about 400 million – live under the national poverty line defined by the Planning Commission of India. At the same time, India has a huge middle class, estimated to range in size from 30 million to 300 million depending on how the term is defined. Over the past decade and more, India has been experiencing some of the highest growth rates in the world, and this economic prosperity has had a role to play in the growth of the media industries. The 1990s began on a low note with a GDP growth rate of 1.4 per cent in 1991–1992. This was a watershed, preceded by a balance of payments crisis and tided over with major economic reforms. As a result of these reforms, the GDP growth rate jumped to 5.4 per cent in 1992–1993 and rose every succeeding year to hit 8.0 per cent in 1996–1997. In the last decade, growth rates have remained consistently high, exceeding 9 per cent in many years.

Over the last 60 years, India's GDP growth has outstripped its population growth. Figure 7.15 shows the relative growths of population and the GDP, the latter considered at constant prices indexed to the base year 1951. In the two decades since the launch of economic reforms in India, the growth of GDP has accelerated. Between 1991 and 2001, the decadal growth of population was about 21 per cent, but the GDP grew more than 72 per cent. In the decade 2001–2011, population grew by 17.7 per cent while GDP climbed by 141 per cent.

Thus, the growth of news media in India is inextricably tied up with the macro picture of demographics and the economy, including the phenomena of population growth, higher literacy rates, increasing urbanization and rising standards of living. The average Indian is becoming richer (or less poor), more educated and moving to cities, and this process of empowerment and greater engagement with local and national processes is the core engine that is fuelling

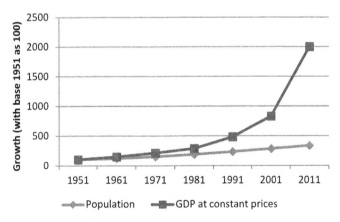

*Figure 7.15* Relative growth of GDP and population
Source: Census of India

growth in the media. For the most part, the benefits of this growth are accruing to the newspaper and television sectors, which have not yet been adversely impacted by the rise of the mobile and Internet sectors.

## Diversity

India's diversity makes India both difficult and very fertile for media operations. In many senses, India's media is becoming increasingly differentiated, in keeping with its geographical, linguistic, cultural and political diversity. The political boundary of India incorporates multiple nationalities, cultures, languages and ethnicities. India's population is not only diverse, it is also very large. India's smallest state has a population comparable to Finland or Denmark and its most populous state houses about 200 million people, which is three times that of the UK, two and a half times that of Germany, and one-third more than Russia.

Culturally, India is more diverse than any other country in the world – the only land mass more diverse than India is the continent of Africa. In religious terms, too, India is not homogenous. More religious traditions have a home in India than in any other country, and almost all major religions have a sizeable number of followers. Linguistically, it has 22 'official' languages and, in addition, English serves as a link language. More than 10 million people speak each of the 14 major languages, 29 languages are spoken by more than one million, 60 languages are spoken by more than 100,000 people and 122 languages by more than 10,000 Indians. Indian languages belong to four different language groups – the Indo-European, Dravidian, Sino-Tibetan and Austro-Asiatic or Mon-Khmer.

These wide divergences of language, culture and ethnicity are coupled with differences of political culture in different Indian states. The various regions of India have different political histories and political cultures, ranging from the highly personalized to deeply ideological, and variously linked with religion, culture, ethnicity and caste groupings. Some Indian states repeatedly vote in Hindu right wing governments, others elect communists for decades at a time.

India's states are broadly demarcated on the basis of language, and the cultural, literary and political histories of these states affect the media in those languages. There has been a reinvigoration of various linguistic spaces, and thus of the media in these languages, since the late 1980s. Changing power equations have resulted in a shift away from the language of power, English, and the designated national language, Hindi to other languages, bringing with it a shift in the media consumption in various languages. Large media groups in a number of languages have begun to attain the size and prominence that was earlier associated with the 'national' media in English and Hindi. At the same time, the 'national' media have started catering to the growth in regional languages. *The Times of India, The Hindu* and *Hindustan Times* are just a few of the 'national' media groups that have started moving into the language market in response to media consumption shifts and the consequent shift of advertising revenue to language media.

This move away from Hindi and English towards other languages is also evident in news and entertainment television, with a large number of channels having sprung up to cater to the growing appetite for content in regional languages. Most major television organizations have a bouquet of regional language channels, and of course there are a number of media groups that have emerged in various regions.

## Issues in Indian media

If there is one characteristic of the Indian media landscape that demands attention, it is the intense competition that marks each of its sectors. Whether it is newspapers (more than 94,000) or television channels (more than 800), the sheer number of media titles manoeuvring for market space and advantage has begun to define the media landscape (Thussu, 2012).

The results of this competition are manifest in many different aspects. One is the desperate search for profitability. In each segment of the market, whether by language, geography or genre, there is space for only a limited number of winners (Ram, 2011). Market leaders succeed in being profitable, but the vast numbers of second- and third-tier media companies in each market are lucky merely to survive (Kohli-Khandekar, 2010; Ram 2011). Low profitability also has an impact on ownership – if direct returns from media operations are not an option, investors in media are instead seeking overt returns through the political power and influence of the media. The ownership of media is increasingly being sought by politicians and their associates, or businessmen who want to use media for their ends.

One of the areas in which these pressures are reflected is media output. The large number of players might be expected to lead to a number of strategies that would differentiate one from the other, but this is not the case. What is observed instead is an increasing homogeneity as each of the media outlets at the bottom of the pyramid vie to become clones of the market leaders. Competitive pressures are also thought to be leading to deepening trends of tabloidization and sensationalism in the media. This, combined with a trend towards the instru-mentalization of journalism by media owners, is thought to be responsible for some of the lowering of standards that is observed (Ram, 2011).

Indian media are vast, diverse and complex, and necessarily operate at a number of political, financial and linguistic or geographic levels. This, combined with the shifts taking place because of the economic growth, demographic movements and cultural developments, makes Indian media both a difficult and an exciting object of inquiry.

## References

Census of India [online]. Available at www.censusindia.gov.in. Accessed 3 October 2013.

FICCI (2006) *The Indian Entertainment and Media Industry: Unravelling the Potential.* New Delhi: Federation of Indian Chambers of Commerce and Industry.

——(2008) *The Indian Entertainment and Media Industry: A Growth Story Unfolds*. London: PricewaterhouseCoopers in association with Federation of Indian Chambers of Commerce and Industry.

FICCI-KPMG (2010) *Back in the Spotlight: FICCI-KPMG Indian Media and Entertainment Report 2010*. Mumbai: KPMG in association with Federation of Indian Chambers of Commerce and Industry.

——(2011) *Hitting the High Notes: FICCI-KPMG Indian Media and Entertainment Report 2011*. Mumbai: KPMG in association with Federation of Indian Chambers of Commerce and Industry.

——(2012) *Digital Dawn: The Metamorphosis Begins: FICCI-KPMG Indian Media and Entertainment Report 2012*. Mumbai: KPMG in association with Federation of Indian Chambers of Commerce and Industry.

——(2013) *The Power of a Billion: Realizing the Indian Dream: FICCI-KPMG Indian Media and Entertainment Report 2013*. Mumbai: KPMG in association with Federation of Indian Chambers of Commerce and Industry.

——(2014) *The Stage Is Set: FICCI-KPMG Indian Media and Entertainment Industry Report 2014*. Mumbai: KPMG in association with Federation of Indian Chambers of Commerce and Industry.

Hallin, D. and Mancini, P. (2004) *Comparing Media Systems: Three Models of Media and Politics*. New York: Cambridge University Press.

IMF (2014) *World Economic Outlook April 2014: Recovery Strengthens, Remains Uneven*. Washington: International Monetary Fund.

IRS (2012) *Indian Readership Survey*. Available at http://mruc.net/sites/default/files/IRS%202012%20Q2%20Topline%20Findings_0.pdf. Accessed 20 October 2012.

Jeffrey, R. (1993) Indian Language Newspapers and Why They Grow, *Economic and Political Weekly* 28(38): 2004–2011.

Kohli-Khandekar, V. (2010) *The Indian Media Business* (third edition). New Delhi: Sage.

Mehta, N. (2008) *India on Television: How Satellite News Channels Have Changed the Way We Think and Act*. New Delhi: Harper Collins.

Ministry of Information and Broadcasting (2012) *Annual Report*. New Delhi: Ministry of Information and Broadcasting, Government of India.

Ministry of Information and Broadcasting, India (2014) [online] Website, 'Ministry of Information and Broadcasting, Government of India'. Available at http://mib.nic.in/. Accessed 6 July 2014.

Ninan, S. (2007) *Headlines from the Heartland: Reinventing the Hindi Public Sphere*. New Delhi: Sage.

Page, D. and Crawley, W. (2001) *Satellites over South Asia: Broadcasting Culture and the Public Interest*. New Delhi: Sage.

Parthasarathy, R. (1997) *Journalism in India* (fourth edition). New Delhi: Sterling.

Ram, N. (1997) Foreword in Parthasarathy, R., *Journalism in India* (fourth edition). New Delhi: Sterling.

——(2011) *The Changing Role of the News Media in Contemporary India*. Indian History Congress. Punjabi University, Patiala, December.

RNI (2014) 'The Office of the Registrar of Newspapers for India'. New Delhi. Available at http://rni.nic.in/.

Sen, A. (2005) *The Argumentative Indian*. London: Penguin.

Telecom Regulatory Authority of India (TRAI) (2011) *Annual Report 2010–2011*. New Delhi: Telecom Regulatory Authority of India.

——(2013) *Annual Report 2012–2013*. New Delhi: Telecom Regulatory Authority of India.

Thomas, P. N. (2010) *Political Economy of Communications in India: The Good, the Bad and the Ugly*. New Delhi: Sage.

Thussu, D. K. (2012) A Million Media Now! The Rise of India on the Global Scene. *The Round Table: The Commonwealth Journal of International Affairs* 101(5): 435–446.

Vilanilam, J. V. (2005) *Mass Communication in India: A Sociological Perspective*. New Delhi: Sage.

WAN-IFRA (2008) *India: Media Market Description*. Paris: World Association of Newspapers.

——(2010) *India Country Report*. Paris: World Association of Newspapers.

——(2011) *World Press Trends 2011*. Paris: World Association of Newspapers.

'WAN-IFRA World Press Trends Database' (2011) Available at www.wptdatabase.org/. Accessed 15 October 2012.

World Bank (2014) [online] *World Development Indicators*. Available at http://wdi.worldbank.org/table/1.1. Accessed 08 August 2014.

# Chapter 8

# China: media and power in four historical stages

*Zhengrong Hu, Peixi Xu and Deqiang Ji*

The current media landscape in China is the result of a series of significant processes of configuration and reconfiguration during the long river of Chinese history in general, and a turbulent modern period in particular, and is characterized by several contradictory and contesting logics. The first historical stage of Chinese media in the modern period can be briefly referred to as decolonization from colonial powers. Chinese newspapers in their modern sense were mainly born in the midst of the nineteenth century for a unique function – saving China and ensuring survival. This strategy aimed to address both the internal corruption of the late Qing Dynasty and the external invasions of foreign colonial powers. The former aim was subordinate to the latter, as internal pulses for change were stimulated by the looming danger of complete Western colonial domination. It continued until 1949, when the second stage started with Socialism. The third stage followed in 1978, when the market became a priority in the context of the concept of the 'socialist market economy'. Currently we are living during the fourth stage with a new emphasis on social justice. Hence four stages or dimensions are recognized: decolonization (before 1949), Socialism (1949–1978), market (1978–2003) and justice (2003–present).

## The 'birth mark' of Chinese media: decolonization (before 1949)

Modern Chinese newspapers were born when China was in a comprehensive state of crisis, both internally and externally. Externally, China was an ancient agrarian civilization, which, in a phase of economic decline, was on a direct collision course with the fledgling Western industrial powers in their most brutal and aggressive phase of expansion. China was defeated by Britain in the first Opium War in 1840–1842, by British and French allied powers in the second Opium War in 1856–1860, by France in the Sino–French War in 1883–1885, by Japan in the First Sino–Japanese War in 1894–1895, by an Eight-Nation Alliance (Britain, France, Germany, Russia, the US, Japan, Italy and Austria–Hungary) in 1900, and was finally dragged into two World Wars and a full scale civil war.

Internally, China was shaken by the Taiping Rebellion, a Christian funda-
mentalist movement from 1850 to 1864, which claimed the lives of around
20 million before it was brutally suppressed by the Boxer Rebellion from 1898
to 1901, an anti-imperialism and anti-Christianity movement, whose followers
believed their flesh could withstand bullets and cannons. This was followed by
the 1911 Revolution, which overthrew the Qing dynasty and created the
first – though premature – republic in Asia in the ruins of thousands of years
of imperialism and was ended by the Communist movement in 1949 after
three years of civil war.

These external and internal turbulences shaped the development of newspapers in China. From a macro perspective, Castells aptly describes these years as:

> a time of crisis for state bureaucracies and moral traditions, of globalization
> of trade, of profitable drug traffic, of rapid industrialization spreading in
> the world, of religious missions, of impoverished peasants, of the shaking
> of families and communities, of local bandits and international armies, of
> the diffusion of printing and mass literacy, a time of uncertainty and
> hopelessness, of identity crisis.
>
> (Castells, 1997: 6)

The *Chinese Monthly Magazine* is generally regarded as the first Chinese language
magazine on Chinese soil. It was launched by a Protestant missionary to China,
William Milne, on 5 August 1815, in an effort to assist his religious mission.
There was a tradition of newspapers in China being established by the colonist
masters, with content often glorifying colonial activities. However, Chinese
language newspapers were being launched at this point – in an era of radical
change – by Chinese people themselves, and many of them were motivated
by reform and decolonization. It was a process of learning from the West to
defend against the West. Three waves of these launches of Chinese newspapers are evident: the Hundred Day's Reform; the 1911 Revolution; and the
May Fourth Movement. Unlike Western modern newspapers, which were
created as a commodity, these Chinese newspapers came into being with a
mission to rescue China from a deep-seated crisis.

### First wave: the Hundred Days' Reform

The period from 1895 to 1898 constitutes the first peak of setting up newspapers by Chinese people. A total of 120 newspapers mushroomed during the
three years, and nearly 80 per cent were established by Chinese founders. This was
in sharp contrast to early nineteenth century, during which over 70 newspapers
and magazines were set up and only one third were Chinese (Li, 2009: 76).
Kang Youwei, a progressive intellectual of the late Qing Dynasty, launched
newspapers to campaign for a top-down political reform. They described a
looming crisis of being fully occupied by foreign powers: Britain, Czarist

Russia, France and Japan. They warned that countries such as India, Vietnam, Myanmar, Korea, Turkey and Afghanistan had suffered such a fate and called for a reform movement to learn from the West to save China.

The founding of these newspapers preceded a top-down reform movement known as the 'Hundred Days' Reform'. Reformers gained support from the young Emperor Guangxu and initiated a nationwide reform. What they had in mind was a transplantation of the Japanese Meiji Restoration. Their radically-enacted reform proposals covered nearly all aspects of Chinese society: politically changing an absolute monarchy into a constitutional monarchy; educationally replacing a traditional examination system emphasizing humanities with a modern examination system emphasizing maths and science; economically applying capitalist principles to industrialize the nation; and militarily building a new army. The reform survived for only 104 days and was crushed in 'the Coup of 1898' by conservative forces led by the Emperor's mother, Dowager Cixi.

### Second wave: 1911 Revolution

The 10 years before the 1911 Revolution was the second peak of launching newspapers by Chinese people. In the 10 years from 1901 to 1911, more than 1,100 newspapers and magazines appeared, with over 100 titles on average per year. Newspapers gained readership in all Chinese provinces and covered topics about women, children and peasants (Li, 2009: 92). Topics that featured in the newspapers in this period were: '"Decolonization" or "enlightenment", which one takes priority?', 'Revolution or reformation, which recipe is more applicable?', '"Focusing on concrete problems" or "reaching consensus on broad -isms", which one comes first?', 'Decolonization, revolution, and upholding −isms won out as primary cures for the social challenges.' As a result of the 1911 Revolution, the Nationalist Party of China came into power and the Republic of China was founded, which lasted in Mainland China from 1912 to 1949. It survived wars with the warlords, Japanese invaders, but was defeated by the Communists in the civil war. It was nicknamed as the 'Flowery Republic'. The media under the Republic of China was controlled by the government, though there was a robust private media industry with some degree of freedom, tolerating Communist editorials calling for a democratic polity with multi-party governance.

### Third wave: May Fourth Movement, 1917–1921

Over 1000 newspapers and magazines appeared during the May Fourth Movement period from 1917 to 1921, setting off the third peak of the growth of media in China. On average, 200 titles of newspapers and magazines appeared annually. The May Fourth Movement was triggered by China's diplomatic failure at the Versailles Peace Conference. The Allied Powers betrayed China: instead of giving the German colonized city Qingdao back to China, the conference decided to hand it over to Japan. Student demonstrations on 4 May 1919 in Tiananmen Square turned into a national campaign merging with workers' movements. China's traditional culture, with its backward military technology and political system, was blamed for its overall failure. The movement proposed a new way of writing, of dressing and a new calendar. The main message of the movement was nicknamed as 'Mr. Democracy' and 'Mr. Science' as solutions to the social and cultural dilemma. While the movement was essentially a progressive movement promoting democracy, it worked also as a foretaste of the Cultural Revolution nearly 50 years later, when anti-tradition actions reached its height.

It can be observed from these earlier journalistic practices that Chinese media were born with a birthmark and a mission of decolonization and democratization. Such an appeal was enshrined by one revolution after another. The influence of this birthmark on the current media landscape is evident in at least three aspects: implanting an emotional trope; marking the start of modern Chinese history; and insisting on the importance of national sovereignty. Originating from this negative context is a style of journalism that carries a lack of confidence in China's own system and self-victimizing when faced with the Western powers.

## State control: politics takes command (1949–1978)

Huang (1999) views the rule of the Republic of China from 1912 to 1949 and its being toppled by the Communists in Mainland China in a constructive way. The Jiang Kai-shek administration of the new Republic erected a superstructure on top of the existing system. While the Nationalists abolished unfair treaties, established a constitutional framework, defended the country against Japanese aggression and attended the drafting of the Universal Declaration of Human Rights, their vision of democracy was not fully developed because its influence was confined to the cities. Mao Zedong and his Communist comrades succeeded in mobilizing the Chinese peasantry by combining Marxist thought with Chinese reality. They created a new structure from the grassroots. By that time, China was so divided that Jiang's top-down urban structure and Mao's rural grassroots structure failed to make connections with each other. A full-scale civil war solved this split in a bloody way. The confrontation between Nationalists and Communists between 1945 and 1949 drove the Nationalists away to Taiwan.

In the new Communist China, no private ownership was allowed – of either media or land, after the Three Great Remould in 1952–1956. Chinese revolutions, whether undertaken in the name of God (Taiping Rebellion) or in the name of getting rid of God (Boxer Rebellion), in the name of capitalist democracy (1911 Revolution) or in the name of communism (1949), all had in common the drive for land reform. Of these, the Taiping Rebels' proposal and the Communist one were the most similar. The purpose of land policy in the Taiping Rebellion was to set up a utopian society in which people collectively shared land, food, clothes and money so that everyone was equal and nobody was starving. The concept of collective ownership of land was inherited by the Communist revolutionary movement, which introduced state and collective ownership and collective labour through People's Tribunes. Like land ownership, media ownership did not avoid the fate of being nationalized.

On the eve of the founding of the People's Republic of China, *China Business Daily* – based in Hong Kong – debated whether private newspaper ownership should be removed. Half of the six commentators believed that private ownership should be immediately or gradually prohibited, promoting a dual system of state and community-run newspapers. The other half believed that private newspaper ownership is a healthy contribution to the society. Though the Party-state confirmed the necessity of having private newspapers, it was simply impossible for private media to survive under an overall radical social context. Among a total of 281 newspapers in February 1950, 55 were private newspapers; however, only five months later this number dropped to 25 titles and three years later all the private media outlets were effectively gone. Official media restored themselves as dominating voices as they had always been in traditional China (Liu, 2010).

Unlike the earlier overthrow of dynasties, the revolutionary pulse did not wane with regime change, and the Communist Party, as a new ruler, did not acknowledge the legitimacy of the Confucian codes. Rather, this period witnessed a grassroots revolution and mobilization against these codes in words and in practice. The revolution was so radical that the whole class of landlords and 'capitalists' was completely erased. Two decades before the Communist victory, Mao's resentment of all the symbols of authorities and traditions was already evident. Mao (1927) made the following announcement in his report on the peasant movement in Hunan Province:

> A man in China is usually subjected to the domination of three systems of authority: (1) the state system (political authority), ranging from the national, provincial and county government down to that of the township; (2) the den system (clan authority), ranging from the central ancestral temple and its branch temples down to the head of the household; and (3) the supernatural system (religious authority), ranging from the King of Hell down to the town and village gods belonging to the nether world, and from the Emperor of Heaven down to all the various gods and spirits belonging to the celestial world. As for women, in addition to being dominated by these three systems of authority, they are also dominated by the men (the authority of the husband). These four authorities – political, clan, religious and masculine – are the embodiment of the whole feudal-patriarchal system and ideology, and are the four thick ropes binding the Chinese people …

With the victory of the revolution in 1949, Mao mobilized all available resources to promote a complete liberation of the Chinese population from these perceived feudal ropes. This Chinese version of Communist ideology, propagated through various art forms and media, was a radical reconfiguration of the previous Confucian codes. With revolution as the central spirit, a Communist vision of Chinese society would resemble nothing else in history. Under it, traditional values were condemned. Buddhist temples were torn down. Family-tree books were burned. Confucian teachings were treated with utter contempt. Worship of ancestors was abandoned. Traditional cuisine and furniture were redesigned. Stone arches erected by former dynasties to show women's loyalty/virginity were smashed. All the symbols conveying traditions were deemed to be feudal. Documents as diverse as a textbook, a diploma, a birth certificate, a wedding licence, a death penalty sentence, a certificate of house property, a receipt of telephone bill, an instruction manual for electric appliances, a driving license, a household registration form, a letter of reference and a hospital diagnosis shared one thing in common: Chairman Mao's instructions.

In keeping with the overall political culture, the media also turned radical. In broadcasting media, any content damaging the image of workers, peasants and soldiers, or praising enemies was forbidden. Any content describing romantic love and capitalist lifestyles typified by the US, or revisionist Communist ideas represented by the then USSR was forbidden. Content describing the life of Chinese emperors and ghosts was regarded as feudal and backward and thus forbidden. Broadcasting was filled with material repeating the political line of the Cultural Revolution.

In 1966, the first year of Cultural Revolution, almost half of the broadcasting programmes were political and revolutionary: 'One Song per Week' was renamed as 'One Revolutionary Song per Week'. 'Tell Stories' was renamed as 'Telling Revolutionary Stories'. Newly created radio programmes included 'People across the World Love Chairman Mao and New China', 'Songs Adapted from Chairman Mao's Words', and 'Selected Readings of Chairman Mao's Works'. One year later, the percentage of political programmes further increased to 72 per cent and arts programmes decreased to 24 per cent. Mao's cult of personality and the notion of continuing revolution under the proletariat dictatorship were central topics of the political content. In these fanatic years of the Great Cultural Revolution from 1966 to 1976, the Socialist New Arts occupied all platforms. It took decades for the Communist Party to transform itself from a revolutionary party into a ruling party.

## Rise of the market: development as a priority (1978–2003)

This period marks the expansion of market forces by leaps and bounds, and yet another reconfiguration process. Two years after Mao Zedong's death, China's Communist experiment was halted, together with its static mode of economic development and revolution-based mentality. Though the country was badly damaged by these changing political movements, the legacies of the

Communist era included a comprehensively-structured economic system, a well-designed educational system, an egalitarian land distribution system and a fully mobilized Chinese population. The new legitimacy of the Chinese Communist Party was founded on economic growth, under the overarching and 'undebatable' banner of 'development is the hard truth' and it focused initially on poverty reduction, or more broadly, the improvement of people's living standards.

The Third Plenary Session of the 11th Central Committee held in 1978 paved the way for the introduction of a market mechanism in pursuit of a socialist form of modernization. This shift happened 10 years earlier than in the Soviet Union. In the general social transformation of the post-Cultural Revolution period, China embraced the neo-liberal turn of the Reagan–Thatcher administrations in the economy, '[w]ith Chinese characteristics' (Harvey, 2007) and 'neoliberalism as exception' (Zhao, 2007: 25–26). It then jumped on board the information revolution, which, as Dan Schiller once contended, was one of the two poles of the twenty-first century for the global capitalist economy, together with the rise of Chinese economic power (Schiller, 2007).

Consistent with the dramatic turn of events in the political arena, from 1978 onwards there has been a similar transition in public and media discourses. A new logic regarding history/society was established. This is a seemingly neutralized but essentially capitalist conception of history/society as a linear line of transition from agrarian, industrial and post-industrial/information societies, to the most recent one: a low-carbon society. It replaced the Marxist view of this linear history as progress from slavery; feudal; and a capitalist to a communist system, with an emphasis on the transformations of both the production relations and the class struggle, which was quietly suspended. However, it seems that a dual system of rhetoric still operates, since courses on Marxism are still being taught from high school to universities. In order to justify the capitalist policy initiatives, what has been in reality a commoditization or commercialization process is described as 'marketization' or 'industrialization'. This innovation or linguistic turn has been an ongoing phenomenon.

The works of futurologists such as Alvin Toffler have been widely criticized in Western academic literature for their over-simplification and techno-centric enthusiasm, but the third wave rhetoric fitted perfectly with the then Chinese context and was regarded as a new Bible. *The Third Wave* was translated into Chinese in 1983 and touched the souls of the generation of Chinese intellectuals and politicians, who were, at the time, tired of political ideology and eager to seek new ways to overtake the West. The wave rhetoric spared the communists-become-capitalists the trouble to justify their legitimacy to rule after the demise of the statist system. Toffler's popularity in China in the 1980s reached such an extent that he was enlisted by the *People's Daily*, the central propaganda organ of the Chinese Communist Party, as one of the top 50 foreigners that had had the greatest influence on modern Chinese history, along with others as diverse as Karl Marx, Richard Nixon and Marie Curie. Taking into consideration

China's social context in the 1980s, it makes sense that the status of Toffler was elevated to the historical status of Marx, as he represented a new framework of thinking for China that enabled it to put aside its past.

The agendas of top Chinese officials, newly-fledged businessmen and people at the grassroots all converged, dreaming of riding the tide of the third wave. Imitating Japanese and American models of economic development, in a fanciful hope of leapfrog, in 1984 China recruited the information sector into its opening-up experiment, under the slogan of 'developing information resource, serving the course of modernization'. Two years later, in March 1986, a national long-term 10 billion Yuan innovation plan, the '863 Plan' (named after the initiating year and month) was launched for the purpose of improving advanced science and technology, especially information technology.

In this new logic of social evolution, Chinese society was undergoing a period of rapid transformation on three levels: an agricultural level, an industrial level and an informational level. Between these three levels, two jumps can be distinguished: one jump from the agricultural level to the industrial, the other from industrial to informational. An important feature for China, and perhaps also for other developing countries, is that these two transitions were happening simultaneously, which is arguably rooted in the processes of a capitalist-oriented uneven development. Many aspects of the society were in a state of flux, be it politics, economy or culture.

The media industry thrived during this process: the management, writing style, topics of interest and operating logic of the purely official media could not meet the new needs of an audience created by the process of industrialization, marketization and urbanization. Three types of newspapers emerged from the state organs: evening, metropolitan and economic. These new publications were essentially different from their official precursors in that they were driven by commercial logic and the tastes of readers. The newspaper industry prospered significantly during this period: 133 of 146 titles of evening newspapers available in 1999 were created after the 1978 Reform and Open-up policy (Liu, 2010). Metropolitan newspapers started in the 1990s – *Guizhou Metropolitan* was the first newspaper to use the word. By 2002, there were over 70 metropolitan newspapers.

During this period, the newspaper industry experienced marketization (1978–1996) followed by conglomeration (1996 onwards). With marketization, nearly 30 years of Party-state monopoly was broken and the media sector in a large measure is now supported by advertising. The other trend was conglomeration: although the Party-state still functioned as the owner of newspapers, in practice this was in name only and the first conglomerate, Guangzhou Daily Group, was set up in 1996. By 2002, there were 39 newspaper groups. Another breakthrough happened in 2003, when the first case of cross-regional ownership was approved by the Administration of Press and Publications. *The Beijing News* was co-founded by Guangming Daily Group in northern China and Nanfang Daily Group was established in southern China.

As far as broadcasting is concerned, a four-layered administrative structure at the state, provincial, city and county level was introduced in 1983 to assign more autonomy to provincial and local entities to enable them to launch their own broadcasting stations. There were 118 radio stations and 47 television stations in 1982; by 1988, the number of radio stations increased four-fold to 461 stations and the number of television stations increased nine-fold to 422 stations. By 2012, after a series of administrative conglomerations of radio and television stations at all levels, the number of radio stations declined to 169, while the number of television stations also reduced to 183. The national penetration rate of radio and television services stood at 97.51 per cent and 98.20 per cent respectively (Pang, 2013). At the end of the twentieth century, the total advertising turnover of broadcasting reached 16.9 billion Yuan (Liu, 2010) and the general income of the broadcasting industries by 2013 had reached a historical height of around 37.3 billion Yuan (Pang, 2013).

In-depth reports, investigative news programmes and traffic information radio channels became popular and lucrative. Unlike the other reconfiguration processes, there has been a rich academic debate over the impact of this market reconfiguration on party politics. Critical communication researchers raised questions about transplanting a market mechanism into a body of socialism. In the two visits to China before and after 1978 reform and opening-up policy, foreigners used metaphors like 'After Bicycles, What?' and 'You can't be a little pregnant' to predict the consequences of the capitalist turn upon Chinese society and media. Their predictions were proved true 20 years later, when capitalism blossomed in China. These were the typical questions asked by communication researchers about the Chinese social context in the 1990s:

> In what ways do market forces influence the media? How does the commercial imperative both accommodate and challenge Party control? What are the political implications of the current fusion of Party control and market forces in the Chinese news media? To what extent does the market present a democratizing alternative to Party control?
>
> (Zhao, 1998)

Overall, Yuezhi Zhao (1998) observed a set of contradictions about the identity of Chinese media: 'between the Party line and bottom line'; 'profit or ideology', 'power and money', 'servants of the state or the market'. These formulations reduced the Chinese media system into a state-corporatist model driven both by market competition and elements of the old Communist/ Confucian legacy of state control. According to them, the Chinese media landscape in the 1990s was like the bats in one of Aesop's fables: 'The bats, the birds, and the beasts.' Like bats, the Chinese media struggled between two mutually exclusive identities, wanting to be both the singing birds for the Party-state and the running beasts in the market, reducing themselves to 'propagandists or entertainers'.

In addition to critical discussions on either the dichotomy of an emancipatory market and the repressive state or the mutual constitution of both, scholarly attention also shifted to the constructive role of marketized media in promoting media freedom and democracy, particularly in the post-1978 period. Lee (2001) pointed out that, during the Republic of China years (1911–1949), the fight for media freedom was about how much freedom; during Mao's years (1949–1978), the question was whether there was any freedom, and after two decades of economic reform (1978–1990s), the question had returned to the first question: how much freedom?

In the new millennium, the consequences of the introduction of a market mechanism remain a central topic for discussion, but one has to take into account a third dimension: the rise of the grassroots as a societal agent. This has led Lee to ponder 'what will the emerging global network of communication technology do to China's state-controlled commercialized journalism' (ibid.) and Zhao (2007) to write 'After Mobile Phones, What?' to include 'grassroots participation' as a new dimension of communication research.

## Rise of the grassroots: justice as a priority (2003–present)

Looking back over China's history of reform, a contradictory pattern of both continuity and dialectical change emerges. More than two decades of neoliberalism has transformed the political economy, as well as cultural politics. China has entered a critical phase of rebalancing the triangular relationship between state, market and society, as Zhao argues, 'subordinating both state and market to social needs' (2007: 49). Hu Jintao's presidency at first countered the policies of the former capitalist-led, economic-driven development by repositioning 'society' and 'justice' at the centre of sustainable development to build a 'harmonious society'. This, to a certain extent, pulled the state back to 'a just path for humanity' (Renjian Zhengdao) (Hu, Wang, Zhou and Han, 2011), halting the further incorporation into socialism of the capitalist logic of 'accumulation by dispossession' (Harvey, 2003). Seeing the impact of this on an already fractured and polarized society since the 1990s, with structural inter-class tensions, inequalities and social instabilities – exemplified by the nationwide privatization of state-owned enterprises and the corresponding reconfiguration of capital-labour relations – from 2012, Chinese President Xi Jinping and his consultant team proposed an even more radical approach. This was, on the one hand, to confine capitalist expansion inside the state administration, and, on the other hand, to revitalize the socialist legacy as the legitimacy of the new China, serving the people instead of capital, both domestically and globally.

However, it would be wrong to characterize these changes as merely driven from the top by the leadership in a bureaucratic system, or to undervalue them as just political rhetoric. Instead, serious social analysis sees them as a reflection of the comprehensive transformation of Chinese society, involving agencies of all classes and groups, but particularly from the 'grassroots'. Against this background during the past decade, more uncertainties have appeared for Chinese society, concurrently with the dramatic transformations in an enlarging and integrated media sector, as coined by Zhao in her 2011 book chapter 'Chinese media, contentious society'. This is also exemplified in studies of communicative practices in China and beyond, such as the 'ambiguities in communicating with the world' in a multifaceted international communication environment, discussed by Hu and Ji (2012), underlining the problems of taking an essentialized concept of China as the starting point of analysis.

In terms of the changes in the media landscape and the instrumental role of media in social reform since the beginning years of the new millennium, more uncertainties and even contestations are present. Although the process of commodification of media sector is still 'controlled' (Weber, 2010), due to the Party-state's historically-rooted concern about the challenges from both a completely capitalist industry inside and political threats from global imperialist powers outside, mediated by a domestic capital-driven media market, China has indeed seen a new phase of further commodification and marketization in media, which might reach the limit of the socialist state's containment of a capitalist development.

Following a zero-sum logic of competing capitals via advertising subsidies or investment, the press industries are shrinking because of the comparatively low return from getting audience's attention and following market behaviour, while the broadcasting industries are increasingly digitized and concentrated on urban-based middle-class tastes in, for example, stylized TV dramas and reality shows. The latter are targeting a national marketplace, especially for those provincial satellite TV stations such as Hunan and Jiangsu, and therefore caught the attention of investors who were seeking for more profitable spaces across different industries.

Regardless of the reconfiguration of the conventional media market, the emerging Internet platform is becoming the major force to shape a more integrated media or digital market economy, particularly through mass participation in the use of quickly evolving hardware, as well as the production, circulation and consumption of content.

In this expansionary and competitive digital market, the increase in the power of the audience/users has been acknowledged, while the state's policies of bridging the digital divides between affluent and poor regions, developed urban and underdeveloped rural areas are progressing. As a result of these power restructurings, more voices have been heard, increasing discursive conflicts in transitional China today. As well as the continuing intellectual debates between leftist and rightist intellectuals on the changing nature of the state and the approach China might take towards future developments in democracy, popular debates mediated by both conventional media and (mobile) Internet platforms also deserve careful attention. In the case of the Wenzhou high-speed train collision in 2011, which killed 40 passengers and injured around 200, Chinese Twitter service 'Weibo' was used by passengers and other witnesses to spread news of the tragedy at least 40 minutes ahead of the conventional media and to criticize the state's mega-project. On 30 August 2013, a photo of a local official in Shaanxi province – with a smiling face and a luxury watch – in front of a car accident, hit the national news headlines. Dacai Yang, the smiling official, was soon identified by Chinese Internet users through 'human flesh search'. Afterwards, his improper and irresponsible behaviour, as well as his luxury watch, became the focus of online discussions, including a national Internet search on the corrupt officials and the luxury watches that they own. Thus, debates on the Chinese Internet, triggered by breaking news, reflect a fractured social structure as well as ideological conflict.

This new media environment, spear-headed by the Internet is becoming more conducive to the ideals contained in *glasnost*. Unlike the former Soviet Union, the Chinese experiment towards 'publicity and openness' is being executed in a gradual way. There are three important differences between China and the former Soviet Union in this context that are worthy of mention.

First, reform in China started in the realm of the economy. Secondly, Chinese economic reforms were launched in 1978, almost a decade earlier than in the Soviet Union, where *perestroika* started in 1986. Thirdly, the Chinese case was a unified effort based on the consensus of people from all walks of life and bringing together both top-down initiatives and bottom-up grassroots participation. The Soviet case was more or less driven from the top.

With the rise of the Internet as a revolutionary form of new media, a new approach to scholarly analysis is required, one with a societal perspective. With regard to the role of the state, the grand design of numerous development initiatives was seriously flawed in its inability to maintain justice and equality. In fact, injustice and inequality were implicit in the policy: 'Let some areas and some people get rich first, then other areas and people will follow, and finally all will get rich.'; 'No matter if it is a black cat or a white cat, as long as it catches mice, it is a good cat.'; 'Take efficiency as the top priority, take also into account justice.'; 'Cross the river by touching the stones.'

In the post-2003 period, the state pragmatically switched its policy from 'let some get rich first' to 'let us get rich together', from 'black cat theory' to 'green cat theory', and from 'efficiency first' to 'justice first'. But in terms of essential political and economic reform, the Party-state is still lagging behind: because of the deeply-rooted middle and upper-class bias of the previous reform and the overbearing bureaucratic systems as an independent interest group, the developmental state has fallen victim to various entrenched *ad hoc* interests and its credibility is eroding away in the networked new media environment in which people are expressing their soaring dissatisfaction about the widening gap between rich and poor, urban and rural, capitalist reality v. proclaimed socialist ideals.

## Grassroots and the Internet

While the deficit in the environment, human rights, freedom and justice keeps growing, the Internet industry thrives courtesy of the prevailing post-1978 market logic. On 20 September 1987, the first email entitled 'across the Great Wall we can reach every corner in the world' was sent out successfully from the Computer Application Technology Center of the Chinese Academy of Sciences in Beijing to Germany. On 20 April 1994, as a result of the joint efforts of the scientific community, China 'achieved its full-functional connection to the Internet' by opening a line through Sprint Co. Ltd and 'has been officially recognized as a country with full functional Internet accessibility'. By June 2014, China had 632 million Internet users and 527 million mobile Internet users (CNNIC, 2014), with the potential to fully reactivate a conventional media landscape comprising over one billion television viewers, nearly 700 million radio listeners, 200 million regular newspaper readers and a mobile network of 900 million mobile phone users, each of them the largest in scale in the world.

The Chinese experience with the Internet has had a different trajectory from its counterparts in the developed North. Castells (2004: 14–22) attributes the birth of the Internet in the US to the interactions of three independent processes: the crisis of industrialism, the rise of freedom-oriented social movements, and the revolution in information and communication technologies. Following this reasoning, the growth and maturity of civil society forces was an essential factor for the birth and spread of the Internet in the US and Europe. That is not the case for China: the Internet was brought into China at a time when networking among civil society members was extremely difficult.

Nevertheless, the voices of civil society groups and individuals at the grassroots level are suddenly being heard. A symbiotic relationship between the grassroots and new media is developing. Neither the capital nor the state has so far been able to break this intimacy between the grassroots and new media, and in fact the state and capital themselves are locked in a both allying and competing relationship with people's voices. Unlike their media predecessors – broadcasting and newspapers – the Internet and other new communication technologies are not easy prey for state and market power. They greatly facilitate expressions by the grassroots and empower disadvantaged groups, who are raising their voices and raising their profiles. This ascendance is paralleled by the wide adoption and spread of information and communication technologies.

In this sense, the arrival of a free communication tool was bound to be revolutionary. The Internet has been used to feed and coordinate civil society movements. This impact was not evident in the initial years of the Internet in the 1990s. After the turn of the new millennium, however, the potential of this new communication technology to connect people and fight against injustices was suddenly realized. These contestations are now unfolding in present-day China. Numerous spectacles and events led by new media platforms like Weibo and WeChat are re-shaping the media and public opinion landscape. Official media, market-oriented media and private Internet companies, as well as grassroots media, un-peacefully co-exist in China, forming a unique media matrix.

Along with the ongoing political reform, official media are still playing a dual role of propaganda and profit-making, but in a sense turning back from further marketization in order to be consistent with the commanding heights of the Party-state, which has become the biggest potential client for the media system, with accumulated capital and increasing redistributive power. Provincial TV stations, Beijing TV, for example, receive millions of dollars from the Beijing Municipal government as subsidies in a fiercely competitive media market in the capital city, as well as soft regulations to keep in line with the government's overall propaganda system. A new role played by the government, which is different from that in the pre-reform period, should be taken into account. Against the backdrop of 'the state advances while the private sector retreats' (Guojin Mintui) criticized by liberal intellectuals, market-based media with little commitment to the propaganda role are finding that capital is taking control. Instead of making innovations in production for target consumer groups by capital accumulation, those market entities are striving for cross-industrial capitals to raise the production level. As Chinese TV filmmakers are eager to make their own blockbusters to compete with Hollywood, TV stations and other content-driven industries are also following a market logic, which explains the triumph of singing competition show 'Voice of China' and reality show 'Where Are We Going, Dad?'. As a result, capital investment is becoming increasingly concentrated on such dominant and monopolistic players, while the remaining majority is reaching a point of survival or death.

The Internet, especially private Internet companies, is redrawing the picture of Chinese media, with its conventional media partners lagging far behind. Through not only the technical power of integrating all existing media markets by digitization and the Internet, but also well-developed business models, represented by rising ARPU revenue, and less intensive regulations from an informationalized economy-led state governmentality, private Internet companies have been incorporated into a capital-driven market and have in fact enjoyed a comparatively 'free market' ever since their birth. However, with rising concern about potential political challenges from a market-freedom-based communicative space, together with worries about national cyber security, the state has issued much stricter rules over the last decade to regulate Internet companies and their market behaviour.

Grassroots media, mainly based on easy access to affordable mobile Internet by the majority, are mushrooming in a fractured Chinese society. Despite those common appeals to justice and equality, grassroots media are highly divided in forming specific, even individualized, communication circles and showing particular political, economic and cultural concerns and interests, as demonstrated in social media events. Different definitions of justice, equality and democracy are proposed by different constructs of the grassroots to reflect their political and economic interests and ideological standpoints. Therefore, deconstructing the grassroots is key to understanding the complex restructuring and polarization of Chinese society and its relationship to the development of new media.

## References

Castells, Manuel (1997) *The Power of Identify*, The Information Age: Economy, Society and Culture Vol. II. Oxford: Blackwell.

Castells, Manuel (ed.) (2004) *The Network Society: A Cross-Cultural Perspective*. Cheltenham, UK: Edward Elgar.

China Internet Network Information Center (CNNIC) (2014) 'Basic Statistic Data (2014-06-30).' Available at www.cnnic.net.cn/hlwfzyj/jcsj/.

Harvey, David (2005) *The New Imperialism*. Oxford: Oxford University Press.

——(2007) *A Brief History of Neoliberalism*. Oxford: Oxford University Press.

Hu, Zhengrong and Ji, Deqiang (2012) Ambiguities in Communicating with the World: the 'Going-out' Policy of China's Media and Its Multilayered Contexts. *Chinese Journal of Communication*, 5(1): 32–37.

Hu, Angang, Wang, Shaoguang, Zhou, Jianming and Han, Yuhai (2011) *Renjian Zhengdao* (The Right Road of Human Beings), Beijing: People's University Press.

Huang, Ray (1999) *Broadening the Horizons of Chinese History*. Armonk, NY: M.E. Sharpe.

Lee, Chin-Chuan (2001) Servants of the State or Market? Media and Journalists in China, in Jeremy Tunstall (ed.) *Media Occupations and Professions: A Reader*. Oxford: Oxford University Press.

Li, Bin (2009) *A Social History of Journalism in China*. Beijing: Tsinghua University Press.

Liu, Jialin (2010) *Compiling 60 Years History of Journalism and Communication in China*. Guangzhou: Jinan University Press.

Mao, Zedong (1927) Investigation Report of Hunan Peasants Movement, in Mao, Zedong (1961) *Selected Works of Mao Zedong*. Beijing: People's Publishing House.

Pang, Jingjun (ed.) (2013) *Annual Report on China's Radio, Film and Television*. Beijing: Social Science Academic Press.

Schiller, Dan (2007) *How to Think About Information*. Champaign, IL: University of Illinois Press.

Toffler, Alvin (1983) *The Third Wave* (in Chinese, translated by Zhu, Zhiyan and Pan, Qi). Shanghai: SDX Joint Publishing Company.

Weber, Ian (2010) Commodifying Digital Television in China: A Socio-linguistic Analysis of Media Discourse, Technology Deployment and Control. *New Media and Society*, 12 (2): 89–308.

Zhao, Yuezhi (1998) *Media, Market, and Democracy in China: Between the Party Line and the Bottom Line*. Urbana and Chicago, IL: University of Illinois Press.

——(2007) After Mobile Phones, What? Re-embedding the Social in China's 'Digital Revolution'. *International Journal of Communication*, 1(1): 92–120.

——(2008) *Communication in China: Political Economy, Power and Conflicts*. Lanham, MD: Rowman & Littlefield.

——(2011) Chinese Media, Contentious Society, in James Curran (ed.) *Media and Society*, Fifth edition, London: Bloomsbury.

Zhao, Yuming (ed.) (2004) *History of China's Radio and TV*, Beijing: Beijing Broadcasting Institute Press.

# Chapter 9

# South Africa: a free media still in the making

*viola candice milton and Pieter J. Fourie*

Historically, South Africa was characterized by a social and media landscape based on racial exclusion, with a white presence and a structured black absence as its defining characteristic. With the shift to democracy in 1994, the South African media have had to reposition themselves ideologically, politically and culturally. Today, South Africa is a multi-party constitutional democracy with a vibrant media that, while often at odds with the country's post-apartheid media policies, also bears some striking similarities to the media landscape under apartheid and colonial rule. In this chapter, we give a brief overview of the South African media system and landscape, followed by a transitory synopsis of regulation and the state of freedom of expression in South Africa.

Looking at the South African media from the vantage point of different media models, one could argue that, historically, South Africa has combined several of these: the authoritarian model (evident in the prohibition of independent, private-owned newspapers by the British Governor, Lord Charles Somerset, in the apartheid-era state broadcasting as well as the stringent censorship of the press), the libertarian model (manifested in the relatively unregulated press environment of the late nineteenth and early twentieth century) and the social responsibility model (the establishment of, for example, the Newspaper Press Union in 1882, as well as the South African Broadcasting Corporation's transition from state to public broadcaster). In recent years, there has also been pressure from the South African government to ascribe to a development model (here, it is argued that the media should also be used to promote national development and cultural identity).

## South Africa's post-apartheid media landscape

South Africa has a population of nearly 52 million. Of these, 79 per cent are black African; 9.6 per cent are white, 8.9 per cent are coloured and 2.5 per cent are Indian (OMD Media Facts, 2013). To comply with affirmative action and black economic empowerment policies, the country's media landscape therefore should reflect these realities in terms of ownership structures, media content, media diversity and access to the media. The architects of the post-apartheid

South African constitution envisioned a media that could function within the overlapping models of libertarian theory, social responsibility theory and development theory. Though it is seen to be slipping in recent years, the constitutional commitment to freedom of expression, including media freedom, and the right of access to information and the independence of broadcasting legislation are marked departures from the colonial and apartheid past. In terms of regulation and legislation, the scene was therefore set for a media environment committed to growth in ownership, outlets, content and access; and with a commitment to fair and equal representation of citizens and their diversity of opinions.

In theory, contemporary South Africa has a dynamic media landscape. The country has six public service radio stations, 18 commercial national and regional radio stations, 10 public service African language stations and over 60 community radio stations. As far as print is concerned there are 21 daily national, regional and city-based newspapers, 24 weekly newspapers, 25 community papers and over 400 consumer magazine titles. In terms of online media, there are 17 major news sites, apart from the online sites of newspapers and broadcasters (OMD Media Facts, 2013: 10). This impressive spread, however, does not necessarily translate to a more equal media environment. A closer scrutiny of the statistics reveals some latent issues with regard to media access, growth and ownership structures.

## Print

When the issues of access and distribution are considered, it is clear that the history of segregation and systematic underdevelopment of the majority of South Africans, which started in the nineteenth century under British rule, has had a profound impact on the ways in which South African media is consumed. South Africa is still one of the most unequal societies in the world, with the majority of the poor still primarily among the black population. With regard to print it should be noted that, while only 14.3 per cent of South Africans are Afrikaans and 10.8 per cent are English, most of South Africa's mass media publish in English or Afrikaans and only three of the major newspapers publish in isiZulu (the most widely spoken South African language at 23.2 per cent). OMD Media Facts' study of media access for South Africans above the age of 15 reveals that, while the South African media landscape may be characterized by the availability of a wide range of media, accessibility remains an impediment, as there are many people in remote rural areas who still do not have access to a diverse range of information (OMD Media Facts, 2013: 10). Access to newspapers is highest among coloured, Indian and white South Africans and lowest among black South Africans (ibid.). In terms of distribution, smaller media groups face huge challenges as the major distribution networks and the big media players control the printing presses. With few exceptions, news-papers are primarily distributed in metropolitan areas and not always easily accessible in poor rural areas. The costs of purchasing newspapers for poor people are thus prohibitive if one considers transport costs (Lloyd, 2013).

In terms of media growth one might be tempted to laud the growth in terms of media outlets. The country's broadcasting and digital landscape is impressive in this regard (OMD Media Facts, 2013: 10). The broadcasting sector, which was previously almost completely state-owned, has seen the introduction of a number of new private and community broadcasters that are independently owned and controlled, while the Internet is also making inroads, especially among the more affluent classes. In contrast to these, there has been no such similar growth or change in the print sphere. In spite of the fact that the number of consumer magazines and newspapers and business-to-business publications has more than doubled, the number of mainstream dailies and weeklies has stagnated. In 1991 there were 22 daily newspapers; there were still 22 dailies in 2012. There were 25 major weeklies in 1991, there were 28 in 2012 (OMD Media Facts, 2013: 10). This might be a result of the growth in online publications, which has seen print media take a hit globally. More disturbingly, perhaps, is the finding that, where ownership of print media is concerned, the past is very much present. Today, South Africa has a broad range of individual newspaper titles, but, as was the case under apartheid, four major companies dominate the South African newspaper and magazine industry and between them own the majority of mainstream titles and control 90 per cent of the print media sector. Angelopulo and Potgieter's extensive study into the economic specification of media ownership in South Africa clearly illustrates the dominance of the so-called Big Four in print media, i.e. Caxton/CTP Pty Lt, Naspers/Media24; Times Media Group and Independent News and Media South Africa (2013: 4). This pattern is exacerbated when ownership patterns of magazines are considered. South Africa has a large and diverse number of magazine titles, however the range of ownership is significantly lower; with the big four companies also dominating in this respect (OMD Media Facts, 2013: 17).

Angelopulo and Potgieter (2013: 12) note that, although these groups have undergone significant transformation in ownership, their constituent newspapers have remained dominant and the underlying structure of the sector has not changed significantly. Lloyd (2013) adds to this that:

> In, 2011 during parliamentary hearings into print media transformation it emerged that the average black ownership of the press was 14 per cent, while female representation at board level was only 4.44 per cent. Print owners defended this at the hearings, stating that the number of black editors of newspapers had grown from 7 per cent in 1994 to 65 per cent in 2011. However, as online independent publication, the *Daily Maverick,* wrote early in 2013, '[w] atching print media engage with transformation is pretty much like witnessing an unwilling schoolboy being hauled off to the principal's office, screaming and resisting every step of the way.'

'The Big Four' has become a thorn in the South African government's side, which sees their news coverage of corruption, scandals and outrages of various kinds as anti-ANC and thus dangerous to the ruling party. Amid accusations of preferential treatment of political parties, sensationalist reporting and a lack of focus on the positive aspects of South African life in general, and government in particular, the ruling party's discontent with mainstream newspapers reached a peak in 2007, resulting in calls for more stringent regulation of the press in the form of a state-regulated media appeals tribunal (the so-called MAT). In response to this, civil society pressed for a more transparent independent co-regulatory system, resulting in a major overhaul of the South African Press Council.

In addition to the big four newspapers, there are also a few smaller but significant media outlets – over 200 non-profit and community newspapers. Lloyd (2013) notes that some of the alternative journals have survived, such as the feminist journal *Agenda* and the *Labour Bulletin*, while a number of other left-wing publications have emerged recently (such as *New Agenda* and *Amandla*). Perhaps the most controversial of the smaller media groups is Infinity Media. Infinity Media is a joint venture between India's Essel Media and Oakbay Investments, which is owned by the controversial Gupta family. The Gupta family is close to President Jacob Zuma, and has managed to attract massive amounts of government spending. Through the publication of a newspaper (the *New Age* established in 2012), as well as their 24-hour television news channel ANN7 (launched in 2013); this outlet strives to provide an alternative viewpoint in a market where the established viewpoint is considered anti-ANC. As such, the Gupta-titles are unapologetically pro-government and pro-ANC, though less forthrightly so than had been initially expected (De Wet, 2013).

Ownership of the remaining titles is varied; some are closely-held private companies, others have empowerment owners, others still are effectively foreign-owned. The influential *Mail & Guardian*, for example, is Zimbabwean-owned, while the *Citizen's* parent company, Caxton, publishes apolitical free local newspapers, yet, from the point of view of the ANC, these independents are nearly indistinguishable from many other outlets in their coverage of corruption, scandals and opposition parties. The independent titles' positioning in relation to government varies but more often than not they act as watchdogs for the government (De Wet, 2013).

## Broadcasting

After 1994, South Africa's broadcasting sphere has seen some radical changes that coincided with the changes in the country's political public sphere. Traditionally, broadcasting in South Africa was dominated by the state-controlled South African Broadcasting Corporation (the SABC). After the unbanning of opposition political parties and the release of Nelson Mandela in 1990, the National Party set in motion a gradual privatization of the broadcaster that would free it from government control and rule. This resulted in the sale of a number of

SABC radio stations to commercial bidders, as well as the development of community radio. Berger (2004: 55) posits that, since the economic policy in post-apartheid South Africa was capitalist, the government and other players looked to the private sector as the engine of the media's growth. Consequently, the SABC Board and management started to restructure the SABC into business units in preparation for a more competitive and commercialized broadcasting environment.

The SABC was transformed into a national public broadcaster, funded through TV licence fees, advertising and sponsorship revenue, as well as other business services. It was put under the control of a board, selected through public hearings (of Parliament) and appointed by the country's president. Under the Broadcasting Act of 1999, the SABC became a limited liability company with the state as the 100 per cent shareholder and was restructured into two arms: commercial (SABC3) and public services (SABC1 and SABC2). Until 1995, the SABC monopolized the country's airwaves, with M-Net (established in 1986) as its main competitor in television broadcasting. In the 1990s, SABC television changed from a one-channel television broadcasting in two languages, to six television channels broadcasting in 11 languages. Four were free-to air, namely SABC1, SABC2, SABC3 and Bop-TV, while Africa2Africa and SABC Africa were pay-per-view channels, broadcasting into the rest of Africa by satellite. The SABC had scaled down to only the three SABC channels in South Africa broadcasting on free-to-air analogue and one 24-hour news channel, launched on the DStv platform in 2013. Multichoice's DStv was established in 1995 and eTV, the country's first free-to-air commercial television station on a terrestrial frequency launched in 1998, while On Digital Media's TopTV entered the market in 2010. The SABC also owns 18 radio stations, broadcasting in all 11 official languages.

In terms of ownership, the SABC is a public broadcaster with Government as its main shareholder; Multichoice is owned by Naspers, while eTV is a subsidiary of PRIMEDIA, whose ownership is made up of trade-union pension funds, broad-based empowerment groups and others (De Wet, 2013). PRIMEDIA's radio stations and satellite broadcaster eNCA,

> present a quandary of sorts to the ANC. Their ownership borders on the impeccable, with union money backing both. Primedia also drives pro-citizen (and sometimes sunshine) initiatives such as LeadSA. Yet their coverage of both the ANC and government failures is often scathing, which puts the ANC in a difficult position: admitting they are considered anti-ANC would mean admitting ownership is not the reason behind negative coverage.
>
> (De Wet 2013)

Statistics from OMD Media Facts (2013: 10) reveal that radio reaches the most South Africans (93.1 per cent), with television a close second (at 91.7 per cent).

Community radio, with its focus on community issues, regionalized local content, retail and religious interest, seems to lead the audience ratings with over 25 per cent of listeners during OMD Media Facts' (2013: 15–16) period of observation. This is followed by the SABCs radio stations, whose focus on African languages make them popular choices for South African listeners. South African audiences clearly prefer local content and, if it is presented in one of the 10 official (African) languages, listenership as well as television viewership increases dramatically. This is borne out by the statistics for television viewing, which shows a clear preference for the SABC channels and eTV (OMD Media Facts, 2013: 12). Cost is not necessarily a factor as on the pay-per-view DStv platform, the channel touting a local focus, Africa Magic, is the second most popular channel, while the most popular television programme on M-Net is the locally produced magazine and reality programme, *Carte Blanche* (ibid.).

South Africa has approximately seven million licensed television households (Armstrong and Collins, 2004), with 91.7 per cent of South Africans above the age of 15 watching television daily (OMD Media Facts, 2013: 10), making it one of the largest television audiences in Africa. Satellite television developed rapidly after 1995, when the first commercial satellite television broadcasts were made. MultiChoice dominates satellite broadcasting in Africa with a presence in 48 countries in Sub-Sahara Africa and the adjacent Indian Ocean islands, and a subscriber base of more than two million (Naspers, 2013). MultiChoice's DStv offers South African viewers the internationally dominant news channels BBC, CNN, CNBC and Sky News, as well as PRIMEDIA's award-winning 24-hour news channel, eNCA. Two new players to the DStv news environment in 2013 deserve mention here. In August, 2013, both the Gupta-affiliated ANN7 24-hour news channel and the SABC's round-the-clock news channel, SABCN, launched on the DStv platform. ANN7 explicitly states its intention to focus on presenting the government in a more positive light.

While there was considerable (often vitriolic) discontent with the introduction of ANN7, more serious responses were reserved for SABCN. Discontent in this regard centred on two issues. First, the fact that the public broadcaster launched its 24-hour news channel on a digital platform to which the majority of its viewers have no access was seen as problematic. Secondly, the deal between Multichoice and the SABC is seen as potentially devastating to South Africa's fledgling democracy as 'it all but gives a commercial broadcaster total control over a public broadcaster, which is unheard of' (Bird in Business Day Online, 2013). Media Monitoring Africa's (MMA) William Bird questioned Multichoice's motives for granting money to the SABC to launch SABCN on a DStv platform when the implementation of Digital Terrestrial Television (DTT) is imminent; while the Communications Workers Union's Mathopo is quoted as saying '[w]e are happy with the progress that the SABC is making. We hope that this launch will afford job opportunities to many young people. We hope that poor people will be able to access to the channel [*sic*]' (in Mhlana, 2013).

The comments by the Communication Workers Union is especially apropos, given that prices for satellite decoders and DStv packages, while decreasing over the last few years as the demand grows, ensures that they remain largely off-limits to all but a small elite (see OMD Media Fact, 2013: 12 for viewership statistics). The SABC contends that this is an interim arrangement and that the SABC News channel will also be available on the DTT platform, once the switch from analogue to digital signal takes place in 2015. As of the time of writing, all of the SABC's DTT channels will be free-to-air (Channel24, 2013).

In terms of its licensing agreement as regulated by the IBA Act of 1993, about 50 per cent of all SABC programs transmitted are produced in South Africa; the remainder are mainly popular American and European television productions. Local programs include every possible genre from children's television and soap opera, to serious drama and documentaries about what it means to be a South African in the rapidly transforming country. Jacobs (2004) also observes that news production in South Africa is thoroughly modern and technically on par with most Western European countries. Television news is fed by SABC news teams reporting from all parts of the country, using modern portable electronic cameras and line-feed equipment via more than 220 television transmitters. Between radio and television, more than 98 news bulletins are broadcast in all 11 languages weekly (Jacobs, 2004).

The SABC competes with eTV, M-Net, DStv and Top TV for audiences, with eTV emerging as the broadcaster's main competition in this regard (OMD Media Facts, 2013: 12). When viewership is calculated in terms of Living Standard Measures (LSM), the impact of the economy on access is clear.[1] Duncan and Glen note in this regard that 'the South African television system has become characterised by uneven development with those who participate in the economic mainstream having access to a plurality of television services and to viewing options that expand all the time as the multi-channel environment matures' (2010: 40). This also has implications for advertising, as the old adage that advertisers want viewers (with money) holds true.

In South Africa, race is still a key factor in market segmentation, with the higher LSM, representing the most affluent viewers – still predominantly white (although this is rapidly changing) – while LSM 1, the least affluent, are predominantly black. Holborn (in South Africa.info, 2012) posits that Africans made up 99.7 per cent of those in LSM 1 in 2001, but only 3 per cent of those in LSM 10. He notes that while there have been significant changes in terms of South Africans living standards, in 2010 Africans still made up the majority of those in LSM 1 (98 per cent), while only 19 per cent of Africans are in LSM 10. Of adults in LSM 10, 65 per cent were white. When the SABC thus lays claim to an increase in audience numbers (as current Chief Executive Officer Lulama Mokhobo recently did), from an advertiser's point of view this audience includes a large percentage of (black) viewers from the lower LSM's – traditionally the 'have-nots', which is not an audience segment that appeals to advertisers.[2]

The implementation of Digital Terrestrial Television (DTT) is touted to change this status quo dramatically. In 2006 the South African Department of Communications (DoC) announced that South Africa would switch from analogue to DTT and, in November 2008, the South African government declared that broadcasters would have three years to switch from analogue to digital. They argued, along with the International Telecommunications Union, that the switch from analogue to digital is necessary in part because of escalating costs of repairing the ageing analogue infrastructure, which in SABC's case dates back to the 1970s. Apart from the cost benefits of switching to digital, there is also a general consensus that DTT will bring superior picture quality, a wider range of channels, greater interactivity, capacity to broadcast content in several languages and greater access for the majority of the people. However, the government's decree to switch from analogue to digital was not without problems, as a result its implementation has been considerably delayed. To date, after expenditure in excess of several million, there is still little agreement about what DTT in South Africa would or should entail, whether to implement it, whether 'more channels' will translate into a more diversified content platform and, if DTT is to be implemented, when this will happen.

While the changes in the print and broadcasting landscape can generally be considered as positive, they also led to an interesting shift in terms of how newspapers and broadcasters now view and approach audiences.

## Impact of changing print and broadcasting landscape on media audiences

Arguably the most significant change to the media landscape in South Africa is the manner in which race and the market intersects in ways that suggests a continuation of the apartheid-era segmentation of audiences. In electing to adopt a liberal democratic framework after 1994, the country was led to believe that economic growth happens through the market, most notably through the pursuit of neoliberal economic policies (see Duncan, 2000). What this means for media segmentation of audiences is that the public envisioned by the media is one that would be favourable to advertisers, i.e. the affluent, urban sectors of the community. Given South Africa's troubled history of disenfranchising black, coloured and Indian citizens, race intersects with the market in interesting ways: the most affluent viewers remain white and thus more attractive to advertisers, while the least affluent viewers remain black and a poor market for advertisers.

This intersection of race and market also has other consequences. Most significantly, it results in curious alliances that defy simplistic racial classifications. For example, the ownership structures of the press, while continuing to be referred to as 'white' and 'black', actually mask more complex interrelations between Afrikaners and newly-created black capital, or black capital and

English capital (Tomaselli and Louw, 1989; Louw, 2004). Jacobs (2004) quotes Harvey, who contends that the black elite – which he largely equates with the ANC and the various business and intellectual strata whose emergence is tied up with the transition – 'elevates questions of racism and suppresses questions of class' for its own interest. Tomaselli (1997) adds that, irrespective of their colour, capitalists, who have greater access to mainstream channels of communication, will use it to further their own class interests. The profit motive marginalizes and indeed misrepresents peripheral communities in programming and content decisions (Horwitz, 2001; Barnett, 2003; Duncan and Glen, 2010).

As is the case in broadcasting elsewhere, the post-apartheid government's move to downscale direct state support in the form of subsidies to the public broadcaster led to a greater reliance on programme funding through advertising. In television, the results have been major cuts in programming and its replacement with infomercials, rebroadcasts of local as well as cheap imported programmes and a re-racialising of the audience into 'market' segments which coincide with the racial divide and the emerging class divisions within the majority black population (Jacobs, 2004). Thus, as South Africa witnessed the separation of state and broadcasting, reduction in state subsidies have meant that, just as television held the promise of greater access for the black majority, it would be governed more indirectly by the market.

Commercialization has eclipsed the public-service nature of media system (Horwitz, 2001), and has thus restricted access in terms of media ownership to privileged private interests. Now, instead of being 'merchants of news', editors have become 'dealers in public opinion' (Jacobs, 2004). One consequence of this transition for the public sphere is that the poor are left out, caricatured or stereotyped in such discourses and debates (Jacobs, 2004; Milton, 2006). Thus the media, and specifically the public broadcaster, like other arenas in the South African public sphere, is favouring the elite (be they black and/or white) while any benefits to the poor are incidental, rather than planned. This situation did not go unnoticed by civil society as indicated by COSATU's 2002 march to the SABC headquarters to protest the broadcaster's pro-business model, which they accused of neglecting blacks, the poor and the working class.

To be fair, under pressure, the government set in motion structures to ensure that all sectors of the populace could benefit from broadcasting and communication. The setting up, in 2002, of the Media Development and Diversity Agency (MDDA) by an Act of Parliament (Act 14 of 2002) comes to mind here, but as is the case with the SABC, the MDDA is constrained by a lack of funding, making it difficult for the institution to carry out its mission (Sparks, 2009). In fact, in spite of clear incentives to transform the media landscape into a more equitable environment, free of political (and for public broadcasting also commercial) influence, some argue that the transformation process is too slow and is not yielding the desired results.

## New/online media

We have briefly touched on the digitalization of broadcasting when we discussed the post-apartheid broadcasting landscape. In this section, we review and analyse issues of access, ownership and control in the South African new media sector with specific focus on the Internet and mobile-based technologies. As happens almost universally, the impact of new media on the South African media system can be seen in terms of the creation of new distribution platforms; giving rise to multi-media approaches; a high level of interactivity between communicators and users (audiences); convergence of public and private media; niche markets; and creating new economic, social and political contexts for and in which the media have to operate.

As is the case with broadcasting, the Internet industry experienced a high growth rate between 1998 and 2008 (Z-Coms, 2009). The State of Broadband Report released by the UN Broadband Commission in September 2013 shows that 41 per cent of South Africans use the Internet, thus making it one of the top five countries in Africa (United Nations Broadband Commission, 2013: 98, 100). The report breaks down Internet access in terms of access to fixed broadband and mobile broadband. With regard to the first, South Africa is ranked 111th worldwide, with 2.2 out of every 100 people subscribing to fixed broadband. The global average is 9.1 (ibid.: 93). The report concurs with World Wide Worx's (2012) finding that smartphones are the main driver in Internet growth, noting that mobile broadband subscriptions (which allow users access to the Internet via smartphones, tablets and Wi-Fi- and Bluetooth-connected laptops) are growing at a rate of 30 per cent per year. During the survey period of 2012, mobile broadband penetration in South Africa stood at 26 per cent, and the UN Broadband Commission Report predicts that, by the end of 2013, there will be more than three times as many mobile broadband as there are fixed broadband connections (ibid.: 94). Finally the report reveals that 25.5 per cent of South African households have Internet access – that is a growth of 15.5 per cent from where we were in 2012 (ibid.: 96).

While there is remarkable growth in access to the Internet, as with all other aspects of the South African media industry, access remains problematic, with more than half of the South African population still totally unconnected. Among those with access, distribution is not equally spread across provinces. Of the 25.5 per cent of households with Internet access (or for which at least one member has access to the Internet at other venues), penetration is greater in provinces with large cities, than in less urbanized areas (MyBroadband, 2013).

Ownership patterns of online titles for newspapers and magazines are similar to the ownership patterns for print. Naspers leads the pack with 27 online titles, followed by Independent News and Media (17) and Avusa (14). Caxton has been bumped from the top four by Tabloid Media, who owns 10 titles to Caxton/CPT's 4 titles (Z-Coms, 2009). Independent News and Media's content is not necessarily accessible to all browsers – subscribers have access to all articles, but the general public only has access to those titles and content as determined by the publisher (Z-Coms, 2009). Avusa's online titles include 'The Times/Sunday Times' online; 'Sowetan Online' and the 'The Weekender' online, of which the company has a 50 per cent shareholding. Avusa has Mvelaphanda, a BEE company, as one of its major shareholders (ibid.). A similar pattern is discernible for online magazine ownership, with only one of the big four – Independent News and Media – missing from the picture. Established media owners have not only made some of their published newspapers and magazines available online, but they have also made it possible for such publications to be conveniently accessed via mobile devices. Added to this, social media such as blogs, micro blogs, wiki's, etc., are changing the ways in which news and other information is accessed.

New media, like other media in South Africa, are dominated by the major media companies such as Naspers/Media24 and Avusa. Small and specialized publications like the Mail & Guardian have created new business models by adopting new technologies that have enabled them to extend their reach beyond the print version of their newspapers (Z-Coms, 2009). Yet others, like newcomer to the field, the Daily Maverick, have opted for a purely online presence, as it markets its content to left-leaning, middle-class audiences. Telecommunications companies like Telkom and Vodacom not only own and provide the technology infrastructure required to access the Internet; they also have content provision spaces through which they establish a web presence.

While there is definite (and sporadic) growth in terms of access to the Internet, South Africa's most disadvantaged groups are still being left out of the loop. Accessibility in this respect is hindered not only by low computer literacy rates in general and in black communities in particular (Z-Coms, 2009), but also because the high costs of broadband and cell phones in the country are barring many South Africans from accessing their basic right to communicate. The issue of cost is deemed a serious human rights violation by the Right2Know campaign, which notes that the right to communicate is a basic human right that should not be hampered by unattainable cost structures. To this end, the campaign staged protests against cell phone companies in 2013 to fight the high costs of broadband and cell phones, noting that the right to communicate in South Africa will be the next step in their campaign towards ensuring an accessible media environment where freedom of expression is foregrounded.

## Media regulation and freedom of expression in South Africa

In this section, our focus shifts to how the media are regulated in South Africa and on freedom of expression which, as a cornerstone of South Africa's fledgling democracy, remains a crucial matter. To contextualize this shift in focus, we briefly consider the situation under apartheid, before outlining the contemporary legislative environment.

Under apartheid, there were numerous threats of legal action against the media. An example was the dreaded Publications Act of 1974, which made provision for extreme censorship of all media based on the concept of undesirability. The act was instrumental in the banning of newspapers (and editions thereof), films, books, magazines and works of art, etc. The act was instrumental in the banning of *The World* in October 1977. *The World* became the first white-owned South African newspaper to hire a black editor without white supervision when the late Percy Qoboza (arguably the most well-known black journalist in South Africa) was appointed in 1976. On 19 October 1977, the newspaper was banned as part of the government crackdown that followed the Soweto uprisings against Afrikaans-medium education in black schools. Today, 19 October is dedicated to seminars on media freedom and freedom of expression at universities across South Africa. The *CS Monitor* (Van Slambrouck, 1984) further notes the detainment of 73 black journalists in the late-1970s/early-1980s, of which 15 were subsequently banned in terms of the Publications Act of 1974 and the Internal Security Act of 1976. The Internal Security Act (1976) empowered the Minister of Justice to ban organizations or publications and to imprison or otherwise restrict persons without proof of their membership of organizations. The South African Communist Party, the African National Congress and other anti-apartheid political parties were also banned under this act.

The enforced 'State of Emergency' of the 1980s solidified the apartheid government's control of the media who, under the guise of 'national security', brought in censorship and restrictions that amounted to prohibiting publication of information about security forces, any restricted gatherings, boycotts, illegal organizations, people's courts, restricted persons or detainees, etc. (cf. Fourie, 2002; 2009 for more detail about legislation under apartheid).

In direct response to the laws of apartheid (of which the above are only a few examples to illustrate how severe censorship of the media was under apartheid), South Africa's new Constitution following the first democratic elections in the 1990s, makes special provision for the right to freedom of expression. The Constitution guarantees and protects the right to freedom of expression, including media freedom, the right to access to information and the independence of broadcasting legislation (KAS, 2003). Section 192 of the Constitution provides for the establishment of an independent broadcasting regulatory authority that must 'regulate broadcasting in the public interest and to ensure fairness and a diversity of views broadly representing South African society' (ibid.).

The introduction of an independent regulator with constitutionally guaranteed independence was a significant step forward for the broadcasting industry. Where broadcasting is concerned, the Independent Broadcasting Authority (IBA) and the Independent Communications Authority of South Africa (ICASA) deserve special mention. To comply with the provisions towards freedom of expression, a number of statutory bodies and laws are in place, including the ICASA as a sector-specific regulator for the broadcasting and telecommunication sectors; the MDDA, which aims to promote media development and diversity; the Films and Publications Act, which governs the pre-classification of films and publications, and the Protection of Information Act, which regulates the protection of official secret state information.

A primary goal of post-apartheid communication policies was to establish 'democratic communication' as a means to 're-distribute power' and to not have the same social framework of old to dictate communication and policy frameworks in the future. In terms of the media, this meant addressing inequalities in ownership, representation and access. A key feature of this redress is a focus on affirmative action and black economic empowerment. In line with affirmative action and black economic empowerment policies, a focus on local content has been central to post-apartheid broadcasting regulation. To this end, the MDDA was set up by an Act of Parliament to enable 'historically disadvantaged communities and persons not adequately served by the media' to gain access to the media.

In terms of media performance, three codes of conduct applying to print and broadcast media were initiated post-apartheid. For broadcasting the following applies: the Code of the Broadcast Complaints Commission of South Africa, which is a statutory code administered by the Broadcasting Monitoring and Complaints Committee (BMCC) under the IBA Act No. 153 of 1993 (the IBA is the frontrunner to ICASA); and the Broadcasting Complaints Commission of South Africa (BCCSA) Code, which is a voluntary code administered by the BCCSA, with the backing of the National Association of Broadcasters (NAB) – the industry body for the broadcasting sector. The purpose of the two Broadcasting Codes is to lay down standards of conduct for broadcasters operating in South Africa. The BCCSA Code applies only to members of the NAB. The objective of channelling disputes through the BCCSA is to achieve a speedy and cost-effective settlement of complaints against members of the NAB who have submitted themselves to the jurisdiction of the BCCSA. The BMCC Code otherwise applies to all broadcasters who are not members of the BCCSA. The code of conduct for the print media is the Press Code of Professional Practice ('the Press Code'), which is a voluntary code administered by the Press Ombudsman. The purpose of the Press Code is to lay down standards of conduct for the print media. Many of the provisions in the Press Code mirror the provisions in the Broadcasting Codes.

However, despite the Constitution, institutions and measures in place to internally regulate and monitor the media, two landmark cases tested South Africa's commitment to freedom of expression and media freedom in recent years. With regard to freedom of expression, the Promotion of Access to Information Act (2000) and the Protection of Information Act 84 (1982) came under scrutiny by government and eventually also civil society. Neither act encompasses media-specific statutes, but many of their provisions have a direct influence on the ability of the media to gather information. The Protection of Information Act especially has gained notoriety in recent years as the post-apartheid government seeks to redress it, ostensibly in line with the libertarian ideals of the post-apartheid state. It was passed by the apartheid government and was designed to 'provide for the protection from disclosure of certain information', which meant any information dealing with the government's actions (Protection of Information Act 84, 1982: 1). The act allowed the ruling government to arrest and detain any person who entered a 'prohibited place', as defined by the government.

The post-apartheid government stated its commitment to freedom of information throughout the early years of rule, signing into legislation the Promotion of Access to Information Act, which further indicated the government's concentration on freedom of information: 'To give effect to the constitutional right of access to any information held by the State and any information that is held by another person and that is required for the exercise or protection of any rights' (Government Gazette No.20852, 2000: 2). In 2010, however, security Minister Siyabonga Cwele introduced the Protection of Information Bill (the so-called 'Secrecy Bill'), which, if it were to be accepted in its original format, would have effectively shielded government officials from public scrutiny and which, as was the case under apartheid, would have criminalized activities essential to investigative journalism. How this bill is interpreted will clearly have consequences for the ways in which the media report on issues such as crime, corruption or protests. As will be pointed out later, the Secrecy Bill galvanized South African citizens into action and tested the ability of civil society and non-government organizations to organize around a common cause and form a pressure group to intervene when government oversteps its bounds.

A second case concerns the now defunct Public Service Broadcasting Bill (PSB Bill) of 2009. In October 2009 the South African Department of Communications ('DOC') found itself in conflict with civil society organizations following the publication of a draft 'PSB Bill, the Charter of the Corporation and the Charter of Community Broadcasting Services', which called for fundamental changes to the South African broadcasting landscape. The proposed PSB Bill was in part a response to the deep and very public crisis of South Africa's public (service) broadcaster, the SABC.[3] Since the glory days of the first free and democratic elections in South Africa – when the SABC was hailed for its relatively balanced account of the election processes – the public broadcaster had come under increasing fire for perceived bias towards the ANC government. Recent years have witnessed an increase in reports and concerns about political interference in the country's public broadcaster. Its board selection process is viewed with suspicion, while revelations about self-censoring through omission, blacklisting and biased reporting of politics in general has led many to conclude that the ANC, like its predecessor the National Party, is turning the broadcaster into its own special propaganda machine (Louw and Milton, 2012).

In spite of the big-scale changes to the South African broadcasting landscape that marked the end of the state monopoly of broadcasting, as well as the introduction of policies designed to generate 'procedures for accountability, transparency and public participation in communications policy' (Barnett, 2003: 175), there is a growing concern for the editorial independence of the public broadcaster and indeed the sustainability of public-service broadcasting in an increasingly commercialized media environment, which, amongst others, had dire consequences for the Broadcaster's ability to meet its financial obligations. In reaction to these issues, the PSB Bill proposed, amongst others, a radical change in the SABC's funding model.[4] However, inconsistencies in the phrasing of the bill and the threat to broadcasting and media freedom meant that the PSB Bill was shrouded in controversy from its inception.

In essence, the PSB Bill proposed that in future, direct parliamentary appropriations and television license fees be replaced by an earmarked tax on income. The accrued funds for public broadcasting were to be paid into a PSB Fund, to be administered by the MDDA. All broadcasters would be allowed to apply for funding through this mechanism. The bill stipulated that public broadcasting should be funded from personal income tax (not more than 1 per cent), money appropriated from Parliament, contributions from broadcasting services licensees, contributions from business and money accruing to the PSB Fund. It further proposed a cap on commercial revenue, stipulating that this may not exceed the income from the PSB Fund and other non-commercial revenue. The bill also outlined Board and Chief Officer appointments for the SABC that would make the SABC much more dependent upon the DoC and the Minister of Communications in its decision-making processes. Critics argued that the SABC 'is headed for a complete editorial independence meltdown if the Bill is enacted' (Da Silva, 2010) and civil society organizations, under the leadership of the Support Public Broadcasting Campaign immediately started their efforts to petition the Bill. Though civil society action eventually forced government to abandon the Bill, the very fact that it was introduced in the first place signals a worrying trend in terms of government's commitment (or lack thereof) to media freedom and the independence of public broadcasting in the country.

What emanates from the discourses about freedom of expression is challenging discussions of what can be described as different cultural perceptions and understandings of key concepts such as 'public interest' and 'freedom of expression', with the government often claiming that the media still holds a Western-biased view and that there is a need to indigenize journalistic practices and ethics. In this respect, the concept of 'Ubuntu'[5] is often evoked as a moral–philosophical point of departure for debating the role and functions of the media in society. The argument is raised that the political economy of media systems in Africa are still guided and dominated by Western views and values related to ownership, control, management and journalism practices, and Western-dominated views of freedom of expression, public opinion and public interest.

Ubuntuism represents a subtle shift from a libertarian model to a developmental model of the media, and the emphasis of the latter on foregrounding national developmental goals and cultural/national identity elevates fears of government interference in *how* news is produced and *what* news would be considered relevant and newsworthy. The implications of an indigenous world view, such as ubuntuism on the ontology and epistemology of contemporary South African thinking about the media is clear. Whereas 'the West' focuses on media primarily in terms of (i) its information, surveillance, entertainment and educational role; (ii) journalism's freedom and right to protection in order to be able to fulfil its social responsibility; and (iii) the individual's right to information, surveillance, entertainment and education, Ubuntu shifts the focus towards (i) the media's role in community bonding and in (ii) dialogue towards reaching consensus based on the (iii) cultural and social values and morals of a community. This has far reaching theoretical (and practical) consequences as pointed out by Fourie (2007) in his seminal essay on ubuntuism and its impact on journalism.

In the immediate aftermath of apartheid, South Africa went to great pains to ensure a free and independent media. Today, few would argue the fact that media freedom and independence have come a long way since the dark days of apartheid that saw the state utilizing the SABC as its own personal propaganda machine and the marginalization and indeed blocking out of voices not espousing the government's point of view. However, many would also note with concern recent developments in the South African political sphere that threatens to erode the progress made in this regard. As Berger notes in his study on media legislation, 'South African media operate with substantial impunity in a free environment ... however, there is a certain amount of harassment' (Berger, 2007: 108). The concern is that the number of 'buts' might rise – though this would not happen silently given the vocal and vibrant media and civil society sector in South Africa.

## The future of a free media: the role of civil society

Civil society has an established history of engaging with government over issues threatening media independence in South Africa's fledgling democracy. The Campaign for Open Media's (COM) march on Auckland Park, the headquarters of the SABC, on 25 August 1990 comes to mind as one example. On that date over a thousand people marched towards the SABC in a bid to, amongst others, demand that the restructuring of broadcasting take place on a democratic basis (Louw, 1993: 47). This incident marked the first time that ordinary members of the public mobilized around broadcasting matters, and followed the controversial appointment of the Viljoen Task Group on Broadcasting in March 1990. Media activists took issue with the lack of representativeness of the Group's membership as well as the fact that its deliberations were held in secret.

The Film and Allied Workers Organisation (FAWO) and COM formed an alliance in protest against this state of affairs, organized the march and succeeded in placing broadcasting, heretofore treated as an issue that should be 'de-politicized', squarely into the political arena (ibid.: 11–12). The march on the SABC was followed by a series of other high-profile public events staged by members of civil society, including the trade unions, civic organizations, cultural and political formations, academics, journalists and media practitioners. In November 1992, the COM was replaced by the Campaign for Independent Broadcasting (CIB), whose primary aims included, inter alia, that it should be acknowledged that broadcasting was a constitutional issue and therefore needed to be dealt with through the process of constitutional negotiations.

Today, not unlike in the 1990s, it is civil society that is reclaiming the SABC and redefining how the media in general should be viewed within a democracy. Current concerns regarding media policy in general, and broadcasting policy and freedom of expression in particular, seem poised on three primary questions: who should control the SABC, how should it be funded and how should the media system be positioned in relation to the country's normative understanding of the role of the South African media?

Where broadcasting is concerned, civil society organizations started developing concrete policy papers for broadcasting reform in 2008. In this respect, the SOS coalition, with its strong resemblance to the 1990s CIB, is taking the lead. According to their manifesto, the SOS is a membership-based coalition representing unions, NGOs, CBOs, community media, independent film and TV production sector organizations, academics, freedom-of-expression activists and concerned individuals. They aim to create a public-broadcasting system dedicated to the broadcasting of quality, diverse, citizen-orientated public programming committed to deepening South Africa's Constitution, particularly the Bill of Rights and socio-economic rights. Specifically, they focus on strengthening the SABC (and also community radio and TV). Their current efforts are geared in particular towards ensuring that new comprehensive legislation is drafted for the SABC (and community media) that ensures their effective governance and funding (SOS Support Public Broadcasting).

With regard to media freedom and freedom of expression, the Right2Know Campaign (R2K) is taking the lead. R2K officially launched in August, 2010 as a civil society reaction and opposition to the proposed Protection of State Information Bill (the so-called Secrecy Bill). Apart from R2K, more than 30 non-government organizations, including academic associations, the Human Rights Commission, Corruption Watch, the Law Society of South Africa, the Nelson Mandela Foundation, the Public Protector, Higher Education South Africa and numerous media NGOs such as the SOS Campaign, the South African National Press Club and the South African National Editors' Forum, continuously protested and presented new submissions to public hearings against the Secrecy Bill.

Civil action forced government to rethink key aspects of the Secrecy Bill and, while many of the concerning clauses were not revised or removed, some of the more controversial issues were significantly toned down. In spite of protests from civil society and opposition parties that more revision was needed, the revised bill was recently passed in Parliament and, at the time of writing, is waiting to be signed into law by President Jacob Zuma. The R2K has since expanded its focus and is currently actively involved in activism around access to information and the right to communicate (Right2Know).

Organizations like SOS and R2K enter the public arena at a time when the role of social media in civic and civil discourse is widely debated. Aware of the potential of social media networks, they have established a digital presence through their engagement with Twitter, Google groups, Facebook and organizational websites. Through the use of social media networks (which supplement their more hands-on efforts), these groups provide not only an important context and necessary background about the issues that South African citizens should take heed of, but they also attempt to move citizens to take a stand.

## Conclusion: looking towards the future

Since the demise of apartheid in 1994, the issue of black media ownership and the expansion of online media are the focal points for South African media history. With regard to print media, it is clear that four groups still dominate media ownership, there are still major challenges with regard to access and distribution and the often requested 'diversity of voices and opinions' are still hampered in a media environment where convergence and revenue is king.

With regard to voice, the online media environment, which is less stringently controlled and where spaces such as blogs, wikis and even comment sections in newspapers allow for input from a diversity of voices and opinions. News content itself has to undergo fast editing as micro blogging sites such as Twitter and Facebook often 'scoop' traditional media. Like print media globally, newsrooms will have to rethink the ways in which they package and distribute news content. Some newspapers (and broadcasters) in South Africa already have an established Twitter presence with relatively big followings, while others are still lagging behind. While social media sites are relatively easily accessible Internet platforms (also easily accessible on mobile platforms), cost remains a serious detriment to Internet penetration in South Africa. In spite of the exploding figures for mobile Internet access, more than half of South Africa's citizens still cannot access the Internet at all. As noted by the R2K campaign, the issue of cost with regard to access of information and the right to communicate deserves serious attention.

As far as broadcasting is concerned, given the growing problems with the political independence and financing of the public broadcaster since its inception in 1936, South Africa needs a new dispensation. In this regard it is probably one of the country's biggest challenges to design and implement a new broadcasting model, departing from the present three-tier system (public, private and community). In such a model a clear balance between economic, social and cultural goals will need to be achieved and sustained. This could be done, amongst other things, by acknowledging and grasping the opportunities of digitization towards increased access (for broadcasters and audiences) and new ways of thinking about the different relations between the media and democracy. It remains to be seen if South Africa will grasp the possibilities of multi-platforms created by digitization to address minority audiences (linguistic and cultural) and communities, a diversity of interests and the production of quality content and form.

In short, as far as policy and strategy is concerned, it is a challenge for all involved to grasp the opportunities of the new media environment to rethink the functions of the media in the South African society. Such rethinking could gain from a broader and changed understanding of the social responsibilities of the media in a developed but also developing, rich but also poor, literate but also illiterate, unified but also divided, country.

## Notes

1 The Living Standards Measure (LSM) is used in South Africa as an audience ratings measure that values level of income above racial categorization. Of course, this discourse masks the fact that in South Africa, all of the above (with the possible exception of age) intersects with race.
2 Here, it is of course necessary to acknowledge that advertisers that are referred to in this case are the advertisers attractive to broadcasters – those with big items to sell and who are willing to also pay big money to advertise.
3 To read more about the crisis, see Lloyd, Duncan, Minnie and Bussiek, 2010.
4 At present, the SABC is funded through a mixed model that includes commercial funding, licence fees, a small percentage from Government funding and a small percentage from 'other' sources. See Louw and Milton (2012), Chapter 8 for a detailed discussion.
5 Ubuntu is a Nguni Bantu term roughly translating to 'human kindness'. It is an idea from the southern African region which means literally 'human-ness', and is translated as 'humanity towards others', but is often used in a more philosophical sense to mean 'the belief in a universal bond of sharing that connects all humanity'.

## References

Angelopulo, G. and Potgieter, P. (2013) The economic specification of media ownership in South Africa, *Communication: South African Journal for Communication Theory and Research*, 39(1): 1–19.

Armstrong, C. and Collins, R. (2004) *Digital Dilemmas for South African TV*. LINK Centre Public Policy Research Paper 6. Graduate School of Public and Development Management. University of the Witwatersrand, Johannesburg.Available at http://link.wits.ac.za/papers/ddtvcarc.pdf. Accessed: 18 June 2013.

Barnett, C. (2003) *Culture and Democracy: Media, Spaced and Representation*. Edinburgh: Edinburgh University Press.

Berger, G. (2004) More media for Southern Africa? The place of politics, economics and convergence in developing media density. *Critical Arts*, 18(1): 42–75.

——(2007) Media legislation in Africa: A comparative legal survey. Available at http://unesdoc.unesco.org/images/0015/001570/157072e.pdf. Accessed: 10 June 2011.

Business Day Online (2013) SABC, DStv broadcasting deal spells bad news for e.tv. *Business Day Online*. Available at http://bit.ly/1s0JAYC. Accessed: 1 November 2013.

Channel24 (2013) SABC announces that set-top boxes will be free-to-air. *Channel24. Entertainment now*. Available at www.channel24.co.za/TV/News/SABC-announces-that-set-top-boxes-will-be-free-to-air-20131031. Accessed: 1 November 2013.

Da Silva, I. S. (2010) Lobby group cries foul over 'unconstitutional' Public Service Broadcasting. *Bizcommunity.com*. Available at http://bit.ly/5zKi6M. Accessed: 1 June 2011.

De Wet, J. (2013) South Africa's political media landscape. *Mail and Guardian*, 30 August.

Duncan, J. (2000) *Broadcasting and the National Question: South African Broadcast Media in an Age of Neoliberalism*. Braamfontein: Freedom of Expression Institute.

Duncan, J. and Glen, I. (2010) South African television: Turning points, in Moyo, D. and Chuma, W. (eds.) *Media Policy in a Changing South Africa: Critical Reflections on Media Reforms in the Global Age*. Pretoria: UNISA Press.

Fourie, P. J. (2002) Rethinking the role of the media in South Africa. *Communicare*, 21(1): 17–41.

——(2007) External media Regulation in South Africa, pp. 30–69 in Fourie, P. J. (ed.) *Media Studies: Policy, Management and Media Representation*. Second edition, Cape Town: Juta.

——(2009) 'n Terugkeer na die onderdrukking van vryheid van spraak? Ooreenkomste tussen die apartheidsregering(s) en die ANC se optrede teen die media/A return to the repression of freedom of speech? [Similarities between the apartheid government(s) and the ANC's actions against the media]. *Tydskrif vir Geesteswetenskappe*, 49(1): 62–84.

Government Gazette No.20852 (2000) Promotion of Access to Information Act, 2000. *Republic of South Africa Government Gazette No.20852*. Cape Town, 3 February 2000.

Horwitz, R. B. (2001) *Communication and Democratic Reform in South Africa*. Cambridge: Cambridge University Press.

Jacobs, S. (2004) *Mapping the Public Sphere after 1994: The Media Set-up*. Available at www.newschool.edu/tcds/Sean%20Jacobs.pdf. Accessed 1 August 2005.

Konrad-Adenauer-Stiftung (KAS) (2003) *SADC Media Law: A Handbook for Media Practitioners. Volume 1: A comparative overview of the laws and practice in Malawi, Namibia, South Africa and Zimbabwe*. Johannesburg: Konrad-Adenauer-Stiftung.

Lloyd, L. (2013) *South Africa's Media, 20 Years after Apartheid. A Report to the Center for International Media Assistance*. Available at http://issuu.com/cima-publications/docs/final/1?e=3797659/4077297. Accessed: 27 September 2013.

Lloyd, L.; Duncan, J.; Minnie, J. and Bussiek, H. (2010) *South Africa: Public Broadcasting in Africa Series*. Johannesburg: Open Society Institute Network.

Louw, E. (2004) Political power, national identity and language: The case of Afrikaans. *International Journal of the Sociology of Language*, 170: 43–58.

Louw, E. and Milton, V. C. (2012) *New Voices over the Air: The Transformation of the South African Broadcasting Corporation in a Changing South Africa*. New York: Hampton Press.

Louw, P. E. (ed.) (1993) *South African Media Policy: Debates of the 1990s. Studies on the South African Media*. Belville: Anthropos.

Mhlana, Z. (2013) TV channel raises questions. *Media Monitoring Africa*. Available at www.mediamonitoringafrica.org/index.php/news/entry/tv_channel_raises_question_mmas_william_bird_comments_on_the_sabcs_24-hour_/. Accessed: 27 September 2013.

Milton, V. C. (2006) *Combating HIV/Aids on the SABC: Public Service Broadcasting, Rainbowism and Media Advocacy*. Ann Arbor, Michigan: UMI Dissertation Services.

MyBroadband (2013) South Africa's Internet access stats revealed. *mybroadband.co.za*. Available at http://mybroadband.co.za/news/internet/85165-south-africas-Internet-access-stats-revealed.html. Accessed: 7 October 2013.

Naspers (2013) Pay-Television. *Naspers.com*. Available at www.naspers.com/pay-television_detail.php?MultiChoice-Africa-GOtv-5. Accessed: 7 October 2013.

OMD Media Facts (2013) *The Future of Media: Blueprint, 2013. OMD South African and SADC Media Facts, 2013*. Available at www.omd.co.za/media_facts/FOM029_Blueprint_OMD_mediafacts2013.pdf. Accessed: 27 September 2013.

Republic of South Africa Government (1982) Protection of Information Act 84. *justice.gov.za*. Available at www.justice.gov.za/legislation/acts/1982-084.pdf. Accessed: 7 October 2013.

——(2000) Promotion of Access to Information Act, 2000. *Government Gazette No.20852*. Cape Town, 3 February 2000.

Right2Know (2013) What we do. *Right2Know.or.za*. Available at www.r2k.org.za/about/what-we-do/. Accessed: 27 September 2013.

South Africa.info (2012) South African living standards 'on the up'. *SouthAfrica.info*. Available at www.southafrica.info/about/social/living-standards-030212.htm#.UoYE8_lBOSo#ixzz2kiFgKyG9. Accessed: 7 October 2013.

SOS (2011) Welcome to the SOS: Support Public Broadcasting website. Available at http://bit.ly/9EO4oK. Accessed: 2 June 2011.

Sparks, C. (2009) South African media in transition. *Journal of African Media Studies*, 1(2): 195–220.

Tomaselli, K. (1997) Ownership and control in the South African print media: black empowerment after apartheid, 1990–1997, *Ecquid Novi: African Journalism Studies*, 18(1): 67–68.

Tomaselli, K. G. and Louw, E. (1989) The South African progressive press under emergency, 1986–1988, *Ecquid Novi: African Journalism Studies*, 10(1–2): 70–94.

United Nations Broadband Commission (2013) *The State of BroadBand, 2013: Universalizing BroadBand. A Report by the Broadband Commission*. September 2013. Available at www.broadbandcommission.org/documents/bb-annualreport2013.pdf. Accessed: 07 October 2013.

Van Slambrouck, P. (1984) Muted voice of black press in South Africa is muffled further. *The Christian Science Monitor*, 17 April.

World Wide Worx (2012) *Executive Summary, Internet Access in South Africa, 2012*. Available at www.worldwideworx.com/wp-content/uploads/2012/12/Exec-Summary-Internet-Access-in-SA-2012.pdf. 07 October 2013.

Z-Coms (2009) *Trends of Ownership and Control of Media in South Africa*. Prepared for Media Development and Diversity Agency (MDDA), June15.

# Part III

# Comparative perspectives

## Introduction

Comparative communication research has become increasingly important in a rapidly globalizing media world. In this final part of the book, contributors deploy a comparative framework to explore journalism practices, as well as to examine intra-BRICS media coverage and digital futures, given the unprecedented growth of on-line media in some of the larger BRICS nations, notably China and India.

There has been no comparative study of journalists in BRICS nations so far. In their chapter, Svetlana Pasti, Jyotika Ramaprasad and Musawenkosi Ndlovu first review the state of the journalist profession in four BRICS nations (Brazil, India, China and Russia), based on past worldwide studies –*The Global Journalist for the 21st Century*, and the *Worlds of Journalism Study* – before synthesizing findings about journalists from these diverse countries with distinct media systems and journalistic cultures. The authors then report findings of comparative surveys of journalists in the BRICS countries – a work in progress using the first results from India and South Africa. Central to the study is the character and quality of growing Internet-based new media as an alternative to the conventional media. The chapter discusses similarities and differences between BRICS journalists in terms of their professional structure and values, freedom on the net and engagement with social and political protests.

The second chapter in this section by Herman Wasserman, Fernando Oliveira Paulino, Dmitry Strovsky and Jukka Pietiläinen examines how the respective countries in the BRICS alignment engage in transnational media exchanges and representations. The chapter tracks investments of various BRICS countries in the media industries of their counterparts, for example the expansion of China's print and broadcast media presence in South Africa, the investment of the South African media company Naspers in digital media companies in Brazil, India and China, and Russia's 24-hour television channel Russia Today. This expansion is analyzed in terms of the notion of 'soft power' as a way for nations to extend their influence. The chapter includes the results of exploratory analyses of the representation of the BRICS alignment as a group and as individual nations in the respective media of the member states. These analyses explore how the media in these countries portray their membership of the BRICS group, what types of news (e.g. economic, political, social) about the BRICS alignment receives the most coverage and whether the other member states are portrayed in a positive or negative light. It is clear, though, that while there may be significant potential for intra-BRICS interactions, the primary dynamic and flow of media content for all these countries remains with the West.

The final chapter by Daya Kishan Thussu evaluates how current and potential developments in digital media in the BRICS countries might impact on global communication. The international presence of the BRICS media is likely to expand exponentially, the chapter suggests, with the growing convergence of mobile communications technologies and content via an altered and multi-lingual Internet. The predominance of English on the Internet is increasingly being challenged, he argues, necessitated by the extraordinary expansion of digital media in major BRICS nations – China, India, Brazil and Russia. What implications, asks Thussu, will such digital connectivity have on information and communication agendas, 'soft power' discourses, both in the BRICS countries and beyond? Will this lead to a fragmented and 'nationalized' Internet? The chapter maps these developments and analyses them within the context of questions about Internet governance and suggests that, given the scope and scale of change in BRICS nations – especially China and India – a New World Information and Communication Order is under construction: a NWICO 2.0.

# Chapter 10

# BRICS journalists in global research

*Svetlana Pasti, Jyotika Ramaprasad and Musawenkosi Ndlovu*

## Introduction

This chapter provides an introduction to international comparative research about journalists with a focus on the BRICS countries. It reports the early results of a study of BRICS journalists, from 2012 to 2016, which aims to scrutinize and understand the media systems of BRICS through the human dimension, taking a view from within, from the subjective world of the journalist-practitioners themselves. Even recent global comparative projects, such as Weaver and Willnat's (2012) *The Global Journalist for the 21st Century* (GJ), and the first phase of Hanitzsch *et al.*'s (2012) *Worlds of Journalism Study* (WJS) did not include journalists from all the BRICS countries (Brazil, Russia, India, China and South Africa). Moreover, both projects (GJ and WJS) focus on traditional mainstream media, which does not provide a sufficient understanding of contemporary journalists and global trends in journalism in the context of the omnipresent digitalization of their work and life.

The current BRICS project attempts to fill this gap by studying the BRICS journalists together and comparing them with Western, and at times, non-Western journalists. Focusing on the internal dynamics of their profession, particularly the transition from offline to online, this study in its full scope examines relations between online and traditional news media to understand the changes wrought in the journalism and media systems of the BRICS countries. In mainstream comparative research, online news media still receive little attention. Some (Stetka and Örnebring, 2013; Hanitzsch *et al.*, 2012: 476) refer to online news media's weak institutionalization as a possible reason for their exclusion from journalist surveys. Recent studies of Western media have revealed a tension between the old and new news media and even hostility on the part of the old media towards online news. Online journalism is perceived as less ethical, less autonomous, less objective and accurate, more profit-oriented and in general non-professional (Thompson, 2003; Singer, 2003, 2005; Matheson, 2004, as cited in Bogaerts and Carpentier, 2013:67–69).

This BRICS study defines online news media as separately established Internet media organizations. They are not digital newsrooms or online versions of conventional newspapers, magazines or radio-television stations. Many of them represent a completely different history: some were born, in contrast to traditional media, without the help of media moguls or the government, often from the independent initiative of journalists and active citizens. It is crucially important in this scenario to scrutinize the rise and distinctive features of online news media in the BRICS countries in comparison with traditional news media, and to explore any tension between them. Such a nuanced approach aims to better understand the nature and character of news media and the future of journalism in the BRICS countries.

Towards this end, we are conducting in-depth interviews of journalists in four cities – two metro cities and two provincial cities – in each BRICS country. In each metro city, 48 journalists will be interviewed, two each from 24 media outlets. In each provincial city, 24 journalists will be interviewed, similarly two each from 12 media outlets. Both samples will include traditional and online media. Thus, in each country 144 journalists will be interviewed to make a grand total of 720 journalists from all five BRICS countries. Field work will be completed by the end of 2014. Thus, the main question in this chapter is: what is the profile of the BRICS journalists that emerges from the research? The chapter first reviews past worldwide studies of journalists, and then focuses on the countries in the BRICS coalition. For Brazil, China and Russia, the chapter relies on the recent global studies (GJ and WJS); for India, on past literature; and for South Africa, on preliminary findings from the BRICS survey.

## Past studies of journalists worldwide

Each of the BRICS countries has its particular history of development of media and journalism, and of research about journalists. For example, in the Soviet Union, sociological studies of journalists, of their demographics and working conditions – initiated in the 1920s by the young Communist Party and state – were of an applied nature, with the goal of increasing the effectiveness of journalists' work and influence in society (Gus, 1930; Grushin and Onikov, 1980). However, these studies were little known outside the Soviet Union because they were published in the Russian language and because little communication existed between Western and non-Western communist countries, such as the Soviet Union and China, during the Cold War (Zhang, 1989). In Brazil, systematic research about journalism and journalists began only in the 1960s (Herscovitz, 2012: 368). In India, the first systematic study of journalists and journalism was a doctoral dissertation in 1969 (Eapen, 1969). In South Africa also, such research is young: journalists under apartheid were studied mainly in terms of their political ideological output (cf. Tomaselli, Tomaselli and Muller, 1987, 1989).

These early indigenous efforts to study journalists were small in comparison to the Western, especially English-language, studies that dominated the marketplace of ideas and publications, leading later researchers from non-Western countries to, more or less, use the same methods, approaches and theories. While such simulation may not be completely and culturally appropriate in non-Western journalist surveys, given their widespread use, the next section provides landmarks in the evolution of studies of journalists in the West.

Weaver and Wilhoit's (1986) first study of US journalists surveyed 1,001 journalists from an estimated journalist workforce of 112,072. The authors found that newsrooms had more male than female journalists and that most journalists were satisfied with their jobs. In comparison with the earlier Johnstone *et al.* (1976) study, there was a decline in perceptions of autonomy but a more pluralistic mindset among journalists, with a third subscribing to both the interpretive and disseminator roles.

In their second study, Weaver and Wilhoit (1996) surveyed 1,156 American journalists from an estimated workforce of 122,015. They found that more women and minorities were present in newsrooms but that job satisfaction had reportedly declined, particularly among younger journalists, and so had perceived newsroom autonomy. The journalists ranked speed of information delivery to audiences as extremely important, but they continued to consider the disseminator and interpretive roles as cornerstones of their profession, with interpretation reported as a fundamental function of journalism. The adversary function was a minority mindset in this study, as in their first study, and the role of journalist as populist mobilizer emerged in this study. In essence, the majority of the journalists had a pluralistic orientation to their roles.

Weaver *et al.*'s (2007) third study in 2002 selected 1,149 American journalists from 116,148 full-time editors, reporters and producers. The authors concluded that the statistical profile of US journalists had remained stable, although there was a slight increase in minority representation in American media. Journalists assigned the most value to investigating government claims, followed by getting information to the public quickly. Their pluralistic orientation declined a little, with a majority in favour of the interpretive role.

These landmark studies inspired global efforts, using the original or modified questionnaire, to empirically examine the profession of journalism (Reese, 2001). Weaver's (1998) *The Global Journalist: News People around the World* presented 21 of these studies surveying 20,280 journalists between 1986 and 1996. Weaver concluded that there was no 'typical global journalist' and that in fact many ethical and practical differences existed. A larger per cent of journalists reported autonomy in Finland, Canada and the US than in China, Hong Kong, Taiwan and even Britain. Where the importance of roles was studied, there was considerable agreement on the importance of disseminating information quickly to the public, less agreement on the importance of investigating government claims and providing analysis of complex problems, and considerable disagreement on providing entertainment.

In a more recent book, *The Global Journalist in the 21st Century*, Weaver and Willnat (2012) presented 42 national journalist surveys of 29,272 journalists from 31 countries (for some countries more than one survey was presented) between 1996 and 2011. Their concluding chapter provided comparisons across these countries for shared variables. More men than women were present in the newsroom in 23 out of 29 countries, but the population of female journalists had increased from 33 per cent (Weaver, 1998) to 41 per cent (Weaver and Willnat, 2012). Global journalists tended to be younger, but their educational level varied dramatically from 38 per cent of journalists with a four-year-college degree in Finland to 100 per cent holding this degree in Brazil. Journalists' satisfaction with their job also varied significantly, from 84 per cent being very satisfied in Finland to only 2.5 per cent in the United Arab Emirates.

South Korea, Hong Kong and Taiwan had the lowest per cent of journalists in the *Global Journalist* (GJ) study who were 'very satisfied' with their autonomy, while Finland and Canada had the highest. The highest percentage of journalists who rated the role of watchdog of government as very important was from the US (71 per cent). The roles that had the highest average percentage of GJ journalists rating them as extremely important were 'reporting the news quickly' (53 per cent), 'reporting objectively' (51 per cent) and 'providing analysis of events' (49 per cent). By this measure, the least important role was 'providing entertainment' (19 per cent).

## Brazilian, Russian and Chinese journalists in the global studies (GJ and WJS)

More recently, a coordinated project to study global journalists – *Worlds of Journalism Study* (WJS) – was launched; its pilot study is complete and its second study is in the data collection phase. This section juxtaposes the findings about the BRICS journalists in three countries (Brazil, Russia and China) from the WJS pilot study with findings from the latest GJ study (Weaver and Willnat, 2012 and Hanitzsch *et al.*, 2012), and discusses them in the context of the data collected in the BRICS study. The WJS surveys were conducted between 2006 and 2009 (Hanitzsch *et al.*, 2012: 477–478). Thus, to allow greater validity in comparison, only those surveys conducted between 2006 and 2010 were selected from the GJ studies: Russia in 2008 (Pasti, Chernysh and Svitich, 2012); Brazil in 2009 (Herscovitz, 2012); and China in 2010 (Zhang and Su, 2012) (Weaver and Willnat, 2012: 3–4).

These studies differed in their theoretical underpinnings as well as their research scope and objectives, and thus to some extent in their variables, though sometimes the differences were more a matter of nomenclature. Still, GJ focused on demographics, working conditions and values of journalists, whereas WJS investigated journalism cultures, professional autonomy and influences on news work. Using a comparative framework, this chapter identifies differences and commonalities among journalists both within BRICS and between BRICS and Western and some non-Western countries with the aim to create a picture of BRICS journalists emerging from recent studies and deconstruct existing, often-false, stereotypical dichotomies of the Western and the non-Western.

## Findings from the Global Journalism (GJ) studies

### Demographic profile

According to Weaver and Willnat (2012: 537), the estimated 700,000 Chinese journalists are among the largest group in the world; in comparison, US journalists number about 116,000. These authors indicate that Brazil has only 30,000 journalists, but recent data collected by the Federal University of Santa Catarina and the Federal Union of Brazilian Journalists indicate 145,000 registered journalists, of whom 70,000 are employed by the media with the remaining working for the government (public relations departments) and as teachers (Bergamo et al., 2012). National teams conducting the BRICS survey indicate 35,000 journalists in South Africa, 250,000 journalists in Russia and between 40,000 and 100,000 journalists in India, depending on data source. In Russia, too, it is difficult to get reliable data; the number of journalists is only an approximation, and the government only plans to provide regular statistics on them. Note also that the data on the number of journalists does not include freelancers; national teams indicate that in China freelancers number one million, while in Russia freelancers who have a formal contract with media outlets number 25,000. In reality, there are many more Russian freelancers because working without a contract is common. For other countries, such data were inaccessible. In general, the size of media markets is a possible explanation for the variation in the size of the journalist workforce. In the case of China and Russia, the State and its administrative resources are likely to be equally important in shaping of their media markets and journalist workforce.

BRICS project data indicate that Brazil has considerably fewer newspapers and magazines than Russia and China, but has three times as many radio stations as Russia and 50 times as many as China. The Brazilian researchers working on the project suggest that two factors – social and professional – explain the relatively small number of journalists employed by the media in comparison to a population of 200 million. The first factor is the legacy of illiteracy: currently the illiteracy rate is 8.7 per cent of the population, or 13.2 million people who cannot read (IBGE, 2013). This has resulted in a small number of newspapers versus a large number of radio stations, many of which are community based, formed by young elementary school and journalism students who have acquired popularity as reporters. The second factor is the high status of journalism as a profession identical to that of lawyers and physicians and thus requiring a journalism university degree for entrance into the profession.

Table 10.1 presents empirical data from Brazil, Russia and China on demographic profile, job satisfaction and perception of roles from the GJ

*Table 10.1* Portrait of BRC journalists

| % except where indicated* | Brazil | Russia | China | US |
|---|---|---|---|---|
| Mean age of journalist* | 40 | 41 | 33 | 41 |
| Gender (female) | 45 | 60 | 53 | 33 |
| Educated/qualified in journalism | 100/100 | 90/44 | 93/NA | 89/36 |
| **Role** | | | | |
| Watch the government | 15 | 53 | NA | 71 |
| Analyze events | 72 | 78 | NA | 51 |
| Report news quickly | 38 | 81 | NA | 59 |
| Provide access to public | 38 | 69 | NA | 39 |
| Provide entertainment | 20 | 25 | NA | 11 |
| **Job satisfaction** | | | | |
| Very satisfied | 21 | 19 | NA | 33 |
| Predictors of satisfaction* | *Pay, professional recognition, possibility for promotion* | *Job autonomy, providing help to people, political alignment of media* | NA | *Rating of own institution in informing the public, personal influence on subjects covered, pay* |

Source: *Global Journalist* studies, (Weaver, 2012)

study. The table shows that Chinese journalists are among the youngest (33 years old) in the world, while Brazilian (40) and Russian (41) journalists are older and similar in age to US journalists (41). The journalism profession in Brazil, Russia and China is characterized by trends towards feminization and high education. Female and male journalists are almost equal in number in Brazil (40 per cent), but female journalists exceed the number of male journalists in both China (53 per cent) and Russia (60 per cent). Altogether, 100 per cent of journalists in Brazil, 93 per cent in China and 90 per cent in Russia are highly educated. In Brazil almost all journalists have special education in journalism. In Russia about half (46 per cent) are from other specializations because journalism school graduates do not want to move from large cities, where they studied in universities, to small towns, thus leaving the profession in provinces short of journalism school graduates as staff. In the US, the profession is less feminized (33 per cent female) and less trained specifically in journalism (36 per cent majoring in journalism).

### Working conditions

According to Weaver and Willnat (2012: 534), job satisfaction is an important indicator of the working conditions of journalists because it is linked to their perceived autonomy. In Russia, the US and some other countries (Chile, Colombia, Finland, South Korea, Malaysia, Sweden), perception of freedom is related to high job satisfaction. The level of job satisfaction (per cent of journalists who were 'very satisfied') was lower in Brazil (21 per cent) and Russia (19 per cent) than in the US (33 per cent) and especially in Finland (84 per cent). For China, these data were not collected. Brazil and Russia differed in the three most important predictors of journalists' job satisfaction. For Brazil, it was 'pay', similar to other Latin American countries such as Chile and Colombia. In contrast, in Russia, it was 'job autonomy', as was also the case in Poland, Finland and South Korea. Two other important predictors for job satisfaction were 'professional recognition' and 'possibility for promotion' in Brazil and 'opportunity to help people' and 'political line of their media' in Russia (Weaver and Willnat, 2012: 535). Thus Brazilian journalists were more pragmatic, prioritizing material values such as income and rising mobility, whereas Russian journalists were more oriented to idealistic and altruistic values such as autonomy and helping people. This is not surprising given the lack of political freedom in the majority of Russian media, but it also reveals these journalists' adherence to the roles prescribed by the Soviet theory of journalism to help people concretely, for example, in response to a letter or a phone call from a reader (in other words, an organizer role in the social order).

In addition, journalists' choice of factors that bring them the most satisfaction in work also reflected the state of journalism in their countries. In particular, Brazilian journalists' satisfaction was more self-referential; it depended on benefits to themselves: money, recognition from peers and career growth, all of which are internal to the journalist. This also indicates that journalism is well established as a somewhat independent force driven by journalists. Professional satisfaction among Russian journalists is derived from external factors such as autonomy in their jobs (controlled by the State), on the one hand, and the editorial policy of the media, on the other. In the US, the three important predictors were 'rating of own institution in informing the public', 'personal influence on subject covered' and 'pay' (Weaver and Willnat, 2012: 535). US journalists were both self- and other-referential in their sources of satisfaction, which were their pay and their own independence to shape their journalistic stories as well as their media organization's achievements. For China these data were not collected.

## Roles

Of the six journalistic roles used in GJ surveys, three had the highest per cent of subscribers across the surveyed countries: 'reporting news quickly' (53 per cent), 'reporting objectively' (51 per cent), and 'providing analysis of events' (49 per cent) (see Table 10.1). In Brazil and Russia, respectively, 38 per cent and 81 per cent of the respondents subscribed to 'reporting news quickly' and 72 per cent and 78 per cent subscribed to 'providing analysis of events.' Data on 'reporting objectively' is not available for the three BRICS countries. Russian journalists are very sceptical of the notion of objectivity; they do not believe in the possibility of 'pure objective reporting' because of the political orientations of the media (owner) and the subjective attitudes of journalists. With regard to other roles, in Brazil 38 per cent (close to the 39 per cent in the US) and in Russia 69 per cent subscribed to 'providing access to public' and (only) 15 per cent in Brazil but 53 per cent in Russia subscribed to the 'watchdog' role. For China these data were not collected.

Weaver and Willnat (2012: 539) acknowledges that correlation is not always present between the level of press freedom and the importance of the watchdog function. For example, in the US, rated by Freedom House as having free media, 71 per cent of journalists considered the watchdog role as important, while in Germany, the Netherlands and Sweden, also rated free, journalists were less likely to think that the media should act as watchdogs. Weaver and Willnat (2012: 536) explain that the lower per cent of journalists subscribing to the watchdog role in Brazil (rated as partly free), Germany and Japan (free) is due to the close ties between journalists and government officials and also the increased acceptance of a large role for the government in these societies. However, this explanation may not be generalizable if one considers Russia (rated as not free, as well as China), where half of the journalists support the watchdog role despite the close media–journalist–government official ties. At the same time, it is possible that this support for the watchdog role is not reflected in practice, but is a reference to the ideal role from normative theory about journalism's roles.

In Russia, support for investigative journalism as part of the watchdog role is not to be expected, due to the lack of demand for such journalism in the post-Soviet reality of state capitalism based on the merging of power (the state) and property (capital) into the power–property system – the basis of the 'Vertical of Power' (Nureev, 2013). In addition there is a significant threat to life: investigative journalists in Moscow and other regions of Russia have been murdered, most notably investigative journalist Anna Politkovskaya in 2006, killed for carrying out her professional activity, which must have created a chilling effect.

Russian journalists, including those who were critical of state control in the past, prefer to work in stable, state-owned media organizations. In this system, there is no incentive to adopt the watchdog role because it provides them with the personal comfort of good salaries, social security and the potential to rise in their careers as compared with the existing precarious conditions in many private media: 'grey salaries', non-official employment, lack of tax allocation to the pension fund, pressure to use non-ethical methods of work, and absence of protection from arbitrary owners (Pasti, 2007: 2010).

## Findings from the *Worlds of Journalism Studies* (WJS)

The WJS studies (Hanitzsch *et al.*, 2012) were published as a separate summary chapter in the book *The Global Journalist for the 21st century* (Weaver and Willnat,

*Table 10.2* Portrait of BRC Journalists – II

| Role, ethics and influences | % of Journalists Agreeing | | | |
|---|---|---|---|---|
| | Brazil: Peripheral Western | Russia: Authoritarian | China: Authoritarian | (US): Western |
| Watchdog government | 89 | 57 | 83 | 86 |
| Provide interesting information | 67 | 64 | 50 | 49 |
| Support official policies | 43 | 27 | 60 | 23 |
| Advocate for social change | 53 | 29 | 61 | 25 |
| Influence public opinion | 24 | 62 | 74 | 18 |
| Stay away from unverified information | 54 | 50 | 88 | 72 |
| Journalists can depict reality as it is | 77 | 33 | 62 | 68 |
| What is ethical varies from one situation to another | 27 | 69 | 71 | 29 |
| Avoid questionable methods of reporting | 76 | 36 | 64 | 82 |
| Influence from supervisors and higher editors | 79 | 52 | 80 | 80 |
| Influence from management/ownership | 55/36 | 66/62 | 81/76 | 62/23 |
| Newsroom/professional conventions | 80/78 | 53/52 | 57/60 | 81/79 |

Source: *Worlds of Journalism* study, (Hanitzsch *et al.*, 2012)

2012); this section draws from that chapter, and Table 10.2 presents the main findings from the WJS study for Brazilian, Russian and Chinese journalists.

## Roles

For some roles ('watchdog of the government'), Brazilian journalists were similar to the Chinese, as well as German and Ugandan, journalists; for others ('to provide the audience with the information that is most interesting'), they were similar to Russian journalists and dissimilar from German and Austrian journalists (Hanitzsch *et al.*, 2012: 478). The Chinese and Russian journalists also differed from each other in some role perceptions, for example, with regard to support of official policies and advocating for social change, but were similar in others, for example, influence on public opinion (ibid.: 481). The WJS and GJ studies did not match on findings for the watchdog role; results for the BRICS countries are shown in Table 10.3. Results differed for Brazil (14.6 per cent from GJ and 89 per cent from WJS), Germany (7 per cent GJ and 88 per cent WJS), Switzerland (26.9 per cent GJ and 81 per cent WJS), Indonesia (39 per cent GJ and 80.8 per cent WJS) and Chile (38.9 per cent GJ

*Table 10.3* Professional roles

| Role | % of Journalists Saying 'Extremely Important' from Weaver 2012: 537; and (in brackets) from Hanitzsch et al., 2012: 478 | | | | |
|------|--------|--------|-------|-----|-----------------|
|      | Brazil | Russia | China | US  | Overall Mean    |
| Report news quickly       | 38       | 81       | NA       | 59       | 53 |
| Provide analysis of events | 72      | 78       | NA       | 51       | 49 |
| Be government watchdog    | 15 (89)  | 53 (57)  | NA (83)  | 71 (86)  | 39 |
| Provide access to public  | 38       | 69       | NA       | 39       | 36 |
| Provide entertainment     | 20       | 25       | NA       | 11       | 19 |
| Report objectively        | NA       | NA       | NA       | 52       | 51 |

Source: Weaver (2012) and Hanitzsch *et al.* (2012)

and 64 per cent WJS) (Weaver and Willnat, 2012: 537; Hanitzsch *et al.*, 2012: 478). Other comparisons are difficult because the wording of the role statements differed between the two sources. The GJ surveys were based on national samples of journalists, while the WJS studies had small samples of 100 journalists from each country.

### Influences

Results for the percentage of respondents perceiving censorship as an important source of influence on journalistic work were Chinese (74 per cent), Russian (38 per cent) and Brazil (6 per cent). Freedom House classified countries into three clusters – free, partly free and not free: it identifies Russia and China as not-free and Brazil as partly free (Freedom House, 2013). For China, the opinion about the influence of censorship coincides with this classification with a majority of (self) censored journalists in non-free media but for Russia, it coincides only partly, where two-thirds of journalists are not harassed with censorship in their non-free media. For Brazil, influence of censorship is not a problem at all, although it is identified as partly free in terms of media freedom. Three sources that were perceived as having somewhat similar levels of influence in the three BRICS countries were news deadlines, supervisors and higher editors, and management. For news deadlines, the percentages were: 61 per cent for China, 53 per cent for Russia and 57 per cent for Brazil (ibid.: 490–491); for supervisors and higher editors, they were 80 per cent for China, 79 per cent for Brazil and 52 per cent for Russia; and for management, they were 81 per cent for China, 66 per cent for Russia and 55 per cent for Brazil.

'Ownership' was an important source of influence on journalistic work for China (76 per cent) and Russia (62 per cent) but not very important for Brazil (36 per cent). For Brazilian journalists, two other important sources of influence were 'newsroom conventions' (80 per cent) and 'professional conventions' (78 per cent). For Chinese and Russian journalists, these sources were rated as influential by smaller percentages of respondents: 57 and 60 respectively for 'newsroom conventions' and 53 and 52 respectively for 'professional conventions.' US journalists were similar to Brazilian journalists in importance of some sources of influence: 'newsroom conventions' (81 per cent), 'professional conventions' (79 per cent), and 'supervisors and higher editors' (80 per cent) (Hanitzsch et al., 2012: 490).

China and Russia differed from some Western countries in their perceived influence of 'management' and 'ownership'. These two countries had the largest percentage of journalists who indicated that 'management' (81 per cent and 66 per cent respectively) and 'ownership,' (76 per cent and 62 per cent respectively) were major influences. This provides indirect evidence of the political and economic pressures on the media and journalists in Russia and China, working under the double control of the state as (in)direct media owner or manager, and media businesses as not-free from the political control of the state. In contrast, the percentages for the same factors were small in Germany (15.2 and 10.7 respectively) and Austria (15.0 and 16.1 respectively). Interestingly, in the US, the percentage was rather large for management (61.9 per cent) unlike the other two Western countries, Germany and Austria, and more like China and Russia, but smaller for ownership (23.4 per cent) and thus closer to Germany and Austria. In Brazil, the percentages were not as large as in China and Russia (55.2 and 35.9 respectively) but nowhere as small as in Germany and Austria.

## Epistemologies

In contrast to findings on influences on journalistic work, Chinese and Russian journalists were not similar to each other nor were they different from Brazilian journalists in epistemological orientation. In some orientations ('I always stay away from information that cannot be verified'), Brazilian journalists (54 per cent) were close to Russian journalists (50 per cent) and both were different from Chinese journalists (88 per cent), as well as German (77 per cent) and Austrian journalists (84 per cent). In others ('I think that journalists can depict reality as it is'), Brazilian journalists (77 per cent) were substantially different from Russian (33 per cent), as well as German (35 per cent) and Austrian (39 per cent) journalists (Hanitzsch et al., 2012: 482).

## Ethics

In their ethical ideologies, results did not fall into a pattern by countries. For example, for situational ethics, Chinese and Russian journalists were similar, as distinct from Brazilian journalists who disapproved of situational ethics (ibid.: 485). On the other hand, for avoiding questionable methods of reporting, Chinese journalists were similar to Brazilian journalists (the majority did not accept them) and different from Russian journalists who had high tolerance for questionable methods (ibid.: 485).

## *Journalism cultures*

Attempts to classify media systems based on different criteria have long been part of the literature. For example, the WJS suggested a classification based on findings about professional autonomy, influence on news work and journalism cultures (explored in terms of roles, epistemologies and ethical ideologies): Western, peripheral Western and authoritarian. It concluded that Brazil had a peripheral Western journalism culture, and Russia and China had an authoritarian journalism culture. Based on this classification, would Russia and China be more similar to each other than to Brazil? The answer, based on a comparison of role perceptions of journalists, influences on news work, epistemologies and ethical ideologies is 'no'.

As Table 10.2 shows, clear polarities between authoritarian (Russia and China) and Western (Brazil and US) journalistic cultures do not exist; instead there is a certain hybridity, which reveals the dynamic nature of journalistic cultures and therefore the impossibility of one-dimensional definitions and labels that do not help to understand differing alignments in journalism. Thus, Brazilian journalists are closer to the US and different from Russian journalists in their high support of the watchdog role and low need to influence public opinion, in their ethical positions, and in the high importance they place on newsroom and professional conventions. However, they are different from US journalists and similar to Chinese journalists in such issues as support of official policies, advocacy for social change and amount of influence of management.

Russian journalists are close to the US and different from Brazilian and Chinese journalists in such issues as lack of support of official policies and lack of advocacy for social change. Chinese journalists are close to Brazilian and US journalists and different from Russian journalists in such issues as higher support of the role of watchdog of government, greater influence of supervisor and higher editors and avoidance of questionable methods. However, they are different from Brazilian and US journalists and close to Russian journalists in their desire to influence public opinion and their approval of situational ethics, higher influence of management and ownership, and the lack of importance of newsroom and professional conventions.

As compared with journalists from the other countries, Brazil's journalists rate the entertainment role highest, have the most conviction that a journalist can depict reality as it is, and are the most disapproving of situational ethics. Russia's journalists have the lowest level of confidence that journalists can depict reality as it is and are most tolerant of unethical methods and unverified information. China's journalists have the highest desire to influence public opinion, to advocate for social change, and to verify information and have more support for official policies. US journalists harbour the lowest support for official policies and for advocacy for social change, do not want to influence public opinion, have the highest disapproval of unethical methods, feel minimal influence of management, and place the highest importance on newsroom and professional conventions.

In summary, the most prominent characteristics of journalists in Brazil, Russia and China are as follows. Brazil's journalists are socially responsible, conscious of their profession's high status in society, devoted to their profession and organization, committed to professional rules and traditions and ethical principles, see a central role in the analysis of events and do not desire to influence society. Russia's journalists have a libertarian attitude to personal freedom, the lowest support for official policies, a low level of confidence in their ability to change anything in society and are tolerant of unethical behaviour. China's journalists are disciplined, socially responsible, flexible in dealing with situations and seek to influence society.

## Indian and South African Journalists

The next section is based on national surveys of journalists in India and South Africa, which were not included in the global projects of GJ (Weaver and Willnat, 2012) and WJS (Hanitzsch et al., 2012).

### India

India has roughly 82,000 registered newspapers, 831 television stations and 245 radio stations. To the best of the authors' knowledge, no study using a probability sample has been conducted to provide a representative picture of Indian journalists, making ascertaining a demographic profile difficult. However, other literature, including studies using non-probability samples, is available, and provides a picture of these journalists' beliefs, attitudes, norms and practices among other things.

### Profile

Given the tremendous growth of news media in India (Thussu, 2013), it may be inferred that more and more young people and women are joining what has been traditionally a male-dominated profession. This growth, however, has also led to the increased hiring of people without adequate training in journalism (Rao and Johal, 2006; Rao, 2009). Little empirically sound information is available on other demographic variables such as age, education and income, though reports indicate that journalism in India is not in general a highly paid profession (Rao and Johal, 2006). One survey of 410 journalists (Press Trust of India, n.d.) from both the regional and English press, conducted after 2002, indicated that gender inequality was prevalent in the media. Female journalists often worked on contract by daily wage, did not always have maternity and child-care benefits and experienced some sexual harassment; still they kept a positive attitude towards their career.

*Working conditions*

Using Shoemaker and Reese's (1996) theory of content, which provides five levels of influence on journalists – personal beliefs/values, media routines, organization, extra-media, ideology – as they create content, Colaco and Ramaprasad (2008a) found that Indian journalists' made finer discriminations in these influences. They perceived the following influences in order of importance: media routines, organization, personal values/opinions, extra media, career advancement, public/government and political/religious beliefs. Journalists in this same study were reasonably satisfied with their jobs (on a five-point scale, job satisfaction was 3.92).

*Roles*

With the advent of the vernacular press in the mid-nineteenth century (before that newspapers were in the English language), India's newspapers began to focus on issues of importance to Indians, but were restricted from writing stories that would cause dissatisfaction with the British colonial government (Pandey, 1999). As the Indian press grew, it became critical of colonial rule and advocated self-rule (Pandey, 1999). With independence came the constitutional guarantee of a free press. Since then, the role of the Indian press has included development advocacy, protocol news coverage and, with time, a watchdog function in a democratic political system (Aggarwala, 1979; Rao, 2008; Relly and Schwalbe, 2013). Ram (2011) suggests two central functions of Indian journalists, '(a) the credible-informational and (b) the critical-investigative-adversarial' (ibid.: 13) and a third, 'pastime' function. He further includes several derivatives of the central functions: public education, a forum for analysis, comment and criticism and agenda building.

In what might be the first empirical study of Indian journalists' beliefs, using a convenience sample of 216 journalists from four geographically representative metros, the perceived roles that emerged were as follows in order of assigned importance: provide information fast, educate citizens, sustain democracy (all three being democracy related functions); discuss social policies; practice development journalism (both representing critical development journalism); be public advocate, provide cultural stimulation (both embodying public service); and support country, support government (both indicating uncritical 'development' journalism) (Colaco and Ramaprasad, 2007).

*Ethics*

Various codes of ethics, such as the Parliamentary Codes (Ravindranath, 2004, as cited in Rao and Johal, 2006) and the Norms of Journalistic Conduct (Bertrand, 1997; Press Council of India, 2005) are available for Indian journalists. These codes focus on roles and responsibilities, as well as journalism standards such as accuracy, fairness, source confidentiality and not engaging in plagiarism. It appears, however, that guidance for daily ethical practice is missing in these codes. Colaco and Ramaprasad (2008b) measured whether journalists found certain practices acceptable. On a five-point scale where a number below three indicates not acceptable, means for the five practices in descending order were: 2.58 for breaking trust/masquerading, 2.20 for paying/ inventing sources, 1.95 for staging/altering photographs, 1.88 for accepting gifts and 1.62 for disclosing harmful facts. Thus journalists found these practices more or less unacceptable.

Another study (Ramaprasad, Liu and Garrison, 2012), using in-depth interviews with a convenience sample of 15 journalists found that opinions about ethical news practice using new technology were mixed. Journalists from English-language national newspapers indicated that their newspapers' standards were strict and pointed a finger at the vernacular media. Overall, the responses of the sample journalists indicated areas of uncertainty about ethical practice. For example, some believed that information on the Internet was in the public domain and thus the media could just use it. At the same time, the respondents would not use an individual's private information, a corporation's proprietary information or government's confidential information from the Internet.

## South Africa

The exact number of South African journalists is basically unknown. There is no legislative framework in South Africa that compels journalists to register. However, the Media Institute of Southern Africa (MISA) estimates the number of newsroom employees to be 6,000. The last study to look into numbers, *Glass Ceiling Two: An audit of women and men in South African Newsroom* (Morna, 2007), also uses this estimate.

### Profile: race and gender

Using a sample of nine newsrooms from three TV stations – CNBC Africa, EWN and SABC – as well as six newspapers – *City Press, M& G, Sunday Times, Beeld, The Witness* and *Sowetan* – Daniels (2013) provides a race and gender profile of South African journalists in the metro cities of Johannesburg and Durban and the provinces Gauteng and KwaZulu-Natal. He indicates changing demographics in terms of race and gender between 2002 and 2012. Race is an important factor because during the apartheid period, newsrooms were dominated by white males. Daniels found that in 2012 the majority (61 per cent) of journalists were black and that there was near gender equality with women journalists comprising 49 per cent of the newsroom (most of the nine newsrooms had equal or near equal and sometimes higher numbers of women than men). Daniels also found that 55 per cent of the editors were black and 45 per cent were white. The gender split among editorial ranks was 55 per cent male and 45 per cent female. The picture was slightly different for editors countrywide from the main commercial newspapers, belonging to the five print companies: out of 42 editors, 23 (55 per cent) were white and 19 (45 per cent) were black; 29 (69 per cent) were male and 13 (31 per cent) were female (Daniels, 2013).

The BRICS-specific research had some more nuanced findings for gender. In one community TV station, a female journalist pointed out that the editors did not want female journalists to interview certain traditional leaders. This was however an exceptional case. On other matters, journalists did not feel that gender was a factor: it did not affect their pay, assignments or opportunities, nor did it hinder their work and career. Opinions about the effect of race were different though: black journalists strongly felt that race affected their work and career more than did gender. With respect to education, the ongoing BRICS study has so far found that, across gender and race, middle-aged and younger journalists have university degrees, diplomas or equivalent, while some of the older journalists were trained in-house.

### Working conditions

South African journalists in the BRICS study indicated they were generally satisfied with their jobs (scale ranged from 'somewhat' to 'a lot'). Their greatest satisfaction derived from producing stories that helped to transform the lives of poor communities. For example, if they reported on a problem faced by a community hospital and it was solved immediately, journalists received great satisfaction. Their second source of satisfaction was holding public officials fully accountable to citizens, followed by their and their profession's ability to educate the public.

Complaints about working conditions differed by race, length of service and medium. Some journalists complained of nepotism, uneven pay grades, racism and 'being handled'. In particular, junior journalists were not satisfied with management, the allocation of story assignments and pay. Black journalists complained about the slow pace of social transformation, while white journalists complained about what they believe amounts to reverse racism when they have to make way for black journalists. Print journalists who had been in their jobs for a long time were not satisfied due to their low pay and the uncertain future of the industry. Broadcast journalists complained about irregular working hours and its effect on their family life.

Junior journalists and those who had joined the industry more recently expressed greater long-term commitment to their jobs, a desire to stay in the industry for a long time, to grow and to make changes. Community media journalists apart, South African journalists expressed fascination with the technological changes (innovations) in their media organizations that allow them to record, edit and publish the story from any location. These changes have made it easier for them to do their work.

## Roles

Other than those who worked in sports, the journalists were not restricted to covering specific beats; instead they worked across a whole range of story types. The South African journalists were highly motivated people who said they joined the profession because they liked working with people and transforming people's lives. They see themselves as truth-tellers. Following the liberal philosophical tradition that humans are rational and can make up their minds about whatever media content is out there, they suggest that there should be no restrictions on their public service and watchdog roles. They believe there is no need to control political and entertainment content in the media. They are averse to and sensitive about any attempt to stifle the media and their own freedom of speech. They collectively and consistently reported shock at the introduction of the Information Bill in South Africa, the law that could get them jailed if they were found to be in possession of state classified information, even if possession of that information was in the public interest.

These journalists saw themselves as possessing the characteristics of a professional journalist: integrity, objectivity and fairness. None of them had ever produced a story to gain financial reward or services. They did, however, acknowledge that some South Africa journalists engage in paid news, thus degrading the integrity and professionalism of journalism; these journalists are frowned upon by the journalistic establishment.

## Conclusion

The BRICS countries are among the top ten growing economies with the greatest share of investments in global advertising markets in 2012–2015 (ZenithOptimedia, 2013): China holds the second place (after the US), Brazil the third, Russia the fifth and India the ninth. In the list of top 10 advertising powers in the world, China occupied the third position in 2012 after the US and Japan, and it will keep the third position in 2015. Russia will rise from the 11th position in 2012 to the seventh position by 2015. Brazil will keep its sixth position in 2015 (ZenithOptimedia, 2013). This rapid growth has led to an explosion of media and thus of the related professions of journalism and public relations/advertising (Sparks, 2014).

It needs to be acknowledged that the BRICS countries lack sufficient information and reliable statistics about their journalists and media, a situation quite distinct from that in many Western countries, and that the two recent global projects (Weaver and Willnat, 2012; Hanitzsch et al., 2012) and local surveys in India and South Africa reported herein have limited generalizability because they did not always use a valid sample. Still, a tentative image of BRICS journalists working mostly in traditional media does emerge from the available information and reflects some commonalities among journalists within the BRICS countries. More important, within the context of the tradition of building macro typologies, it captures national and regional peculiarities and paradoxes caused by the internal and external influences on the profession and on journalists within the framework of their media systems and societies. What are these commonalities and peculiarities?

Journalism is a popular profession in the BRICS countries, especially among the young, particularly in China and South Africa. In Russia, although young journalists comprise one third of this profession's population, the mean age of Russian journalists is 41 years because they can simultaneously hold a staff job as well as a second job and pension. Journalism's popularity is associated with the rapid growth in media and also the growing number of journalism schools, where, as in Russia, large numbers of applicants come from wealthy families. In some countries, for example in Russia, the relatively high status of journalists in the social structure is also a factor; it promises large possibilities for professional and social mobility. In most of the BRICS countries, journalists belong to the middle class in terms of education, occupation and income, but also, as posited by Bourdieu (Benson and Neveu, 2005), owing to their social position (journalistic field) that locates them in elitist communication environments (political and economic fields).

BRICS journalists are generally educated, though they may not always have a degree or diploma in journalism; however the Brazilian journalist must be educated in journalism to enter the profession, while the Russian journalist, especially the regional Russian journalist, on the other hand, often comes from other areas of study.

Of considerable significance is the fact that feminization of the profession is occurring in these countries; many more females work as journalists today than in the past. This may be a reflection of the growing number of females entering the workforce in general, but it is particularly noteworthy in journalism given its unusual working hours, in some cases the unusual degree of danger associated with journalism and in some countries the rather protective or restrictive nature of the upbringing of girls. In the post-communist countries of China and Russia, feminization is connected with the political liberalization of journalism in the context of the transition from 'hard power' to 'soft power' and with the shift in emphasis from the propagandist function (entrusted mostly to males to defend communist values) to a plurality of functions to satisfy varied consumer interests, including those of women consumers that female journalists may be better able to present.

BRICS journalists are reasonably satisfied in their profession; however their satisfaction is associated with different aspects of their work that cannot be understood separately from the level of development of their markets and of media freedom. For Brazilian journalists, job satisfaction is related to pragmatism and expectations for better income and rising mobility; for Indian journalists, it is professional benefits; for Russian journalists, it is helping people and the job flexibility that allows them to combine work as journalists with other jobs; and for South Africa, it is educating and helping people to change their life for the better and to watch officials be made accountable to society. Many BRICS journalists work for human rights: Anna Politkovskaya's work is a case in point in Russia. At the same time, some BRICS journalists increase their income by writing articles for money within the overall context of widespread economic corruption and rather non-transparent media economies.

While the popularity of journalism, considerable education, feminization of the profession and reasonable job satisfaction are commonalities among BRICS journalists, there are differences too. In their perceptions of roles and ethical rules, BRICS journalists differ, based on the level of press freedom in the country, national traditions of journalism and the condition of ethics in the profession and in society. According to Western media monitoring sources (Reporters without Borders, 2014; Freedom House, 2014) BRICS countries are either 'partly free' or 'not-free' countries with completely different working conditions for their journalists than in 'free' Western countries. Their national traditions of journalism are part of their cultural code: collectivist, paternalistic and status-oriented as per Hofstede's (2001) dimensions, unlike the Western cultural code which is individualistic, based on principles of consultation and mutual trust as a basis for compliance with regulations (Mishra, 2008 cited in Pasti and Nordenstreng, 2013: 259–260). This suggests that journalism, as well as society, operates rather within informal rules and personal networks than by formal laws.

The review of previous scholarship revealed a lack of attention to the BRICS group that is not surprising given the long domination of Western research and its natural interest in Western media and journalists. Even the recent most known global studies led by Weaver and Willnat (2012) and Hanitzsch (2012) had in their national samples only three countries (Brazil, Russia and China) from the BRICS group, necessitating the sourcing of past local research for India and preliminary findings of the BRICS project for South Africa. While such a heterogeneous combination of studies, of different scale, approach and time, does not make this review elegant and structurally balanced, it does present a tentative portrait of BRICS journalists and their working environments in national contexts. However, a critical assessment of past studies also makes obvious the need for a more current, comparative and systematic empirical study of BRICS journalists, particularly prioritizing the inclusion of journalists working for online news media. Such a study will provide a comparison of traditional media journalists and online journalists at a transitional juncture in journalism's history, where traditional news media and their journalists are under pressure to digitalize.

There are further pressing and important reasons for studying BRICS journalists: the interest in BRICS countries obviously lies in their economic growth, including an optimistic forecast for even greater development of media and advertising markets. But another major reason lies in its own success in forming a coalition of non-Western countries, symbolizing cultural globalization and representing the era of multiple modernities. According to Eisenstadt

(2000: 2), 'modernity and Westernization are not identical. Western patterns of modernity are not the only "authentic" modernities, though they enjoyed historical precedence and continue to be a basic reference point for others' (Baysha, 2012: 2986). This era of globalization, which is witnessing 'the rise of the rest' not only economically but also in terms of education, makes it possible for non-Western intellectual perspectives to emerge and circulate. It is necessary to seize the moment and engage in study situated within local and national contexts that provide more nuanced pictures of the world and, in this case, of the journalists. It is important to capture the subtleties that make for finer representations than the reductionism that occurs under macro-level typologies that additionally may have their genesis in Western paradigms. De-linking from Western normative judgments, which are conventionally used to evaluate and compare national cases in global studies, is thus critical.

The study of BRICS journalists referenced in this chapter is in its early stages. Using primarily qualitative in-depth interviews, the project will present the BRICS journalists' profile in the context of their societal and professional dynamics comparing across media type (online/traditional), age and location (metro/provincial cities), within BRICS, and between BRICS and the West. The core task of the study is to derive current journalist profiles in all their complexity while at the same time trying to understand whether the BRICS coalition has any influence on the professional foundation and practice of journalism in these countries.

## References

Aggarwala, N. (1979) What Is Development News? *Journal of Communication* 29(2): 181–182.

Baysha, O. (2012) Mythologizing Modernity through Vernacular Discourses. *International Journal of Communication*, 6: 2985–3005.

Benson, R. and Neveu, E. (2005) *Bourdieu and the Journalistic Field*. Cambridge: Polity.

Bergamo, A.; Mick, J. and Lima, S. (2012) Perfil do jornalista brasileiro: Características demográficas, políticas e do trabalho Síntese dos principais resultados. Available at http://perfildojornalista.ufsc.br/files/2013/04/Perfil-do-jornalista-brasileiro-Sintese.pdf.

Bertrand, C. J. (1997) *Quality Control: Media Ethics and Accountability Systems*. Paris: Presse Universitaires de France.

Bogaerts, J. and Carpentier, N. (2013) The Postmodern Challenge to Journalism: Strategies for Constructing a Trustworthy Identity, pp. 60–71 in Peters, C. and Broersma, M. (eds.) *Rethinking Journalism Trust and participation in a transformed news landscape*. Routledge: London.

Colaco, B. and Ramaprasad, J. (2007) Indian Journalists: Democracy Builders or Government Supporters? AEJMC National Convention, Washington, August.

——(2008a) Job Influences of Indian Journalists: What Pushes and Pulls their Pens, AEJMC National Convention, Chicago, August.

——(2008b) 'Receptions and Rejections: Professional Ethics of Indian Journalists'. International Association for Media and Communication Research Annual Congress, Stockholm, Sweden, July.

——(2009) The Grass is Greener on This Side: Indian Journalists' Job Satisfaction, Media Freedom Rating, and Perceived Importance of Profession, ICA Annual Conference, Chicago, May.

Coppedge, M. (2012) *Democratization and Research Methods*. Cambridge: Cambridge University Press.

Daniels, D. (2013) *The State of the Newsroom in South African 2013: Disruptions and Transitions: JHB* Wits Journalism, University of Witwatersrand.

Eapen, K. E. (1969) Journalism as a Profession in India: Two States and Two Cities. Unpublished doctoral dissertation. University of Wisconsin.

Eisenstadt, S. N. (2000) Multiple Modernities. *Daedalus*, 129(1): 1–29.

Freedom House (2013, 2014) Available at http://www.freedomhouse.org/.

Grushin, B. A. and Onikov, L. A. (1980) *Massovaya informatsiia v sovetskom promyshlennom gorode* [The Mass information in the Soviet industrial city]. Moskva: Politizdat.

Gus, M. (1930) *Za gazetnye kadry* [For the newspapers' personnel]. Moskva: Leningrad.

Hanitzsch, T.; Seethaler, J.; Skewes, E. A.; Anikina, M.; Berganza Cangöz, R. I.; Coman, M.; Hamada, B.; Hanusch, F.; Karadjov, C. D.; Mellado, C.; Moreira, S. V.; Mwesige, P.G.; Lee, P.; Reich, P. Z.; Noor, D. V. and Yuen, K. V. (2012) Worlds of Journalism: Journalistic Cultures, Professional Autonomy, and Perceived Influences across 18 Nations, pp. 473–494 in Weaver, D. H. and Willnat, L. (eds.) *The Global Journalist in the 21st Century*. New York: Routledge.

Herscovitz, H. G. (2012) Brazilian Journalists in the 21st Century, pp. 365–381 in Weaver, D. H. and Willnat, L. (eds.) *The Global Journalist in the 21st Century*. New York: Routledge.

Hofstede, G. (2001) *Culture's Consequences: Comparing Values, Behaviors, Institutions and Organizations across Nations*. Second edition. London: Sage.

IBGE (2013) Brazilian Institute of Geography and Statistics. Available www.ibge.gov.br/english/.

Johnstone, J. W. C.; Slawski, E. J. and Bowman W. W. (1976) *The News People*. Urbana: University of Illinois Press.

Matheson, D. (2004) Weblogs and the Epistemology of the News. Some Trends in Online Journalism, *New Media & Society*, 6(4): 443–468.

Mishra, G. (2008) Using Geert Hofstede Cultural Dimensions to Study Social Media Usage in BRIC Countries, *International Values and Communication Technologies*. Available at https://blogs.commons.georgetown.edu/isdyahoofellow/using-geert-hofstede-cultural-dimensions-to-study-social-media-usage-in-bric-countries/.

Morna, C. L. (2007) *Glass Ceiling Two: An Audit of Women and Men in South African Newsroom*. JHB: SANEF (South African National Editors' Forum) and Gender Links.

Nureev, R. (2013) Power-Property in Post-Soviet Russia as a Path Dependence Problem, Paper presented in Nordic Russian and Eastern European Studies Conference 'Intentions, Interactions and Paradoxes in Post-Socialistic Space' Helsinki, 24 May.

Pandey, G.P. (1999) *Press and Social Change*. New Delhi: Manak Publications.

Pasti, S. (2007) *The Changing Profession of a Journalist in Russia*. Tampere: Tampere University Press. Available at http://acta.uta.fi/english/teos.php?id=11005.

——(2010) A New Generation of Journalists, pp. 57-75 in Rosenholm, A.; Nordenstreng, K. and Trubina, E. (eds.) *Russian Mass Media and Changing Values*. London: Routledge.

Pasti, S.; Chernysh, M. and Svitich, L. (2012) The Russian Journalists and Their Profession, 267–282 in Weaver, D. and Willnat, L. (eds.) *The Global Journalist in the 21st Century*. New York: Routledge.

Pasti, S. and Nordenstreng, K. (2013) Paradoxes of Journalistic Profession: Case of Russia in the Context of the BRICS Countries, pp. 243–268 in Vartanova, E. (ed.) *World of Media: Yearbook of Russian Media and Journalism Studies 2012.* Moscow: Lomonosov Moscow State University.

Press Council of India (2005) *Norms of Journalistic Conduct.* Retrieved from http://press council.nic.in/Content/62_1_PrinciplesEthics.aspx.

Press Trust of India (n.d.) *Status of Women Journalists in India.* New Delhi: National Commission of Women.

Ram, N. (2011) *The Changing Role of the News Media in Contemporary India.* Indian History Congress, Punjabi University, Patiala, December.

Ramaprasad, J.; Liu, Y. and Garrison, B. (2012) Ethical Use of New Technologies: Where Do Indian Journalists Stand? *Asian Journal of Communication,* 22 (1): 98–114.

Rao, S. (2008) Accountability, Democracy, and Globalization: A Study of Broadcast Journalism in India. *Asian Journal of Communication.* 18(3): 193–206.

——(2009) Glocalization of Indian Journalism. *Journalism Studies,* 10(4): 474–488.

Rao, S. and Johal, N. S. (2006) Ethics and News Making in the Changing Indian Mediascape. *Journal of Mass Media Ethics,* 21(4): 286–303.

Ravindranath, P. K. (2004) *Press Laws and Ethics in Journalism.* New Delhi: Authors Press.

Reese, S. D. (2001) Understanding the Global Journalist: A Hierarchy-of-influences Approach, *Journalism Studies,* 2(2): 173–187.

Relly, J. E. and Schwalbe, C. B. (2013) Watchdog Journalism: India's Three Largest English-language Newspapers and the Right to Information Act, *Asian Journal of Communication,* 23(3): 284–301.

Reporters without Borders (2014). Retrieved from http://en.rsf.org/.

Shoemaker, P. J. and Reese, S. D. (1996) *Mediating the Message: Theories of Influence on Mass Media Content.* White Plains, NY: Longman.

Singer, J. (2003) Who Are These Guys? The Online Challenge to the Notion of Journalistic Professionalism, *Journalism,* 4 (2): 139–163.

——(2005) The Political J-Blogger 'Normalizing' A New Media Form to Fit Old Norms and Practices. *Journalism* 6(2): 173–198.

Sparks, C. (2014) Deconstructing the BRICS, *International Journal of Communication,* 8: 392–418.

Stetka, V. and Örnebring, H. (2013) Investigative Journalism in Central and Eastern Europe: Autonomy, Business Models, and Democratic Roles. *International Journal of Press/Politics,* 18 (4): 413–435.

Thompson, B. (2003) 'Is Good Too Powerful?', BBC News website, 21 February. Available at http://news.bbc.co.uk/1/hi/technology/2786761.stm.

Thussu, D. K. (2013) India in the International Media Sphere. *Media, Culture & Society.* 35(1): 156–162.

Tomaselli, K.; Tomaselli, R.T. and Muller, J. (1987) *Narrating the Crisis: Hegemony and the South African Press.* Johannesburg: Richard Lyon and Co.

——(1989) *The Press in South Africa.* Cape Town: Richard Lyon and Co.

Weaver, D. H. (ed.) (1998) *The Global Journalist: News People Around the World.* Cresskill: Hampton Press.

Weaver, D. H. and Wilhoit, G.C. (1986) *The American Journalist. A Portrait of US News People and Their Work.* Bloomington, Indiana: Indiana University Press.

——(1996) *The American Journalist in the 1990s. US News People at the End of an Era,* Mahwah,NJ: Lawrence Erlbaum.

Weaver, D. H.; Beam, R.A.; Brownlee, B. J.; Voakes, P.S. and Wilhoit, G. C. (2007) *The American Journalist in the 21st Century: US News People at the Dawn of a New Millennium* Mahwah, NJ: Lawrence Erlbaum.

Weaver, D.H. and Willnat, L. (eds.) (2012) Journalists in the 21st Century: Conclusions, pp. 529–551 in Weaver, D. H. and Willnat, L. (eds.) *The Global Journalist in the 21st Century*. New York: Routledge.

ZenithOptimedia (2013) 'The Countries with the Biggest Investment in the Growth of the Global Advertising Market'. Available at www.gipp.ru, April.

Zhang, H. and Su, L. (2012) Chinese Media and Journalists in Transition, pp. 9–21 in Weaver, D. and Willnat, L. (eds.) *The Global Journalist in the 21st Century*. New York: Routledge.

Zhang, X. (1989) Wo Guo Nongcun Xinwen Chuanbo Xianzhuang Yanjiu (A Study of Media Communication in China's Rural Regions), pp.146–166 in Chongshan Chen and Xiuling Mi (eds.) *Zhongguo Chuanbo Xiaoguo Toushi (A Perspective on Media Effects in China)*. Shenyang: Shenyang Chubanshe.

# Chapter 11

# Intra-BRICS media exchange

*Herman Wasserman, Fernando Oliveira Paulino,[1]
Dmitry Strovsky and Jukka Pietiläinen*

In the shifting geopolitical relationships exemplified by the BRICS formation, transnational flows of media content, capital and human resources are already displaying new emerging South–South trajectories. Of these, the steep escalation of China's involvement in the media landscape in Africa has perhaps been the most visible (and most controversial). Examples of this increased presence of Chinese media in Africa, which include China Central Television, Xinhua News Agency and the newspaper *China Daily,* will be discussed later in this chapter. It is, however, important to note that these flows are multi-directional, as can be seen for instance in the case of the South African media company, Naspers, which has also invested in other BRICS countries like China, Brazil and India, in the Russian television channel, Russia Today that broadcasts internationally, and in the Indian film industry, which has shown a tremendous growth in reach and influence globally.

These flows and contraflows between BRICS members – the intra-BRICS exchanges – will form the focus of this chapter. The chapter will include perspectives on transnational media exchanges in the form of investments, as well as intra-BRICS media representations. Instead of discussing these questions for each country in turn, the chapter opts for a thematic rather than a nation-based approach. Three key themes have been identified and will be discussed from the perspectives of various BRICS countries. These themes are, firstly the flows and contraflows of media capital; secondly, the representation of other BRICS countries in domestic media; and, lastly, soft power initiatives – BRICS media 'going out' to others.

## Flows and contraflows of media capital

In 2002, an amendment to the Constitution in Brazil allowed foreign investment in Brazilian media companies, following which partnerships with companies from the US and Europe (mainly Portugal and Spain) were established. However, investment from Chinese, Indian, Russian and South African companies in Brazilian media and telecommunications are still dwarfed by European and American capital investments. Portugal Telecom, for example, has more customers and revenues in Brazil than in Portugal (Reis, 2013). Brazilian companies have also not invested directly in media markets in other BRICS countries, although Globo, the main Brazilian media enterprise, has exported *telenovelas* for broadcast on Russian television since 1988, when the Brazilian soap opera *Slave Izaura* impressed Soviet audiences, who had up until then not been exposed to much international fare. This series had a significant cultural impact in Russia, as it stimulated not only widespread discussion about the fate of the poor slave girl character, but also the learning of Portuguese (Estadão, 2001). Later, Russian television actively began to broadcast cultural events from Brazil, including the famous carnivals.

Flows between South Africa and other BRICS countries have also not been just in one direction. The South African media company Naspers, for instance, has been benefiting greatly from its investment in the media platform Tencent in China, which now accounts for more than 80 per cent of the media conglomerate's R200 billion (approximately $25 billion) market capitalization (Steyn, 2012). The Naspers subsidiary, MIH also owns a 9.9 per cent stake in Beijing Media Corporation, a leading newspaper company in China, which publishes Beijing Youth Daily. Naspers' investment in China and other BRICS countries is therefore largely responsible for the repositioning of a media company that was built on Afrikaner capital during the apartheid era and was largely supportive of the apartheid regime, to become a global media conglomerate. This South African company, through its various subsidiaries, has interests in the Internet, pay-television and print media across the world, including BRICS countries.

The history of Naspers' expansion into the Russian market started as early as 2006, after it was unveiled that the company planned to buy a blocking stake of the national newspapers *Trud* ('Labor') and *Argumenti i fakti* ('Arguments and facts'). In 2007 Naspers Limited purchased 30 per cent of the Internet portal Mail.ru from the Russian company, ForexAW for $165 million. The Mail.ru group in Russia owns Russia's leading Internet service, its largest Internet portal and two of the largest Russian-language social networks, *Odnoklassniki.ru* ('Classmates') and *Moi Mir* ('My World'), as well as the Avito online classifieds site in Russia (see naspers.com for details of these and other holdings). Shares acquired by Naspers were previously owned by Digital Sky Technologies and Tiger Global Management as minority shareholders of Mail.ru. The Mail.ru General Director, Dmitry Grishin, said that it was good for his company to have Naspers as its business partner. At the time there was a prediction that Naspers would pursue the developing Russian Internet market (Goncharova and Noskovich, 2007), which it then went on to do. Its subsidiary MIH now owns a 43 per cent stake in Mail.ru, as well as a 100 per cent stake in Slando, an online classified advertising concern. Another example of Naspers' activity in Russia is its investment of $50 million in Avito Holdings, gaining 18.6 per cent of its entire stake. The money received from this deal was directed towards strengthening positions of

Avito.ru especially in 'Auto' and 'Property', which were increasing trends in online shopping in Russia. As a result, in March 2013 Naspers became the biggest stakeholder in free announcements in the country (CNews, 2013), leaving far behind those Scandinavian media companies actively investing in Russia's media business.

In Brazil, Naspers has several interests in media companies, including a 30 per cent stake in the leading media company, Abril, a 91 per cent interest in the Buscapé group – the largest e-commerce-company in that country – and a stake in the Internet company Compera 'n Time. Naspers is also a partner of the Brazilian online publishing platform Movile. In India, Naspers has an interest in the biggest e-commerce destination in that country, Flipkart.com, as well as in the leading online travel groups, Ibibo and TravelBoutiqueOnline, and the Internet company ACL Wireless.

Naspers therefore seems to be at the forefront of companies playing successfully in foreign markets. The achievements of Russian companies investing money in overseas media business are much more modest. In 2011 a business investor Yuri Milner – whose career spans the World Bank and the Russian financial sector, and whose interests include computer technologies, specializing in Internet assets – negotiated the purchase of shares in several Indian Internet companies. As reported by Indian media, initial investments have been counted between $100 million and $200 million. Milner's investment company, Digital Sky Technologies (DST) Global, offered to initiate this deal to Flipkart, as well as to the local company, Just Dial. However the preliminary negotiations were not easy, and Just Dial in the long run refused to look for investors. Also, the Yuri Milner Foundation intended to participate in funding online-shop Flipkart wishing to raise $150–200 million investment to China and India. It is worth mentioning that in terms of Internet penetration, prospects in India are more promising than even China. If the Chinese online audience is about 500 million out of 1.3 billion, then in India the number of Internet consumers is approximately 100 million out of a population of 1.2 billion. By end of 2011, the Mobile Association of India and research firm IMRB expected growth of the Internet audience India to 121 million (DST, 2011). However, the competition in Indian and Chinese markets made this deal only partly successful.

## Representation of other BRICS countries in domestic media

The emergence of BRICS as a construct seems to have led to an increase in attention to other member states in the media of these respective countries. Two features of this intra-BRICS coverage stand out: first, not all BRICS countries are covered with an equal amount of prominence or frequency – some countries are seen as more deserving of media coverage than others – and, secondly, when other BRICS countries are reported on, such coverage often takes place via the prism of the local – in other words, media tend to foreground the implications of the BRICS alignment, or developments in other members states, for their local economic or political situation.

BRICS countries continue to be on the agenda of their counterparts. In contemporary Russian national newspapers, for instance, Brazil, China, India and South Africa were and still are among the 30 most often mentioned foreign countries. However, these countries are not always mentioned in the context of the BRICS alignment and it is not clear to what extent the acronym is understood by Russian media audiences. In Brazil, as in other BRICS countries, the BRICS configuration remains viewed through a local lens. For instance, coverage of the economy of other BRICS countries often compares their economic growth with that of Brazil. An example of this is the 2012 interview with the economist Jim O'Neill, creator of the BRIC concept, in the editorial of the 'Economy' section of *Correio Braziliense*, Brazil's leading newspaper, based in the capital Brasilia. He was quoted as saying: 'Brazil has grown and garnered the attention of other countries. It is seen as one of the highlights among BRICS and has many opportunities' (*Correio Braziliense*, 2012a). A similar line of thought was present in a report in the same newspaper about Brazilian President Dilma Rousseff's visit to the US. The article, entitled 'The Giant's Appetite', indicates the importance of Brazil on the contemporary international scene as a potential ally for the US, and identifies Brazil as a democratic institution in comparison to other BRICS countries: 'the country is an ally, yet at the same time has its own voice. Out of the BRICS countries, it is the closest to the United States yet North American politics still does not see this' (*Correio Braziliense*, 2012b).

In Brazil, coverage of the BRICS countries tends to focus on political and economic matters, with little attention to social and cultural aspects. This was a finding from an analysis of Brazilian media coverage of other BRICS members using the *Correio Braziliense* (Paulino, Bolaño and Holanda, 2013). *Correio Braziliense* is a newspaper of record, and has a large impact inside and outside the Federal District of Brasilia, a region of almost 2.5 million inhabitants. This newspaper was chosen for analysis because Brasilia is Brazil's diplomatic headquarters, houses the BRICS country embassies and sells close to 55,000 copies daily, with a permanent section dedicated to international news. Even though the number of readers is not comparable to those of a major US newspaper, the *Correio Braziliense* helps to shape the news agenda for media in Brazil, influencing other newspapers, radio and TV stations, as well as Internet websites.

Reporting of BRICS in this newspaper was analyzed using the composed month methodology: a random sample of 31 editions was developed from within 366 newspapers in 2012. The analysis involved applying the notion of the 'imagined community' (Anderson, 1991) and techniques concerning content and discourse (Rocha and Deusdará, 2005). It took the thematic focus of the texts into account and was not based on the size of the reports or the comparison of each one of the published discourses (interviewees, analysts or journalists). Out of the 31 editions analyzed, 13 texts directly referenced BRICS or BRIC. The majority of these were in the Economy and Politics sections, with a minority in the Opinions, World and Art and Entertainment sections.

This study of intra-BRICS media coverage in Brazil found that reporting is dominated by political and economic news (what Park and Alden, 2013 refers to as 'upstairs' relationships), and that the social and cultural dimensions of the BRICS relationship ('downstairs', in Park and Alden's terminology) are neglected. This is also true of media coverage in South Africa, where coverage of BRICS in general, and the China–Africa relationship in particular, has been fairly balanced and optimistic, probably because these relationships have largely been seen in terms of the economic and developmental opportunities these geopolitical shifts hold for South Africa (see Wasserman, 2014, for a detailed analysis). Reporting on BRICS as an emerging economic power bloc, the establishment of a BRICS development bank and business prospects in the BRICS countries have all been topics that received coverage in the South African business media.

In Russia, China is covered mainly in terms of economics and international relations, but less in the fields of culture, sports and daily life. The construction BRICS (or BRIC) itself is seldom present in Russian national newspapers. BRICS is mentioned most often in economic newspapers *RBK-daily*, *Kommersant*, *Vedomosti* and the government newspaper *Rossiiskaya Gazeta*. This can be easily explained by the economic context being more important on the BRICS agenda for the Russian press than any other issue. In those newspapers which mention BRICS most often, it appears only 30–40 times per year. Other newspapers – popular tabloids and politically oriented newspapers – mention BRICS less often. For example, the nationalist newspaper *Zavtra* has mentioned it only twice, and usually in relation to BRICS as a counterweight to the US. BRIC was practically never mentioned in the Russian press before 2006, when it started to appear simultaneously in several Russian newspapers. BRICS became more prominent after 2009 and the first BRICS summit in Ekaterinburg in Russia. Russians saw BRICS as a contrast to G7 and as a form of potential economic cooperation for Russia. Russian economic newspapers also pointed out that Russia was the most developed of all the BRICS countries.

In South Africa, contesting views of China can be found in the media, with some examples of stereotyping and fear-mongering still existing. However, on the whole, the media seem to have developed an attitude of 'cautious optimism' with regard to BRICS as a group and South Africa's place in it (Wasserman, 2014). A recurring theme in the responses is the view that South Africa's inclusion in the BRICS alignment is a positive development, as it gives the country a seat at the 'big table' of emerging powers. The benefits from South Africa's association with the group are seen mostly in economic terms. One journalist responded that 'the creation of more trade opportunities is always positive', while another saw BRICS as a 'prestigious club to be a part of' (Wasserman, 2014). Editors are, however, not blind to the fact that South

Africa does not 'belong' in the BRICS group on the strength of its economy (Olsen, 2013).

The availability of Chinese media to South African journalists has also led them to develop a more nuanced understanding of China. South African journalists have indicated that they consult Chinese media platforms like the news agency Xinhua from time to time to ascertain themselves of the official Chinese views on news events and international affairs. In this regard (although based on a small exploratory study) it would seem that Chinese soft power exercised via media may start to have an effect in South Africa.

It is clear from the intra-BRICS coverage that not all BRICS countries are viewed as being of equal importance. In Russian, Brazilian and South African media, China is a clear leader. In Russian and South African newspapers, India is the second and Brazil the third. In Russian newspapers, South Africa receives the fourth most coverage. There are of course peaks when significant news events are happening in a specific country, like in 2010 when South Africa got slightly more attention than usual in Russian newspapers because of the FIFA Soccer World Cup being hosted in South Africa.

Content analysis of coverage of BRICS countries in South African media in recent years (see Wasserman 2014 for a detailed discussion) displayed China's clear dominance. Its closest competitor in terms of volume of coverage, India, received almost half the amount of coverage, followed by Brazil and then Russia. As far as tone of coverage is concerned, reporting on all four of South Africa's BRICS partners in the South African media was quite balanced. With the exception of Russia, which received more negative coverage than positive or neutral reports, the tone of most reports on China, India and Brazil can be described as neutral or balanced.

The South African media clearly considers China to be the most important of the BRICS partners. When the coverage of China and India as the two most dominant BRICS countries is combined, it further confirms the trend that 'Chindia' (*Global Media and Communication*, 2010) as a region is emerging as a focus point for the South African media, as this region is a bigger trade partner for South Africa than Brazil and/or Russia. The tone of the reports on most of the BRICS countries, specifically China, also continues the earlier trend of balanced views rather than a stark positive/negative binary discourse.

The Indian media presence in South Africa is primarily focused on the huge South Asian diaspora – estimated to be more than 1.3 million strong – who live mainly in Durban and Johannesburg. Indian connections with South Africa have a long history: Mahatma Gandhi, who was involved in founding the Transvaal-based British Indian Association in 1903, started the newspaper *Indian Opinion* in the same year, published in four languages, which was to become the prime vehicle for the dissemination of Gandhi's thoughts. A number of Indian television channels are available via DStv, one of the largest pay television networks in Africa, including the Tamil-language Sun TV, NDTV in English, Zee TV, and Sony Asia's Hindi channels. In addition, since

2008, a locally produced entertainment channel on DStv network called Saffron TV has been promoting the 'South African Indian experience', at different levels. A Bollywood-driven lifestyle magazine, called *SA India*, is also popular among young ethnic Indians (Thussu, 2013).

As is the case in the South African and Russian media, China received the most coverage of all the BRICS countries in the Brazilian press. Most of the texts published in relation to China (107 references) highlight the fact that the country has the largest consumer market and the second largest economy in the world. Many published texts refer to the fact that China is Brazil's main economic partner. Reports in *Correio Braziliense* dealing with India specifically used that country as an economic parameter for comparison with Brazil. India also received substantial cultural coverage alongside economic coverage. One example of BRICS cultural exchange was the successful Brazilian soap opera *Caminho das Índias* (India – A Love Story), screened in prime time on TV Globo, and winning the 2009 International Emmy Award for Best Telenovela. This 206-episode soap, set in India and Brazil and dealing with Indian themes, including caste, gender and class, with Brazilian actors playing the Indian characters, was one of the most expensive productions in TV Globo's history (Thussu, 2013).

Russia, in contrast, received much coverage of conflict and politics in *Correio Braziliense*, notably its position on the crisis in Syria. It can be concluded that most of the texts published by *Correio Braziliense* on BRICS in the collected sample editions from 2012 addressed the main issue of economic issues, a direct consequence of the prevalence of trade between countries compared to other areas of exchange such as sports and culture. Besides economic and financial issues, it is also important to highlight the coverage the *Correio Braziliense* gives to Russia and China's political position regarding Syria, to their sports activities in the Olympic Games and to Indian cultural activities.

Individual BRICS countries are still tagged with cultural marks or stereotypes in the Brazilian press, such as 'Russians and authoritarianism'; 'India and its statistics and culture'; 'China, closed regime and economical threat'; and 'South Africa and its apartheid heritage'. Beyond that, the people in the bloc states do not have a way to voice their opinion or cultural themes in civil society, different than coverage on the United States' or Europe's facts.

Similar focus areas linked to BRICS countries can be found in the Russian media. In the second quarter of 2013, China was present in Russian national newspapers mostly in connection with economics and secondly with international relations. For Russia, China is an important neighbouring country and the most important trading partner. China appears as a competitor of Russia, for example in Africa or in space, but also as a neighbouring country with foreign trade connections, or as a source of narcotics exported to Russia. In international politics China is mentioned often in connection with Russia and the US, or in connection with India. Also the situation in Korea resulted in a lot of mentions of China in Russian newspapers. If the press in many ways treats China positively by considering it a great neighbour, then the Russian population, especially in its Far East region, seems to be more sceptical about the close presence of China. The Russian people are not very happy about China's perceived dominance in all spheres, including trade and financiers, which therefore is seen to undermine economic opportunities in the same fields in Russia.

China appeared also as an alternative to Europe in Russian discussion, especially on such topics as economic cooperation or the death penalty. China appears as one of the sources of illegal economic migration to Russia. Swine influenza and threat of it (to Russia) was also linked with China. It seems that, in comparison with other BRICS countries, China is reported in Russia not from as pluralistic a perspective as, for example, India is. Regional differences in covering China are great in different parts of Russia; in Siberia and Far Eastern parts of Russia it is much more present than in the European part.

In contrast to China, India has been seen as a strategic partner in Russia, but economic relations with India are less active than with China. In the second quarter of 2013, India appeared in the Russian press in many different ways. India was mentioned often in connection with international politics, but also in relation to the economy, internal politics, education, science, culture and tourism. India was mentioned in comparison with Russia more often than other BRICS countries, whether about, for example, school uniforms or elections. Also India's (as well as China's) desire to become members of the Arctic Council was mentioned in several newspapers. India is one of the most important export partners of the Russian arms industry as well as the second biggest export market (after Belgium) for Russian jewels. The Russian fashion industry manufactures its products in India (and China).

The economic press defines India as one of the rapidly growing economies with which Russian companies cooperate. Many newspapers also mentioned the Indian ban on foreign financing of civic organizations which criticize the state. In the sports pages, India was mainly present in connection with chess. In the television pages, India also appeared because Indian soap operas are shown on Russian television. In 2014, Russian channel NTK9 acquired a drama series from India – *Iss Pyar Ko Kya Naam Doom* (*How Do I Call This Love?*) from Indian channel Star TV and Intellecta, a media consultancy that works to sell Indian series and Bollywood movies to Russia. Indian popular cinema has a long association with Russia: during the Soviet period Indian Bollywood films were very popular among Russian citizens and even today they have a small audience. The state-owned channel *Domashny* (Home) shows Bollywood, while India TV, a corporation owned by the Moscow-based Red Media Group, has been broadcasting Indian films and other programming in Russia since 2006 (Thussu, 2013).

Brazil was mentioned in leading Russian newspapers most often in connection with sport, mainly soccer. Other stories about Brazil were related to economics, foreign policy and culture. Usually in these stories, Brazil is mentioned in connection with other countries, for example, listed as one of the G20 countries, one of the countries in which same-sex marriage is legal, as one of the largest postal services in the world or as a country into which a Russian online dating service was planning to expand. Sports comprised two-thirds of the coverage of Brazil in current affairs newspapers. In popular newspapers there were various human interest and entertainment topics stories involving Brazil, including one about a female doctor who killed 320 sick people (*Komsomolskaya Pravda*, 29 March 2013). There were also many mentions of Brazil in the television pages, since a Brazilian telenovela *Avenida Brasil* (in Russian, *Prospekt Brazilii*) was being broadcast during the period of the study. There was also a report that millions of people protested in Brazil about spending on sports events, given the social problems (*Komsomolskaya Pravda*, 2013).

*Rossiiskaya Gazeta*, the government newspaper, has its own correspondent in Brazil, unusual in Russian media with their limited finances, and so can provide a more varied picture on topics such as the economy, internal politics, etc., and often mentions Brazil in connection with BRICS. Also, the economic press regularly refers to BRICS and Brazil, making comparisons, often with Russia or other BRICS countries. For example, in Brazil small businesses have similar problems with taxes and bureaucracy as in Russia (Vedomosti, 2013). There were also reports on Russian arms exports to Brazil and on Brazil's economic potential. While coverage of Brazil was dominated by sport, South Africa can be found in Russian media in connection with both economy and sport. In the Soviet period, South Africa was seriously criticized in the media for apartheid, but those times are long past. South Africa now is more visible in business-oriented media than in general outlets. South Africa is seen as one of the new markets in which Russian companies may expand their activities. The BRICS summit in Durban in April 2013 was mainly covered in economic newspapers and state newspaper *Rossiiskaya Gazeta*. In sport news, South Africa was visible mainly in soccer and tennis.

## Soft power initiatives – BRICS media 'going out' to others

The notion of 'soft power' (Nye, 2005) – defined as a means to achieve desired political outcomes by using influence and persuasion rather than force – can be seen as one of the objectives of the development of media that can promote national interests globally, and within the BRICS group. One should however remain cautious about the extent to which these initiatives can be successful – too overt support from a government might mean that it is viewed as propaganda, and will backfire on the sender of the message.

Western reportage about China's investments in Africa has often been characterized by fear-mongering or a paternalism that emphasizes the threat China poses to African countries. The increased presence of Chinese media on the continent may be seen as an attempt to counter those stereotypes, as part of China's 'going out' strategy and the more assertive foreign policy that

China has adopted in recent years. Kurlantzick (2007) has reported the attempts made by China to 'professionalize' the international broadcasts of China Central Television (CCTV) so as to come across as less propagandistic and more in line with the expectations of global media audiences.

Examples of China's media presence on the African continent include the launch of the state broadcaster, China Central Television (CCTV), with its African head office operation in Nairobi in 2010. This presence makes it possible for CCTV news reports to be broadcast across the continent. The state news agency Xinhua has been present on the continent since the 1980s, but in 2011 it also launched a mobile application that makes its news service available to the continent's millions of African mobile phone users. Xinhua's English channel, CNC World, is now also being broadcast to subscribers to the digital satellite television platform DStv, after the South Africa-based company MIH agreed to carry it on its African networks. On the print news front, the opening of bureaus in Johannesburg and Nairobi of the English-language edition of *China Daily* has extended the newspaper's reach to English-language readers in these major African centres, as well as online. Exchange programmes for media groups and journalists to visit China and vice versa have also been seen as a way to further extend its cultural influence.

The appearance in 2005 of the TV channel Russia Today (http://rt.com) from the very beginning was determined by the needs of the state to initiate broadcasting to foreign audiences. Initially, broadcasts were limited to English but Arabic and Spanish were added later. Today, this TV channel also broadcasts online, transmitting information via Twitter, Facebook and YouTube, into more than 100 countries; it has about 200 million regular users mostly living outside of Russia. The channel is popular abroad, largely due to its corresponding to the format of Western broadcasting companies. In that sense, Russia Today is similar to Al-Jazeera that drew heavily on former BBC staffers and, to a lesser extent CCTV, which also went through a period of 'professionalizing' and 'polishing' its international broadcasts as part of such a global 'charm offensive' (Kurlantzick, 2007: 63) and a means to counter negative stereotyping in African media.

The Internet has provided Russia with a useful space for the exercise of soft power. Several Russian websites are published in English and aimed at foreign audiences. The main objective of these websites is to encourage the development of international contacts between Russia and its foreign partners, and to extend Russia's influence globally. This is supported by the information policy of the web-blog *Modern Russia* (http://twitter.com/modernrussia), Internet portal *Russia Beyond* (www.facebook.com/russiabeyond) and others. The web-blog *Modern Russia* was designed by the public relations and lobby firm Ketchum, registered in the US and involved in the promotion of PR-projects on the Internet, including those initiated by governmental organizations. The main purpose of this blog, which registered 11,453 users (measured in October 2012) is to create a positive image of Russia among the world community.

It is possible to find here much information emphasizing the importance of Russia in the modern world, yet the economic issue turns out to be a priority. Great attention is paid to projects aimed at promoting Russia's attractiveness to investors. The focus falls on topics like the real estate market, the development of the northern territories and the introduction of information technologies in different fields of business. A lot of information is provided as interviews with Western business people, which seems to be of some help for the foreign audience to understand the 'theme of Russia'.

The English-language portal *Russia Beyond*, with its nearly 4,000 users and a presence on Twitter, also looks like a source of information destined to improve the international image of Russia. However, compared to the first web-blog, the local information is more diverse and discusses such topics as politics, sports, history, technological developments introduced in domestic industries. There were also reports on religion and national identity (which never appear in the blog *Modern Russia*) – in other words the 'downstairs' dimension of public diplomacy. It is noteworthy that the portal provides a consumer with both problematic and critical information (such as extracts from the speeches of Russian opposition leaders and of member of the infamous punk band *Pussy Riot*, etc.). The page 'Russia Beyond the Headlines' (www.facebook.com/russiannow?v=wall), initiated in 2007 by the state-run newspaper *Rossyiskaya Gazeta* and regularly updated on Facebook, became a subsidiary platform of the portal *Russia Beyond*. The success of this soft power initiative may be measured by the fact that *Russia Beyond the Headlines* is from time to time quoted by authoritative international newspapers such as *The New York Times*, *The Daily Telegraph*, *La Repubblica* and others.

Another source of information aimed at foreign audiences is the news agency *RIA-Novosti* (http://en.rian.ru/). Funded by the Russian government, it has news bureaus in 45 countries and translates information into 14 languages. The agency has initiated the English-language web-site 'The RealRussia' (www.facebook.com/TheRealRussia?sk=app_197936773558886), the main goal of which is to provide international users with various facts about Russia, including on the topics of tourism, sports and culture.

The above-mentioned Internet sites and the TV-Channel *Russia Today* provide the audience with information concerning the relations between Russia and foreign countries. However, the theme of BRICS almost seems to be of no importance at all in the coverage on these platforms. It would seem that these 'soft power' initiatives do not include the active promotion of the ideas of BRICS to international audiences. Both the Russian and overseas audiences are essentially left in the dark about the prospects for Russia to be an active member of this international project. The lack of coverage of BRICS in these public diplomacy channels also casts doubt on the regular public statements by Russian leaders from the mid-2000s onwards that the relationships within the BRICS organization are a priority for the national economic strategy.

As a recent Working Paper from the Russian International Affairs Council states: 'The Russian and Indian mass media both fail to perform its primary function of unbiased coverage of events that take place in two countries. Attention is primarily focused on negative events and problems in bilateral relations, particularly when it comes to defence-tech cooperation' (RIAC, 2013: 21). It recommends establishment of an English-language Russian online publication for India and suggests opportunities for Indian media to open Moscow bureaus.

Indian media have also been central in the country's construction of 'Brand India', which entailed a redefinition of public discourse (Chaudhuri, 2010: 70). Diasporic Bollywood actors and soap opera and reality TV stars have made their mark in international media, and have also achieved fame domestically (Chaudhuri, 2010: 69). The Indian film industry has become well-known globally as a result of its popularity among diasporic audiences. The visibility of Indian film has increased in the West in recent years, partly as a result of coverage of this industry in the Western press (Athique, 2005: 117).

Indian media content is now also reaching China, where Bollywood films with their larger-than-life narratives used to be popular during the communist period as a useful alternative to state propaganda and a cheap substitute for a Hollywood extravaganza. As China opened to the West during the 1980s and gradually developed its own film industry, interest in Indian films declined. In more recent years, there has been a modest revival, signalled by the release in 2000 of a shortened, digitized, and dubbed version of historical drama *Lagaan* (Land Tax) which was released across 25 theatres in China. The success in China of the 2009 campus-based comedy *3 Idiots* has brought Bollywood back into Chinese popular consciousness, especially among the younger generation. The correspondent of *The Hindu* newspaper in Beijing reported the reaction of a senior Chinese official: 'The film entirely changed mindsets, of even Ministers and entire Ministries. It mesmerized people and convinced them that there was a lot in common between both countries, and that Indian entertainment did have a market in China' (cited in Thussu, 2013). In 2012, Zee TV became the first Indian network to be granted landing rights in China to supply dubbed Indian content to the world's largest television audience. There is very limited reverse flow of media content from China to India. As for Indian journalism, despite being a country with a highly developed – and English-language – news media, BRICS countries are not a priority area for them, instead their focus remains on the South Asian issues and on huge Indian diaspora, especially based in the Gulf Arab states, Britain and the US.

## Conclusion

From the increased interpenetration of media capital, the increased amount of coverage and the debates in the media about the BRICS formation in the respective member countries, it is clear that the shifting geopolitics will increasingly be mirrored on media platforms. But these shifts are not only mirrored, they are also facilitated and played out through mediation. The flows and contra-flows of media capital are part and parcel of shifting economic relations, and the media provide a key platform for 'soft power' and public diplomacy initiatives that are bound to impact on the intra-BRICS relations in future.

Although a fair amount of intra-BRICS coverage could be noted in the various countries studied, it also became clear that attention is mostly paid to political and economic issues. The cultural and social dimensions of these global shifts are not yet finding their way into the media of these countries in rich and meaningful ways. For the coverage to become more textured and to contribute to a better understanding of not only the economic and political impacts of the BRICS alignment, but also the social and cultural implications, media would have to give more attention to the 'downstairs' relationships that evolve through the new geopolitics, and not only the 'upstairs' trade and exchange (cf. Park and Alden, 2013). The media is likely to remain a central space where ideological battles, political tugs-of-war and cultural engagements are contested among the BRICS countries and between the BRICS group and other regions of the world.

## Note

1 With the assistance of Fernando Molina.

## References

Anderson, B. (1991) *Imagined Communities: Reflections on the Origin and Spread of Nationalism*. London: Verso.

Athique, A. (2005) Watching Indian Movies in Australia: Media, community and con-sumption. *South Asian Popular Culture* 3(2): 117–133.

Chaudhuri, M. (2010) Indian Media and Its Transformed Public. *Contributions to Indian Sociology* 44(1 and 2): 57–78.

CNews (2013) Available at www.webground.su/topic/2013/03/12/t239, 12 March. Accessed 4 June 2013.

*Correio Braziliense* (2012a) Editorial, February 6, page 9. Available for subscribers on http://buscacb2.correioweb.com.br/correio/2012/02/06/AXX09-0602.pdf.

*Correio Braziliense* (2012b) Economy section, September 4, page 7. Available for subscribers http://buscacb2.correioweb.com.br/correio/2012/04/09/AXX07-0904.pdf.

DST (2011) 'Gotov vlozhit' sotni millionov dollarov v Indiiskiy Internet [DST is ready to finance Indian Internet with hundred millions of dollars]'. Available at http://mediabusi-ness.com.ua/content/view/27014/125/lang,ru/, 21 November. Accessed 4 June 2014.

*Estadão* (2001) 'Novelas brasileiras conquistam a Rússia'. Available at http://www.estadao.com.br/arquivo/arteelazer/2001/not20010513p7613.htm,13 May. Accessed 5 December 2013.

*Global Media and Communication* (2010) Editorial: 'Chindia' and Global Communication. *Global Media and Communication* 6(3): 243–245.

Goncharova, O. and Noskovich, M. (2007) 'Naspers kupil tret' Mail.ru [Naspers has bought one third of the Mail.ru]', 24 January. http://www.burocrats.ru/ismi/070124115131.html. Accessed 4 June 2014.

Kurlantzick, J. (2007) *Charm Offensive: How China's Soft Power Is Transforming the World*. New Haven, NJ: Yale University Press.

Nye, J. (2005) *Soft Power: The Means to Success in World Politics*. New York: Public Affairs.

Olsen, K. (2013) Xi Trip Highlights China's Africa Influence. *Mail & Guardian*. 21 March.

Park, Y.J. and Alden, C. (2013) 'Upstairs' and 'Downstairs' Dimensions of China and the Chinese in South Africa, pp. 643–662, in Pillay, U., Hagg, G. and Nyamnjoh, F. (eds.) *State of the Nation 2012: Tackling Poverty and Inequality*. Pretoria: HSRC Press.

Paulino, F.; Bolaño, C. and Holanda, M. (2013) The Other BRICS Countries in Brazilian Media: Stereotypes and states over society. Paper presented at ICA Preconference, London: University of Westminster, June.

Reis, A. (2013) Oi, Portugal Telecom to Merge, Creating $17 Billion Giant. *Bloomberg Technology*. Available at http://www.bloomberg.com/news/2013-10-02/portugal-telecom-to-combine-with-oi-into-carrier-led-by-bava.html, 2 October. Accessed 5 December 2013.

RIAC (2013) *Postulates on Russia–India Relations*. Working Paper No. 3. Moscow: Russian International Affairs Council.

Rocha, D. and Deusdará, B. (2005) Análise de Conteúdo e Análise do Discurso: Aproximações e afastamentos na (re)construção de uma trajetória. *ALEA* 7(2): 305–322.

Roughneen, S. (2011) After BRIC Comes MIST, the Acronym Turkey Would Certainly Welcome. *The Guardian* Available at http://www.guardian.co.uk/global-development/poverty-matters/2011/feb/01/emerging-economies-turkey-jim-oneill, 1 February. Accessed 18 March 2013.

Steyn, L. (2012) Naspers Rides Big Chinese Wave. *Mail & Guardian*. Available at http://mg.co.za/article/2012-08-31-naspers-rides-big-chinese-wave, 31 August. Accessed 21 March 2013.

Thussu, D. K. (2013) *Communicating India's Soft Power: Buddha to Bollywood*. New York: Palgrave/Macmillan.

Wasserman, H. (2014) South Africa and China as BRICS Partners. Media perspectives on geopolitical shifts. *Journal of Asian and African Studies* 49 (5): published online, doi:10.1177/0021909613514191.

# Chapter 12

# Digital BRICS: building a NWICO 2.0?

*Daya Kishan Thussu*

The international presence of BRICS media is likely to become more noticeable with the growing convergence of mobile communications technologies and content via an altered and multi-lingual Internet. The predominance of English on the Internet might also be undermined, creating tendencies towards a fragmented Internet. China, which hosts the world's largest blogging population and whose version of Facebook – *QZone* – had more than 600 million users by 2014; while *Weibo* (the Chinese version of Twitter), has an equally large following and is increasingly influencing mainstream journalism within the Sino media-sphere. Internet users in India are expected to reach 600 million by 2020, driven by wireless connections. Russia already has the highest Internet penetration among the BRICS nations. In Brazil too, the Internet is expanding at a rapid pace, while the growth of mobile Internet in South Africa is likely to increase as 3G becomes more affordable. What implications will such digital connectivity have for global news flows, information and communication agendas, both in the BRICS countries and beyond? This chapter aims to evaluate how current and potential developments in digital, Internet-based media in the BRICS countries might impact on global communication. It maps these developments and analyses them within the context of questions about Internet governance and suggests that, given the scope and scale of change in BRICS countries, a New World Information and Communication Order may be evolving – a NWICO 2.0.

## BRICS in the context of NWICO

Despite its many internal differences and complex external affiliations, the BRICS group shares their non-Euro-Atlantic origins as well as their consistent calls to redress power imbalances in existing international institutions and structures. In this respect, these nations represent a much older and often forgotten demand for a fairer and more just international order, with its roots in the Non-Aligned Movement, of which India was a founding member and a leading exponent. The demand for a New World Information and Communication Order (NWICO), which dominated international communication debates during the 1970s and 1980s, most significantly within UNESCO, in its essence argued that the international information system, because of its structural logic, reinforced and perpetuated inequality, with serious implications for the countries of the Global South, which were heavily dependent on the West for both information software and hardware (Nordenstreng and Padovani, 2005; Pickard, 2007; Nordenstreng, 2012; Thussu, 2015). It was argued by NWICO supporters that, owing to economic, political, social and technological imbalances, there was 'a one-way flow' of information from the 'centre' to the 'periphery', which created a wide gap between the 'haves' and the 'have nots.' This 'vertical' flow (as opposed to a more desirable, horizontal flow of global information) was dominated by Western-based transnational corporations, which treated information as a 'commodity' and subjected it to the rules of the market. It was argued that there existed a 'flagrant quantitative imbalance between North and South created by the volume of news and information emanating from the developed world and intended for the developing countries and the volume of the flow in the opposite direction'. Therefore, 'by transmitting to developing countries only news processed by them, that is, news which they have filtered, cut, and distorted, the transnational media impose their own way of seeing the world upon the developing countries' (Masmoudi, 1979: 172–173).

Western governments, led by the US, saw in the call for a NWICO a 'Soviet-inspired', Third-World design to control the media through state regulation. As a concept it was seen as one fundamentally in conflict with liberal Western values and the principle of the 'free flow of information'. Their response was also affected by Cold War assumptions that made the West place the issues regarding global newsflow in the context of East–West rivalry. The opponents of NWICO argued that it was a pretext for Third-World dictators to stifle media freedom and to impose censorship. The Western governments and their commercial media viewed the NWICO demands as 'entailing too interventionist a role for the state and also as likely to result in the exclusion of foreign journalists, with consequent restriction of information flows' (Wells, 1987: 27).

As a result of the protracted debates, the International Commission for the Study of Communication Problems was set up in 1977. The MacBride Commission, as it was popularly known, submitted its final report to UNESCO in 1980, a document which, for the first time, elevated information- and communication-related issues onto the global agenda. Out of the 16 members of this Commission, only two represented the BRICS nations – India and Russia (then Soviet Union). The other three BRICS countries had virtually no contribution to the NWICO debate: China was conspicuously absent from the deliberations; Brazil was ruled during that period by a pro-US military dictatorship; while South Africa was under an apartheid regime with very limited international diplomatic exposure.

Much has changed in the world since those ideologically-charged days of East–West/North–South dichotomies. In the post-Cold War, post-Communist, neo-liberal globalized world, new geo-political and economic constellations are emerging and old ones being reconfigured. The BRICS nations represent a striking example of this changed globe, also notable in the field of media and communication. As Castells has suggested, 'communicative action' remains the key to power (Castells, 2009: 50) and, as their communicative power increases, what will be the impact of the BRICS nations on the global information and communication system?

## Digital growth and BRICS

The most significant change in global media is the exceptional growth in digital communication. According to PricewaterhouseCoopers' report, *Global Entertainment and Media Outlook 2014–2018*, global mobile Internet penetration will reach 55 per cent by 2018, which will enable digital advertising to increase its share of total advertising revenue to an estimated 33 per cent, up from 14 per cent in 2009. Industry reports suggest that the BRICS nations are likely to see a surge in the TV subscription market, as well as in the advertising sector, since they 'possess both high growth rates and major scale' (PwC, 2014). According to PwC, China, with total Internet advertising revenue of more than $30 billion in 2018, will be the largest of the 'higher-growth, larger-scale' markets. In newspapers too, China, India and Brazil are likely to witness impressive expansion. The 2013 World Press Trends survey by the World Association of Newspapers and News Publishers reports that 800 million now access news online, an increasingly large number of them among BRICS nations (WAN-IFRA, 2014). Though the US will be the world's biggest entertainment and media market in 2018, in terms of digital revenues and Internet advertising, China will have 'dramatically narrowed the gap' (PwC, 2014). China will also become the world's largest film market by 2020, says a UNESCO report, noting that Brazil, Russia, India and China are increasing the share of the world film market (both production and admissions), with China being 'the main star of this story: based on conservative estimates, by early 2020 the Asiatic giant will surpass US as the main film market in the world' (UNESCO, 2013: 34).

The growth is also remarkable in the other Asian giant, India, where it took a decade for the number of Internet users to grow from 10 million to 100 million, but just three years to double that number to 200 million (FICCI-KPMG Report, 2014: 98). India's Minister of Communications and IT, Ravi Shankar Prasad, told Parliament in August 2014 that the number of Internet users in the country had reached nearly 252 million by March 2014. An estimated two million new users are added every month to social media networks in India, which is expected to have the largest Facebook population by 2016, surpassing the US (FICCI-KPMG Report, 2014: 119). The projected growth in India's Internet users is likely to be 'the highest incremental growth in the world', says a McKinsey report, noting:

India has significant advantages that make it fertile ground for an internet-enabled transformation: a youthful demographic profile that will produce a large future wave of early adopters of technology; a large pool of workers with technical education; and a strong culture of entrepreneurship and the ability to adapt business models for a resource-constrained environment.

(Gnanasambandam *et al.*, 2012: 11)

With the expansion of 3G and gradual introduction of 4G services, paralleled with the affordability of smartphones as telecom companies achieve economies of scale, more and more Internet users are likely to be mobile-only subscribers using Internet-enabled devices (ibid.). In 2013, India had 42 million 3G connections, expected to grow to about 369 million by 2018 (FICCI-KPMG Report, 2014: 102). Industry estimates suggest that digital advertising spending will reach about $2 billion by 2018, compared to $26 billion for China and nearly $80 billion for the US. However, the biggest potential change is in the countryside – in 2013, for the first time in India's history, there were more rural than urban readers of newspapers (UNESCO, 2014).

As India's ambitious National Optical Fibre Network is completed, with a plan to provide broadband connectivity to 250,000 *gram panchayats* (village councils) serving 600,000 villages and over 1.15 billion people, it will considerably improve access to citizen services and the quality of information collected at the grassroots level. As a result, the rural communication scene is likely to be transformed (FICCI-KPMG Report, 2014: 98). Another feature of this transformation is the increasing realization that, while English remains a link language within India and a vehicle for global communication, the real growth is in India's indigenous languages. Already Google has launched a Hindi handwriting tool for search, and Mozilla Firefox a Tamil version of its browser, while Samsung announced the launch of regional language user interface and applications for its Indian customers (FICCI-KPMG Report, 2014: 106). As the McKinsey report observes: 'The next wave of internet adoption in India will be dominated by local language speakers' (Gnanasambandam *et al.*, 2012: 17).

Such connectivity is encouraging businesses to invest in communication infrastructure: in 2014, one of India's biggest corporations, Reliance Industries, acquired Network 18 – the country's premier news and entertainment channel – and is introducing a 4G broadband network in a phased manner under the brand of 'Reliance Jio' Infocomm ('live' in Hindi). The suggestion is that, as the Internet infrastructure is strengthened and millions of Indians start using digital platforms and services, corporatized news from Network 18 – which owns many channels – will provide the content for the telecom company. India's e-retailing market, too, is predicted to reach $20 billion by 2020. In 2014, India's response to Amazon – Flipkart.com, the country's largest e-commerce company – attracted $1 billion in funding from investors – unprecedented in Indian corporate history (Thoppil, 2014).

As the McKinsey report notes: 'If India achieves its potential for growth in the number of internet users and internet technology-related consumption and investment, the internet's contribution to GDP would be nearly $100 billion in 2015' (Gnanasambandam *et al.*, 2012: 2). However, in comparison to its BRICS partners, India lags behind considerably: in contrast to Brazil and South Africa it has only approximately 6 per cent of the number of secure Internet servers per capita. Also impeding its growth is high cost of access and usage, one of the highest costs of broadband access: more than four times that of China and Brazil (ibid.).

In China, where nearly half the population was online in 2014, the scale of the digital revolution is even greater and the impact of this is being experienced across the globe. The 2014 announcement of the public offering of Alibaba, China's largest e-commerce company on the New York Stock Exchange – valued at $200 billion – generated much interest in the global business press, an indication of the changing contours of global digital capitalism. WeChat, an app owned by Chinese firm Tencent, which allows users to create personal profiles or subscription profiles, in 2014 had 400 million users. Apart from providing consumer brands to reach a tailor-made audience, such digital connectivity has also helped WeChat to emerge as a platform for critical journalists in China to work around state censorship. *China Daily*, the English-language mouthpiece of the government, is available as *Real Time China* on WeChat. Like many Chinese-language publishers, they use WeChat to share articles and pictures about topics trending on the web. In India, Brazil and South Africa, journalists are increasingly using social media to supplement mainstream media and, in some cases, also to demand greater transparency from governments.

Among the BRICS nations, Brazil has the highest Internet penetration after Russia. Brazilians are 'among the world's top users of blogs and social networks (in 2013, there were 80 million Facebook users in Brazil) and use of online media is growing fast, attracting foreign outlets like *BuzzFeed*, the Spanish newspaper *El País* and the *Huffington Post*, which launched their Portuguese versions' (Newman and Levy, 2014: 36).

In Russia, the Internet industry is characteristically indigenous, as its social networking sites (*VKontakte*), blogging platforms (*LiveJournal*) and search engines (*Yandex*), are largely in Russian. Known popularly as the 'RuNet', the Russian-language Internet has demonstrated exceptional growth: in the period 2003–2013, the main Russian top level domain '.ru' grew from 200,000 to about 4.5 million. Internet usage in South Africa has more than doubled in the last four years. According to the State of the Newsroom SA 2013 study, one third of the country's adult population were on the Internet and that figure is expected to double by 2016. The Government is planning for broadband access for every citizen by 2020 (quoted in FICCI-KPMG Report, 2014). One reason for this expansion is the growing use of mobile Internet across the world. According to 2014 *Ericsson Mobility Report*, there were 1.9 billion smartphone subscriptions in 2013 and a ten-fold growth in mobile data traffic between 2013 and 2019 is predicted, mostly in the developing world. Mobile broadband subscriptions had reached 2.3 billion in 2014 – by 2019 these were expected to account for more than 80 per cent of all mobile subscriptions (*Ericsson Mobility Report,* 2014: 6).

## Surveillance and security: a cyber Cold War?

This global connectivity is raising concerns about security in the digital domain. Countries, corporations and individuals are increasingly anxious to protect their cyber assets as the 'Internet of things' begins to take firmer shape (US Government, 2014). According to the research firm Gartner, organizations around the globe spent $67 billion on information security in 2013. Despite the rhetoric of a cyber war or a terrorist attack on electrical grids and communications networks – a 'cyber 9/11' – it has been argued that the real threat is espionage, sabotage and subversion (Rid, 2013). However, it is not state-less terrorist outfits but national governments which have been blamed for digital sabotage. One example was 'the destruction in 2010 of centrifuges at a nuclear facility in Iran by a computer programme known as Stuxnet', the handiwork of US and Israeli 'software experts' (*Economist,* 2014).

Some BRICS members have contended that the US wields great influence on Internet infrastructure, thus undermining the security and sovereignty of other nations (Ebert and Maurer, 2013). Given that the Internet was developed in the US – within its military-industrial-complex, evolving from a network infrastructure created by the Department of Defense – it has a strong American stamp on it. This goes back to the 1990s when the Internet was privatized and globalized and the creation of ICANN (1998) (the Internet Corporation for Assigned Names and Numbers), the US-based non-profit organization which coordinates a vital aspect of online communication – the Internet Protocol addresses and domain names system (DNS), so that users can send and receive information from any web-connected device. It was set up under contract to the US Department of Commerce, with its National Telecommunications and Information Administration assuming a lead role within the organization (Kruger, 2014). These issues have become prominent since the Internet is increasingly affecting all aspects of life for people across the globe. As ICANN's draft Five Year Strategic Plan 2016–2020, released in April 2014, notes: 'By the end of 2020, it is estimated there will be as many as one trillion "things" connected to the Internet, using the DNS as a platform for a range of services for the world's users. This will expand the very nature of the Internet from an on-demand human service to an always on, near continuous use service for sensors and machines' (Cerf *et al.,* 2014).

The age of ubiquitous digital services and 'cloud computing', with services like iCloud, Google Drive and Dropbox, will transform data storage and access across the globe with implications for data-mining and trading (Fuchs *et al.,* 2011; Mosco, 2014). Corporations are particularly concerned about the security of intellectual property rights in the digital realm. A study by the US-based Centre for Strategic and International Studies estimates that globally the annual cost of digital crime and intellectual-property theft was $445 billion (Lewis and Baker, 2013). Given that it is mostly US-based and owned corporations – notably Microsoft, Google, Facebook, PayPal, Amazon, Twitter and Yahoo – which effectively control global Internet traffic, questions have been raised about data protection and the issues of digital surveillance and spying (Fuchs *et al.*, 2011; Mosco, 2014, among others). A vast majority of Internet users – over 90 per cent – deploy tools and platforms developed by these companies, making them vulnerable to consumer surveillance and worse. Google, for example, accounts for nearly 70 per cent share of the global search engine market, while global paid search Internet advertising has the largest share of total Internet advertising revenue, at $48.4bn in 2013 (PwC, 2014).

The 2013 exposés by former National Security Administration (NSA) contractor Edward Snowden about NSA spying revealed 'the US government's vast capacity to intercept communications around the world'. These not only 'appear to have damaged one major element of America's global image: its reputation for protecting individual liberties', as a Pew Survey found (Pew Research Center, 2014: 6), but also contributed to what has been termed as a cyber Cold War among the main protagonists of the original Cold War – US and Russia (the country where Snowden has been granted political asylum). Apart from revealing the extent of global surveillance that the US government was routinely undertaking – ranging from diplomatic negotiations to corporate spying, to issues of individual privacy – the Snowden affair also demonstrated the collusion of major Internet corporations in this enterprise.

The BRICS countries – especially Russia – were particularly exercised by this, prompting President Putin to even suggest that the Russian search engine *Yandex* was controlled by Western intelligence agencies. In Brazil, following the news that the NSA had listened to the private phone conversations of President Dilma Rousseff, the image of the US declined considerably – from 69 per cent in 2013 to 52 per cent in 2014 – among those questioned in a multinational audience research survey conducted by the Pew Research Center (Pew Research Center, 2014). Brazil also announced the creation of fibre-optic submarine cables which will link up Brazil directly with Western Europe (thus bypassing the US). In addition, it introduced a bill that would mandate the storing of digital data on Brazilians in Brazil, thus contributing to the emergence of a 'national Internet'.

## Safeguarding cyber sovereignty

In the Internet age of global and globalized communication, the governance of the Internet becomes a crucial element and the BRICS nations, given the scale and scope of their digital growth, are key players in this global tussle

(Ebert and Maurer, 2013). Of the five BRICS nations, there are strikingly different approaches with regard to the governance of the Internet: while the members of IBSA – India, Brazil and South Africa – by and large, follow the US-led model championing a 'multi-stakeholders' approach, Russia and China have argued for a UN-approved and managed governance structure, with such intergovernmental organizations as the International Telecommunications Union (ITU) undertaking a primary role in defining and implementing governance, and for a reduced role for ICANN. At the heart of the debate are two competing views – the 'sovereignist' where national governments take the major decisions, and a market-led privatized network – on how the most significant global network should be governed.

The Snowden disclosures of US government surveillance practices, including the monitoring of foreign leaders, have reignited an international debate over Internet governance. The US modelled regulation for the new areas of communication, it has been argued, applies 'neo-liberal logics as a part of its efforts to recreate the transnational hegemonic communication system' (Bhuiyan, 2014: 38). Governing the Internet has been a deeply contested issue. In 2005, the UN-sponsored World Summit on the Information Society (WSIS) defined Internet governance as 'the development and application by governments, the private sector and civil society, in their respective roles, of shared principles, norms, rules, decision-making procedures, and programs that shape the evolution and use of the internet' (WSIS, 2005). Under pressure from many member states, the UN's response to US-influenced ICANN was the establishment in 2006 at the WSIS of the Internet Governance Forum (IGF), an international group of governments and nongovernmental entities, to discuss Internet-related policies (Nordenstreng and Padovani, 2005; Pickard, 2007).

Since then, the Internet has grown exponentially and a range of issues – from cyber security to digital property rights to electronic commerce – have complicated the governance discourse (US Government, 2014). As Mueller has suggested, the Internet's 'transnational scope, boundless scale, distributed control, new institutions, and radical changes in collective action capabilities ... are transforming national control and sovereignty over communication and information policy' (Mueller, 2010: 5). He has argued that Internet governance can be best conceptualized as 'networked governance', which provides 'one possible way of bridging the gap between national institutions and global connectivity' (ibid.: 6). Networks that 'combine state and non-state actors', Mueller has argued, 'can overcome some of the limitations of the government based on territorial sovereignty' (ibid.: 7).

The IGF followed a 'multi-stakeholder model' promoted by ICANN, where governments shared policy debates with private sector and civil society groups (Pickard, 2007; Bhuiyan, 2014). Mueller has called multi-stakeholder governance a 'pluralization of international institutions' (Mueller, 2010: 8). Some BRICS governments saw this as a cloak for legitimizing a commercialized neo-liberal policy structure developed to protect and promote digital corporations, most of which are based in the US. China's attitude on this issue is clearly stated in its 2010 White Paper:

> China believes that the UN should be given full scope in international internet administration and supports the establishment of an authoritative and just international internet administration organization under the UN system through democratic procedures on a worldwide scale. All countries have equal rights in participating in the administration of the fundamental international resources of the internet.
>
> (Government of China, 2010)

Russia, too, prefers a model that is state-centric and based on the inviolability of state sovereignty, favouring a greater role for the UN. Both countries have serious concerns about the control of the Internet by the US and its capacity to compromise security both in the virtual and real world.

There is a domestic dimension of this attitude as well: both countries exercise extensive and deeply embedded control and censorship regimes: the so-called 'Great Firewall of China' – an effective information filtering mechanism – is the most cited example of this (Yang, 2009; Ng, 2013). In Russia, too, governmental control over Internet intermediaries and service providers is strong. However, unlike Russia, Chinese global presence is growing and digital capitalism is increasingly important to its version of capitalism 'with Chinese characteristics', which is very open to foreign investment and international trade but still closed to political pluralism.

At the UN-sponsored World Conference on International Telecommunication held in Dubai in December 2012, Russia and China, as two key countries, introduced a proposal stating: 'Member States shall have equal rights to manage the internet, including in regard to the allotment, assignment and reclamation of internet numbering, naming, addressing and identification resources to support for the operation and development of basic internet infrastructure' (ITU, 2012a). Unsurprisingly, it was rejected by the US, asserting that 'the United States continues to believe that internet policy must be multi-stakeholder-driven' and that it 'should not be determined by member states, but by citizens, communities, and broader society' (US Government, 2012). The proposal was subsequently withdrawn and the ITU adopted a non-binding resolution, '[t]o foster an enabling environment for the greater growth of the internet', which stated that 'all governments should have an equal role and responsibility for international internet governance' and invited governments to 'elaborate on their respective positions on international internet-related technical, development and public policy issues within the mandate of ITU at various ITU forums' (ITU, 2012b).

The US declined to sign the treaty, and the head of the US delegation stated that the Internet had 'given the world unimaginable economic and social benefits during these past 24 years – all without UN regulation. We candidly cannot support an ITU treaty that is inconsistent with a multi-stakeholder model of internet governance' (US Government, 2012). Of the 144 members of the ITU, 89 nations signed the treaty, while 55 either chose not to sign or abstained from voting, including the other three BRICS nations – India, Brazil and South Africa. While supporting the role of governments in Internet regulation, these three argued for the representation of private interests and civil society groups. The Dubai meeting was labelled by *The Economist* as 'a digital version of the Cold War' (*Economist*, 2012).

Despite their differences over this, the BRICS nations have been increasingly challenging the US-created global Internet regime and demanding greater internationalization of Internet governance. China and Russia submitted a joint proposal on information security to the UN in 2011, while India, Brazil and South Africa have been focusing on the information society since their 2003 Brasilia Declaration. Brazil's has been an important voice with regard to Internet governance issues, for example, by promoting open source software (against strong US opposition). In March 2014, a month before NETmundial, an international conference organized by Brazil in São Paulo, the US government announced plans to relinquish its control over the Internet Assigned Numbers Authority (IANA), which is operated by ICANN and seen by many as a damage-control exercise post-Snowden revelations. NETmundial, described as a 'global multistakeholder meeting on the future of internet governance', produced a non-binding 'NETmundial Multi-stakeholder Statement', essentially reaffirming the multi-stakeholder model of Internet governance. This demonstrated once again rifts among BRICS nations, who had been demanding that Internet governance should reflect the fact that the Internet was becoming more international: it stated that 'internet governance must respect, protect and promote cultural and linguistic diversity in all its forms' (NETmundial, 2014).

This internationalization was also emphasized by the Indian submission to the conference: 'The structures that manage and regulate the core internet resources need to be internationalized, and made representative and democratic' (Government of India, 2014a). The statement by the Indian representative at the São Paulo meeting talked of a 'trust deficit' in the system and criticized the multi-stakeholder model itself, demanding that 'the internet governance ecosystem [should] be sensitive to the cultures and national interests of all nations, not just of a select set of stakeholders'. Interestingly, the Indian position also questioned the presence of the non-governmental sector in governance negotiations: 'Given the important role that non-government stakeholders play', the Indian representative said, 'there should also be a clear delineation of principles governing their participation – including their accountability, representativeness, transparency, and inclusiveness. Clearly, it makes it even more important that we define multistakeholderism' (Government of India, 2014b).

This is a concern shared by other BRICS nations. The non-governmental sector has grown in size and influence over the past two decades, the large majority of which are based in the West but operate across the world. They wield increasing clout within international forums, including Internet governance deliberations, and this has been seen by many as benefitting Western-based digital corporations. In countries with a democratic polity and an open economy, such as Brazil, India and South Africa, their presence is strong, while in Russia and China they remain marginal actors.

In the West, though, the so-called non-governmental sector is crucial in policy discourse, not least in relation to the future of the Internet. One significant entrant is the Global Commission on Internet Governance, established in January 2014 by the US-based Centre for International Governance Innovation and UK's Chatham House, 'to help educate the wider public on the most effective ways to promote internet access, while simultaneously championing the principles of freedom of expression and the free flow of ideas over the internet'. This invoking of 'free flow' doctrine is reminiscent of the NWICO debates referred to at the beginning of this chapter.

As BRICS gain greater salience in global governance issues, will the Internet infrastructure and architecture need reformulating? Will it lead to new cracks appearing in cyberspace? If China, Russia, Brazil and India, among other large nations, had their own 'national' Internet, insulated from the prying eyes of US corporate advertisers or intelligence agencies, what would happen to the World Wide Web? In the first paper released by the above mentioned Global Commission on Internet Governance, Joseph Nye writes: 'it is unlikely that there will be a single overarching regime for cyberspace any time soon. A good deal of fragmentation exists now and is likely to persist. The evolution of the present regime complex, which lies halfway between a single coherent legal structure and complete fragmentation of normative structures, is more likely' (Nye, 2014)

Eric Schmidt, Executive Chairman of Google and Jared Cohen, Director of Google Ideas, predict that the World Wide Web will 'fracture and fragment', leading to the 'Balkanisation' of the Internet, with 'co-existing and sometimes overlapping but in important ways, separate' national systems. The Internet in each of these 'Internet Balkans', as they refer to them, 'would take on its national characteristics' the process would 'at first be barely perceptible to users, but it would fossilize over time and ultimately remake the internet' (Schmidt and Cohen, 2013: 85). Another form of 'Balkanization of the Internet' has more serious economic implications if proposals in the US by some Internet Service Providers to create fast digital lanes for 'paid prioritization', come about, whereby websites could charge for quality content delivered to subscribers at a faster speed. These digital lanes and by-lanes will also be aggressively utilized by governments to protect and promote their global interests.

## Soft power in the digital domain

In his widely cited book *Soft Power*, Joseph Nye suggested one key source for a country's soft power is its foreign policies 'when they are seen as legitimate and having moral authority' (Nye 2004: 11). Despite Nye's focus being primarily on the US, the concept of soft power has also been adopted by BRICS nations, recognizing the centrality of communication in contemporary international relations in a digitally connected and globalized environment with multiple media flows, involving both state and non-state actors and networks (Thussu, 2013).

The growing globalization of media content from BRICS countries – in terms of international television news emanating from China and Russia and the deepening globalization of Bollywood and *telenovelas* from Brazil – offers new opportunities for soft power discourse. As the world becomes increasingly mobile, networked and digitized, will such cultural flows erode US hegemony? In his 2011 book *The Future of Power,* Nye explored the nature and shift in global power structures – from state to non-state actors and suggested that governments have to use 'smart power' ('neither hard nor soft. It is both'), making use of formal and informal networks and drawing on 'cyber power' (Nye, 2011).

The use of international broadcasting and personalized social media is adding another dimension to communicative power of governments and corporations, in a 'global networked society' (Castells, 2009). Soft power is increasingly communicated within a digital environment, as part of what is described as 'Public Diplomacy 2.0.' Castells has argued for a broader understanding of public diplomacy in such a connected space. He suggests that it seeks to build a public sphere in which diverse voices can be heard in spite of their various origins, distinct values, and often contradictory interests,' and recommends using it for developing 'a global public sphere around the global networks of communication, from which the public debate could inform the emergence of a new form of consensual global governance (Castells, 2008: 91).

BRICS nations can learn from the US experience in this field. A US government report, *National Framework for Strategic Communication,* called for 'engagement' with foreign audiences to make public diplomacy more effective, using the possibilities offered by 'Web 2.0' to 'engage people directly', adding that such connectivity 'allow[s] us to convey credible, consistent messages, develop effective plans and to better understand how our actions will be perceived' (US Government, 2009: 1). However, what makes the US a formidable media and cultural presence around the world is not government propaganda channels but a thriving and globalized private media. BRICS countries can provide a much needed corrective to a US-centric debate about soft power, especially by bringing culture into the global discourse. As Zaharna argues, '[t]he role of culture as a force shaping public diplomacy represents a pressing research need, which at present is curiously unexplored' (Zaharna, 2010: 182).

In recent years, soft power initiatives have much progressed beyond the Western world. Both Russia and China have launched US-specific television operations, RT America and CCTV America, employing American staff, in an interesting example of news contra-flow. Russia, particularly, has experience of operating an extensive global propaganda machinery during the Soviet era, supporting anti-colonialism and anti-imperialism and promoting progressive causes around the Third World. During the NWICO debates, the issue of 'information imperialism' was widely discussed within anti-Western groups. In the digital age, the Russian media is increasingly using its online presence. The website of the Arabic version of Russia Today – *Rusiya Al-Yaum* – claims to draw on average 100,000 visitors every day, while RT's YouTube presence is also impressive.

China has used a combination of instruments, including public diplomacy, economic assistance, cultural exchanges and international broadcasting to promote its geopolitical and economic agenda. As Daniel Bell has noted, 'copying Western ways won't be sufficient for China to project its soft power' (Bell, 2008: 19). A Chinese version of soft propaganda, largely circulated via CCTV News (with prominent operations in Kenya and the US), as well as international newspapers, such as the English-language *China Daily*, is resolutely delivered to an international audience by the Party-state in the form of an unabashedly official discourse promoting notions of the peaceful 'rise' of China on the global scene. Outside the official circuits, the growing global presence of Chinese students, business executives and tourists contribute to a people-to-people conversation, arguably more effectively than state-sponsored, external communication projects, which include broadcasting and online presence, as well as the proliferation of Confucius Institutes across the globe (Wang, 2010; Lai and Lu, 2012).

Indian soft power in the digital domain remains limited, although the Indian government has belatedly woken up to the need to expand its external broadcasting. A high-powered committee in 2014 recommended that Prasar Bharati, India's public broadcaster, should have a 'global outreach'. Its vision is ambitious.

> [to] create a world-class broadcasting service benchmarked with the best in the world using next-generation opportunities, technologies, business models and strategies. The platform should be designed for new media first and then extended to conventional TV. Outline an effective content strategy for Prasar Bharati's global platforms (TV and Radio) focused on projecting the national view rather than the narrow official viewpoint.
>
> (Prasar Bharati, 2014: 15)

Such attitudes will certainly help to increase the Indian presence in the international sphere, especially with the growth of English-language media in India and the globalization of Indian media industries. The expert committee has proposed the establishment of Prasar Bharati Connect, which would be tasked with managing the state broadcaster, Doordarshan's websites 'to make them more appealing, interactive, and engaging, and also integrate them with the existing social media channels' (Prasar Bharati, 2014: 33). In August 2014,

Doordarshan signed an agreement with Deutsche Welle to distribute Indian public television to the European market. According to Prasar Bharati CEO, Jawahar Sircar, this aims to 'provide an important platform to position DD's content globally and projecting India's viewpoint to a global audience' (Quoted in *Business Line,* 2014).

News 18 India, the country's leading 24/7 news network, also launched a channel in the US, its mission described by its CEO as 'at a time when the world is watching India, News 18 India will serve as the world's window into India'. (*Television Post,* 2014). News 18 India, along with many other Indian news channels, is available to South Asian diaspora markets, including in Britain, Singapore and the Arabian Gulf states.

For private news networks, the need for global expansion is limited, since, in market terms, news has a relatively small audience and therefore meagre advertising revenue. For the other two major BRICS countries – China and Russia – these commercial considerations are not particularly significant as their news networks are generously funded by their respective governments. For India, Brazil and South Africa, entertainment is what defines their global media presence and, as digital connectivity grows in these countries, media products such as Bollywood and Bollywoodized content from India, *telenovelas* from Brazil and television entertainment from South Africa are likely to increase circulation in global digital space. In 2013, there was more material from Bollywood than Hollywood on YouTube (Thussu, 2013). As social media proliferate further and become more multi-lingual, user-generated content will be produced by many more consumers in much higher volumes and velocity in an open and leaky information system, making governments' attempts to control information increasingly difficult, even if the Internet is 'nationalized'. In such a rapidly changing communication ecology, the mandarins of Public Diplomacy 2.0 have to adapt to this reality to understand how the politics of cyber-space influence international relations (Choucri, 2012).

## BRICS building a NWICO 2.0?

Will the rise of BRICS create a New World Information and Communication Order for the digital age? The issues surrounding global information imbalances was one of the central planks of the NWICO debates, and much of the debate – led by the Non-Aligned countries – was framed in the context of news agencies. In today's transformed media environment, new issues have emerged, as noted above, but old concerns about asymmetries in media power persist and have even been consolidated, though geo-political and economic equations are changing with BRICS nations – particularly China – emerging as a significant global voice. A World Bank report predicts that 'China will account for 30 per cent of global investment by 2030, while Brazil, India, and Russia, together, will account for more than 13 per cent of global investment in 2030, more than the United States' (World Bank, 2013: 5).

The state remains an extremely important actor among BRICS nations – particularly in China and Russia – in some way an antidote to the globalization theorists' notions of the 'withering away' of the state under the pressures of market forces. Braman has argued that states retain huge power, including informational power 'that shapes human behaviour by manipulating the informational bases of instrumental, structural, and symbolic power' (Braman, 2006: 25). In a globalized knowledge economy, the state's role is likely to continue to define international relations. The Thomson Reuters Derwent World Patents Index reported that in 2011 China overtook the US to become the world's top filing country for invention patents, with 526,412 applications compared to the US count of 503,582. More Chinese residents were granted patents than Americans (112,347 compared to 108,626). Brazil and India also showed impressive progress in patents in pharmaceuticals, while Russia was notable in medical technology. Apart from electrical machinery, apparatus and energy, Chinese patents were in such areas as digital communication and computer technology (Adams *et al.*, 2013).

A possible synergy of cyberspace with efforts toward sustainable development is an arena where BRICS nations could contribute significantly. BRICS countries have sophisticated space and satellite programmes: Russian expertise in this field is well-established, being the first country to send a human to space; China has demonstrated exceptional growth in this sector, while the Indian Space Research Organization, which has built and launched a range of satellites at affordable rates, can provide communication infrastructure to counter the traditional domination of this field by the US and the European Union. Brazil's plan to build an undersea cable – to link South America to Europe – is another example of this shift – though the initial idea of building a BRICS undersea cable was dropped (see Zhao in this volume).

The aid budget of BRICS nations is also growing, with China emerging as the largest donor from the developing world, followed by India: Indian foreign assistance has tripled in the last decade. Russia has a particularly significant role in terms of energy support and in the field of defence industries (Graham, 2013), while Brazil has significantly increased its foreign aid to many countries in Africa. BRICS champions a qualitatively different development discourse and these nations can benefit from greater policy synergies and intellectual exchanges to share experience on such issues as Intellectual Property Rights, climate change, health and education (Amar, 2012; Hurrell and Sengupta, 2012). Already, these conversations have begun: a recent Working Paper from the Russian International Affairs Council states: 'The prospects of building further links between Russian research (and its resources) and India's engineering skills (which can be witnessed already in the military realm) supplemented by low-cost Chinese labour with sufficient quality level look extremely promising' (RIAC, 2013: 14).

India could learn from China's exceptionally successful programme of drastically reducing if not eliminating poverty and Brazil's clean-fuel energy programmes (Cepaluni and Vigevani, 2012; Trinkunas, 2014). The 'Civil Law Marco internet' – dubbed the Internet Bill of Rights – passed by Brazil at the launch of the NETmundial conference referred to earlier, stipulates that companies such as Google and Facebook will be subject to Brazil's laws and courts in cases involving information on Brazilians, even if the data is stored on servers abroad. Such laws help to protect citizens from any violations of their digital rights and should encourage other nations to follow suit. As DeNardis has stressed, it is a crucial imperative for the public to actively engage in issues surrounding Internet governance as they will ultimately determine Internet freedom (DeNardis, 2014).

BRICS nations could provide a new impetus to digital education, too. The creation of a BRICS Academic Forum that meets annually could consolidate this agenda. Given its strong information technology sector – it accounted for 58 per cent of the global outsourcing industry in 2012 – India could play a useful role within the BRICS constellation. Such programmes as *Aadhaar* (Sanskrit for foundation) – the world's biggest IT project aimed to provide a unique identification number for every Indian citizen to ensure that they receive entitlements under various welfare schemes – could be replicated in similar situations in other developing countries. India was the first country to deploy satellite television for developmental communication through its 1970s SITE (Satellite Instructional Television Experiment) programme. Its Open Universities could provide online education in English to students across the globe: a government initiative – the National Programme on Technology Enhanced Learning – to provide online lectures through YouTube, received 62 million views (Government of India, 2012: 23). From tele-medicine, to tele-education and from mobile banking to e-governance, the opportunities that the digital connectivity offers are tremendous.

As one of the founding members of the Non-Aligned Movement, India was a leading voice during the NWICO debates and a key component of the Non-aligned News Agencies Pool, an attempt to encourage South–South news exchange to counter Western information hegemony. In the age of BRICS, coinciding with cracks within the neo-liberal model of US-led capitalism, there is now talk of Non-Alignment 2.0 (Khilnani *et al.*, 2012). Could such a media discourse contribute to finding approaches that transcend the binaries of Orientalism and Occidentalism to create a new paradigm within which to understand a more inclusive version of globalization, beyond Western formulations? Castells has argued that 'power is primarily exercised by the construction of meaning in the human mind through processes of communication enacted in global/local multimedia networks of mass communication, including mass self-communication' (Castells, 2009: 416).

BRICS could be an important voice in articulating Southern viewpoints and perspectives in global forums like UNESCO, ITU and WIPO on such diverse and contested issues as sustainable development, multiculturalism, intellectual property rights in the digital environment, safeguarding of media plurality and indigenous media. However, as elsewhere, most of media in BRICS countries is entrenched in a culture thriving on entertainment and infotainment-driven programming, and rooted in a commercial system, which has even affected state-controlled media as in China. In the age of what has been termed 'spreadable media', content is increasingly produced, distributed and consumed by a myriad of networked audiences, who communicate through formal and informal nodes (Jenkins, Ford and Green, 2013). By overwhelming public discourse with infotainment, egalitarian aspects are marginalized in the news media, at a time when at least four out the five BRICS nations are home to nearly 600 million people living in poverty and enduring deeply unequal social and economic relations, which, despite economic growth are, in some cases, being exacerbated, a trend seen globally, and eloquently expounded by French economist Thomas Piketty (Piketty, 2013).

The issues that confront many BRICS nations – about good governance, sustainable development and poverty – have striking resonances in many other countries in the Global South. Despite the BRICS nations' gradual integration with the US-led neo-liberal economic system, there is a strong tradition of intellectual and political engagement among BRICS populations, whether socialistic approaches in Russia and China, community activism in Brazil or anti-colonial sentiments in India and South Africa. As the BRICS media globalize, will this critical mass contribute to strengthening the voice of the South on the global scene, or will they act as surrogates to the US-dominated entertainment-driven media?

The US and Europe are to initiate a 'Transatlantic Trade and Investment Partnership', to further integrate trade and investment structures and policies to counter such groupings as BRICS, an indication of the changing global power equations (Gilboy and Heginbotham, 2012; Goldstein, 2013; Sidhu, Mehta and Jones, 2013; Narlikar, 2013; Johnston, 2013; Acharya, 2014). A 2014 Pew Survey showed that, in 2008, in France, Germany, Poland, Spain and Britain, 44 per cent considered the US to be the world's top economy, while just 29 per cent said it was China. By 2012, the percentage naming the US had declined to 28 per cent, while the share saying China had nearly doubled to 57 per cent' (Pew Research Center, 2014: 12).

As Chin and Thakur suggest, 'The multilateral order cannot hold if the power and influence embedded in international institutions is significantly misaligned with the real distribution of power' (Chin and Thakur, 2010: 119). However, the BRICS nations remain divided on crucial policy issues, as noted above in relation to Internet governance. As yet, it has been suggested, there is not 'a shared vision of what a radically *different* world order might look like. Rather, the agenda seems to focus primarily on the redistribution of power within the existing order' (Breslin, 2013: 629, italics in original).

ICANN notes that the Internet has 'allowed for the sharing of knowledge, creativity and commerce in a global commons', but this commons has been transformed in the years since ICANN was formed in 1998, when merely four per cent of the world's population was online, with half of those users in the US. By 2020, it estimates that 63 per cent of the world's population will be online (five billion users), many of whom will not use Latin keyboards' (Cerf *et al.*, 2014). This multi-lingual Internet will contribute to its long overdue internationalization and encourage its study to go beyond Anglophone approaches (Goggin and McLelland, 2009). However, what Schmidt and Cohen have called 'a digital caste system' will probably remain (Schmidt and Cohen, 2013: 254), as the US domination of the Internet is not likely to disappear in the foreseeable future, although it will be a different Internet: China and India will account for nearly half of new mobile Internet users in the next five years, but this 'will come with significant cultural, commercial and political challenges' (PwC, 2014).

According to India's twelfth Five Year Plan (2012–2017), the country requires $1 trillion to improve its backward infrastructure. China is in possession of more than $3 trillion in reserves and keen to invest in stable markets. The pro-business new government in New Delhi led by Narendra Modi is trying to encourage Chinese investment. This 'Chindian' exchange is likely to strengthen the BRICS bloc, especially now that a BRICS bank has been set up and may lead to a new kind of economic globalization, almost parallel to the Western-dominated Bretton Woods system. As a World Bank report notes: 'in a multipolar world, South–South monetary policy coordination will become more critical in promoting stable financial and macroeconomic conditions in developing countries' (World Bank, 2013: 144). The US is still recovering from what Nobel laureate Joseph Stiglitz has called a 'three trillion dollar war' – the 'war on terror' (Stinglitz and Bilmiss, 2008) – while the Euro continues to be weak. It may be a mere coincidence that the currencies of the BRICS countries all start with the letter R: Real, Rouble, Rupee, Renminbi, Rand. There is little doubt, however, that the BRICS should contribute to a more pluralistic and multi-perspectival media globe and that a BRICS Internet would be a crucial node within this networked world. Will a NWICO 2.0, fuelled by rising powers like BRICS, reconfigure the global communication discourse?

## References

Acharya, Amitav (2014) *The End of American World Order*. Cambridge: Polity

Adams, Jonathan; Pendlebury, David and Stembridge, Bob (2013) *Building BRICKs: Exploring the Global Research and Innovation Impact of Brazil, Russia, India, China and South Korea*. London: Thomson Reuters. February.

Amar, Paul (2012) Global South to the Rescue: Emerging Humanitarian Superpowers and Globalizing Rescue Industries, *Globalizations* 9(1): 1–13.

Bell, Daniel (2008) *China's New Confucianism*. Princeton: Princeton University Press.

Bhuiyan, Abu (2014) *Internet Governance and the Global South: Demand for a New Framework*. London: Palgrave Macmillan.

Braman, Sandra (2006) *Change of State: Information, Policy, and Power*. Cambridge (Mass.): MIT Press.

Breslin, Shaun (2013) China and the Global Order: Signalling Threat or Friendship? *International Affairs* 89(3): 615–634.

*Business Line* (2014) Doordarshan Signs Pact with German Channel, *Business Line*, 5 August.

Castells, Manuel (2008) The New Public Sphere: Global Civil Society, Communication Networks and Global Governance, *The ANNALS of the American Academy of Political and Social Science* 616: 78–93.

——(2009) *Communication Power*. Oxford: Oxford University Press.

Cepaluni, Gabriel and Vigevani, Tullo (2012) *Brazilian Foreign Policy in Changing Times: The Quest for Autonomy from Sarney to Lula*. Lanham, MD: Lexington Books.

Cerf, Vinton *et al.* (2014) Strategy Report: ICANN's Role in the Internet Governance Ecosystem. ICANN. Available at http://goo.gl/9Wr0CD.

Chin, Gregory and Thakur, Ramesh (2010) Will China Change the Rules of Global Order?, *Washington Quarterly* 33(4): 119–138.

Choucri, Nazli (2012) *Cyber-Politics in International Relations*. London: MIT Press.

DeNardis, Laura (2014) *The Global War for Internet Governance*. New Haven: Yale University Press.

Ebert, Hannes and Maurer, Tim (2013) Contested Cyberspace and Rising Powers, *Third World Quarterly* 34(6):1054–1074.

*Economist* (2012) Internet Regulation: A Digital Cold War? *The Economist*, 14 December.

——(2014) Defending the Digital Frontier: A Special Report on Cyber-security, *The Economist*, 12 July.

*Ericsson Mobility Report* (2014) *Ericsson Mobility Report: On the Pulse of the Networked Society*. Stockholm: Ericsson, June.

FICCI-KPMG (2014) *The Stage is Set: FICCI-KPMG Indian Media and Entertainment Industry Report 2014*. Mumbai: KPMG in association with Federation of Indian Chambers of Commerce and Industry.

Fuchs, Christian; Boersma, Kees; Albrechtslund, Anders and Sandoval, Marisol (eds.) (2011) *Internet and Surveillance: The Challenges of Web 2.0 and Social Media*. New York: Routledge.

Gilboy, George and Heginbotham, Eric (2012) *Chinese and Indian Strategic Behavior: Growing Power and Alarm*. New York: Cambridge University Press.

Gnanasambandam, Chandra; Madgavkar, Anu; Kaka, Noshir; Manyika, James; Chui, Michael; Bughin, Jacques and Gomes, Malcolm (2012) *Online and Upcoming: The Internet's Impact on India*. McKinsey & Company, December.

Goggin, Gerard and McLelland, Mark (eds.) (2009) *Internationalizing Internet Studies: Beyond Anglophone Paradigms*. London: Routledge.

Goldstein, Andrea (2013) The Political Economy of Global Business: The Case of the BRICs. *Global Policy* 4(2):162–172.

Government of China (2010) *The Internet in China*, chapter 6, Beijing: Information Office of the State Council of the People's Republic of China, 8 June.Available at www.gov. cn/english/2010-06/08/content_1622956.htm.

Government of India (2012) *Ministry of Human Resource Development, Education Annual Report 2011-2012*. New Delhi: Ministry of Human Resource Development.

——(2014a) *Government of India's Initial Submission to Global Multi-stakeholder Meeting on the Future of Internet Governance*; São Paulo, Brazil on 23–24 April. Available at http://mea. gov.in/Images/pdf/official_submission_to_the_conference.pdf.

——(2014b) Statement by Vinay Kwatra, Indian representative at the Global Multi-stakeholder Meeting on the Future of Internet Governance in Sao Paulo, Available at http://mea.gov.in/Speeches-Statements.htm?dtl/23246/Statement+by+Mr+Vinay+Kwatra+Indian+representativ.

Graham, Loren (2013) *Lonely Ideas: Can Russia Compete?* New Haven: Yale University Press.

Hurrell, Andrew and Sengupta, Sandeep (2012) Emerging Powers, North–South Relations and Global Climate Politics, *International Affairs* 88(3): 463–484.

ITU (2012a) *Document 47-E, Proposal by Algeria, Saudi Arabia, Bahrain, China, UAE, Russia, Iraq and Sudan,* World Conference on International Telecommunications, 11 December, International Telecommunications Union. Available at http://files.wcitleaks.org/public/S12-WCIT12-C-0047!!MSW-E.pdf.

——(2012b) *Final Acts of the World Conference on International Telecommunications, Dubai,* International Telecommunications Union, December. Available at http://www.itu.int/en/wcit-12/Documents/final-acts-wcit-12.pdf.

Jenkins, Henry; Ford, Sam and Green, Joshua (2013) *Spreadable Media.* New York: New York University Press.

Johnston, Alastair (2013) How New and Assertive is China's New Assertiveness? *International Security* 37(4): 7–48.

Khilnani, Sunil; Kumar, Rajiv; Mehta, Pratap Bhanu; Menon, Prakash; Nilekani, Nandan; Raghavan, Srinath; Saran, Shyam and Varadarajan, Siddharth (2012) *Nonalignment 2.0: A Foreign and Strategic Policy for India in the Twenty-First Century,* New Delhi: National Defence College and Centre for Policy Research, 30 January.

Kruger, Lennard (2014) *Internet Governance and the Domain Name System: Issues for Congress.* Washington: Congressional Research Service.

Lai, Hongyi and Lu, Yiyi (eds.) (2012) *China's Soft Power and International Relations.* London: Routledge.

Lewis, James and Baker, Stewart (2013) *The Economic Impact of Cybercrime and Cyberespionage.* CSIS report. Available at http://csis.org/files/publication/60396rpt_cybercrime-cost_0713_ph4_0.pdf.

Masmoudi, Mustafa (1979) The New World Information Order, *Journal of Communication,* 29(2): 172–185.

Mosco, Vincent (2014) *To the Cloud: Big Data in a Turbulent World.* New York: Paradigm.

Mueller, Milton (2010) *Networks and States: The Global Politics of Internet Governance.* London: MIT Press.

Narlikar, Anita (2013) India Rising: Responsible to Whom? *International Affairs,* 89(3): 595–614.

NETmundial Multistakeholder Statement, 24 April 2014. Available at http://goo.gl/f3ziWZ.

Newman, Nic and Levy, David (eds.) (2014) *Reuters Institute Digital News Report 2014: Tracking the Future of News.* Oxford: Reuters Institute for the Study of Journalism.

Ng, Jason (2013) *Blocked on Weibo: What Gets Suppressed on China's Version of Twitter (and Why).* New York: The New Press.

Nordenstreng, Kaarle (2012) The New World Information and Communication Order: An Idea That Refuses to Die, pp 477–499, in Nerone, John (ed.) *Media History and the Foundations of Media Studies, Volume 1, The International Encyclopedia of Media Studies.* Oxford: Wiley-Blackwell.

Nordenstreng, Kaarle and Padovani, Claudia (2005) From NWICO to WSIS: Another World Information and Communication Order, *Global Media and Communication* 1(3): 264–272.

Nye, Joseph (2004) *Soft Power: The Means to Success in World Politics.* New York: Public Affairs.

——(2011) *The Future of Power.* New York: Public Affairs.

——(2014) *The Regime Complex for Managing Global Cyber Activities.* Paper Series: No. 1, May, London: Centre for International Governance Innovation and the Royal Institute for International Affairs.

Pew Research Center (2014) *Global Opposition to U.S. Surveillance and Drones but Limited Harm to America's Image,* July. Washington: Pew Research Center.

Pickard, Victor (2007) Neo-liberal Visions and Revisions in Global Communication Policy from NWICO to WSIS, *Journal of Communication Inquiry,* 31(2): 118–139.

Piketty, Thomas (2013) *Capital in the Twenty-First Century.* Cambridge (Mass.): Harvard University Press.

Prasar Bharati (2014) *Report of the Expert Committee on Prasar Bharati. Vol. I and II,* New Delhi: Government of India: Prasar Bharati.

PwC (2014) *PwC Annual Global Entertainment and Media Outlook,* London: Pricewater-houseCooper.

RIAC (2013) *Postulates on Russia-India Relations.* Working Paper No. 3. Moscow: Russian International Affairs Council.

Rid, Thomas (2013) *Cyber War will not take Place.* New York: Oxford University Press.

Schmidt, Eric and Cohen, Jared (2013) *The New Digital Age: Reshaping the Future of People, Nations and Business.* London: John Murray.

Schneier, Bruce (2013) The Battle for Power on the Internet, *The Atlantic,* October 24.

Sidhu, Waheguru Pal Singh; Mehta, Pratap Bhanu and Jones, Bruce (2013) A Hesitant Rule Shaper? pp. 3–22 in Sidhu, Waheguru Pal Singh; Mehta, Pratap Bhanu and Jones Bruce (eds.) *Shaping the Emerging World: India and the Multilateral Order.* Washington: Brookings Institution Press.

Stiglitz, Joseph and Bilmiss, Linda (2008) *The Three Trillion Dollar War: The True Cost of the Iraq Conflict.* New York: W.W. Norton.

Television Post (2014) News 18 India launches in the US. *Television Post,* 1 August, Available at www.televisionpost.com/television/news18-india-launches-in-the-us/.

Thoppil, Dhanya Ann (2014) India's Flipkart Raises $1Billion in Fresh Funding. *Wall Street Journal,* 29 July.

Thussu, Daya Kishan (2013) *Communicating India's Soft Power: Buddha to Bollywood.* New York: Palgrave/Macmillan.

——(2015) *International Communication: Continuity and Change,* Third Edition. New York: Bloomsbury Academic.

Trinkunas, Harold (2014) *Brazil's Rise: Seeking Influence on Global Governance.* Washington: Brookings Institute.

UNESCO (2013) *Emerging Markets and the Digitalization of the Film Industry. An Analysis of the 2012 UIS International Survey of Feature Film Statistics.* Paris: Institute for Statistics, United Nations Educational, Scientific and Cultural Organization, August.

——(2014) *World Trends in Freedom of Expression and Media Development.* Paris: United Nations Educational, Scientific and Cultural Organization.

US Government (2009) *National Framework for Strategic Communication.* Washington: The White House.

——(2012) Statement delivered by Ambassador Terry Kramer from the floor of the WCIT, 13 December 2012. U.S. Department of State, *Press Release,* 'U.S. Intervention at the World Conference on International Telecommunications'. Available at http://www.state.gov/r/pa/prs/ps/2012/12/202037.htm.

——(2014) *Big Data: Seizing Opportunities, Preserving Values.* Washington: The White House, May.

WAN-IFRA (2014) *Trends in Newsrooms 2014.* Paris: The World Association of Newspapers and News Publishers.

Wang, Jian (ed.) (2010) *Soft Power in China: Public Diplomacy through Communication.* New York: Palgrave Macmillan.

Wells, Clare (1987) *The UN, UNESCO and the Politics of Knowledge.* London: Macmillan.

WSIS (2005) *Tunis Agenda for the Information Society,* 18 November 2005, WSIS-05/TUNIS/DOC6(Rev.1)-E, p. 6. Available at http://www.itu.int/wsis/docs2/tunis/off/6rev1.pdf.

World Bank (2013) *Global Development Horizons 2011 – Multipolarity: The New Global Economy.* Washington, DC: World Bank Publications.

Yang, Guobin (2009) *The Power of the Internet in China: Citizen Activism Online.* New York: Columbia University Press.

Zaharna, Rhonda (2010) *Battles to Bridges US Strategic Communication and Public Diplomacy After 9/11.* New York: Palgrave Macmillan.

# Index

Page numbers in *italics* denotes a figure/table

CPSIA information can be obtained
at www.ICGtesting.com
Printed in the USA
BVOW06s1549231116

468302BV00014B/9/P